Lonely Planet Publications
and | London

Beth Greenfield

Miami
& the Keys

WITHDRAWN

Contents

Published by Lonely Planet Publications Pty Ltd
ABN 36 005 607 983

Australia Head Office, Locked Bag 1, Footscray,
Victoria 3011, ☎ 03 8379 8000, fax 03 8379 8111,
talk2us@lonelyplanet.com.au

USA 150 Linden St, Oakland, CA 94607,
☎ 510 893 8555, toll free 800 275 8555,
fax 510 893 8572, info@lonelyplanet.com

UK 72–82 Rosebery Ave, Clerkenwell, London,
EC1R 4RW, ☎ 020 7841 9000, fax 020 7841 9001,
go@lonelyplanet.co.uk

Destination Miami & the Keys

If you've never been seduced by a place, chances are you've never been to Miami – or at least not given it a fair shake. Because not only does this city know how to work its Latin-fusion charms, but it's also got pizzazz enough to tantalize you with its future – and soul enough to remind you of its past.

Miami Beach shimmers and glimmers and poses but it also has depth and warmth and intelligence, and a sensuousness that's downright addictive. Much of that is thanks to its scantily clad, sun-loving people, who perfectly embody their home. Across the sluice of Biscayne Bay, the City of Miami nurtures its culture, fights its demons and builds high and hopefully into the sky. And way south in the Florida Keys – the southern string of islands teeming with tropical flora and fauna and fun – the mood is so compelling that it lures even the Miami minions for sexy, slow-paced getaways.

If you're not been to Miami in 10 or 20 years, wipe all that you know of the place out of your mind – likewise if you've not been here in a few months. Because details don't stay the same for long in Miami, and we're not just talking about South Beach. Sure, those hot clubs and hotels and eateries and their jazzed crowds shift rapidly (with the exception of that gorgeous, you-can-count-on-me art deco), but so do the rhythms above 20th St and over the many Miami causeways. Go from Cuban, Argentine and Haitian flavors to opulent Coral Gables villas and the sweeping peacefulness of Key Biscayne beaches. See high-art chic in the Design District bleeding into gussied-up seediness along Biscayne Boulevard, Downtown hubs teeming with worker bees and cruise-ship tourists, pockets of Coconut Grove funkiness welcoming sleek suburban malls, and swampy Everglades environments crawling with wonderful wildlife. You'll also find glorious public-art projects and impressive museums, magnificently preserved architecture, vast sandy beaches, nightclubs and eateries to rival any top global city, and work-of-art hotels that are good enough to live in. Greater Miami has it all, and plenty more.

MICHAEL AW

South Beach & Miami Beach

Beach Patrol Headquarters (p34) resembles a ship run aground

Palm trees and car chrome capture the Miami vibe (p19)

JON DAVISON

ALFREDO MAIQUEZ

LEE FOSTER

Whiz through South Beach – the choice of wheels is yours (p131)

A lifeguard hut is painted with the full blaze of a South Beach (p50) sunset

WITOLD SKRYPCZ

The combination of sun, sea and sand has lured countless tourists to South Beach (p50)

Bed down art deco–style in Avalon Hotel (p151), South Beach

In-line skates (p131) and Miami are a natural fit

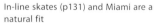

Nighttime neon transforms hotels (p150) on Ocean Dr

Neighborhoods

Public art and Cuban culture in one neat, tiled package in Little Havana (p65)

RICHARD CUMMINS

RICHARD CUMMINS

Coral Gables' Venetian Pool (p73) was once a limestone quarry

The Italian Renaissance–style Vizcaya Museum (p70) was built in 1916 in Coconut Grove

JON DAVISO

Listen to the click of dominoes tiles at Máximo Gómez Park (p66), Little Havana

JEFF GREENBER

Freestyle, breaststroke or dog paddle – there's room enough for it all at the Biltmore Hotel (p71), which boasts the largest hotel swimming pool in the USA

The Metromover (p61) is a unique way to take in the sights of Downtown Miami

Visit the Ancient Spanish Monastery (p74), Northern Miami Beach

The Design District's Living Room (p64) plays with perspective

Food & Drink

Refuel at Van Dyke Café (p96), South Beach

LEE FOSTER

Food, culture and geography come together in Floribbean cuisine (p95)

LEE FOSTER

The lobby of the Marlin Hotel (p111) is like a silver-nitrate dream.

LEE FOSTER

JEFF GREENBERG

Little Havana (p103) is a prime location for Latin American cuisine

Shopping & Nightlife

RICHARD CUMMINS

Shop up a storm at CocoWalk (p146), Coconut Grove

Admire the lights at Las Olas Riverfront (p205), Fort Lauderdale

RICHARD CUMMINS

Splashes of fluorescent color illuminate art-deco hotels along Ocean Dr, South Beach (p50)

JON DAVISON

Florida Keys & Key West

Introduce yourself to loggerhead turtles (p172)

LEE FOSTER

WILLIAM HARRIGAN

Exploration doesn't have to stop at land's edge – divers off Looe Key (p174)

Islamorada (p170), in the Florida Keys, is just a ribbon of land

LEE FOSTER

Sample older, more graceful modes of transportation (p132)

WITOLD SKRYPCZAK

LEE FOSTER

Relax on Duval St in Key West (p177)

WILLIAM HARRIGAN

Nature paints with its full palette
over Key Largo (p165)

LEE FOSTER

Pay homage at Hemingway House (p181), Key West

In Key West (p177) when the sun goes down, everyone comes out to watch

LEE FOSTER

Everglades & Fort Lauderdale

Stroll along the Fort Lauderdale Beach Promenade (p208)

PETER PTSCHELINZEW

Kayak (p200) your way through the Everglades

JIM WARK

MARK & AUDREY GIBSON

Dine next to bobbing boats in Fort Lauderdale (p204)

Savor the dramatic views of the Everglades from the Shark Valley observation tower (p194)

WITOLD SKRYPCZ

The Author

BETH GREENFIELD

Beth made her first trip to Miami Beach as a toddler, in 1972, to visit her retired grandparents. The annual December pilgrimages – made from her native New Jersey in the family station wagon – continued for years. Eventually Beth went to college to study English, followed by journalism in graduate school and the big move to New York City, where she now lives, writing for various publications (including *Time Out New York* and the *New York Times*) and teaching travel-writing classes. Beth is the coordinating author of Lonely Planet's *New York City* guidebook and a contributor to the latest *USA* and *Mexico* titles. When she started visiting Miami again as an adult, she yearned for the good ol' days – of blue-haired Jewish ladies at Publix, tales of a mythically scary Downtown and, most of all, Grandma's homemade blintzes. But she quickly fell in love with the bold and beautiful new Miami, too.

Lowdown

- Population (Greater Miami) 2.25 million
- Time Zone Eastern Standard
- Moderate hotel room $200
- Bus ride $1.25
- Cup of coffee $1
- Cuban sandwich $4
- Essential drink Mojito $10
- No-no Sunburn

Lonely Planet books provide independent advice. Lonely Planet does not accept advertising in guidebooks, nor do we accept payment in exchange for listing or endorsing any place or business. Lonely Planet writers do not accept discounts or payments in exchange for positive coverage of any sort.

BETH'S TOP MIAMI DAY

First things first: food, in the form of an awesome omelette breakfast in South Beach at the **Front Porch Café** (p92). Then comes a stroll around the 'hood – north along Ocean Dr and over the **Lincoln Road Mall** (p55). Here I'll people watch for a while; shop for avocados, papayas and orchids at the **Farmers' Market** (p88); pick up a new item of cool clothing at one of various boutiques; do a shot of Cuban coffee from **David's Cafe** (p94) and then skedaddle, ready for some real fresh air. I find it in the form of a leisurely bike ride along the breezy paths of **Key Biscayne** (p67). On the drive back to the mainland I'll meander through the lush roads of **Coral Gables** (p71) before hightailing it to the Mid-Beach **Boardwalk** (p55) for a sunset run. After a shower, bring on the nightlife: listen to music while sipping a Design District cocktail at the **District** (p101), perhaps, along with peek at a neighborhood art-gallery opening, followed by dinner at any one of the city's wonderful eateries – **Soyka** (p102), maybe? Or will it be **Nemo** (p90)? Or **Miss Yip** (p95)? My nightcap could come in many forms, but preferably one of the following: a Downtown cocktail at **Bahia** (p110), an indie film at **Miami Beach Cinematheque** (p125), or an elegant moonlight stroll along the beach.

Essential Miami & the Keys

Beach (p57) Sun, sand, scene.

Art Deco Historic District (p53) Pastel hotels and nostalgia.

Design District (p62) It's industrial chic – with a purpose.

Lincoln Rd (p54) Stroll, shop, eat and gawk. It's quintessential South Beach.

Cuban coffee windows (p104) Have a shot or a sandwich, and barely stop long enough to notice you've done it.

City Life

City Life

MIAMI TODAY

In-the-moment Miami is difficult to pin down – but future Miami is easy. At least that's the way it looks from the ground, where cranes and construction sites shoot up to the sky, new hotels pop up every few months and new Miami converts just keep on a comin'. It's a city of hope with an eye on tomorrow, where development has surpassed tourism as the strength of the local economy. The real-estate boom – a game of seemingly endless condo building and ever-affordable options – moves excited locals to line up for open houses the night before they begin, and lures New Yorkers with a promise of quality of life. Tourism comes in a close second to development, with Miami the current darling of travel magazines. It's no wonder, with all the new hotels and hot dining spots and growing cultural offerings that help to keep it on the international radar. Partially responsible for its rise are the influences of New York City and Los Angeles, 1300 and 2760 miles away respectively, but closer and closer all the time – both through Miami's visitors and transplants, celebs especially, and new outposts of New York and Los Angeles hotspots (thank you, Andre Balazs, Ian Schrager, Jenny Yip, Govind Armstrong and all the rest).

But what about all of Miami's troubles, from racial tensions and drug crimes to political corruption and natural disasters? Today's Miami seems to be keeping it all at bay. No matter what new immigrant groups settle on these shores, the cultural landscape expands to make room for all; no, the Nicaraguans don't necessarily live next door to the Argentines, and there are certainly natural tensions, but for now there doesn't appear to be any threat of a riot redux. The lurid murders made infamous by *Miami Vice* 20 years ago have declined to a level that's in keeping with the other major cities of the USA – so much so that Miami's powers-that-be seem to have embraced the pastel-clad TV show: the shooting of an on-location Hollywood film version has just wrapped, with the city's heartfelt blessing. And political corruption? Well, it still goes on – to a point, like everywhere – but new mayor Manuel Diaz, a big improvement over the administration that oversaw the 2000 presidential-election disaster here, is trying hard to keep it under control. And though hurricanes are a constant threat to South Florida, the city has been charmed for years, escaping major destruction while communities less than 100 miles away have been devastated.

Miami today is a spunky city, pulsing with people who know how to remain strong and positive no matter what new challenge comes along. It's been there, done that and will do it again, and it continue, like a phoenix, to rise up from any ashes.

CITY CALENDAR

No matter when you choose to make your way to Miami, you're bound to find something fun going on – especially in high season, when folks flock here to escape the cold and play in the sun. For information on official holidays, see the Directory, p221. And see Nightlife, p110, for more extensive information on arts and entertainment festivals.

JANUARY

The beginning of the new year also happens to be the height of the tourist season in these parts. Expect fair weather, crowds of visitors, higher prices than usual and a slew of special events. New Year's Eve brings fireworks and festivals to South Beach and Downtown's bayfront.

FEDEX ORANGE BOWL FOOTBALL GAME

☎ 305-341-4700; www.orangebowl.org; Pro Player Stadium, 2269 NW 199th St, Opa-Locka

In early January, flocks of football fanatics descend on Pro Player Stadium in Opa-Locka for the Orange Bowl – a major, classic college football game.

ART DECO WEEKEND
☎ 305-672-2014; www.artdecoweekend.com; Ocean Dr btwn 1st & 23rd Sts
This weekend fair featuring guided tours, concerts, classic-auto shows, sidewalk cafés, and vendors of arts and antiques is held in mid-January.

ART MIAMI
☎ 866-727-7953; www.art-miami.com; Miami Beach Convention Center, 1901 Convention Center Dr, South Beach
Also in mid-January is this massive fair, a display of modern and contemporary works from more than 100 galleries and international artists.

KEY BISCAYNE ART FESTIVAL
☎ 305-361-0049; Crandon Blvd, Key Biscayne
Held in late January since the early 1960s, this is a showcase of more than 150 local artists, from painters to glass blowers.

FEBRUARY
The last hurrah for Northerners needing to escape the harsh winter, February brings arts festivals, and street parties, as well as warm days and cool nights. February 14 is Valentine's Day, when lovers celebrate their amour.

MIAMI INTERNATIONAL FILM FESTIVAL
☎ 305-377-3456; www.miamifilmfestival.com
This early-February (sometimes late-January) event, which is sponsored by Miami-Dade College, is a two-week festival showcasing documentaries and features from all over the world.

COCONUT GROVE ARTS FESTIVAL
☎ 305-447-0401; www.coconutgroveartsfest.com; Biscayne Blvd btwn NE 1st & 5th Sts, Coconut Grove
One of the most prestigious arts festivals in the country, this late-February fair features more than 300 artists.

MIAMI INTERNATIONAL BOAT SHOW & STRICTLY SAIL
☎ 305-531-8410; www.discoverboating.com/miami; Miami Beach Convention Center, South Beach
With more than 250,000 attendees, this late-February event is a serious water lovers' extravaganza and one of the largest new-boat shows in the world.

SOUTH BEACH WINE & FOOD FESTIVAL
☎ 305-460-6563; www.sobewineandfoodfest.com
In late February, *Food & Wine* magazine presents this fest of fine dining and sipping to promote South Florida's culinary image. Expect star-studded brunches, dinners and barbecues.

MARCH
Spring arrives, bringing warmer weather, world-class golf and tennis tournaments, outdoor festivals and the Irish party holiday of St Patrick's Day, on March 17.

CARNAVAL MIAMI
☎ 305-644-8888; www.carnavalmiami.com
In early to mid-March, this is a nine-day party of festivals, concerts, a beauty contest, an in-line skating contest, a Latin drag-queen show and a Calle Ocho cooking contest.

MIAMI ORCHID SHOW
☎ 305-255-3656; 2700 S Bayshore Dr, Coconut Grove Exhibition Center, Coconut Grove
Held since the mid-1940s, this annual mid-month show of flowers comes from statewide growers.

NASDAQ 100 TENNIS TOURNAMENT
☎ 305-230-7223; Tennis Center at Crandon Park, 7300 Crandon Blvd, Key Biscayne
In late March, and formerly known as the Lipton and Ericsson Open, top-ranked tennis pros play for hordes of spectators.

WINTER MUSIC CONFERENCE
☎ 954-563-4444; www.wmcon.com
Party promoters, DJs, producers and revelers come from around the globe to hear new artists, catch up on technology and party the nights away.

Hot Conversation Topics
- 'South Beach is *so over*!'
- 'I can't believe the Performing Arts Center hasn't opened yet.'
- 'Let's buy in North Miami before it's too late.'
- 'Shaq's gonna save the Heat this year.'
- 'That's it, I'm finally getting hurricane insurance!'
- 'Did you see J Lo at Skybar last night?'
- 'Let's go for Argentine-Italian in Normandy Isle.'
- 'Did you vote in favor of the slot machines?'

WINTER PARTY WEEK
☎ 305-572-1841; www.winterparty.com
The gay-circuit party bonanza, in mid-March, benefits gay-rights organizations, including the National Gay & Lesbian Task Force.

APRIL
Welcome to the shoulder season, bringing quieter days, lower prices, balmier temperatures and a few choice events. The religious holidays of Easter and Passover fall in April, as does the final of the Nasdaq 100 Tennis Tournament.

BILLBOARD LATIN MUSIC AWARDS
☎ 646-654-4660; www.billboardevents.com
This prestigious awards show, in late April, draws tops industry execs, star performers and a slew of Latin music fans.

MIAMI GAY & LESBIAN FILM FESTIVAL
☎ 305-534-9924; www.mglff.com
Held in late April to early May, this annual event features shorts, feature films and docs screened at various South Beach theaters.

MAY/JUNE
May and June boast increased heat, fewer visitors and several cultural events. Memorial Day is the official start of summer, bringing a beach-oriented three-day weekend.

FASHION WEEK OF THE AMERICAS
☎ 305-604-1000; www.fashionweekamericas.com
This annual May showcase features runway shows from Latin, Caribbean, American and European designers.

GOOMBAY FESTIVAL
☎ 305-567-1399
A massive fest, held the first week of June, that celebrates Bahamas culture.

FLORIDA DANCE FESTIVAL
☎ 305-674-6575; www.fldance.org
In mid-June, this festival brings performances, classes, workshops and seminars on dance to Miami.

JULY/AUGUST
The most beastly, humidity-drenched days are during these months, when many locals vacation elsewhere and others spend their

Top Five Unique Events
- The **King Mango Strut** (opposite) is old-school Coconut Grove: wacky and fun.
- Chow on lo mein and watch festive dragon boats race along the waterway during the **South Florida Dragon Boat Festival** (below).
- Early March brings **Carnaval Miami** (p17) – 10 days of parades, fashion shows and concerts, ending with an over-the-top fest along Calle Ocho.
- Skip the Bahamas and head to Miami in the first week of June for the **Goombay Festival** (left), a colorful Caribbean food and arts fest.
- Come to town during **Winter Party Week** (left) and spend a week among 10,000 hot, shirtless boys cruising dance floors all over town.

days melting on the beach. Official celebrations are few and far between.

INDEPENDENCE DAY CELEBRATION
☎ 305-358-7550; Bayfront Park, Downtown
July 4 features an excellent fireworks and laser show with live music that draws more than 100,000 people to breezy Bayfront Park.

MIAMI SPICE RESTAURANT MONTH
☎ 305-358-7550; www.miamirestaurantmonth.com
Top restaurants around Miami offer prix-fixe lunches and dinners to try to lure folks out during the heat wave.

SEPTEMBER/OCTOBER
In September the days and nights are still steamy. The start of the school season brings back college students. There are just a couple of tourist-oriented events in September, but they're followed by a slew of cultural offerings come October.

HISPANIC HERITAGE FESTIVAL
☎ 305-541-5023; www.hispanicfestival.com
Held in late October, it's one of the largest festivals in the country, commemorating the discovery of the Americas with concerts, food, games and folkloric groups.

SOUTH FLORIDA DRAGON BOAT FESTIVAL
☎ 305-633-0168; www.miamidragonboat.com;
Haulover Beach Park, Bal Harbour
This new event brings thousands for Chinese food, a crafts fair and the main event: festive

dragon-boat races along the Florida East Coast Canal, accompanied by dramatic drumming.

MIAMI REGGAE FESTIVAL
☎ 305-891-2944; Bayfront Park, Downtown
It's been one of the largest reggae events in the country, happening since the 1980s.

NOVEMBER
Tourist season kicks off at the end of the month, bringing more crowds and slightly cooler, more bearable days. Thanksgiving falls on the last Thursday of the month.

RASIN
☎ 305-751-3740
This annual Haitian cultural festival hits in early November with music, food, crafts and more.

MIAMI BOOK FAIR INTERNATIONAL
☎ 305-237-3258; www.miamibookfair.com
Occurring in mid- to late November, this is among the most important and well-attended book fairs in the USA, with hundreds of nationally known writers joining hundreds of publishers and hundreds of thousands of visitors.

WHITE PARTY
☎ 305-667-9296; www.whiteparty.net
This weeklong extravaganza draws more than 15,000 gay men and women for nonstop partying at clubs and venues all over town.

DECEMBER
Tourist season is in full swing, with Northerners escaping south and booking rooms so they can bask in sunshine and be here for Christmas and New Year's Eve festivities.

ART BASEL MIAMI BEACH
☎ 305-674-1292; www.artbasel.com/miami_beach
Occurring in early December, this is one of the most important international art shows in the US, with works from more than 150 galleries and a slew of trendy parties and events.

KING MANGO STRUT
☎ 305-401-1171; Main Ave & Grand Ave, Coconut Grove
Held each year just after Christmas, this quirky 24-year-old Coconut Grove parade is a politically charged, fun freak that began as a spoof on current events and the now-defunct Orange Bowl Parade.

City Life – Culture

CULTURE
IDENTITY
According to one New York transplant and longtime Miami Beach resident, Miamians are basically 'New Yorkers with shorts.' It may sound simplistic, but it's really not far from the truth – in both attitude *and* demographics. A majority of Miami's residents are focused, fast-paced, hard working and concerned with trends, styles and hip culture. But they make all their serious moves while wearing casual – and sometimes very little – clothing, from the shorts-and-bikini-top combo to sandals. They dress up for nightclubs, though, where they may very well cross paths with an A-list Hollywood celeb; but, just like cool New Yorkers, they will certainly not let on that they've noticed.

A large number of Miamians are transplants from elsewhere – whether it's New York or Cuba or rural Florida – and about 60% of both Miami and Miami Beach's residents are foreign born. It's also become a city of youngsters: while the median age in Miami Beach was 65 in the 1980s, these days it's 39.

In talking about Miami-area residents, it's important to differentiate between the mainland city, which has a total population of 362,000, and that of Miami Beach, which has 88,000 residents – though its other statistics are quite similar. Both have a Latino majority – 55% in Miami Beach and 65% in Miami – with most Latinos being Cuban (see p20). All this may explain much of what makes many folks tick down here: Fidel Castro, his refusal to back down and America's stance on the Cuba embargo. In general, Miami's older Cuban exiles are a one-issue voting block (anti-Castro), which explains why there's such an unwavering Republican voice bellowing forth from what appears to be a liberal, or at least Democratic, city.

Miami is also home to a significant Haitian population, though census figures fail to differentiate Haitians from other groups of Black residents.

One widely held belief about Miamians is that they are all vapid, plastic-surgery-obsessed, bulimic party animals who spend their lives preening in preparation for being let

19

Northern Capital of the Latin World

Miami may technically be part of the USA, but it's widely touted as the 'capital of the Americas' and the 'center of the New World.' That's a coup, really, when it comes to marketing Miami to the rest of the world, and especially to the USA, where Latinos are now the largest minority. Miami's pan-Latin mixture makes it more ethnically diverse than any Latin American city.

How did this happen? Many of Miami's Latinos arrived to this geographically convenient city as political refugees – Cubans fleeing Castro starting in 1959, Venezuelans fleeing President Hugo Chavez, Brazilians and Argentines running from economic woes, Mexicans and Guatemalans long arriving to find migrant work. And gringos, long fascinated with Latin American flavors, now visit Miami in part to get a taste of the pan-Latin stew without even having to leave the country.

It's all led to the growth of Latin American business here, which has boosted the local economy. Miami is the US headquarters of many Latin companies, including LanChile, a Chilean airline; Televisa, a Mexican TV conglomerate; and Embraer, a Brazilian aircraft manufacturer. It's home to Telemundo, one of America's biggest Spanish-language broadcasters, as well as MTV Networks Latin America and the Latin branch of the Universal Music Group. It's also the host city of the annual Billboard Latin Music Conference and Awards.

Cubans do still lead the pack of Latinos in Miami, though – and Cubans have a strong influence on local and international politics. Conservative exile groups have often been characterized as extremists; many refuse to visit Cuba while Castro is still in power. A newer generation, however – often referred to as the 'YUCAs' (Young Urban Cuban Americans) – are much more willing to see both sides and not nearly as caught up in ending Cuba's current way of life as their parents are.

While many of the subtleties may escape you as a Miami visitor, one thing is obvious: the Latino influence, which you can experience whether you seek it out or wait for it to fall in your lap. Whether you're dining out, listening to live music, overhearing Spanish conversations, visiting Little Havana or Little Buenos Aires or simply sipping a chilled *mojito* (a Cuban rum-based cocktail) at the edge of your hotel pool, the Latin American energy is palpable, beautiful and everywhere you go.

past the velvet ropes (thank you, *Nip/Tuck*). While this description may be apt for many among the nightclub-loving hordes who flock to South Beach, it's not the whole picture. Twenty percent of Miami Beach's residents live below the poverty line, while the median income is only $40,000.

LIFESTYLE

How do Miamians live? Depends on their income and neighborhood, of course, but one typical scenario would be in a high-rise condo, with cool, spare furnishings, decent space and a big and beautiful view. Or it could be in a house, big or small, with a small yard and possibly a pool. On the mainland you might find an artist living in a large, dusty loft on a seemingly abandoned urban stretch of street. Poor residents could live in a tiny apartment or a ramshackle house – maybe without a phone or kitchen or proper plumbing, and filled with a large family.

Nearly 40% of both Miami and Miami Beach residents own their own home; while the median value of those homes in the Beach is $330,000, it's about half that in Miami. The majority of those who rent their homes pay an average of $875 per month. Low-income housing is a serious issue in the Miami area. The biggest growth has been in the development of luxury condo high-rises; by the end of 2004, there were 70 condominium projects being planned or built – in Downtown Miami alone. And if all goes as it should over the next 10 years, about 55,000 condo units, at an investment of $9.9 billion (and with price tags starting at $200,000 and rising sharply from there), will be built in and around the Downtown area. A major housing trend in Miami Beach, has been that of hotel-condominiums; allowing folks to own a piece of the luxury pie and also make money from it, too.

This is all done through a range of salaries. While a successful real-estate agent or attorney in Miami might make over $200,000 per year, a journalist might make $50,000, a public-school teacher about $30,000 for a starting salary, and Florida's minimum wage is $6.15 per hour. If you're not a realtor (or at least real-estate investor), you probably will be soon – or you may work in the industries of tourism, fashion, higher education, publishing, retail, furniture making or aircraft repair. Median income, though, stands at about $40,000.

The Glamorous Life

Playgrounds, of course, breed vanity, and vanity is a big part of what makes Miami go 'round. Blame the heat, the skimpy bikinis, the fabulous nightlife scene or the influx of celebrities who vacation here. Either way, folks who live in Miami or Miami Beach want to look their hottest. This is, after all, the inspiration and setting for the popular *Nip/Tuck* plastic-surgery drama series, and it is truly a plastic-surgery hotspot; pay attention when you walk around, and you'll be sure to notice the slew of folks who have had Botox injections, eyelid lifts, tummy tucks, liposuction and breast enhancements. Miami is also a model magnet, boasting both on-location spots for photo shoots, from expansive beaches to glitzy hotel lobbies, and plenty of nightclubs for the skinny minnies to unwind and party down with the various other celebrity beauties who vacation here – Paris Hilton, Cameron Diaz, J Lo and Jessica Simpson among them. The influence of Miami-chic is far reaching, not only through *Nip/Tuck*, but through events that draw hip and urban national crowds (**Art Basel, p19**; **Winter Music Conference**, p118; **Winter Party Week, p18**), hotel lobbies that appear in fashion spreads of national magazines (**Marlin**, p156; **Ritz-Carlton South Beach**, p157) and LA or NYC outposts of eateries and hotels (**Table 8**, p157; **Standard**, p162) that are already on the global map of fabulousness. Also having global impact is the diet craze known as the South Beach Diet – a good-carb, good-protein plan popularized by Miami's own Dr Arthur Agatston that, by name alone, could lure you into believing that you'll soon look as good as the sun-kissed Miami jetsetters.

Whether you're at the low or high end of the pay scale, it's likely you drive a sport utility vehicle (SUV) – a sign of either prosperity or debt. More and more, you may drive to your job from an outlying area of Miami – one of the suburban neighborhoods that make up the sprawling Miami-Dade County region. You may come home to children, although only 23% of families in Miami have children, and average family size is 3.2.

Miamians are generally relaxed when it comes to accepting others' diversity, and a lot of that is signaled by local administrations. Miami Beach, for example, became the third Florida municipality (after Broward County and Key West) to offer domestic-partnership registration with a law passed in 2004. This gives same-sex partners valuable rights, from hospital visitation to making joint healthcare decisions. The state, meanwhile, is more conservative: it's the only state in the country with a blanket law that forbids gay couples from adopting children. But Miami's LGBT voice continues to grow, and gay Americans consider the city to be among the most prominent gay playgrounds in the country.

FOOD & DRINK

It wasn't so long ago that the idea of fine dining in Miami drew guffaws from serious foodies; it meant, after all, choosing between the standard-red-sauce options of Italian and the steak-fish-chicken menus of Continental, with no excitement to speak of. Today, along with practically every other aspect of Miami, that has changed – for the better. Foodies are flocking to area restaurants, chefs are making names for themselves with a blend of Latin, Caribbean and local cuisines (known as 'Floribbean') and the city is becoming a serious global-food melting pot, offering everything from Cuban sandwiches to Brazilian *feijoada* (a meat stew with rice and black beans), Thai curries, stellar Japanese sushi, Argentine-Italian pastas and Asian-Caribbean fusion. Events such as the **South Beach Food & Wine Festival** (p17) draw cuisine junkies from around the country. Street food in the Downtown area still includes hot-dog carts – but now you'll find *arepas* (cornmeal cakes), fresh mangos and empanadas for sale, too. And don't worry, the Jewish delis, Chinese take-outs and American standards haven't disappeared; the only difference is that they no longer stand alone.

Though the influence of nearby Caribbean and Latin cultures have always made its way into the foods of Miami, it wasn't considered hip until one talented and forward-thinking chef, Douglas Rodriguez, turned up the heat and busted out with fabulous fusion entrees at **Yuca** (p96). He sparked a trend that hasn't stopped, bringing to the region attention that has inspired other chefs either to rise above the local fray or hightail it to Miami from other big-city dining capitals. Restaurant openings in Miami are big news more often than not – especially when they come courtesy of celebrity chefs with preexisting followings. Take, for example, the latest outpost of Table 8, made hyper-famous in LA by owner-chef Govind Armstrong. Table 8 created a buzz simply by reporting that it would open in spring 2005 at the new hotel, **Regent South Beach** (p157). Whether it will be as good as its West Coast location remains to be seen. For more details about Miami's restaurant scene, see p88.

FASHION

With Miami now a hub of cool food, night-life and arts, it makes sense that it would gain acclaim as an influencer in the world of fashion. And it has, with the annual **Fashion Week of the Americas** (p18) playing a large role in putting this region on the most stylish global maps. The showcase of Latin American designers is the biggest-known fashion event in Miami, drawing designers and fans from around the world each May since it was brought to town from Ecuador by Beth Sobel of Sobel Fashion Productions in 2003.

The event is renowned globally, from Paris to Hong Kong – but it's by no means the only game in town. Miami draws hordes of designers who are ever-searching for sensuous inspiration, both for creations and photo-shoot locations, and it's the base city for fashion company Perry Ellis International. GenArt, a national nonprofit organization dedicated to film, art and fashion, holds an annual Fresh Faces in Fashion showcase here, focusing on Miami's burgeoning designer scene. The 20-year-old local designer Esteban Cortezar has received global acclaim, and the Miami International University of Art & Design began taking itself a lot more seriously a couple of years ago, moving into massive new digs in Biscayne Boulevard's Omni Building. Amateur fashionistas can get a taste of Miami's stylish vibe anytime by hitting any one of the various high-fashion retail boutiques, most of which are clustered around Lincoln Rd, or the wholesale fashion shops on the mainland in Wynwood. For more information on Miami's fashion world, see Shopping, p136.

SPORTS

Spectator sports in Miami are a thriving part of the cultural landscape, with the **Miami Heat** (p128), in basketball, and **Miami Dolphins** (p128), in football, being the teams that most easily work the masses into a frenzy. The Heat, a relatively young team by franchise standards, came into the NBA (National Basketball Association) in the 1988–9 season and has had plenty of ups and downs in seasons since then. The club made headlines in 1995 by acquiring coach Pat Riley and star player Alonso Mourning (both have since moved on), and the biggest excitement these days has been the addition of two all-star players, Shaquille O'Neal and Dwayne Wade, who have truly pumped up the volume. During basketball season, October through March, you can catch the Heat at the American Airlines Arena.

Football, which happens from September until January, is also extremely popular in Miami, where the team is the aqua-clad Miami Dolphins. For much of its history, the team was coached by the spectacular Don

---

Mixing the Perfect *Mojito*

Cuba's most popular cocktail – a rum-based, Latin take on the mint julep – is also Miami's. And though it's most fun to go out and be served the refreshing drink in style, here's a sure-fire recipe for making your own:

- 1.5oz of light rum (choose a good one – Havana Club, Bacardi, etc)
- 2 tsp finely-ground sugar
- 3 tsp (or more) fresh lime juice
- splash of club soda
- a few sprigs of fresh mint

Crush the fresh mint in a tall glass, coating the inside of the glass with mint oil. Mix the sugar and lime juice into the mint, top with ice cubes, then pour in the rum and the club soda. Garnish with mint.

Top Five People-Watching Spots

- Spy shoppers, scenesters and a celeb or two at **Lincoln Road Mall**.
- On **Ocean Drive** clueless tourists mix with locals and everyone in between.
- The bustling strip of Downtown, **E Flagler St** is where scurrying businessmen mix with cruise-ship tourists.
- At the **Bal Harbour Shops** watch chichi shoppers with nose jobs and gold cards burning holes in their pockets.
- Enjoy an ocean view from the **Mid-Beach Boardwalk**, which is crisscrossed with Orthodox families, Fontainebleau guests and local joggers.

Shula, who coached the most wins (347) in football history and now runs a chain of steak restaurants around Miami. Though they've not yet matched their record of 1972 – when the Dolphins became the first NFL team to have an undefeated season – they continue to be a top-ranking team. Games are played at Pro Player Stadium.

Other spectator sports in the city include college baseball, basketball and football; the pro-baseball **Florida Marlins** (p129), who share the Dolphins' stadium; horse and greyhound racing; ice hockey (via the Florida Panthers); and jai alai, a Basque import, played on an indoor court, which involves a speedy ball and unique equipment. For more details on jai alai or other sports, see the Sports, Health & Fitness chapter, p128.

Top Five Media Websites

- **Miami Herald** (www.herald.com) The best stop for local and regional news.
- **Miami Beach 411** (www.miamibeach411.com) A great guide for Miami Beach visitors, covering just about all concerns.
- **Miami Today News** (www.miamitodaynews .com) An excellent online source for business and other daily updates.
- **City Search** (www.miami.citysearch.com) Particularly useful for finding detailed nightlife and dining reviews, often with photos.
- **Cool Junkie** (www.cooljunkie.com/miami) A must for trendies, with info on nightclubs, fashion and more.

MEDIA

Most everyone reads the *Miami Herald* in Miami – and throughout the state – as it's the daily newspaper of record. Some do opt for the *Sun-Sentinel,* which comes out of Fort Lauderdale, but the *Herald,* with a circulation of 325,000, is what most would agree is the best provider of local, national and international news coverage. Plus it's got an excellent entertainment section, a great online version (www.herald.com) and beloved columnists – chief among them Dave Barry, who, after 22 years of writing humorous observations, retired in January 2005. On the downside, it's owned by the media conglomerate Knight-Ridder and is 'partners' with most of Miami's other news sources (a common American problem these days) including the local public radio station, WLRN (an excellent NPR affiliate, by the way); the Spanish-language daily *El Nuevo Herald;* the local TV news of both CBS 4 WFOR-TV and UPN 33 WBFS-TV; and radio's Sports Talk 790 The Ticket. There are some great alternative sources, though, mainly the weekly newspaper the *Miami New Times,* which tends to explore the sides of politics that the mainstream may shy away from. *Miami Today* (www.miamitoday.com), serving the business community, is also a good source, especially for financial and economic news. For more details on local media sources, see the Directory chapter, p216.

LANGUAGE

'One of the nicest things about Miami,' goes an old adage, 'is how close it is to the USA.' Indeed, while English is still the official language here, Miami has an above-average number of non-English-speaking residents: more than 60% of the population speaks predominantly Spanish, in fact. This bilingualism has been woven seamlessly into everyday life in Miami; watch for Spanish business names and for English-Spanish menus, street signs and directions when you do anything from dial an automated information line to use local transportation. Miami is home to the largest Spanish-language daily in the country, *El Nuevo Herald,* as well as Spanish papers including *Libre, Exito* and *El Diario Americas.* Creole is also spoken in big numbers in the Haitian community.

As for English speakers, they may be living in America's South, but don't expect to hear any sign of a Southern accent. Instead, say linguistic experts, the 'Miami accent' is a distinct cadence that's borrowed from that of Spanish, even if the speaker can't speak a word of *Español.*

Getting by on a visit here with no Spanish yourself is no problem. But learning a few phrases could greatly enhance your time in Little Havana as well as traditional Latino restaurants. See the Language chapter (p228). If you plan to spend a lot of time in Spanish-speaking neighborhoods, take along Lonely Planet's compact *Latin American Spanish Phrasebook.*

ECONOMY & COSTS

Miami's economy relies heavily on tourism, but its position as gateway to Latin America has given it powerhouse status as an international business city. More than 150 multinational companies have operations in Miami, including Burger King, Carnival Cruise Lines, Citizen Savings Financial and Knight-Ridder; and at least 100 have their Latin American headquarters here, from Johnson & Johnson to the Gap. The city is also establishing itself as an international banking center – almost 45 international banks call it home. But leading the way today is the business of development, causing investors and builders to jump for joy.

While the growth of the nation is at its weakest in years, Miami's economy is booming. And that could mean high prices for the traveler. It's still possible to experience Miami on about $75 a day – $40 for a room in a hostel, $20 on a combo of diner and take-out food with the rest spent on drinks and/or transport – but the reality is that you will be tempted to spend quite a bit more to truly enjoy your time here. Depending on the location and time of year, a nice hotel room is going to cost you at least $100, with popular South Beach midrange haunts going for closer to $150 to $250. On the high end, expect to pay anywhere from $400 to $1000 a night. Then there's food. The preponderance of ethnic cuisines, delis and diners means that it is possible to find dinner for as little as $10 – but throw in some ambience and alcohol and you'll find it's $10 just for your glass of wine and at least $25 per person for the food. Other costly activities will seduce you, as well – nightclubbing, with entrance fees of about $20 and cocktails that cost about $10 apiece; bicycling, with rentals averaging $20 daily; sky's-the-limit shopping; children's attractions such as the Seaquarium (p68), with an entrance fee of $19 to $24; and live entertainment and sporting events, where ticket prices can cost anywhere from $15 to $100 or more. Expect to spend about $200 a week on a rental car – more if it's peak tourist season.

Bargain seekers, take note: while museums do charge entrance fees, usually around $5, many have free days or hours, including the Bass Museum of Art (p52; 6pm until 9pm second Thursday of the month), Historical Museum of Southern Florida (p60; Sun) and Miami Art Museum (p61; Sun).

How Much?	
Gallon of gas	$2.20
8oz bottle of water	$1
Martini	$8
Souvenir T-shirt	$5
Cuban sandwich	$4
Sunscreen	$9
Beach towel	$8
Club admission	$20
Oceanfront hotel room	$400
Car rental per week	$200

GOVERNMENT & POLITICS

Miami-Dade County, which includes the separate cities of Miami and Miami Beach and environs, has a two-tiered governmental system including a large unincorporated area and 27 separate municipalities. Miami-Dade provides services such as the police and fire departments, and trash collection to the unincorporated areas, which make up about 60% of the county. In some cases, such as police and fire coverage, Miami-Dade may overlap with an incorporated municipality. Buses and other public transportation within the entire county fall under the domain of Miami-Dade. Each municipality within Miami-Dade has its own city government, police force, fire department etc. The Miami-Dade board of county commissioners consists of 13 commissioners elected by districts.

When the last mayor was removed from office following the recount scandal of the 2000 Presidential Election, the current mayor, Manny Diaz, was elected. And in a county known for its political shenanigans, the first-term, Cuban-born mayor has been widely praised for feats including turning around the troubled economy, creating education and antipoverty initiatives and luring more tourists to Downtown Miami by launching a city tourist campaign.

Miami has certainly been less mired in political scandals than in its not-so-distant past. That's not to say, however, that messy politics have ceased. As this book went to press, for example, the trial of Miami Commissioner Arthur Teele was beginning. Teele was arrested on two separate charges – receiving bribes as head of the Miami's Community Redevelopment Agency and trying to run down undercover police officers who were following him.

ENVIRONMENT

CLIMATE

If you know anything about weather in Miami, you probably know that it's a warm place – tropical, actually, which means you should expect humidity and summer temperatures almost all year round. The climate can be oppressive in summer months, with temperatures climbing regularly over 90°F (32°C) from about June through September, which is why the tourism industry experiences a lull during that time. The humidity creates a breeding ground for mosquitoes, adding further to the discomfort. It's not unusual, though, for Miami to experience bouts of chilliness (though locals and weathermen alike keep this info close to their chests). In midwinter, when the biggest flocks of snowbirds head here to escape the cold, temperatures can often dip into the low 40s at night, and hover in the barely warm 50s during the day – despite unwavering forecasts that claim 'tomorrow will bring highs in the 70s!' If it's between December and February, don't believe that till you feel it, and be sure to pack for a variety of possibilities.

THE LAND

Miami is situated in a delicate and fascinating ecosystem that's made up of many parts, one of which is the 40-mile-long Biscayne Bay, a bay with mangrove shorelines, underwater coral reefs and waters teeming with pink shrimp, stone crabs and manatees. The bay forms part of the Atlantic Intercoastal Waterway and is a shallow inlet of the Atlantic Ocean. While many of its mangrove forests have been lost to development, those that remain help stabilize the shoreline and provide shelter for birds and animals. Its lush seagrass beds and coral reefs – many of which have been replaced through Miami's Artificial Reef Program (p52) – are also important elements of the system. The bay's eastern edge contains the northernmost islands of the Florida Keys, protected from development by the establishment of Biscayne National Park in 1968.

The bay is not the only form of water-based life in Miami, of course. There are the coastal strand of beaches and sand dunes; the maritime hammock, made up of dunes old enough to sprout delicate trees; coastal wetlands, consisting of swamps and salt marshes; and freshwater marshes, mostly evident throughout the Everglades. It's a beautiful and compelling ecosystem, and therefore one that is forever luring developers and visitors, and needing protections from these 'admirers.'

Hurricane Forecasting

Though Miami has been lucky in recent years, the threat of a hurricane, during a season that lasts from June through November, is always looming – and memories of past destruction make that a very scary threat indeed. The most devastating hurricane to ever rip through town was back in 1926, when a mighty storm destroyed much of the city. Other biggies were on Labor Day in 1935, killing 400 people, and 1992's Hurricane Andrew. While a nasty series of storms wreaked serious havoc on most of South Florida in 2004, Miami got off easy with just minimal damage. But is the worst still to come? If so, the National Hurricane Center (NHC) hopes to minimize the damage, as it's focused on tracking these storms as early as possible and then issuing warnings, allowing folks to prepare. The NHC uses sophisticated tracking systems, including satellite photos and advanced computer systems; as of 2005 these systems will be faster than ever, with strong backups and a processing speed that has just jumped from 450 billion calculations per second to a whopping 1.3 trillion. It's heady stuff, but comforting, especially to the residents of the vulnerable Miami area.

GREEN MIAMI

Development-loving though they are, the residents of Miami realized a while ago that the beautiful land that lured or kept them here in the first place was in serious danger. Luckily, voters approved a two-year property tax back in 1990 to fund the Environmentally Endangered Lands (EEL) program, which has since acquired and protected more than 21,000 acres of endangered land. Newly nominated parcels are considered every year; those chosen are often boosted with matching funds from the State of Florida's Preservation 2000 program as well as the conservation group Florida Forever.

Other efforts to save the earth include an aggressive motor-oil recycling program, a response to the serious issue of illegally dumped oil – more than 300 cases of which were reported in 2000 alone, costing the city $45,000 to clean up. Miami is also home to one of the largest curbside recycling programs in the nation; it's an extensive plan that recycles items including newspapers, batteries, plastic bottles, glass containers and, in a recent addition, computers, VCRs and televisions. Miami's commercial recycling has been mandatory since 1992.

The Miami area boasts some lovely green spaces and parklands – 9000 miles throughout Miami-Dade County – in addition to the Biscayne National Park (p201) and, of course, the nearby Everglades National Park (p194). Nature and city streets often make for strange bedfellows, such as when the occasional manatee gets lost in a city sewer or when, in 2004, a crocodile was discovered living among the wilds of the University of Miami Campus. The voice of local environmentalists is strong, and can get loud when potentially destructive development plans are announced, but more often than not it's the builders who win.

URBAN PLANNING & DEVELOPMENT

The most burning environmental issue in these parts is that of Everglades restoration, and what'll happen to the $8.4-billion plan that was approved by Congress in 2000 and is being chipped away at by developers at every turn. In 2004 the Bush administration began efforts to bring the Scripps Biomedical Institute – a development that would span the area of 13 shopping malls – to land set aside for preservation, leading to much anger and a massive lawsuit (see Restoration of the Everglades, p191). And now it's looking like the land abutting the Everglades could be in for serious trouble, too. Known as the Urban Development Boundary (UDB) and established in 1975 as a green buffer between densely populated areas and the Everglades, developers have been eyeing the swatch, arguing that it's the only land left for building affordable housing. In 2003 the Miami-Dade Department of Planning and Zoning did a study that determined there is enough developable land to last until 2020 – without moving the UDB. But this latest battle has pitted environmentalists, who argue for the safety of the Everglades, against developers, who argue that surging population and home prices have set off an affordable-housing crisis. Both are worthy arguments here in Miami, and one thing is for sure: this is only the beginning of a fierce and lengthy battle, and one that is symbolic of Miami's myriad issues.

Arts

Arts

It's nothing new that Miami boasts culture. Gentrification and redevelopment, as well as the constant influx of foreigners, have resulted in an explosion of artistic activity for at least the past decade. What is new, however, is that the rest of the world has begun to sit up and take notice. That's mainly thanks to a lineup of special events that draws folks here and then sends them away pumped and inspired, ready to spread the gospel of Miami as a burgeoning arts capital of America. While DJs, pop artists and creatures of the night have the **Winter Music Conference** (p17), lit fans have the November **Miami Book Fair International** (p19). Then there are constant film, dance and classical-music festivals, all high-quality showcases that bring in crowds. But perhaps most transformative to how the rest of the world views artistic Miami has been the 2002 introduction of **Art Basel Miami Beach** (p19), which has created a major buzz throughout the national arts scene.

There are plenty of year-round treats for fans of creativity, of course, most recently Wynwood and the Design District, the scruffy but chic homes to many a gallery, studio and lofty workspace. The creative hubs of Coconut Grove and Coral Gables have plenty to offer, as do the diverse collection of museums all over town. There are also movie houses that may look mall-like but screen an eclectic array of indie treats, beautiful deco theaters showcasing drama and dance spectaculars and, not soon enough, the much-anticipated Downtown **Performing Arts Center** (p121). For a full-on artistic experience, we recommend opting for all.

VISUAL ARTS

The latest boost to the local art scene here has been Art Basel Miami Beach, the US outpost of an annual erudite gathering that's based in Switzerland. By its second year, the event had created electricity throughout the national art world – and had succeeded in wooing 175 exhibitors, more than 30,000 visitors and plenty of celebs to take over the galleries, clubs and hotels of South Beach and the Design District. It's grown, in both size and strength, each year since, and its impact on the local art scene here cannot be overstated.

Though Miami's art scene was virtually nonexistent as recently as the early 1980s, by the mid-1980s artists from around the country discovered that they could get more space and live more cheaply in South Beach than in other art centers such as New York and Los Angeles. About the same time, the South Beach boom began, which in turn supplied the cash to fuel an explosion in local art. Unfortunately – but not surprisingly – as the gentrification of Miami Beach became more complete, the very artists who made the scene had to move on to find new, cheaper digs. The wonderful artist-run **ArtCenter/South Florida** (p54) on Lincoln Rd, which helped to bring around the renaissance, is just about the only such place to have stayed put, still supporting artists

Leslie Hotel (p34), South Beach

with space for working and exhibiting. But for the most part, the art nurturers have moved elsewhere.

That's where Art Basel came in, bringing with it global attention, glitzy glamour and serious money. And it's also where the Design District comes in. This small region, north of Downtown Miami and comprising just about 18 square blocks, is fast becoming, as its name suggests, the heart of interior design and furniture arts in South Florida. (It was what inspired chic *Wallpaper* magazine to declare Miami 'best city' in its 2004 Design Awards). It's home to showrooms from luminaries including **Holly**

Top Five Art Museums

- For big names and an on-the-edge aesthetic, visit the **Museum of Contemporary Art** (p75).
- The **Bass Museum of Art** (p52) has masters, beauties and classics.
- For a gem of design in a treasure of a space, swing by **Wolfsonian-FIU** (p54).
- The last holdout in gentrified South Beach is **ArtCenter/South Florida** (p54).
- The **Rubell Family Art Collection** (p63) boasts names that will wow any art fan.

Hunt (p144), Knoll, Luminaire, Ann Sacks and **Kartell** (p144). But it's also location central for the most up-and-coming, cutting-edge art galleries in the region, from the **Bernice Steinbaum Gallery** (p64) to Adamar Fine Arts and the Silvana Facchini Gallery, as well as various public-art displays. In Wynwood, just south of the Design District, one of many notable spaces is the **Rubell Family Art Collection** (p63), a modern-art collection displayed in a former Drug Enforcement Agency confiscated-drug warehouse. And a small stretch on NW 23rd Street has become a bustling hub, with spaces belonging to *über*-dealer Frederic Snitzer, the nonprofit Locus Projects, and other heavy hitters.

The new art spaces aren't the only good ones, though. The **Museum of Contemporary Art** (p75), designed by Charles Gwathmey and opened in 1996, fused urban and cultural planning by placing a civic and cultural center within a residential and commercial area. It's thriving, known for its provocative, cutting-edge exhibits and wonderful permanent collection. The **Bass Museum of Art** (p52) in South Beach, the **Miami Art Museum** (p61) Downtown and the **Lowe Art Museum** (p73) in Coral Gables deliver the goods when it comes to more Eurocentric works, and the **Wolfsonian-FIU** (p54) in South Beach is a wonderful house of design. Even hotels, aware of the city's art draw, are getting in on the action; check out the excellent exhibits at the **Sagamore** (p111) and the **Four Seasons** (p160), which has a permanent exhibit of Botero sculptures.

Also, as you can imagine, Cuban and Latin American artists have a major impact on Miami's growing art community. You'll find a great array of galleries in both Coral Gables and Little Havana; pick up the detailed *Miami Visual Arts Guide* (available at galleries), which maps the locations of art galleries throughout most every neighborhood in Miami and Miami Beach.

PUBLIC ART

When Art Basel comes to town, artists tend to kick into high gear, gleaning inspiration from the droves of excited artists and fans from around the world. And public art has traditionally been a part of what happens – especially in 2004, when a slew of creators treated Miami as their medium and public-art projects sprang up around the city. The well-known Xavier Cortada painted his colorful *Miami Mangrove Forest* underneath overpasses around town, and they still remain. But the public-art tradition started long ago.

Miami and Miami Beach established the Art in Public Places program way back in 1973, when it voted to allocate 1.5% of city construction funds to the fostering of public art; since then more than 700 works – sculptures, mosaics, murals, light-based

Top Five Public Artworks

- The **Holocaust Memorial** (p53), by Kenneth Treister, South Beach.
- **Living Room** (p64), by Roberto Behar and Rosario Marquardt, Design District.
- **Harmonic Runway** (p30), by Christopher Janney, Miami International Airport Concourse A.
- The **Miami Line** (p30), by Rockne Krebs, Metromover.
- **Mermaid** (p54), by Roy Lichtenstein, Jackie Gleason Theater of Performing Arts.

installations and more – have been created in public spots. *Harmonic Runway* livens up the interior of Concourse A at the Miami airport, while a piece by Rockne Krebs, *The Miami Line*, adds joy to Downtown's Metromover. The team of Roberto Behar and Rosario Marquardt, hailing from Argentina, have been among the most prolific; they created the giant red *M* at the Metromover Riverwalk Station for the city's centennial back in 1996, and are also known as the makers of the giant *Living Room* in the Design District. Other artists involved in the program have included sculptor Isamu Noguchi, muralist Carlos Alfonzo and installation artist Nam Jun Paik. In Miami Beach, you'll see the sculpture *Mermaid,* by Roy Lichtenstein, in front of Jackie Gleason Theater of the Performing Arts; the lovely neon work of Jim Morrison, *A Celebration of Light,* as you enter the Beach via the Julia Tuttle Causeway; and the moving murals of the Electrowave bus fleet, giving colorful character to each of these South Beach buses.

Real-estate developers have even used public art to win political battles: Pinnacle Housing Group, a Miami-based developer of affordable-housing projects, commissioned renowned pop artist CJ Latimore to paint *The Playground,* a colorful, 40ft-tall mural of children, on the side of a new housing development to help it win support from the community in 2003. It worked – just as it did earlier that year, when Pinnacle commissioned fiber-optic sculptures of butterflies and the sun to enhance a housing project in Little Havana.

MUSIC

Miami's music scene has long had a booming reputation for being a leader in Latin and Caribbean sounds, turning out singing stars from Gloria Estefan and Celia Cruz to Ricky Martin and Albita. But it's also developed a sound all its own, called Miami Bass, it nurtures a thriving hip-hop scene and has had a brush with country-rock fame (courtesy of The Mavericks, who disbanded in 1999 but recently reunited to produce a live album). Dance and lounge music is huge here, too, and is best evidenced by the annual **Winter Music Conference** (p17) each March, which brings thousands of DJs and producers to town for workshops and parties. And in recent years Miami has been host to an exciting world of indie rock.

'The bands say the freshness of the Florida audiences is a plus,' penned *Herald* music writer Evelyn McDonnell in a 2004 piece about the indie music boom. It's mostly been in the form of bands coming from elsewhere to perform here, but even the fact that there are venues and

Latin and Caribbean Music Primer

So how can you tell the difference between one Latin and beat and another? And is all Caribbean music reggae? Below, a quick crib sheet for your Miami nightclub explorations.

Salsa is the most commonly heard word used to reference Latin music and dance, and it's no mystery why: it's actually a generic term, developed in the mid '60s and early '70s as a way to pull all Latin sounds under one umbrella name for gringos who were unable to recognize the subtle differences between beats. From the Spanish word for 'sauce,' salsa has its roots in Cuban culture and has a sound that's enhanced by textures of jazz. Music that lends itself to salsa dancing has four beats per bar of music.

One specific type of Cuban salsa is *son* – a sound popularized by the release of 1999's *Buena Vista Social Club* film and soundtrack. It has roots in African and Spanish cultures and is quite melodic, usually incorporating instruments including the *tres* (a type of guitar with three sets of closely spaced strings), standard guitars and various hand drums.

Merengue, meanwhile, originates from the Dominican Republic and can be characterized by a very fast beat, with just two beats to each bar. It's typically played on the tambora, guira (a ridged cylindrical percussion instrument made of metal or dried gourd) and accordion.

Hailing from the Andalusian region of Spain is the folk art of flamenco, which consists of hand clapping, finger snapping, vocals, guitar and the flamboyant dance.

The popular reggae sound, originating in Jamaica and having strong Rastafarian roots, is a total movement most popularly associated with Bob Marley. It's characterized by rhythm chops on a backbeat and, at least in its beginnings, a political-activist message. There are various styles within reggae, including roots (Marley's sound), dancehall, raga and dub.

crowds jostling for the sound is new. Weekly Pop Life party nights at the Design District club I/O (p119) attract fans of pop and electronica and have featured live performers including Peaches, the Remnants and Breaker, Breaker (who toured with Le Tigre). The crop of home-grown bands is still thin compared to many other cities, but it's starting to grow; you can expect to find bands including Sparkydog, Nothing Rhymes With Orange and 10 Sheen rocking out in local live-music venues, such as Churchill's Hideaway (p118).

Miami bass, meanwhile – also sometimes

called 'booty bass' and 'bass music' – has its roots in electro and is known for deep, pounding beats and sexually explicit lyrics. The most famous Miami bass group has been 2 Live Crew, and though the high point for this genre ended in the late '90s, it's still a claim to fame in these parts, and has spawned many other groups – 69 Boyz, Uncle Al and more. It's mainly a subgenre of hip-hop, which is still alive and well in these parts thanks to the acclaimed producers who keep their bases in Miami, including Red Spyda, Cool and Dre, and dirty-mouthed performers who are local hip-hop heroes: DJ Smallz, Pitbull (known for his debut album *Miami*) and Uncle Luke.

The biggest story in Miami, though, is still Latin and Caribbean music. Think salsa, reggae, merengue, mambo, rumba, cha-cha and calypso (see boxed text, opposite), because you'll find it all here, in spades – especially during the Billboard Latin Music Conference & Awards (p18) held here each April. And now, thanks to the emergence of a new local fusion sound, you can often hear them all blended together. The Spam All Stars mix hip-hop, Jamaican, funk, salsa and jazz, for example, while the Latin Jazz Explosion, the Latin-pop band Bacilos, and New York transplant and congo master Sammy Figueroa (who's played with Miles Davis) are also striking a chord with fans.

And then, of course, there's the stalwart world of classical music. What this lacks in numbers of performers it makes up for in fans, as the Florida Grand Opera (p119) and New World Symphony (p119) are both highly respected, often host celebrity conductors and maintain a fierce following among melody junkies all over the region. See the Nightlife chapter (p116) for more music venues.

LITERATURE

Each November the nationally renowned Miami Book Fair International (p19) brings a slew of high-profile authors to town. But many of those writers, of course, already live right in Miami. Though it's certainly not a hotbed of high-brow lit like Key West – which boasts a huge population of authors and was home to late luminaries including Ernest Hemingway, Tennessee Williams and Elizabeth Bishop – Miami has certainly made a name for itself in the genres of mystery and crime lit. Which is not all that surprising. Beginning with former *Miami Herald* crime-beat reporters Edna Buchanan and Carl Hiaasen, and leading up to new names like Jeff Lindsay, the Miami crime-writing scene is alive and well. And other writers, including Carolina Garcia-Aguilera, have managed to focus on other topics, from immigration to love. Books & Books (p122) is an excellent source of local lit, both through its stock and its schedule of readings. For more on readings and spoken word, see the Nightlife chapter (p122). What follows is a sampling of what you'll find on the shelves.

The Between (Tananarive Due, 1996) Due's debut novel focused on Hilton, who is haunted by powerfully frightening nightmares when his wife – the only elected African-American judge in Dade County – begins receiving racist hate mail.

Cold Case Squad (Edna Buchanan, 2004) Buchanan's 13th novel, done in her typically mesmerizing style, is all about Sergeant Craig Burch, who leads the Miami Police Department's cold case squad by trying to track killers whose 'trails vanished long ago like footprints on a sea washed beach.'

Miami Crime Queen: Edna Buchanan

In a recent *Miami New Times* feature about the local lit scene, Delray's Murder on the Beach bookstore owner Joanne Sinchuk said it best: 'There are two people in South Florida who don't need a last name – Fidel and Edna.' And how true it is. With a Pulitzer Prize, stacks of *Miami Herald* clippings, one memoir and 13 novels under her belt, Edna is one of the most quintessential Miami writers of all time.

In her first book, *The Corpse Had a Familiar Face,* Buchanan writes in her signature hardboiled-yet-seductive prose about her humble New Jersey beginnings as Edna Rydzik and how she instantly fell in love with Miami during a visit. Before long, she had secured a job as a police-beat reporter at the *Herald,* and was covering stories from serial murders to the historic race riots of 1980. She eventually traded the newsroom for a fiction-writing career, and for years the subject of her novels was the familiar hard-nosed newswoman Britt Montero. But she's taken a different tack in her latest release, *Cold Case Squad* (see review, p31). Through it all, though, Buchanan, who appears on the book-signing circuit whenever she puts out a new novel, writes about her adoration of Miami with a romanticism that's strong enough to ignite any reader's passions.

Continental Drift (Russell Banks, 1985) It's all here – morals, tragedy, love and sex – in the American classic novel about a blue collar New Hampshire worker who flees for shallow promises in the south of Florida. Banks explores the Miami story in beautiful, haunting prose.

Darkly Dreaming Dexter: A Novel (Jeff Lindsay, 2004) Dexter Morgan is a lab technician who specializes in blood splatter for the Miami-Dade police department. He's also a serial killer. And he's also the good guy. A follow-up to this well-received tale is due out in mid-2005.

Hoot (Carl Hiaasen, 2002) This time the crime master writes for young readers aged nine to 12, weaving a colorful tale of Roy, the new kid in his Coconut Grove school, whose first 'friend,' unfortunately, is a bully. It's a wonderfully quirky Hiaasen intro.

Labrava (Elmore Leonard, 1983) Learn to love (or at least understand) a variety of lowlifes and sleazy folks in the best of the bunch from Leonard. In this suspenseful novel, Joe Labrava is a former secret-service agent who gets mixed up in a Miami scam revolving around a Cuban hitman, a redneck former cop and a fading movie starlet. It's a fast-paced character-driven tale, both intriguing and wacky.

Miami Blues (Charles Willeford, 1984) The late Miami underworld master Willeford first made it big with this addictive novel about a denture-wearing detective's chase after a cold and quirky criminal. It was the basis for the 1990 film of the same name, starring Alec Baldwin.

Miami Purity (Vicki Hendricks, 1996) Hendricks' debut novel is noirish tale of a stripper who tries to go straight, written in trashy, crisp language that's impossible to turn away from.

One Hot Summer (Carolina Garcia-Aguilera, 2003) Margarita Solana, a Cuban-American Miami Beach wife and mother, must re-evaluate her life: her lawyer husband is encouraging her to have another child, but meanwhile, her first love has reappeared on the scene. Conflicts of passion sizzle in Solana's hands.

Tropic of Night (Michael Gruber, 2003) This debut thriller takes readers to Mali, Siberia and Nigeria before settling in Miami, where protagonist Jane Doe assumes a new, faceless life among the city's underclass in order to escape a frighteningly powerful new acquaintance. It's a gripping and fascinating read.

FILM & TV

Like just about everything else in Miami right now, the film and TV businesses are growing all the time – from new TV shows (and recycled incarnations) popping up to a preponderance of directors choosing Miami as an ideal shooting location for their features.

It's not an altogether new idea, of course, and South Florida had a viable cinematic industry way before Hollywood became the filmmaking capital of the western hemisphere. In the 1920s, DW Griffith produced *White Rose* (and other producers followed with their own features) out of Miami Movie Studios in Hialeah. Sam Katzman chose the city for B-movies about gang wars, and several (lowbrow) classics – as well as the *Jackie Gleason Show,* shot here for TV – came out of 1960s Miami. Two of the on-screen images with the most lasting impressions, though, have been *Scarface,* Brian DePalma's over-the-top story of a Cuban drug lord (Al Pacino), and *Miami Vice,* the 1980s TV series about a couple of pastel-clad vice-squad cops that put Miami back on the international map. The images – of murders, rapes and drug-turf wars – were far from positive, however, and the powers-that-be in the city were not happy. Ironically, *Miami Vice* is now credited for bringing South Beach back to life, proving, ultimately, that no press is bad press. The entire first season of the series has just been released on DVD, and a new Hollywood film version is currently being shot on location. Miami and Miami Beach governments love the idea of producers coming to town so much, in fact, that in early 2005 they instituted the One Stop Permitting system, providing a streamlined, online way for makers of films, TV shows and commercials to apply for permits (at www.filmiami.org). At the time of writing, there were more than 60 films, TV shows, commercials and music videos being shot in Miami-Dade.

Below is a list of various films and TVs shows that'll give you a taste of Miami, both past and present.

Top Five Films/TV Shows

- *Scarface* (1983)
- *Miami Blues* (1990)
- *Miami Vice* (1984)
- *Nip/Tuck* (2003)
- *The Birdcage* (1996)

The Bellboy (1960) A baby-faced Jerry Lewis stars in this screwball comedy about, you guessed it, a bellboy at the **Fontainebleau** (p56). Filmed entirely on location (and employing several real-life bellboys in many of the scenes), the film is completely silly, but an interesting look into Miami's storied resort past.

The Birdcage (1996) The Hollywood version of *La Cage Au Folles* stars Robin Williams and Nathan Lane as a gay couple who run a flamboyant South Beach cabaret but try to play it in-the-closet when their son brings his fiancée's right-wing parents to town. It's funny, poignant and a nice visual image of the area.

CSI: Miami (2002) The Miami incarnation of the popular *CSI* TV series about a Crime Scenes Investigation unit revisits Miami's dicey past, but does so from the safety of its now-glitzy present. It's overly produced and a bit too earnest in its writing, but is an interesting peek into some of the city's modern lurid moments.

Get Shorty (1995) Danny DeVito and John Travolta costar in this translation of the Elmore Leonard novel. The smart and hysterical mobster comedy follows a Miami loan shark to Hollywood and Vegas in search of money he's owed.

Mean Season (1985) Loosely based on the experiences of Edna Buchanan and fellow *Herald* newshounds, this drama stars Kurt Russell as Malcolm Anderson, a burnt-out Miami reporter who gets reinspired when his life becomes intertwined with that of a serial killer. It's gripping and good until the overboard Hollywood ending.

Miami Blues (1990) Based on Charles Willeford's novel, this black comedy with a cultish following has Frederick (Alec Baldwin), a sicko thief and liar, worm his way into the world of the very naïve Susie (Jennifer Jason Leigh). It's clever and oddly compelling, with great shots of Coral Gables and the Miami River.

Miami Vice (1984) The series that started it all. Don Johnson and Philip Michael Thomas are vice-squad detectives, which, in 1980s South Beach, means they drive a fancy car, wear pink or yellow blazers and shoot up the bad-guy drug dealers. A wonderful nostalgia trip!

Nip/Tuck (2003) The newest TV series to use Miami Beach as its backdrop, this one uses it well, and is a quirky, funny, far-reaching drama about two not-so-scrupulous plastic surgeons and their complicated personal lives.

Scarface (1983) This classic Miami crime tale stars Al Pacino as a Cuban immigrant who fast learns how to be a big shot in the drug-dealing underworld. It's sheer over-the-top craziness, especially the grand finale scene, shot in the Fountainebleau.

There's Something About Mary (1998) The Farrelly Brothers' hysterical comedy about a grown-up geek who tracks down his high-school sweetheart has some great shots of South Beach.

Hooray for South Beach

Known by many as 'Hollywood of the South,' South Beach boasts enough nightclubs, hotel bars and A-list guests to provide serious fodder for tabloid reporters. It's where they know they'll get a good shot of celebs such as Jessica Simpson, Paris Hilton, Cameron Diaz, Usher, Britney Spears, J Lo and Marc Anthony posing, dancing or lounging among the fabulous set. **Privé** (p115), **Skybar** (p111), **Tantra** (p113), **Rumi** (p116), the **Delano Hotel** (p155) and eateries from **Cafeteria** (p95) to the **Forge** (p97) are all popular star haunts. And some, including Gloria Estefan, Sean 'Puffy' Combs and Mariah Carey own real estate here, making it much easier to track 'em down for a photo session. Jason Priestly and Ashlee Peterson were married on the Miami coast, Calvin Klein is rumored to own a South Beach apartment, and even Al Pacino, apparently ready to return to his roots, has reportedly been scouting for a Miami home.

THEATER & COMEDY

Miami has always enjoyed a rich theater history, but it enjoyed a major coup in 2003. That's when Cuban-born resident Nilo Cruz won a Pulitzer Prize for his *Anna in the Tropics*, becoming the first non–New York production to win. The play had premiered at the **New Theatre** (p122) in Coral Gables, allowing stage fans from all over town to rejoice in Cruz's win. And it's not the only thing going on in Miami, where local-star playwrights such as Teo Castellanos and Marco Ramirez continue to leave big marks on the theater world. Miami's various theater festivals – the International Hispanic Theater Festival in June, Cultura del Lobo in October and the Fringe Festival – bring out heavyweight talents annually. And its rich history, stemming from places including the **Actors' Playhouse** (p122) in Coral Gables, the

Architecture: Art-Deco Miami

During the golden age of travel from the end of WWI in 1918 well into the 1930s, there was a giddy fascination with speed: cars, ocean liners, trains and planes. This transferred to architecture with the popularity of art deco. The term art deco, a variation on 'decorative arts', originated at a 1925 Paris design fair and came to signify a modern style fusing existing forms such as art nouveau, Arts and Crafts and geometric modernism with futuristic lines evoking transportation. After the 1926 hurricane devastated Miami Beach, architectural opportunity came knocking. Miami real estate was up for grabs, and hotel rebuilding began at a frenzied rate. The resulting colorful canvas is known today as the Art Deco Historic District.

Miami Beach developed what came to be known as tropical deco architecture, which organically reflected the natural world around it. Glass architectural blocks let bright Florida light in but kept sweltering heat out. Floral reliefs, popular during the art nouveau period, appeared here, too. Friezes on facades or etched into glass reflected native wildlifelike palm trees, pelicans and flamingos, and took other cues, harmonious and lyrical, from the uniquely American jazz movement. Surrounded by water, Miami Beach deco also developed a rhythmic language, with scalloped waves and fountains.

The clean lines of Miami Beach architecture still made room for playful, hopeful characteristics. Forward thinking, and dreaming about the future, took hold. Space travel was explored through design: buildings began to loosely resemble rockets, and rooflines embodied fantasies about traveling the universe. Curved walls enhanced aerodynamic principles. Racing stripes, alluding to the new speed of cars and trains, furthered the metaphor of efficiency. Nautical elements from the dawning era of ocean liners found expression through porthole windows and metal railings. The wonderful Beach Patrol Headquarters on the sands of South Beach are an excellent example of ship love.

Neon signage helped to individualize buildings. Canopy porches gave hotel patrons a cool place to sit. To reflect the heat, buildings were originally painted white, with animated accent colors highlighting smaller elements. (It was only later, during the 1980s, that interior designer Leonard Horowitz decreed the pastel palette that became the standard.) In Miami today, art deco evokes South Beach, and the Art Deco Historic District, which played a major role in the city's late-20th-century renaissance. With the district the epicenter of Miami's always-hopping hotel and nightlife scene, it's hard to imagine the place as the run-down eyesore it was in the 1970s.

Top Ten Art-Deco Jewels

- The 'deco-Federal' 1939 **Miami Beach Post Office** (p53) features a classical rotunda, marble stamp tables, brass detailing and a striking indoor mural.
- **Jerry's Famous Deli** (p92) is housed in the Hoffman Cafeteria Building, a spacious Henry Hohauser gem from 1939.
- Now home to the Crobar nightclub, the **Cameo Theatre** (p114) still gives a sense of deco-era entertainment with its chrome canopy, glass-block paneling and other unique details.
- The **Beach Patrol Headquarters** is a whimsical take on a ship, not far from the water's edge.
- Gloria Estefan owns the **Cardozo Hotel** (p155), a 1939 Hohauser Streamline-Moderne classic.
- Porthole windows lend the **Essex House Hotel** (p152) the feel of a grand cruise ship, while its spire is rocket-ship all the way.
- **Leslie Hotel** is a classic pastel deco from Albert Anis, with eyebrows that wrap all the way around the side of the building.
- Renovated in 2003, the 1940 **National Hotel** (p156) has a particularly impressive lobby and authentic period murals.
- Check out the dramatic 'R' on the tower roof of the **Raleigh Hotel** (p157), plus the rounded corner and patterned windows.
- **Carlyle Hotel** comes with futuristic stylings, triple parapet and a Jetsons sort of vibe.

Miami Beach post office (p53)

Coconut Grove Playhouse (p122; known for its historic, though disastrous, American premiere of *Waiting for Godot*), and the University of Miami–Coral Gables' acting program (alma mater of both Sylvester Stallone and Ray Liotta), doesn't hurt either. Then there's the whole new armada of cutting-edge venues and troupes, from the innovative **Miami Light Project** (p121) to the City Theater and its series of original summer shorts.

Then take Miami's comedy scene – please! But seriously, folks, while the circuit here may be slightly lacking, there are a few venues and performance troupes worth laughing at. **Impromedy** (p124), an innovative sketch-comedy troupe formed at FIU, performs weekly at the Roxy Performing Arts Center, while **Laughing Gas** (p124), a wacky, costume-heavy improv group does its funny business at various venues around the area and **Just the Funny** (p124) busts out at the Planetarium on weekends. Mostly, though, you'll find big-box theaters, often chains, displaying the mainstream talents of folks seen on HBO or Comedy Central. And sometimes a simple people-watching session on Ocean Dr can be just as amusing. For comedy and theater venues, see the Nightlife chapter (p124).

DANCE

Dance is a relatively new performance genre in Miami, where the oldest companies – Miami City Ballet and Sosyete Koukouy – were both founded in 1985. The strange pairing of these two troupes, one a classical ballet showcase and the other a Haitian dance and theater company (whose name means 'Firefly Society') could not better represent the diversity of the Miami dance scene. While it's the nationally renowned festivals here, namely the Latin-Caribbean flavored **Baila USA Annual Dance & Culture Arts Festival** (p123) and the

Brazilian Fla/Bra that best showcase the international mix of movements here, year-round opportunities abound. **Flamenco Theatre La Rosa** (p120), for example, blends flamenco with Indian styles and even tap dancing. **Momentum Dance** (p120) offers modern works by known choreographers such as Isadora Duncan, while the Maximum Dance Company is Miami's modern star, known for using unexpected musical scores (from U2, for example) for their works. Other troupes blend African, Cuban and Brazilian sounds and styles – a constant on-stage reminder that Miami's culture cannot be narrowed down. For more on dance venues and annual festivals, see the Nightlife chapter (p120).

History

History

Miami Beach and Miami are very new cities, even by American standards. Developed mainly during the 20th century, the region was transformed through a combination of the railroad, hotels, electricity, tourists, and waves of immigrants from empty swampland into a jumping, destination city. It's outside influences that have always made Miami what it is, and they just keep on coming. So whatever you see in this wacky and wild South Floridian world when you visit today, just don't dare expect to find the same place you loved as a kid – or the place you'll love when you're older. Because this city of the future is one hard place to keep up with.

THE RECENT PAST

Miami's entire history is based on riding out a wave of booms and busts instigated by everything from drug-fueled crime to really bad weather. Recent history is no exception, with the only difference being that the space between the highs and lows keeps getting shorter. Just take a look at the past decade: during most of the 1990s, the city rode the peak of a boom sparked in no small part by the trendy allure of South Beach. The city of Miami hosted the Summit of the Americas in 1994 (everyone attended but Castro), celebrated its centennial in 1996 and jumped for joy as the US military moved its Central and South American command center to Miami. But it wouldn't remain smooth sailing for long. The new millennium brought political scandal. First was the Elián Gonzalez nightmare, an international custody fight that ended with federal agents storming the seven-year-old's Little Havana house to have him shipped back to Cuba and anti-Castro Cubans protesting in Miami streets. Then came the removal of Mayor Xavier Suarez from office in 1998, whose election was overturned following the discovery of many illegal votes.

But would this bad image last? Not on your life. A few years later, all is forgiven, with more and more visitors than ever flocking – even moving – to Glitter Beach. New mayor Manuel Diaz has been beloved and scandal-free, new hotels and nightspots can't stop coming, high-end travel magazines can't write enough about the beat, and construction of high-rise condos is on such an upswing that the city looks like a postwar zone that's scrambling to rebuild itself. The new Downtown Performing Arts Center, anxiously anticipated since the project took shape in 2000, is what the government is now counting on as the pièce de résistance of its urbane future (though it's been quite delayed in arriving). And, proving once and for all that the city is charmed, Miami managed to avoid any major damage during a violent series of hurricanes in 2004 that caused mass destruction to much of the rest of the state. Bets are that it'll keep coming out on top.

FROM THE BEGINNING

TEQUESTA INDIANS

Miami's earliest known inhabitants, the Tequesta (Tekesta) Indians, are something of a mystery. Their culture, including their language and customs, did not withstand European settlement long enough to be sufficiently recorded. But the apparently nonagrarian tribal

TIMELINE	10,000 BC	1513	1565
	Tequesta Indians arrive in South Florida	Juan Ponce de León is the first European to land in Florida	Pedro Menéndez de Avilés lands in Florida

group occupied much of South Florida from about 10,000 BC, and the remains of a permanent settlement were recently discovered at the mouth of the Miami River.

Shortly after the Spanish made contact with the Tequesta, the usual tragedy ensued as a combination of disease and violence decimated their population. The Miami River site was probably abandoned shortly after Spanish Conquest. Although no Tequesta tribal members are currently recognized by the US government, it is likely that survivors joined forces with the regional Mikosukee or Seminole tribes.

SPAIN, BRITAIN, & SPAIN AGAIN

The first European to set foot on Florida was Spanish explorer and soldier Ponce de León, in 1513, who was undertaking a painstaking search for the mythical 'fountain of youth.' But the man widely credited for leading Florida to its colonization is Spanish explorer Pedro Menéndez de Avilés. In 1565 – several decades before the Pilgrims landed on Plymouth Rock and before the establishment of Jamestown, Virginia – Menéndez de Avilés landed in what he soon named St Augustine. From there he went north and led massacres on many an encroaching French fleet. The area would become to North America what Poland is to Europe: the flattest piece of land between battling superpowers. Before Florida was officially ceded to the US by Spain in 1821, the entire northeast section of the state was sacked, looted, burned and occupied by Spanish, English and US forces. The Spanish retained control of the region despite repeated British attacks in 1586, 1668 and 1702.

When Spain made a late entry into the French and Indian War, fighting against Britain in 1762, the distraction cost it Florida, which it ceded to Great Britain in a swap for Havana, Cuba, in 1763. The British would hold the territory throughout the American Revolution, though as part of the Treaty of Paris ending that war, it was ceded back to Spain in 1783.

The Seminoles

The story of the native Seminoles – members of a cultured tribe who had developed forms of government, lived in *chickees* (a palmetto thatch over a cypress-log frame), wore heavily beaded outfits and had a deep respect for the South Florida land – is not all that different from the countless Native American horror shows that dot the landscape of early American history. In this particular case, the Seminoles were seen as a barrier to settlers who wanted Florida to be a colony. This sentiment led to a period known as the Seminole Wars, beginning in about 1817. Seminoles, who had been known to harbor escaped slaves and also intermarry with them, were being targeted by US troops, who needed the pesky tribe members out of the way in order to make land grabbing from Spain easier.

The USA began slaughtering large numbers of Seminoles in a battle led by General Andrew Jackson (future president), then captured Pensacola in 1818; by 1819 Spain ceded Florida to the USA. An influx of new colonists kept pushing the Seminoles south and, in 1830, Congress came up with a shockingly Nazi-like scheme: the Removal Act, a law which told Indians they would have to pack up their things and move across the country to the barren plains that would later become Oklahoma. Some went, but the chief, Osceola, refused to sign the treaty and fled into the Everglades with many of his people. Warring broke out weeks later, when US troops arrived to enforce the removal law. This Second Seminole War was the deadliest war waged by the USA on natives, as well as one of the costliest, topping $20 million in resources. The Seminoles were great fighters, and the USA became desperate and dirty: when it agreed in 1837 to negotiate with the tribe and Osceola showed up with a peace flag, the chief was captured and imprisoned as fighting continued. By 1842 the warring had ended, but no peace treaty was ever signed.

Those Seminoles who remained are still living in and around the Everglades, and are now organized under a tribal government and running the Ah-Tah-Thi-Ki Museum (p199) tours and, of course, a casino.

1783	1817	1821	1835–1842
Treaty of Paris	Sir Gregor MacGregor takes over Amelia Island	The USA acquires Florida from Spain	Second Seminole War

Besides one rather significant interruption – when a group of US-backed rebels briefly took over Amelia Island – the Spanish ran the show from 1783 until 1817, when the US moved in to hold the territory 'in trust' for Spain.

In 1817 Sir Gregor MacGregor, a Scottish mercenary with revolutionary experience in Venezuela and the financial support of businesspeople in Savannah, Georgia, and Charleston, South Carolina, hired a force that again took over the island from the Spanish on June 29, 1817. When the money ran out, so did MacGregor, who left two lieutenants in command.

THE US MOVES IN (SURPRISE, SURPRISE)

The two left holding the bag, Lieutenants Ruggles Hubbard and Jared Irwin, formed a joint venture with a Mexico-based French pirate named Louis Aury (who was permitted to fly the Mexican flag anywhere he wanted, so long as he kicked back a percentage of his plunders to the Mexican government). These three managed to turn the place into an even *more* scandalous town – it's said that there were more bars than street corners, and even more brothels.

Perhaps using moral outrage as an excuse to nab some nifty real estate, US troops moved in and took over in December 1817. In a face-saving compromise, Spain officially turned Florida over to the US in 1821 in exchange for US promises to pay the land claims of Spanish subjects (none of which, by the way, were ever paid).

In 1825 the US Army built the Cape Florida Lighthouse. It was the first permanent structure in South Florida, which was then mostly marshy wetlands. A mere 10 years later, the Cape Florida Lighthouse was destroyed during the Seminole Wars. These wars resulted in the massive displacement of the majority of Seminoles to a reservation in Oklahoma. (An interesting note is that the Seminoles are still technically at war with the USA – they say they never signed a valid peace treaty.)

In 1843 William F English settled in Miami, bringing investments, settlers and slaves. By 1850 a post office had been established, and a few dozen handfuls of people had moved into the area; by 1870 William B Brickell had established an Indian trading post at Miami.

In 1881 Henry B Lum bought up and cleared most of Miami Beach (for between 35¢ and $1.25 an acre) in an ill-conceived attempt to grow coconuts on the island. The plants either failed in poor soil or were lost to rabbits and deer, and by 1890 he admitted defeat. But the Lum family held on to much of the land.

TUTTLE & FLAGLER

The first real shot at developing Miami Beach came with John S Collins. He bought the 5-mile strip between the Atlantic and Biscayne Bay (what is now 14th to 67th Sts) and began selling parcels of beachfront property in 1896. But the two most significant arrivals were Julia Tuttle in 1875 and Henry Morrison Flagler in 1895.

Tuttle had stayed in the area earlier with her husband, who had tuberculosis, and after his death she returned to land she had inherited. Over the next 20 years, she bought up quite a bit more property in the area.

Flagler, a developer and the business partner of John D Rockefeller in Standard Oil, had been developing the Florida coast at the northern end of the state, building resorts in St Augustine and Palm Beach. He also built the Florida East Coast Railroad, which extended down as far as Palm Beach. Tuttle contacted Flagler with a proposition: if he would extend his railroad to Miami, Tuttle would split her property with him. Flagler wasn't interested.

Then, in 1895, a record freeze enveloped most of the state of Florida (but not Miami), wiping out citrus crops and sending vacationers scurrying. Legend has it that Tuttle – who

1845	1881	1896	1898
Florida becomes the 27th state in the Union	Hamilton Disston buys a million acres of land in the Everglades	Henry Flagler finishes construction of his railroad	Army camps set up in Miami during the Spanish-American War

is said to have been rather quick both on the uptake and with an 'I told you so' – went into her garden at Fort Dallas on the Miami River, snipped off some orange blossoms and sent them to Flagler, who hightailed it down to Miami to see for himself.

What he found was a tropical paradise that was very warm indeed. Flagler and Tuttle came to terms, after which Flagler announced the extension of the railroad. Soon after, thousands of people whose livelihoods had been wiped out by the big freeze, including citrus growers and workers, and service-industry professionals such as doctors and merchants, headed down to Miami in anticipation of the boom that was to come.

Passenger-train service to Miami began April 22, 1896, the year the city of Miami became incorporated.

SPANISH-AMERICAN WAR

The USA showed the world it was a power to be reckoned with during the 10-week-long Spanish-American War in 1898. As Cuba struggled for independence from Spanish rule, reports drifted back of Cuban farmers being gathered into prison camps. Newspapers such as William Randolph Hearst's New York *Journal* began a campaign of 'yellow journalism' that riled the American public. The stories ostensibly supported the 'humanitarian annexation' of Cuba, which perhaps not coincidentally would have been a culmination of the USA's manifest destiny and a darned happy windfall to US businesspeople.

President William McKinley resisted intervention, but when the battleship *Maine* was destroyed in Havana's harbor, McKinley declared war on Spain. Congress ratified the declaration on April 25. Debate continues today about the *Maine*'s destruction. On one hand, it is suspicious that almost all the ship's officers were ashore at the time of the detonation. On the other, new evidence that the explosion was an accident has also surfaced.

The main fighting took place in two theaters: the North Pacific and Cuba. After handy victories in Manila and Guam, US army and volunteer regiments landed in Cuba in late June, including the Rough Riders (who actually had to leave all their horses in Florida), led by Leonard Wood and Theodore Roosevelt. The Spanish surrendered on July 17, and a week later, the USA invaded Puerto Rico. The Spanish soon asked for terms of peace through a French ambassador, and McKinley, through the signed Treaty of Paris, negotiated US occupation of Cuba (until its independence in 1902), and the acquisition of Puerto Rico and Guam.

EARLY BOOM

Flagler extended his railway into farming-rich areas in Homestead and Cutler, and in 1905 the Overseas Hwy (a railroad causeway connecting the Keys to the mainland) was begun. It fueled yet another, bigger wave of settlement. Development of Miami and Miami Beach kicked off, and in 1914 Chicago industrialist James Deering began building the eye-popping Vizcaya mansion (p70).

The wave peaked during WWI, when the US military established an aviation training facility here. Many of the thousands who came to work and train here also settled in the area.

After the war, the first full-fledged Miami boom (1923–25) was fueled not just by the

Five Who Shaped South Florida

- **Henry Morrison Flagler** The developer whose Florida East Coast Railroad brought scores of visitors to sunny paradise.
- **Julia Tuttle** The woman behind the Flagler man, who lured the skeptical developer to Miami with a handful of orange blossoms.
- **Fidel Castro** He is, after all, the one behind the Mariel Boat Lift, whose150,000 Cubans forever changed the face of modern Miami.
- **Morris Lapidus** The Fontainebleau, Eden Roc, Lincoln Road Mall...is there anything this MiMo (Miami Modern) god *didn't* design?
- **Ian Shrager** The hotelier who forever raised the bar on chic inns, starting with the Delano.

1914	1915	1926	1930s
Miami Beach's first hotel, the WJ Brown Hotel, opens for business	Carl Fischer dredges Biscayne Bay to build Miami	A hurricane demolishes much of the city	Art deco structures go up en masse around the beach area

area's idyllic beachfront location and perfect weather, but also by gambling and a lax implementation of prohibition. Though it was illegal, liquor flowed freely throughout the entire Prohibition period.

HURRICANE, DEPRESSION & WAR

But the perfect weather was not to last – and therefore, neither were any other segments of this boom. The party was cut short by a devastating 1926 hurricane the eye of which trounced Miami and Miami Beach, leaving more than 100 people dead and leading to a statewide recession with national repercussions. Then, still trying to recover from the destruction, the Great Depression hit Miami, and the city and state became major supporters of Franklin Delano Roosevelt and his social-reform plan known as the New Deal. When elected, Roosevelt made his way to Miami to thank South Florida for its support. During that visit an attempt was made on his life by Guiseppe Zangora, a deranged young man. Luckily, FDR escaped unharmed.

In the early 1930s, a group of mostly Jewish developers began erecting small, stylish hotels along Collins Ave and Ocean Dr, jumpstarting a miniboom that resulted in the creation and development of Miami Beach's famous Art Deco district. This, of course, led to a brief rise in anti-Semitism, as the Beach became segregated and 'Gentiles Only' signs began popping up in the north. The election of a Jewish governor in 1933 led to improvement in this area, as did the rise in airplane travel, which brought hordes of Jewish visitors and settlers (and their dollars) from the North.

Meanwhile, the wartime actions in Europe really hit home when a German U-boat sank a US tanker off Florida's coast. The ensuing reaction created a full-scale conversion of South Florida into a massive military base, training facility and staging area. The Army's central Anti–U-boat Warfare School was based in Miami. Miami Beach's hotels were full of soldiers, who marched up and down the beach in full combat gear. After the war, many of Miami's trainee soldiers returned and settled here, and the city maintained its prewar prosperity. In 1947 the Everglades, a sensitive marsh and swamp area that is home to thousands of indigenous wildlife species, was granted national park status by President Truman.

1950s BOOM

In the 1950s, Miami Beach had another boom, and the area became known as the 'Cuba of America.' Gamblers and gangsters, enticed by Miami's gaming, as well as its proximity to the fun, sun and fast times of Batista-run Cuba, moved in en masse. Air travel brought New Yorkers for quick and easy vacations. Even another hurricane didn't discourage people *that* much. In 1954 Leroy Collins became the first Southern governor to publicly declare racial segregation 'morally wrong.' Oranges and cotton were becoming huge business in northern Florida, and as the aerospace industry moved to Florida near the end of the decade, an entire 'Space Coast' was created around Cape Canaveral (between Daytona and Miami on the east coast) to support the development of the Mercury, Gemini and, later, man-on-the-moon Apollo space programs of the National Aeronautics & Space Administration (NASA).

CUBA & THE BAY OF PIGS

After the 1959 Cuban Revolution, Miami was flooded with anti-Castro immigrants who, in gathering to organize a counterrevolutionary force, managed to establish a permanent Cuban community. A group of exiles formed the 2506th Brigade, sanctioned by the US government, which provided weapons and Central Intelligence Agency (CIA) training for the purpose of launching an attack on Cuba.

1935	1954	1956	1959
Miami Beach population hits 13,350 – doubling from just five years earlier	Fontainebleau Hotel opens	Eden Roc Hotel opens	Fidel Castro takes over Cuba and the influx of Cuban exiles begins

In April 1961 the counterrevolutionaries (CRs) launched an attack against the beaches at Playa Girón, a debacle remembered in the USA as the Bay of Pigs. But the US state department had allegedly leaked a warning to the Cubans; a *New York Times* correspondent says he heard about the attack weeks before it happened. The resulting pathetic, half-baked, poorly planned and badly executed attack was little more than an ambush.

To add insult to injury, when the magnitude of the botch-up became clear, President Kennedy refused to send air cover or naval support in the name of 'plausible deniability.' The first wave of CRs, left on the beach without reinforcements or supplies, were all captured or killed (though all prisoners were released by Cuba about three months later).

KENNEDY VS KHRUSHCHEV

Kennedy and the CIA both looked rather silly after the Bay of Pigs fiasco, which is probably why Kennedy stood his ground so firmly during the event that brought the world to the brink of nuclear war: the Cuban Missile Crisis.

Smelling blood after the Bay of Pigs, the USSR's general secretary Nikita Khrushchev began secretly installing missile bases in Cuba. By some stroke of luck or by accident, the CIA managed to take photographs of the unarmed warheads. They were shown to Kennedy in October of 1962, and he went on national TV to announce that the USSR was installing missiles in Cuba, and that doing so in such close proximity to Florida was a direct threat to the safety and security of the country. He then announced a naval 'quarantine' of Cuba (a nice euphemism for a naval blockade, which would have been an act of war), and further, that any attack on the USA from Cuba would be regarded as an attack by the USSR.

As tensions mounted, a flurry of letters passed between Washington and Moscow, beginning with: Well, okay, we *do* have missiles, but they're there as a deterrent not as an offensive threat. The exchange culminated in two offers from the Soviets for ending the stalemate. The first, dated October 26, agreed to remove the missiles in exchange for a promise by the USA not to attack Cuba. The second, on the 27th, tied the removal to the USA's elimination of similar sites it had in Turkey.

Publicly, Kennedy responded to the first offer. When it was announced that the USA would not invade Cuba, the Soviets began removing their missiles. Several months later, and with markedly less fanfare, the US removed its missiles from Turkey.

Miami's population swelled as Cubans immigrated there in record numbers. A special immigration center was established in Miami's Freedom Tower to handle the overflow. It became known as the Ellis Island of the South.

RACIAL TENSIONS

Miami's record of harmonious race relations is not altogether impressive. The Ku Klux Klan has been active in Florida since the 1920s, and bombings of Black-owned housing were not unknown. Blacks were segregated to an area north of Downtown known as Colored Town (p75), later called Overtown. And in the 1950s, as the city grew, many were displaced to the federal housing projects at Liberty City, a misnomer if ever there was one.

During 1965 the two 'freedom flights' that ran daily between Miami and Havana disgorged more than 100,000 Cuban refugees. Sensing the tension that was building between Blacks and Cubans, Dr Martin Luther King Jr pleaded with the two sides not to let animosity lead to bloodshed.

Riots and skirmishes broke out nonetheless, and acts of gang-style violence occurred. But not all were caused by simmering Cuban/Black tensions: Whites got into the fray as well. In 1968 a riot broke out after it was discovered that two White police officers had arrested a 17-year-old Black male, stripped him naked and hung him by his ankles from a bridge.

1961	1962	1966	1973
Botched Bay of Pigs invasion	The Cuban Missile Crisis	The *Jackie Gleason Show* begins broadcasting from Miami Beach	Miami Dolphins win the Super Bowl

In 1970 the 'rotten meat' riot began when Blacks picketed a White-owned shop they had accused of selling spoiled meat. After three days of picketing, White officers attempted to disperse the crowds and fired on them with tear gas. During the 1970s, there were 13 other race-related violent confrontations.

Racial tensions exploded on May 17, 1980, when four White police officers, being tried on charges that they beat a Black suspect to death while he was in custody, were acquitted by an all-White jury. When the verdict was announced, severe race riots broke out all over Miami and lasted for three days. The riots resulted in 18 deaths, $80 million in property damage and 1100 arrests.

Top Five Miami History Books

- *Miami* (1987, Vintage), by Joan Didion. How Cuban politics shape US policy.
- *The Corpse Had a Familiar Face* (1987, Simon & Schuster), by Edna Buchanan. Written by a former *Miami Herald* reporter, this is an addictive read on real-life Miami murders.
- *Black Miami in the Twentieth Century* (1997, University Press of Florida), by Marvin Dunn. This was the first book devoted to the issue of race in Miami.
- *This Land Is Our Land: Immigrants and Power in Miami* (2003, University of California Press), by Alex Stepcik. Stepcik and other authors break it down.
- *Miami, USA* (2000, University Press of Florida), by Helen Muir. A recently expanded 1950s title that's full of anecdotes.

THE MARIEL BOATLIFT

As Florida's economy began recovering in the late 1970s after the oil crisis and recession, Fidel pulled a fast one. He opened the floodgates, allowing anyone who wanted to leave Cuba access to the docks at Mariel. Before the ink was dry on the proclamation, the largest flotilla ever launched for nonmilitary purposes set sail (or paddled) from Cuba in practically anything that would float the 90 miles between Cuba and the USA.

The Mariel Boatlift, as the largest of these would be called, brought 125,000 Cubans to Florida. This included an estimated 25,000 prisoners and mental patients that Fidel had cleverly decided to foist off on the Cuban-American population. The resulting strain on the economy, logistics and infrastructure of South Florida only added to still-simmering racial tensions.

VICES RULE

In the indulgent 1980s, the area gained prominence as the major East Coast entry port for drug dealers, their products and the unbelievable sums of money that went along with them. As if to keep up, many savings and loans (S&Ls) opened here in newly built headquarters. While *Newsweek* magazine called Miami 'America's Casablanca,' locals dubbed it the 'City with the S&L Skyline.'

CenTrust, a particularly wealthy S&L, used a helicopter to load a marble staircase into its IM Pei–designed Downtown headquarters (today the Bank of America Tower), installed gold-plated faucets in the bathrooms and hung several million dollars' worth of art on the walls. A plethora of businesses – legitimate concerns as well as drug-financed fronts – and buildings sprung up all over Miami. Downtown was completely remodeled. But it was still being reborn while in the grip of drug smugglers. Shoot-outs were common, as were gangland slayings by cocaine cowboys.

The police, Coast Guard, Drug Enforcement Agency (DEA), Border Patrol and Federal Bureau of Investigation (FBI) were in a tizzy trying to keep track of it all. Roadblocks were set up along the Overseas Hwy to Key West (prompting the quirky and headstrong residents down there to call for a secession, which eventually sent the cops on their way). Police on I-95, the main East Coast north–south highway, were given extraordinary powers to

1979	1980	1984	1992
The Miami Beach Architectural District gets historic-landmark status with the National Register	Race riots tear up Miami while the Mariel Boatlift brings in 125,000 Cubans	*Miami Vice* hits the air	Hurricane Andrew slams nearby Homestead, but leaves Miami relatively unscathed

stop vehicles that matched a 'drug-runner profile.' According to one public defender who believed in civil rights, this amounted to the power to stop anyone.

Then it happened: *Miami Vice*.

The TV show starred Don Johnson and Philip Michael Thomas as two pastel-clad narcotics detectives who drove around in a Ferrari Testarossa and million-dollar cigarette boats. It was single-handedly responsible for Miami Beach rising to international attention in the mid-1980s. The show's unique look, slick soundtrack and music video–style montages glamorized the rich South Florida lifestyle. Before long, people were coming down to check it out for themselves – especially photographer Bruce Weber, who began using South Beach as a grittily fashionable backdrop for modeling shoots in the early 1980s, leading to imitators and eventually to the situation that exists today: model-jam.

By the late 1980s, Miami Beach had risen to international fabulousness. Celebrities were wintering in Miami, international photographers were shooting here, and the Art Deco District, having been granted federal protection, was going through a renovation and renaissance. Gay men, always on the cutting edge of trends, discovered South Beach's gritty glamour and began holding the annual White Party, an A-list AIDS fund-raiser party, at Vizcaya, and partied along South Beach's oceanfront before and after. The city was fast becoming a showpiece of fashion and trendiness (and party drugs, natch).

CRIME & PUNISHMENT

Policing had never been a strong suit for Miami. After the gangsters and mobsters of the '20s and '50s, and the 1980s *Miami Vice* era, came the serious carjackings and other crimes against tourists in 1993 (see Safety, p224). Miami didn't shake its dangerous reputation until the economic engine of tourism threatened to chug to a complete standstill. Tourist-oriented community policing and other visible programs reversed the curse. Miami went from being the US city with the most violent crime to one with average crime statistics for a city its size. From 1992 to 1998, tourist-related crimes decreased a whopping 80%.

Drug smuggling also became fashionable again in the 1990s. Smaller traffickers, who made runs between the Florida coast and 'mother' ships and air-drops in the Bahamas, reclaimed their voices. During the opening ceremonies for the Brickell Ave Bridge, news cameras panned away from the speaking dignitaries to photograph a speedboat chase right beneath them on the Miami River, a route that one bridge tender said is like a hospital gown – wide open at the back.

As the very fabulous South Beach scene sprouted, so did a drug-dependent club culture. Ecstasy, ketamine and GHB were as popular as topless models. It finally got so bad in the late 1990s that the police couldn't avoid it any longer and started cracking down. While politicians knew the value of clubs to the local economy, they didn't want to be seen as condoning drug use, and very popular spots got shut down.

CUBAN RUN-INS & EMBARGOS

In the early 1990s, the USA stopped instantly accepting Cuban refugees in an effort to keep the hotheads with Fidel rather than on Miami streets. The USA started its Communism deathwatch as anti-Castro demonstrators stepped up pressure, and as Cuba sank deeper into debt and became more desperate for hard currency. Pundits predicting Castro's imminent fall were generally disappointed by a dictator who kept fighting back.

In early 1995, Castro may have made things far more difficult, though, by shooting down two American planes flown by Brothers to the Rescue (BTTR), a Miami-based group that patrols the Caribbean looking for refugee rafters. These rabid anti-Castro, Cubans characterize their work as 'humanitarian aid.' The group claims to have rescued thousands of rafters and

1996	1997	1998	1999
The city of Miami turns 100	Gianni Versace is murdered on the steps of his Ocean Dr home	Mayor Xavier Suarez is ousted from office for absentee-ballot fraud (dead people voting)	Elián Gonzalez is rescued at sea and brought to the USA

boat people, who, it also claims, are shot at by Cuban patrol boats and helicopters. After BTTR planes skirted Cuban airspace as part of a flotilla-and-airborne demonstration, they were downed by the Cuban Air Force. The US government's outrage over the attack raised one of the biggest flaps between the countries since the Bay of Pigs.

Most foreign governments permit their citizens to travel and do business with Cuba; the USA, however, does not. Americans, though, can still surreptitiously visit Cuba via Canada, Jamaica and the Bahamas. Journalists, academics, and families with close kin can officially visit (although families can only visit once yearly). In 1998 sweeping trade embargoes were slightly loosened for the first time since commercial transactions ceased in 1963. Medical supplies were allowed, then came agricultural products, as long as Cuba paid in cash. Although Cuba was struck hard by a hurricane, Fidel's pronouncement in 2000 that he'd not take 'one grain of rice' from the USA was tempered by his cash acquisition in 2002 of $17 million worth of US grain. President Bush, with the support of his brother Jeb, didn't waste much time tightening the embargo again.

Casa Casuarina (p52), South Beach

VERSACE & THE GAP

The highly publicized murder of fashion designer Gianni Versace in 1997 stunned the celebrity world and once again brought negative media coverage to the area (see Casa Casuarina, p52). Despite this, the boom continued. Creeping gentrification has made inroads, and South Beach has long since left the growing stages of a funky, hip destination and become a multinational hot spot. Small family-run shops and restaurants are out, the Gap and Starbucks are in. Miami itself, of course, remains in – way in.

2000	2003	2004	2005
Famed MiMo architect Morris Lapidus dies in Miami	*Nip/Tuck*, a series about Miami plastic surgeons, premieres on TV	The Hollywood version of *Miami Vice* is filmed on location	The most expensive hotel in Miami – the Setai – opens its doors

Neighborhoods

Neighborhoods

Knowing one area from another is your key to the city when it comes to Greater Miami, a region made up of vastly spread-out communities that each have their own distinct, lovable personalities. Neighborhoods are often divided by one of the area's many waterways, whether it's the gritty Miami River, the soothing Indian Creek or the wide and churning Biscayne Bay. And it's this bay, by the way, that separates the city of Miami, on the mainland, from the city of Miami Beach, on a long and skinny island that stands parallel to Miami's shores. Learn this important lesson – that Miami and Miami Beach are not one and the same – and you'll be way ahead of most visitors to these parts.

Also well worth learning are the differences between the vibrant, culturally rich and ever-evolving neighborhoods in Miami and Miami Beach. These 'hoods have the power to make you feel as if you've entered many different cities – even countries – by the time you leave town. Take Little Havana, for example, a part of Miami that started out as a haven for Cuban immigrants but has since expanded into a totally pan-Latin world, full of people from nations including Argentina, Colombia, Brazil and Venezuela. Cubans, meanwhile, have moved into every corner of Miami, making heavenly Cuban coffee and Cuban sandwiches an integral part of the landscape. Little Haiti, also on the mainland, is a massive, rough-and-tumble Haitian community, with markets and restaurants reflecting an entirely different part of the globe. Not far from there is the industrial-chic Design District; attracting top artists and designers from around the world, who offer a stunning array of galleries and showrooms. South of that is the pulsating Downtown, home to businessmen, government workers, gleaming new high-rise hotels, excellent museums and the busiest port in the world, welcoming endless cruise ships, which deposit massive loads of tourists from every corner of this earth. The magnificent Spanish style of ritzy Coral Gables sits south of here, right near the artsy residential (and retail) hub, Coconut Grove. Then, of course, there are the beach communities – the North Beach world of condos and fancy malls and Jewish delis, the quaint and emerging Little Argentina of Normandy Isle, and South Beach, whose trendy nightlife, A-list celebs, top-notch restaurants and flesh-flashing expanses of sand have gained reputations of mythical proportion.

Whatever you do, don't limit your visit to just one of these neighborhoods; you'll be amazed at how crossing just one waterway – or, at the very least, simply venturing up above 21st Street – can add texture, perspective and pure excitement to your trip.

ITINERARIES

One Day

Begin your morning with some Ocean Ave people-watching paired with a fresh-tomato-topped omelette at the Front Porch Café (p92) in South Beach. Walk it off with a stroll through this fabled neighborhood, being sure to include a hop along Lincoln Road (p54), a gander at (or into) some cool deco hotels and a dip into the soft sands of the beach. Take a quick walk along Calle Ocho through Little Havana (p65), stopping for a fresh-fruit shake at Los Pinareños Frutería (Map p255; ☎ 305-285-1135; 1334 SW 8th St), then do a minidrive through Downtown Miami (p58) to get a sense of the urban-ness here. Get to the Design District (p62) before dark and try to catch a gallery show or two, and then settle in here for the evening, grabbing a cocktail at the District (p101), followed by a night of lounging, grooving and dining at Grass Lounge (p113).

Three Days

On the first day, expand your South Beach walk to cover more ground, perhaps going as far south as First Street and as far north as the fabled Delano (p155) for a sneaky peek inside. Include an walking tour with the Art Deco Welcome Center (p50) and a visit to either the Bass Museum of Art (p52) or the **Wolfsonian-FIU** (p54). Grab lunch at a spot of your choice in the 'hood before heading over to Little Havana, where you can stroll around at a leisurely pace and then settle in somewhere such as **Casa Panza** (p103) for dinner and a show. Day two can start out in the Design District, with a no-nonsense breakfast at **Jimmy's East Side Diner** (p103) followed by a walking tour of the area's galleries and showrooms. From there head Downtown, where you can hop on the **Metromover** (p61) for an urban overview and then enjoy a fresh-fish riverside lunch with in-the-know Cuban businessmen at **Garcia's** (p99). Catch sunset back on the beach in South Beach, where you can linger, crowd-free, before dining in the 'hood at a spot of your choice, followed by a night of checking out the SoBe club scene. Shake things up with some still nature on day three, heading over to **Key Biscayne** (p67), where you can rent a bike and explore this mellow island – or visit **Seaquarium** (p68) if you have kids. Catch dinner on the key at **Le Croisic** (p105) and finish the night off at a sleek Downtown spot – **Bahia** (p110) or the **M Bar** (p111) – where you can sip a cocktail with a view.

> ## Top Five Neighborhoods for Cultural Infusions
>
> - It all comes together in **South Beach** (p50) – Latin familias, art galleries, nipped-and-tucked tourists, blue-haired old-timers, plus every cuisine you can crave .
> - It's a Cuban outpost, sure – but **Little Havana** (p65) is also a pan-Latin melting pot.
> - You'll find tons of cutting-edge art galleries in **Wynwood** (p62).
> - Rising modern towers shadow historic buildings **Downtown** (p58), and global tourists and businesspeople mill among it all.
> - It's Latin art galleries galore in **Coral Gables** (p71), plus a palpable Spanish influence via architecture and style.

One Week

A full week gives you plenty of time for exploration. Follow the three-day plan and, on the fourth day, visit the neighborhoods of **Coral Gables** (p71) and **Coconut Grove** (p68), with stops at the **Biltmore** (p71), the **Venetian Pool** (p73) and the gorgeous **Vizcaya** (p70). Alternatively, if you're with children, head to **Parrot Jungle Island** (p78) or **Miami Metrozoo** (p77). Splurge on a serious dinner at **Norman's** (p107) in the Gables. Take a two-night side trip, either to the Everglades' gorgeous region of **10,000 Island** (p200) or down to **Key West** (p177), for a sultry taste of the tropics. Spend your last couple of days visiting the neighborhoods you liked best, catching a live-music or theatre show, and taking an evening boat cruise to gaze at the lit-up skyline. You could also explore more outer regions, such as North Miami and its excellent **Museum of Contemporary Art** (p75) or **Normandy Isle** (p56), where you can try Argentinian food or relish sunset cocktails on the deck at **Roger's** (p98). Whatever you do, don't leave town before hitting **Wolfie Cohen's Rascal House** (p58) for a reminder of the pastrami-Miami days of yore.

ORGANIZED TOURS

More so than many American cities, Miami's outer layer can be tough to penetrate, particularly because its fascinating pockets are so spread out and different from one another, and because its shiny surfaces can be intimidating. But that's where a good tour guide – whether on foot, boat or bus – can come in very handy indeed.

Air/Boat/Bike/Bus Tours
ACTION HELICOPTER TOURS
☎ 305-358-4723; Watson Island; tours $69-149
This company runs 12- to 35-minute jaunts above South Beach, Fisher Island, the Port of Miami, Bayside Marketplace, Coconut Grove and the houses of the rich and famous.

BAYSIDE MARKETPLACE (BOAT TOURS) Map pp252-3
☎ 305-379-5119; 401 Biscayne Blvd; adult/child $14/7; ⏲ 11am-7pm
For harbor tours, head downtown and hop aboard the Island Queen, Captain Jimmy's Fiesta Cruises or smaller speedboat Bayside Blaster. Boats depart hourly. Tours include commentary about the famous folks who live on Star Island and a bit of history, but generally they're alluring because of the skyline views of the dramatic nighttime neon (though you can't see the celebrities' houses at dusk).

ECO-ADVENTURE BIKE TOURS
☎ 305-365-3018; www.miamidade.gov/parks; tours $25
The Dade County parks system leads frequent bike tours through peaceful areas of Miami and Miami Beach, including along beaches and on Key Biscayne. Times vary; call for details.

MIAMI DUCK TOURS   Map pp246-7
☎ 877-DUCK-TIX, 786-276-8300; 1661 James Ave; adult/child/senior $24/17/21; ☒ 10am-6pm
Is it a bus, or is it a boat? No, you won't look too cool gliding through South Beach on this bus/boat hybrid, but the wacky vehicle does provide a nice, high perspective (and amusing commentary) of South Beach and Downtown sites, and, when it enters the water, the moneyed homes of Biscayne Bay shores. Tours depart hourly and last 90 minutes.

MIAMI NICE TOURS
☎ 305-398-0991; www.miaminicetours.com; tours $36-59
This well-established company has a wide range of guided bus excursions to the Everglades, the Keys and Fort Lauderdale, as well as trips around Miami, some including stops at the **Miami Seaquarium** (p68), **Bayside Marketplace** (p59) and **Parrot Jungle Island** (p78).

Walking Tours
ART DECO WELCOME CENTER
Map pp248-9
☎ 305-531-3484; Art Deco Welcome Center, 1001 Ocean Dr; guided tours per adult/child/senior $20/ free/15, self-guided tours per adult/senior $15/10; ☒ 10:30am Wed, Fri & Sat, 6:30pm Thu
Learn the fascinating stories and history behind the wonderful art-deco hotels in the South Beach historic district, either with a lively guide

from the Miami Design Preservation League, or with the well-presented recording and map for self-guided walks. Tours are 90 minutes. The league also leads architectural walks of North Beach, and 'Deco Underworld' tours about the Prohibition era in Miami Beach. Call for reservations and details.

DR PAUL GEORGE
☎ 305-375-1621; tours $15-40; ☒ 10am Sat, 11am Sun
For a really great perspective on many different aspects of the city, call this lively historian for the **Historical Museum of Southern Florida** (p60). He leads a variety of very popular tours – including those that focus on Stiltsville, Miami crime, Little Havana and Coral Gables at twilight – between September and late June. Dr George also offers private tours by appointment.

DOWNTOWN MIAMI WELCOME CENTER   Map pp252-3
☎ 305-379-7070; 174 E Flagler St; tours $5; ☒ 10:30am Sat
See beyond the construction sites and crumbling facades of Downtown for an explanation of historic sites from the original **Burdines** (p143) to the Gesu Church, dating from 1925. The tours are by the Downtown Miami Welcome Center, housed in the historic **Olympia Theater** (p60).

URBAN TOUR HOST
☎ 305-663-4455; www.miamiculturaltours.com; tours from $15
This rich program of custom tours provides walking tours of just about any neighborhood you can think of, from Little Havana and Little Haiti to Coconut Grove and Coral Gables. You can also choose from South Beach architecture, Everglades ecology and Downtown history. All tours are custom.

SOUTH BEACH

Eating p89, Shopping p137, Sleeping p151

Plenty of folks have declared South Beach 'over.' What used to be an exclusive playground for fabulously gorgeous A-listers (mainly a mix of hot gay men, skinny-ass models and various celebs), they say, has been overrun by C-list wannabes – fanny-pack-wearing tourists from the suburbs, stroller-pushing families, and cruise-ship types who drink and holler like frat boys. You can be the judge of how cool or uncool South Beach is. Meanwhile, do head here while you're figuring it out. Whether you find the crowd passé or not, you'll most likely get a kick out of the frenetic energy that it brings to the clubs, shops and hotels, and to the bustling streets and beaches. Pay particular attention to the region south of Fifth St (SoFi), being touted as the *un–South Beach* South Beach (meaning it's even cooler, and less known, or *whatever*). It's bursting with an influx of new nightspots and less scene-obsessed folks. Also seeing a renaissance of sorts is the southern stretch of Alton Rd, where new, low-key eateries have taken locals by storm. But there are many other compelling attractions, from impressive museums to architectural marvels. The area is compact and good for walking, as it's easily covered on foot in just a day or two.

Orientation

South Beach is the part of Miami Beach below about 21st St (though realtors and hoteliers alike have been known to push that border as far north as 40th St). It encompasses the widest section of the island. Streets run east–west; avenues run north–south. Major arteries – Washington, Collins, Alton and Ocean – are named rather than numbered, and their addresses indicate their cross streets (1500 Washington Ave, for example, would be at 15th St).

Washington Ave is the bustling main drag, functioning as the main commercial artery and least trendy strip; Collins Ave is the famous deco-hotel-lined thoroughfare. The chic outdoor cafés and restaurants along Ocean Dr (which only goes as far north as 15th St) overlook the wide Atlantic shorefront. Alton Rd is the utilitarian main drag on the west side, more for driving than strolling, while Lincoln Rd is pedestrian-only between Alton Rd and Washington Ave.

SOUTH OF 5TH STREET (SoFi)

JEWISH MUSEUM OF FLORIDA Map p250

☎ 305-672-5044; www.jewishmuseum.com; 301 Washington Ave; adult/senior & student $6/4, admission Sat free; ☪ 10am-5pm Tue-Sun, closed Jewish holidays

Though images of Jewish grandparents with white shoes and blue hair are practically synonymous with nostalgic 1970s Miami Beach, there was a time when Jews were not welcome above 5th St. Learn all about it – along with the complete chronology of Jewish influences in Florida's political, cultural and artistic worlds at this small museum, housed in a 1936 Orthodox synagogue that served Miami's first congregation. Though there are frequent special exhibits, its mainstay is *Mosaic: Jewish Life in Florida*, which features thousands of items, from photographs to Russian samovar kettles.

SOUTH POINTE PARK Map p250

A recently renovated green space at the southern tip of Miami Beach, this small park has a nice little playground, a fishing pier from which kids (illegally) dive into Government Cut, a short boardwalk and an excellent stretch of beach that's less crowded during the week than those to the near north. There are also volleyball courts and two observation towers, which are great spots for sunset views.

NORTH OF 5TH STREET

ART DECO WELCOME CENTER

Map pp248-9
☎ 305-531-3484; 1001 Ocean Dr; ☪ 9am-7:30pm Mon-Sat, 9am-6:30pm Sun

Be sure to stop in here to get a sense of the much beloved but often misunderstood Art Deco Historic District. You'll find an informative permanent exhibit in the gallery, a bevy of

South Beach Top Five

- Kick off wonderful tours of the Art Deco Historic District here at the **Art Deco Welcome Center** (opposite) – and buy cool deco mementos while you're at it.
- A surprising cultural oasis not far from more vapid trendiness, the **Bass Museum of Art** (p52) has art from some big guns.
- The **Wolfsonian-FIU** (p54) boasts an amazing collection of art and design exhibits in a stunning structure.
- The backbone of the beach culture, the **Promenade** (p53) is where you rub elbows with shirtless posers, rollerblading scenesters and kooky locals.
- A car-free, alfresco mall, **Lincoln Road Mall** (p55) has got it all, from fine dining to a farmers' market.

Artificial Reefs

Initiated in 1981, the Miami-Dade Artificial Reef program came about for one very important reason: to protect natural reefs from humans. The hope is that the program will replenish marine habitats that have been lost due to storms, boating accidents and coastal development. Constructed of durable steel or concrete, the 'reefs' are planted on the ocean floor, where they will act as hosts for barnacles, corals, sponges and clams, which can then grow in population. Eventually, these vital creatures will colonize and inhabit nearly every little bit of these artificial structures as if they were natural. The newest addition to the sea floor was in 2004, namely a massive deck barge was deposited in Government Cut. Other locations, of many, include under the Julia Tuttle Causeway and east of South Beach.

walking tours to join, and a very well stocked gift shop hawking souvenirs from old-fashioned postcards to deco-style jewelry.

BASS MUSEUM OF ART Map pp246–7

☎ 305-673-7530; www.bassmuseum.org; 2121 Park Ave; adult/senior & student $12/10; ⏱ 10am-5pm Tue, Wed, Fri & Sat, 10am-9pm Thu, 11am-5pm Sun
The collection here is a wonderful surprise: permanent highlights range from 16th-century European religious works to Northern European and Renaissance paintings, to impressive old masters such as Peter Paul Rubens. Look for Albrecht Durer, Toulouse-Lautrec and perhaps the finest Flemish tapestries in an American museum. Plus you'll find visiting exhibitions, worthy of only a top museum, rotating through other halls, along with a great gift shop and lunch café (⏱ 11am-3:30pm).

CASA CASUARINA Map pp248–9
1114 Ocean Dr; not open to public
Perhaps more widely known as the Versace Mansion, this was the residence of late fashion designer Gianni Versace. Long before that drama, however, the 1930 building was known as the Amsterdam Palace. A Mediterranean Revival house constructed partially of coral and featuring exposed timbers, the three-story Spanish-style palace was modeled after the Governor's House in Santo Domingo. When Versace purchased the property in the early 1980s, he locked horns for a while with local preservationists after announcing plans to tear down a neighboring hotel so he could build a pool. After a battle, the moneyed designer won – but also struck a deal that would allow

for law changes, saving more than 200 other historic hotels in the process.

None of it seemed important, though, in 1997, when the stalker Andrew Cunanan gunned Versace down in front of the beloved mansion. Now, nearly 10 years after the tragedy, the house attracts a steady stream of tourists with a morbid curiosity and a thirst for celebrity-related photos of any kind. Versace's villa eventually sold for a reputed $35 to $50 million and opened in 2004 as a members-only club with dining options, a day spa and private beach-cabana service.

CORAL ROCK HOUSES Map pp248–9
900 Collins Ave & 1050 Washington Ave; not open to public
These two South Beach relics, both more than 80 years old, are icons built of porous stone from the sea. But it's unclear how much longer either will stick around. While the empty coral rock house on Washington sits on what is now Best Western property and sports a sign claiming its historic shell will soon hold a restaurant, the fate of the house on Collins hangs in the balance. At press time, the city was threatening to use the wrecking ball on the vacant 1918 structure, which inspectors had declared unsound. But historians and preservationists say that the beloved house, built by Avery Smith – the first person to run a ferry service from Miami Beach to the mainland – is as strong as nature itself.

ESPAÑOLA WAY PROMENADE
Map pp248–9
Btwn 14th & 15th Sts, west of Washington Ave
Designed as a replica of a Spanish-style village in the early 1920s, Española Way is lined with charming, pink Spanish-style buildings between Washington and Drexel Aves. Originally created as an artists' colony, today it is a place to stroll and shop, as small storefront galleries and cafés now line the narrow, shaded enclave. A craft market operates here on Saturday and Sunday afternoons.

ESTEFAN ENTERPRISES Map p250
420 Jefferson Ave; not open to the public
You can't miss the dramatic architecture of this place, designed by the internationally renowned Miami firm of Arquitectonica. The dynamic musical duo of Gloria and Emilio Estefan, dubbed 'Miami's Royal Family,' operate their ever-increasing business ventures from here (see Bongos Cuban Cafe, p117, and Cardozo Hotel, p155).

HOLOCAUST MEMORIAL Map pp246-7

☎ 305-538-1663; www.holocaustmmb.org; cnr Meridian Ave & Dade Blvd; admission free; ⊙ 9am-9pm

It's impossible to overstate the impact of this memorial, dedicated to the six million Jews who were killed during the Holocaust. The memorial was created in 1984 through the efforts of Miami Beach Holocaust survivors and sculptor Kenneth Treister. There are several key pieces of the memorial, all utilizing Jerusalem stone and marble, with the *Sculpture of Love and Anguish* the most visible to passers-by. This enormous, oxidized bronze arm bears an Auschwitz tattooed number – chosen because it was never issued at the camp – and terrified camp prisoners who are scaling the sides of the arm. The nearby lily pond and *Garden of Meditation* pay tribute to life, as does the *Memorial Wall,* which is inscribed with the names of those who perished, and the enclosed *Dome of Contemplation,* which shelters an eternal flame.

MIAMI BEACH BOTANICAL GARDEN

Map pp246-7

☎ 305-673-7256; www.mbgarden.org; 2000 Convention Center Dr; admission free; ⊙ 9am-5pm

More of a secret garden, this lush 4.5 acres of plantings flies under most people's radar. And that's a shame, as the patch of green, operated by the Miami Beach Garden Conservancy, is an oasis of palm trees, flowering hibiscus plants and glassy ponds. It's a contemplative place to visit after the nearby **Holocaust Memorial** (left).

MIAMI BEACH POST OFFICE Map pp248-9

☎ 305-531-3763; 1300 Washington Ave

Make it a point to mail a postcard from this 1937 deco gem, the very first South Beach renovation project tackled by preservationists in the '70s. This Depression moderne building in the 'stripped classic' style was constructed under President Franklin D Roosevelt's reign with Works Progress Administration (WPA) funds, which supported artists who were out of work during the Great Depression. On the exterior, note the bald eagle and the turret with iron railings. The interior dome boasts a beautifully restored painted paper ceiling, stamp tables of sturdy marble and a large wall mural of the Seminole's Florida invasion.

PROMENADE Map pp248-9

Promenade 5th–15th Sts

This beach Promenade, a wavy concrete ribbon sandwiched between the beach and Ocean Dr, extends from 5th to 15th Sts. A popular location for photo shoots, especially during crowd-free early mornings, it's also a breezy, palm-tree-lined conduit for in-line skaters,

South Beach Art-Deco Historic District

South Beach's heart is its Art Deco Historic District, one of the largest in the USA on the National Register of Historic Places. In fact, the area's rejuvenation and rebirth as a major tourist destination results directly from its protection as a historic place in 1979. The National Register designation prevents developers from wholeheartedly razing significant portions of what was, in the 1980s, a crime-ridden collection of crumbling eyesores populated primarily by drug-crazed lunatics, Cuban refugees and elderly residents. It's a far cry from that now. Today, hotel and apartment facades are decidedly colorful, with pastel architectural details. Depending on your perspective, the bright buildings catapult you back to the roaring '20s or on a wacky tour of American kitsch.

The National Register listing was fought for and pushed through by the Miami Design Preservation League (MDPL; see p50), founded by Barbara Baer Capitman in 1976. She was appalled upon hearing plans by the city of Miami to bulldoze several historic buildings in what is now the Omni Center. And she acted, forcefully.

The co-founder of the MDPL, Leonard Horowitz, played a pivotal role in putting South Beach back on the map, painting the then-drab deco buildings in shocking pink, lavender and turquoise. When his restoration of Friedman's Pharmacy made the cover of Progressive Architecture in 1982, the would-be Hollywood producers of Miami Vice saw something there, and the rest is history.

The Deco District is bounded by Dade Blvd to the north, 6th St to the south, the Atlantic Ocean to the east and Lenox Ave to the west. One of the best things about these 1000 or so buildings is their scale: most are no taller than the palm trees. And, while the architecture is by no means uniform — you'll see streamline moderne, Mediterranean Revival and tropical art deco designs — it's all quite harmonious. The 1-sq-mile district feels like a small village.

With more than 400 registered historic landmarks, it's hard not to have an interesting walk through the District. And if you know a bit about the architecture, you can follow the Beach boom phases: beginning in the 1930s when 5th St through mid-Beach was developed; moving from the late '30s to early '40s up toward 27th St; and heading north of that into the '50s, when resorts and luxury hotels were interspersed with condominiums.

bicyclists, roller skaters, skateboarders, volleyball players (there's a net at 11th St), dog walkers, yahoos, locals and tourists. The beach that it edges, called Lummus Park, is a sandy expanse sporting six floridly colored lifeguard stands. There's a public bathroom at 11th St, though be aware that its sinks are a popular place for homeless folks to do their bathing.

WOLFSONIAN-FIU Map pp248-9
☎ 305-531-1001; www.wolfsonian.org; 1001 Washington Ave; adult/senior, student & youth 6-18 yrs $5/3.50; ☾ 11am-9pm Thu, 11am-6pm Fri & Sat, noon-5pm Sun

This foreboding Mediterranean-style building served as the Washington Storage Company in the 1930s and '40s, a place where wealthy snowbirds (Northerners who fly south for the winter) could stash their valuables on return trips up north. Now, under the auspices of Florida International University, it houses a different kind of wealth – the stupendous collection of Miami native Mitchell Wolfson, whose family fortune was derived from movie theatres. With gorgeous pieces of furniture, industrial design and home items such as toasters and dishware, many of them deco-inspired, this fascinating collection of 70,000 pieces (dating from 1885 to 1945) is the perfect way to complete the picture that starts with the many gorgeous building facades around here. Be sure to check out the tremendous deco 'waterfall' in the lobby, and the ornate detail of the elevator that whisks you up to the galleries.

LINCOLN ROAD & AROUND
ARTCENTER/SOUTH FLORIDA
Map pp246-7
☎ 305-674-8278; www.artcentersf.org; 800 Lincoln Rd; ☾ 11am-10pm Mon-Wed, 11am-11pm Thu-Sun
Established in 1984 by a small but forward-thinking group of artists, this compound is the creative heart of South Beach. In addition to its 52 artist's studios (many of which are open to the public), ArtCenter offers an exciting lineup of classes and lectures, and is home to a gallery where dynamic, inspired shows are the norm.

JACKIE GLEASON THEATER OF THE PERFORMING ARTS Map pp246-7
☎ 305-673-7300; www.gleasontheater.com; 1700 Washington Ave
The sumptuous theatre housed in the classic, light-blue deco structure is home to the Miami City Ballet and a wonderful venue for traveling Broadway shows and a variety of concerts (p121). And now, following a recent $4.1-million lobby renovation, it's even better than ever. Also, be sure to take a gander at Roy Lichtenstein's *Mermaid* sculpture, gracing the front lawn.

Cyclist, Miami Beach (p55)

LINCOLN ROAD MALL Map pp246-7
Lincoln Rd btwn Alton Rd & Washington Ave

This dynamic pedestrian strip defies expectations: yes, it's a 'mall,' but its vibe remains stubbornly indie. Sure, it gets mobbed with tourists, but the crowd's makeup also includes many locals, with a mix of types including child-laden families, midriff-bearing party girls, Botox babes on hardcore shopping sprees, gay men flocking to Score (p116) and unfazed grandmas doing errands. 'The Road' was conceived by designer and architect Morris Lapidus in the 1950s, when it enjoyed a nice reign until falling into a state of disrepair in the 1970s; a series of multimillion-dollar facelifts throughout the '80s and '90s have helped make it great again. Though its wide, pedestrian-only sidewalk used to be hallowed ground for in-line skaters, it's too mobbed for those sorts of shenanigans at this point. The masses come for galleries, outdoor cafés, various shops (including chain stores), movies at the grandly designed Regal South Beach cinema and prime people-watching. There's an excellent **farmers' market** on Sundays (9am until 6pm) and an **Antiques and Collectibles Market** (☎ 305-673-4991) on the second and fourth Sundays (9am until 5pm).

TEMPLE EMANU EL SYNAGOGUE
Map pp246-7
☎ 305-538-2503; Washington Ave at 17th St

This grand Conservative synagogue, established in 1938 as Congregation Jacob Joseph, features a domed sanctuary and solid stone features. Its membership has grown exponentially over the years. Sabbath services are on Fridays at 6:30pm and Saturdays at 8:45am.

MIAMI BEACH

Eating p96, Shopping p142, Sleeping p159

Much begins to change as you head north on Collins Ave – the view, for one. As you move uptown, it becomes more and more difficult to catch a glimpse of the ocean, thanks to the canyon of condos that rises boldly between the street and the shoreline (though you'll also find some wonderfully wide expanses of sand, such as Haulover Park). The MiMo (Miami Modern) architecture is both bigger and glitzier than the art deco of South Beach. Also much different is the vibe – mellower, older and less up-to-the-minute hip. And then there are the people. Along much of this stretch, the

world of 1950s and '60s Miami Beach comes alive through old-school schmoozers who would call you 'honey' or 'kid' in a heartbeat. The Latin flavor is pronounced, with the Normandy Isle region, at 71st St, fast gaining a reputation as Little Argentina. Do check it out.

Orientation

Maps refer to the swath just above South Beach as, simply, Miami Beach, but know that locals use the jargon Mid-Beach and North Beach, depending on how high up they're talking about. Two northern Miami Beach communities are Surfside (from about 90th St to 97th St) and Bal Harbour (though this is technically just above Miami Beach proper); further north are Sunny Isles and Aventura, which are usually included in spirit, and thus appear on our map. Up through Bal Harbour, Indian Creek separates Collins Ave, almost exclusively lined with high-rise condominiums and luxury hotels, from the residential districts to the west. Alton Rd winds through this exclusive neighborhood and connects with Collins Ave at 63rd St.

MID-BEACH

BOARDWALK Map pp246-7

Stretching between 21st and 46th Sts along the beach, this is a primo spot for jogging or walking, with the ocean spread out along one side of you and the backside pool areas of *über* resort hotels along the other. And, interestingly enough, this length of boards also

Transportation

Bus G, H, J, K, L, S, T.
Car Collins passes through all of these neighborhoods; Alton Rd runs north–south to the west of Indian Creek (cross between the two at 41st St).

Miami Beach Top Five

- Amble or gaze along the **Boardwalk** (p55), along with tourists and Orthodox families pushing strollers.
- Once laughed at for its MiMo design, the **Fontainebleau Hilton** (below), a Morris Lapidus special, has long been the darling of Miami Beach.
- **Haulover Beach Park** (below) boasts miles of unspoiled sand and its own little gathering of nude sunbathers.
- An Argentine enclave, **Normandy Isle** (below) has a clutch of charming eateries and a weekly farmers' market.
- Sample the fare at **Wolfie Cohen's Rascal House** (p58), the pastrami legend of old-school Miami Beach.

Neighborhoods – Miami Beach

serves as a conduit between the area's many Orthodox Jews and their wires, or Eruv (*eh-rev*). The Eruv accommodate Orthodox Jews who leave their homes for various reasons during the Sabbath (which begins Friday evening at sunset), functioning as a connection between the roof of the synagogue and the home.

EDEN ROC RESORT Map p251
4525 Collins Ave

This enormous place was the second ground-breaking resort from Morris Lapidus (the first was the **Fontainebleau**, below), a fine example of the architecture known as MiMo. It was the hangout for the 1960s Rat Pack – Sammy Davis Jr, Dean Martin, Sinatra and crew – and its indoor decor is pretty much left behind from that era. It's worth a look in the lobby, though, as it's a window to another world. Out back, thrilled families lounge by the fancy pool or enjoy cocktails on the ocean-view patio; for inside fun, it's the super rock-climbing facilities (p133).

FONTAINEBLEAU HILTON HOTEL & RESORT Map p251
4441 Collins Ave

This iconic 1954 leviathan, another brainchild of Lapidus, remains an architectural highlight, as it symbolizes the showy and optimistic postwar outlook of MiMo. Note the spectacular tromp l'oeil mural on the southern exterior, designed by Richard Hass and painted over an eight-week period by Edwin Abreu. Also note the lagoonlike water park out back, the famous 'stairway to nowhere' in the massive lobby, and the spots where various films were shot on location here – *The Bellboy*, *Goldfinger* and *Scarface*, to name just a few.

RUSSIAN & TURKISH BATHS Map p251
☎ 305-867-8316; Castillo del Mar, 5445 Collins Ave; $22; ☾ noon-midnight

Places such as this have long been favorite 'hot' spots in New York among folks who want

a spa experience without the glamour, and this new Miami outpost is attracting a similar crowd. Spend a few hours among soothing saunas, steam rooms and whirlpools, and for an extra fee, indulge in a massage or exfoliating salt scrub. You'll feel like jelly for the rest of the day.

NORTH BEACH TO SUNNY ISLES

HAULOVER BEACH PARK Map p251
☎ 305-944-3040; 10800 Collins Ave; per car $4; ☾ sunrise-sunset

This 40-acre sand park has scads of barbecues, picnic tables and volleyball courts, plus a nine-hole golf course and a nearby canoe and kayak rental place, **Urban Trails Kayak Rentals** (p130). Thanks to dense plant growth, it's also relatively hidden from the condos, which is probably why you'll find the rare clothing-optional beach area tucked away at the north end.

NORMANDY ISLE Map p251
71st St west of Collins Ave

Frozen in '50s time until real-estate agents discovered this goldmine of untapped space and low-rise apartment buildings, Normandy Isle is a fast-rising star because of its self-contained commercial area, huge influx of Argentines and new crop of bustling bars and eateries. It's considered by some to be the 'gateway to North Beach' because of its location between the mainland and the Beach via the 79th St (JFK) Causeway. On Saturday mornings the small village green hosts a lovely farmers' market, with fresh produce and especially affordable potted orchids.

OCEAN TERRACE Map p251
Beach btwn 73rd & 75th Sts

While the shopping strip along Collins here is evocative of an old-Miami main street (note the colorful tile facade of Walgreens, formerly

Miami Beaches Guide

Miami Beach has perhaps the best city beaches in the country. The water is relatively clear and warm, and the imported sand is relatively white. Beaches are wide, firm and long enough to accommodate the throngs. A whopping 12 miles from South Pointe to 192nd St (William Lehman Causeway), Miami Beach is said to have an astonishing 35 miles of shoreline when taking into consideration Key Biscayne and the like.

Like a large, accommodating restaurant, Miami's beaches are wordlessly zoned to provide everyone with what they want without offending anyone else. So if you find yourself somewhere where the people around you make you uncomfortable, just move a little further along the beach and you'll be fine. Perhaps surprisingly, topless bathing is legal in most places, a happy result of Miami Beach's popularity with Europeans and South Americans. Generally speaking, skimpy swimsuits seem to be the order of the day, which means you'll see plenty of thongs and other minuscule coverings on the bronzed gods and goddesses (though folks with traditional bathing suits will not feel out of place).

The most crowded beaches are from about 5th St to 21st St. You'll see lots of models preening for photo shoots between 6th and 14th Sts, also known as Glitter Beach. Weekends are usually more crowded than weekdays, but except during special events it's usually not too difficult to find a quiet spot. From 21st St to 46th St, the 1½-mile boardwalk is a nice way to see the beach without getting sand between your toes. Perhaps head out for a sunset stroll before an early dinner?

Don't forget to check out the funky, Ken Scharf–designed **lifeguard tower** at 10th St. Other good, locally designed lifeguard towers dot 5th St to 14th St. You'll notice that art deco was not saved just for hotels.

Elsewhere, notwithstanding the weekend traffic snarls across the Rickenbacker Causeway, Key Biscayne (Map p259) is a prime place to go. The 5 miles of Key Biscayne beaches are relatively undeveloped, commercial-free zones.

Family-Fun Beaches

Families head to beaches north of 21st St, especially the one at 53rd St, with a playground and public toilets, as well as the dune-backed one around 73rd St. They also head south to **Matheson Hammock Park** (Map pp244–5), which has calm artificial lagoons.

Surfing & Windsurfing Beaches

First things first: this isn't Hawaii. In Miami Beach, head north to **Haulover Beach Park** (Map p251) in Sunny Isles or as far south as you can. The breaks between 5th St and South Pointe can actually give pretty good rides (by Florida standards, like 2ft to 4ft). You'll do well with a longboard. **Hobie Beach** (also called Windsurfing Beach; Map p259) rules for windsurfing.

Swimming Beaches

What? You actually want to swim? Head to 85th St in **Surfside** (Map p251). It's devoid of high-rise condos and is watched by lifeguards.

Nude Beaches

Nude bathing is legal at **Haulover Beach Park** (Map p251) in Sunny Isles. Head to the northern end of the park between the two northernmost parking lots. The area north of the lifeguard tower is predominantly gay, south is straight. Sex is not tolerated on these beaches. You'll get arrested if you're seen heading into the bushes.

Gay Beaches

A lesbian, gay, bisexual and transgender (LGBT) crowd traditionally hits the sand at around 12th St, especially after the clubs close on Friday and Saturday. It's not like there's sex going on (there isn't – no big sand dunes); it's just a spot where gay men happen to congregate. Though outnumbered, lesbians gather here, too. Sunday afternoon volleyball at 4pm, after everyone has had a decent night's (morning's) sleep, is packed with fun-loving locals.

Latino Beaches

Latino families, predominantly Cuban, congregate between 5th St and **South Pointe** (Map p250). Topless bathing is unwise and can be considered offensive here.

Party-Scene Beaches

Key Biscayne's ever-popular **Crandon Park Beach** (Map p259) attracts tons of families to its barbecue grills, as well as locals blaring dueling stereos and tried-and-true beach bums.

Quiet Beaches

Despite the presence of families, it's pretty low-key up around 53rd St (Map p251) and down at **Matheson Hammock Park** (Map pp244–5). Or try the spot near the municipal parking lot at around 46th St (just north of the Eden Roc Resort), which is a sort of no-man's land on most afternoons.

Is North Beach the New South Beach?

South Beach, South Beach, South Beach! For years now it's been this rather small swath of Miami Beach that has received all the attention of tourists, hip young residents and developers alike. But plenty of people are hoping for – and slowly witnessing – a shift of attention toward the uptown area. The nonprofit North Beach Development Corporation (www .gonorthbeach.com), for one, has a mission of revitalizing this region, from 63rd St to the city limit at 87th Tce. It raises millions in grant funds to renovate the facades of priceless MiMo structures, spearheads programs to try to bring an infusion of arts and pedestrian-friendly walkways to link together the various neighborhoods, and encourages a variety of development plans. The north has been slowly catching on as the new place to hang, spurred on in no small part by the abundance of MiMo architecture – the glitzy, modern hotels and condos erected between the postwar era and the '70s, with folks like Morris Lapidus and Alber Anis and Roy France leading the way. These buildings tend to attract nostalgia lovers, as do places like the lobbies of the **Fontainebleau** (p56) and **Eden Roc** (p56). Trendsetters, meanwhile, have been congregating at spots such as Normandy Isle, with its fast-growing collection of festive eateries, and **Ocean Tce** (p56), a two-block span of oceanfront cafés and hotels that's been called a 'mini South Beach.' Out on the 79th St Causeway, hipsters gather nightly at the new **Roger's** (p98) restaurant, with big food and strong cocktails served up with prime sunset views on the Biscayne Bay patio. So leave your preconceived notions behind – and go north!

a Woolworth store), the short Ocean Tce behind the sand dunes and along the beach evokes South Beach in miniature. You'll find quaint shops, oceanfront cafés, MiMo apartment buildings and a strong Argentine flavor.

OLETA RIVER STATE RECREATION AREA Map p251

☎ 305-919-1846; 3400 NE 163rd St; per person $2, 2-4 people $4, plus per additional person over 4 $1;
🕐 8am-sunset

As early as 500 BC, the rich Oleta River estuary was home to Tequesta Indians. Today, this recreation area, coming in at almost 1000 acres and certainly the largest urban park in the state, provides a perfect refuge from posing. Snuggled along Biscayne Bay, it's home

to lots of canoes, kayaks and off-road bicycle trails; a sandy swimming beach with calm waters; a mangrove island accessible only by boat; shady picnic areas and a kiddie playground; plus plenty of egrets, eagles and fiddler crabs who make the place their home.

WOLFIE COHEN'S RASCAL HOUSE
Map pp244-5
☎ 305-947-4581; 17190 Collins Ave

Yes, it's a delicatessen. But it's also an icon. From the big yellow-and-brown roadside marquee, which sports catchy, rotating phrases such as 'Ah the smell of pickles brewed in brine and cabbage soup that tastes like wine,' to the '50s-era red-vinyl booths inside, this 24-hour Jewish deli encapsulates a bygone era. And its corned beef on rye is da bomb.

DOWNTOWN MIAMI
Eating p98, Shopping p143, Sleeping p160,

The truly urban Miami, full of dichotomies, is found Downtown. Ragged and gleaming, hopeless and brimming with optimism, the streets down here teem with all sorts of life, from the shady characters that have made this place infamous in Hollywood films to buttoned-up businessmen and foreign tourists fresh off a cruise ship with pockets full of money. While homeless folks and addicts line up in boxes and sleeping bags along NE 1st Ave, most visitors never catch a glimpse of it, sticking instead a couple of avenues east of there, along the bustling bay front. The main streets around the Miami Cultural Center and government offices teem with the energy of any big city, while shop owners hawk cheap luggage and electronics and street vendors offer up hot dogs or fresh *arepas* (cornmeal cakes). And there's the construction. It's everywhere you look. With old facades knocked down and cranes rolled in so fast and furious, it looks like a postwar rebuilding effort. Rebuilding, even a renaissance, is just what those in charge have in mind for these parts, and it's all based upon the upcoming Performing Arts Center – under construction for years, sucking millions from city coffers and with a completion date that's constantly delayed. But it's a symbol of dreams here, and it will not fall by the wayside.

Orientation

Downtown Miami is a fairly straightforward grid, with Flagler St one of the main east–west drags and NE 2nd Ave serving as a major north–south conduit. An international financial and banking center, Brickell Ave runs south to Coconut Grove along the water, boasting new condos and high-rise luxury hotels including the Four Seasons and the Conrad (it also leads to the exclusive Brickell Key, home to the Mandarin Oriental). The lazy, gritty Miami River divides Downtown into north and south, and is crossed by the Brickell Ave Bridge. Biscayne Blvd runs north from the river and Brickell Ave runs south from it; both are on the eastern side of the district.

Transportation

Train Metromover, Metrorail to Brickell Memorial or Government Center.
Bus 2, 3, 8, 6, 7, 9, 77, 95, K, T.
Car From South Beach, the MacArthur Causeway leads you right into Downtown Miami. From further away, I-95 has several downtown exits. From southern Miami, follow Brickell Ave, and from northern Miami, follow NE 2nd Ave or Biscayne Blvd.

BAYFRONT & AROUND

AMERICAN AIRLINES ARENA Map pp252-3
601 Biscayne Blvd
The sleek AA Arena, looking like a massive spaceship that perpetually hovers at the edge of Biscayne Bay, has been home of the Miami Heat basketball team since 2000. The 20,000-seat venue has also hosted major concerts featuring entertainers as diverse as Dave Matthews and Madonna.

BAYFRONT PARK Map pp252-3
301 Biscayne Blvd
A freight port during the first 1920s building boom, this is a relatively calm downtown green space that's mainly south of **Bayside Marketplace** (below) but commingled in places (though the two are separate entities). You'll find two performance venues: the **Amphitheater** is a great perch for the Fourth of July and New Year's Eve festivities, while the smaller 200-seat **South End Amphitheater** hosts free springtime performances featuring local talent. In the southwest corner is the **Challenger Memorial**, a monument designed by Isamu Noguchi for the astronauts killed in the 1986 space-shuttle explosion. Look north for the **JFK Torch of Friendship** and a **fountain** recognizing the accomplishments of longtime US congressman Claude Pepper.

BAYSIDE MARKETPLACE Map pp252-3
☎ 305-577-3344; www.baysidemarketplace.com; 401 Biscayne Blvd
Just south of the **American Airlines Arena** (above) and packed to the gills with chain stores you could find in any other town in the Western world, this waterfront pantheon to consumerism is mysteriously adored by hordes of tourists and the cruise-ship passengers who dock nearby. A quick stroll could be anthropological, though, especially when beautiful days greet the frequent outdoor performers who drive crowds into salsa frenzies. This is also the place to catch one of the many sightseeing boat trips (p49) and to board the **Casino Princesa** (p125).

BICENTENNIAL PARK Map pp252-3
1075 Biscayne Blvd
The barren waterfront park has an amphitheater with occasional free concerts and events, and it's the future site of the Miami Art Museum and Miami Museum of Science, to be known as Museum Park Miami. You'll have to walk here now, as the Metromover Bicentennial Park stop has been closed for the museum construction.

BRICKELL AVE BRIDGE Map pp252-3
Brickell Ave btwn SE 4th & SE 5th Sts
Crossing the Miami River, the bridge is more beautiful than ever after a multiyear, $21-million renovation (components for the raising mechanism had to be manufactured from scratch). Both wider and higher, the dimensions certainly seemed to facilitate the speedboat-driving drug runners being chased by DEA (Drug Enforcement Administration) agents on the day of the bridge's grand re-opening! Best of all, note the 17ft **bronze statue** by Cuban-born sculptor Manuel Carbonell of a Tequesta warrior and his family, which sits perched atop the towering **Pillar of History** column.

Downtown Miami Top Five

- Rising like a phoenix from the construction ashes, the bright yellow **Freedom Tower** (below) is an image of hope.
- The **Miami Art Museum** (opposite) is an oasis of highbrow culture in the midst of lowbrow urbania.
- The romantically seedy **Miami Riverfront** (opposite) is a great place for fresh fish.
- A driverless train, the **Metromover** (opposite) makes revealing loops high above the city.
- Exclusive and peaceful, Brickell Key is home to the lovely **Mandarin Oriental Hotel** (p160).

BRICKELL KEY Map pp252-3
At SW 8th St
It's a wonder this small island off the coast of downtown can even float with all the high-rise condos it's got crowding its surface. A quick visit here can be interesting, though, as there are a couple of cool eateries and, best of all, the stellar **Mandarin Oriental Hotel** (p160), whose lobby and intimate **M Bar** (p111) afford sweeping views of Biscayne Bay.

WEST OF BRICKELL

DADE COUNTY COURTHOUSE
Map pp252-3
73 W Flagler St
When Miami outgrew its first courthouse (see **Old US Post Office**, p62), it moved in to this neoclassical beauty, built between 1925 and 1929 for a cost of $4 million. The top nine floors served as a 'secure' prison, but was the place from which more than 70 prisoners were able to escape over the next several years! Today this is the place for offices, chambers and courtrooms of circuit, county and family courts. Its facade and front steps provide a supremely imposing entryway for anyone on trial these days.

FREEDOM TOWER Map pp252-3
600 Biscayne Blvd; Metromover Freedom Tower
Designed by the New York architectural firm of Shultz & Weaver in 1925, this tower is one of two surviving area towers modeled after the Giralda bell tower in Spain's Cathedral of Seville (the second is at the **Biltmore Hotel**, p71, Coral Gables). The 'Ellis Island of the South,' it served as an immigration processing center for almost half a million Cuban refugees in the 1960s. Placed on the National Register of Historic Places in 1979, it was also home to the *Miami*

Daily News for 32 years. If all goes as planned, the next entity to be housed in this bright yellow tower will be a Cuban-American museum, which the Cuban National Foundation have had in the works for some time now.

GUSMAN CENTER FOR THE PERFORMING ARTS/OLYMPIA THEATER Map pp252-3
174 E Flagler St
Designed by the Chicago firm Eberson & Eberson, this stunning house of performance opened in 1925 as the Olympia Theater. The ceiling features 246 twinkling stars and clouds, along with 12ft-long crystal chandeliers. Today the lobby serves as the new **Downtown Miami Welcome Center** (p50), doling out helpful visitor information and organizing tours of the historic district; at night you can still catch theater or music performances here (p121).

HISTORICAL MUSEUM OF SOUTHERN FLORIDA Map pp252-3
☎ 305-375-1492; www.historical-museum.org; 101 W Flagler St; adult/child 6-12 yrs/senior $5/2/4, admission free on Sun; ☷ 10am-5pm Mon-Wed & Sat, 10am-9pm 3rd Thu of every month, noon-5pm Sun; Metromover Government Center
Within the Mediterranean-style **Miami-Dade Cultural Center**, this historical museum celebrates the multicultural roots that nourish South Florida. It's particularly interesting for kids. Covering a whopping 10,000 years of state history, the far-reaching exhibits start with natural habitats, wetlands, coasts and ridges. They then move through prehistoric Florida, the Spanish invaders and a Spanish galleon before continuing on to wreckers, the cigar industry, Indian tribes and the railroad's importance during the Flagler Boom. Exhibits then proceed through the Great Depression, 1930s tourism, WWII and right up to the present day. The installations aren't huge, but they're very informative. The museum also has excellent visiting exhibits, with recent topics including Calypso music and Florida homes, as well as a good gift shop and an admirable program of special events; check the website for its calendar of events and programs. Historical tours led by Dr Paul George (p50) are in conjunction with this museum.

LYRIC THEATRE Map pp252-3
☎ 305-358-1146; 819 NW 2nd Ave
Built in 1913, the 400-seat Lyric used to be a prime venue for silent movies, talkies, vaude-

ville and live performances by jazz greats like Duke Ellington and his contemporaries. Over the years, it deteriorated along with the neighborhood, Overtown, and by the 1980s, the building was a shell, a roofless shelter for heroin addicts and homeless people. Then the **Black Archives History & Research Center of South Florida** (Map pp244–5; ☎ 305-636-2390; 5400 NW 22nd Ave) stepped up to the plate. Kicking in $1.5 million for renovations, the center completely overhauled the building. The phoenix reopened its doors in 1999 to appreciative neighbors, civic leaders and entertainers alike, and it's now the lynchpin for a complete neighborhood renovation project, which features mixed-income housing and a Historic Folklife Village.

METROMOVER Map pp252-3

This elevated, electric monorail makes wide loops around the edge of the city, carrying an eclectic mix of Miami-Dade College students, locals on their way to work and adventurous tourists. It's kind of like calm anarchy – no one's in control, but no one's out of control, either. A ride on one gives an interesting perspective on the area.

MIAMI ART MUSEUM Map pp252-3

MAM; ☎ 305-375-3000; www.miamiartmuseum.org; 101 W Flagler St; adult/senior & student/child under 12 $5/2.50/free, admission free Sun; ☺ 10am-5pm Tue-Fri, noon-5pm Sat & Sun, noon-9pm 3rd Thu of every month; Metromover Government Center

Also within the **Miami-Dade Cultural Center**, the adjacent museum is ensconced in spectacular Philip Johnson–designed digs. Without a permanent collection, its fine rotating exhib-

its concentrate on post-WWII international art. Look for good Latin American and Caribbean art, as well as artists in the vein of Robert Rauschenberg and Wangechi Mutu. Every third Thursday from 5pm until 8:30pm it's 'Jam at MAM,' a cocktail-fueled gathering featuring live DJs, snacks and a crowd of young professionals. Soon, MAM will be moving to a new waterfront location at Bicentennial Park.

MIAMI-DADE COMMUNITY COLLEGE
Map pp252-3

☎ 305-237-3696; 300 NE 2nd Ave; admission free; ☺ 10am-6pm Mon-Fri; Metromover College/Bayside

Though the college itself isn't very exciting, there are two art galleries with rotating exhibitions at the Wolfson Campus of the Miami-Dade Community College. Both the 3rd-floor **Centre Gallery** and the 5th-floor **Frances Wolfson Gallery** often have photography shows.

MIAMI RIVER Map pp252-3

The Miami River, fed by the Everglades until the early 20th century, is now fed by canals starting at about the 32nd Ave bridge in Little Havana. The colorful, seedy riverfront is one of Miami's most fascinating places – but drive: you won't want to walk around here by night or day. Much of the shore feels abandoned, and is lined with makeshift warehouses, where goods (you can only imagine what, exactly) are loaded and unloaded onto small tugboats bound for and from the Caribbean and other foreign ports. Fisherfolk float in with their daily catch, fancy yachts 'slumming it' dock at restaurants, and nonconformists hang out on their houseboats. In order to have an excuse to linger in the neighborhood, where you are

Pan Am 'Clipper' Air Travel

Pan Am 'Clippers,' big luxurious flying boats really, began taking to the skies off Dinner Key Marina, 3500 Pan American Dr, in 1939. It was a romantic time for air travel, when then-exotic locales such as Honolulu and the shores of South America were filled with wonder and newness. It was a time when overnight flights to China carried only 18 passengers, all in 1st-class (the only class). It was a time when, on flights to Cuba and Key West, pilots would bring along carrier pigeons (rather than radios) to notify the terminal if there was trouble during the flight and the plane had to make an emergency landing.

Although originally headquartered in a houseboat, Pan Am built an art-deco terminal graced with nautical exterior details on Dinner Key in 1930, when it began flying to South America. It was the talk of the town. Although it has been unceremoniously converted into **Miami City Hall** (Map p258; 3500 Pan American Dr; ☺ 9am-5pm Mon-Fri), you can still see a 1938 Pan Am dinner menu and models of the clippers and other seaplanes that flew from here. Head into the lobby and turn left, and left again. You'll get a palpable sense of history sitting near the hangars, which are now used for boatyards. The seaplanes stopped flying in 1945, after WWII had fast-forwarded the development of long-distance land-based planes. Suddenly the exotic locals weren't so remote and, dare we say, the planet not so lonely.

bound to get lost, enjoy lunch or dinner at one of the atmospheric seafood restaurants along the shores or bunk down at the unique **Miami River Inn** (p160).

OLD US POST OFFICE Map pp252-3
100 NE 1st St; ⊙ 9am-5pm Mon-Fri; Metromover College North

Constructed in 1912, this post office and county courthouse served as the first federal building in Miami. The building, which features a low pitched roof, elaborate doors and carved entryways, was purchased in 1937 to serve as the country's first savings and loan. Government prosecutors had outgrown the space anyway, and soon moved into the adjacent Federal Courthouse and Federal Justice Building. Today you can visit the old courthouse to check out Denman Fink's 1940 mural *Law Guides Florida*

Progress in the main courtroom on the 2nd floor. It depicts 1930s Florida, complete with a Cuba-bound Pan Am Clipper. During a winter visit, you may very well see some turkey vultures roosting around the edifice's exterior.

TOBACCO ROAD Map pp252-3
☎ 305-374-1198; 626 S Miami Ave; ⊙ 11:30am-5am Mon-Sat, 1pm-5am Sun; Metromover 8th St

Just south of the Miami River Bridge, a small collection of bars line S Miami Ave. Of these, Tobacco Rd is something of a Miami tradition, having received the city's first liquor license. It's been here since the 1920s and was a speakeasy during Prohibition. Stop in for a drink or a listen to live music while you're in the neighborhood. Film buffs may recognize it as the place where Kurt Russell has a drink in *The Mean Season* (1985).

WYNWOOD, THE DESIGN DISTRICT & LITTLE HAITI

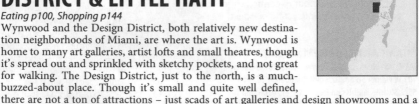

Eating p100, Shopping p144

Wynwood and the Design District, both relatively new destination neighborhoods of Miami, are where the art is. Wynwood is home to many art galleries, artist lofts and small theatres, though it's spread out and sprinkled with sketchy pockets, and not great for walking. The Design District, just to the north, is a much-buzzed-about place. Though it's small and quite well defined, there are not a ton of attractions – just scads of art galleries and design showrooms and a few very trendy bars and eateries. It's easily walkable and definitely worth checking out. Also, many sleek new architectural marvels, from retail centers to leafy plazas, are in the works; visit www.designmiami.com for updates on development.

As with Little Havana, Little Haiti has absorbed waves of refugees during times of Haitian political strife. This is a mainly residential area, whose borders bleed into the Design District in places. Little Haiti struggles with poverty (it isn't a great place to visit after nightfall) and has had limited success in marketing itself as a tourist attraction. But you will find some great eateries and botanicas. And currently in the works is a brand-new Haitian Heritage Museum, a planned culture and art complex with a projected completion date of 2007; follow its progress at www.haitianmuseum.org. The neighborhood is roughly bounded by Biscayne Blvd to the east, I-95 to the west, 90th St to the north and 54th St to south.

Orientation

All three areas are just north of Downtown. While Wynwood is sort of loosely defined as being west of Biscayne Blvd and east of I-95, between 17th and 35th Sts, the Design District is a small, neat grid: between NE 38th and NE 41st Sts and NE 2nd Ave and North Miami Ave. North of all three of these regions is a rapidly gentrifying neighborhood known locally as the Upper East Side.

Transportation
Bus 3, 9, 10, 36, 95, 9, J.
Car From South Beach, the Julia Tuttle Causeway leads you right into the Design District. Follow Biscayne Blvd or NE 2nd Ave south into Wynwood and north into Little Haiti.

WYNWOOD

BACARDI BUILDING Map p254
☎ 305-573-8511; 2100 Biscayne Blvd; admission free;
🕑 9am-3:30pm Mon-Fri

The striking headquarters for the USA's most popular rum company, Bacardi, is made up of two buildings – a beautiful tower with a bright Spanish-tile facade and a smaller 1970s addition. The main space has a small museum dedicated to the history of the family company from 1838 to the present, plus an art gallery that exhibits both local and international artists.

DORSCH GALLERY Map p254
☎ 305-576-1278; 151 NW 24th St

Founded in 1991, Dorsch was one of the first local galleries to exhibit regional contemporary artists. It now counts Rene Barge, George Bethea, Jay Ore and Brian Reedy on its roster of talents, and hosts the SubTropics Music & Sound Arts Festival in spring.

MIAMI CITY CEMETERY Map p254
☎ 305-579-6938; 1800 NE 2nd Ave; admission free;
🕑 7am-3:30pm Mon-Fri, 8am-4:30pm Sat & Sun

The city of Miami's original cemetery was established in July 1897 and contains more than 9000 graves in separate White, Black and Jewish sections. Mayors and politicians lie alongside about 90 Confederate dead and war veterans from the 20th century, and some familiar folks with major headstones include Julia Tuttle and William Burdine. There are also a few curious-looking memorials for 'woodsmen,' realistic-looking logs carved out of cement. But Mrs Carrie Miller, who died in 1926, is the highlight of the cemetery. Her husband, William, wrapped her body in a sheet and encased it in a concrete block 6ft high. 'After the body has gone to dust, her sleeping form will remain,' reads the epitaph. William apparently wanted to join his wife there eventually, but he lost all his money during the Great Depression and died broke. He's buried in an unmarked plot nearby.

RUBELL FAMILY ART COLLECTION
Map p254
☎ 305-573-6090; 95 NW 29th St; adult/senior & student $5/2.50; 🕑 10am-6pm Wed-Sun

The Rubell family – specifically, the niece and nephew of the late Steve, better known as Ian Schrager's Studio 54 partner – operates a couple of top-end hotels in Miami Beach. But they

Top Five Wynwood/Design District Galleries

- **Placemaker Gallery** (p64) Where a homegrown crop of artists, influenced by architecture and the city's phenomenal growth, are making an international name for themselves.
- **Rubell Family Art Collection** (left) The recently renovated warehouse is packed with 1500 works by stars including Cindy Sherman, Damien Hirst and Keith Haring, just for starters.
- **Bernice Steinbaum Gallery** (p64) Bernice Steinbaum is on the map for her diverse and talented roster, which includes women and African-American artists.
- **Dorsch Gallery** (left) This 5000-sq-ft space, filled with cutting-edge paintings, sculpture and installation art, is credited with fueling the art scene of Wynwood.
- **Barbara Gillman Gallery** (p144) Photos of jazz greats and eclectic exhibits fill this massive space at the end of an intimate Design District street.

have also amassed an impressive and pioneering contemporary art collection that spans the last 30 years. Opened in 1996, the 40,000-sq-ft facility houses works by Cindy Sherman, Keith Haring, Damien Hirst, Jean-Michel Basquiat and Jeff Koons. But don't expect just one or two pieces by each artist; the aim is to focus on an artist's entire career. The museum is located in an industrial area, in a large yellow building that once served as a former DEA drug- and weapons-confiscation storage facility. You can call ahead to set up a guided tour.

THE DESIGN DISTRICT

AMERICAN POLICE HALL OF FAME & MUSEUM Map p254
☎ 305-573-0070; www.aphf.org; 3801 Biscayne Blvd; adult/child $12/8; 🕑 10am-6pm

It's not quite like any of the other destinations in this hip 'hood, but it is an interesting stop in its own right. To wit: a police officer is killed in the USA every 57 hours, and this museum memorializes them. You can't miss the boxy building with a 1995 Chevy Caprice Classic police car glued to the museum wall fronting Biscayne Blvd. Inside, you can play detective and work a crime scene, and check out the holding cell for those presumed innocent until proven guilty. While it has some 'fun' collections, like the cop car from Blade Runner, gangster memorabilia,

Art Walks: the New Clubbing?

Grass Lounge (p113) and the **District** (p101) may get all the attention when it comes to nightlife in these parts, but there's another hipster scene too, and it's based right in the spaces that make this area what it is: the art galleries. Following on the heels of other neighborhoods that turn nighttime gallery hours into major social events – Coral Gables, mainly – both Wynwood and the Design District have devoted one night a month to extended exhibition hours mixed with live bands, DJs and a steady flow of wine (a slight problem, considering that many of the spaced-apart galleries require short drives if you want to see them all). The result has been quite fabulous indeed, with the pumped-up crowds who flock here looking more like club kids than art aficionados – and there's not a velvet rope in sight. The Design District's party is on the second Thursday of each month, 6pm to 10pm; Wynwood's follows two days later on the second Saturday, from 7pm to 10pm. Visit www.designmiami .com for information on participating galleries.

confiscated weapons and restraint devices, it's mainly a solemn tribute to slain officers. Murdered officers' names, ranks, cities and states are engraved in white Italian marble, with an interdenominational chapel nearby.

BERNICE STEINBAUM GALLERY
Map p254

☎ 305-573-2700; 3550 N Miami Ave

After two decades in NYC, Steinbaum has moved south, where it's received a grand welcome for its mid-career contemporary artists such as Amalia Mesa-Bains and Deborah Willis.

BUICK BUILDING Map p254
☎ 305-573-8116; 3841 NE 2nd Ave;
⌚ by appointment

This gallery has been known to exhibit some pretty outstanding installation shows, but its most known as the gateway of the Design District because of its striking mural facade. Done on canvas in bright yellow and black, the images of Latin mythological figures were done in 2000 by the married artist team of Roberto Behar and Rosario Marquardt (see the **Living Room**, below).

LIVING ROOM Map p254
Cnr NW 40th St & N Miami Ave

This striking work of public art was created by Argentine husband-and-wife team Rob-

erto Behar and Rosario Marquardt, two of the most prolific public-art creators in Miami today. Though the building that stands behind this creative facade is currently vacant, the installation itself is full of whimsy: an oversized sort of stage set of, you guessed it, a living room, complete with patterned wallpaper and a bright red couch flanked by two tall lamps. The artists have described this work, as well as many of their others, as an 'urban intervention,' blurring the line between art and architecture. *The Living Room* is meant to be a criticism of the lack, and disappearance, of public space.

MELIN BUILDING Map p254
☎ 3930 NE 2nd Ave; ⌚ hours vary

This small art and design 'mall,' for lack of a better word, houses several points of interest, the splashiest of which is the massive shoe sculpture that sits within the vast public atrium inside. Created by artist Antoni Miralda, *Gondola Shoe* is one story high and fabulous. Shops in the Melin include the **Kartell** (p144) design store and the Spanish import **Coma's** (p101).

MOORE SPACE Map p254
☎ 305-438-1163; www.themoorespace.org; 4040 NE 2nd Ave; ⌚ 10am-5pm Wed-Sat

This experimental gallery stands apart from many of the area's galleries for a few simple reasons – its large size, historic structure (the 1920s Moore Furniture Company building) and extensive programming. Conceived in response to the first Art Basel Miami Beach art show, Moore Space, helmed by art collector Rosa de la Cruz, has hosted edgy group exhibitions, lectures and education programs, such as its partnership with the neighborhood's Design and Architecture High School (DASH) and with the New World School of Arts in Downtown Miami. Definitely check out what's going on here when you're in town.

NEWTON BUILDING Map p254
NE 2nd Ave & NE 39th St

Building buffs will want to take a gander at this new and much-touted 'renewal' by architect Walter Chatham. Still vacant at press time, the sleek white facade, rounded corner and nod to deco style brings freshness to what is mainly an industrial-style 'hood.

PLACEMAKER GALLERY Map p254
☎ 305-576-6695; 3852 N Miami Ave

Placemaker Gallery is hot, hot, hot for its outstanding array of young local artists. It is an

Art Basel star and is also the represener of talents such as Daniel Arsham, John Bianchi and Tao Ray.

LITTLE HAITI

HAITIAN REFUGEE CENTER Map p254
☎ 305-757-8538; 119 NE 54th St; ☮ 9am-5pm Mon-Fri

Though it's far from a tourist 'attraction,' this community center is a good stopping point for folks with a particular interest in Haitian culture; it's an invaluable resource for Haitian life in Miami as well as community events.

LIBRERI MAPOU Map p254
☎ 305-757-9922; 5919 NE 2nd Ave

For another taste of Haitian culture, peruse the shelves at this bookstore, bursting with 3000 titles (including periodicals) in English, French and Creole, as well as items such as crafts and recorded music.

LITTLE HAVANA

Eating p103, Shopping p145

After the Mariel Boatlift (p44), Little Havana exploded with Cuban exiles into a distinctly traditional Cuban neighborhood. Now, though, some 25 years later, the makeup of the area has changed significantly, as Cubans who 'made it' have long moved out to the suburbs and newer immigrants from Argentina, Colombia, Nicaragua, Honduras and other Latin American countries have added a new texture to this once strictly Cuban world. Spanish, unsurprisingly, is the predominant language here.

The last Friday night of each month is the most happening in Little Havana. From 6pm to 11pm all the shops and restaurants fling their doors open, and café tables and merchandise spill out onto the sidewalks. Artists and craftspeople show their wares. Folks young and old, well-dressed and not, salsa to live and recorded music in the streets, on sidewalks and in shops.

Orientation

Calle Ocho (SW 8th St) doesn't just cut through the heart of the neighborhood, it *is* the heart of the neighborhood. For the purposes of our exploration, the neighborhood extends roughly from W Flagler St to SW 13th St and from SW 3rd Ave to SW 37th Ave. The Miami River separates Little Havana from downtown on the northeast border.

BAY OF PIGS MUSEUM & LIBRARY
Map p255

☎ 305-649-4719; 1821 SW 9th St; admission free; ☮ 10am-5pm Mon-Fri

This small museum is a memorial to the 2506 Brigade, otherwise known as the crew of the ill-fated Bay of Pigs invasion. The walls are lined with pictures of comrades who were killed during combat and those who participated but have died over the years, without seeing a non-Castro Havana. Though the documents and memorabilia are not all that well organized, it's an interesting and thought-provoking place that certainly puts the fact of Cuban exiles into a political context.

CALLE OCHO Map p255
The heart of Little Havana is Calle Ocho, the Spanish name of SW 8th St, which bustles with the action of local folks running errands and

an increasing flow of tourists who come to see a 'real neighborhood' of Cuban and Latin American shops and cafés. Of particular note are the fragrant cigar shops and intriguing botanicas (religious shops that sell items such as incense, statuettes and herbs). Come here for a mellow slice of true life and you'll be satisfied – just don't expect to see Tito Puente leading a parade of colorfully attired, tight-trousered men through the streets. More likely you'll see old men wearing boxy *guayaberas* (men's

Transportation
Train Metromover to 8th St station.
Bus 6, 8, 17, 42.
Car Follow I-95 to NW 7th St; Calle Ocho only goes one way, east, here, so you'll have to head west on NW 7th St and then circle back around.

shirts with appliquéd designs) arguing politics and playing dominoes.

CASA ELIÁN Map p255
2319 NW 2nd St; donations requested; 🕑 **10am-6pm**

The Elián Gonzales house, where the young boy's life unfolded before cable news channels on a daily basis, is now a shrine and museum. You've probably seen the little house, on an ordinary street, on TV many times. Elián's great-uncle Delfin bought the house in late 2000 and opened it in late 2001 as a shrine honoring Elián's time in the States. The place is filled, floor-to-ceiling, with hundreds of photographs, magazine covers, and belongings of Elián's. His bedroom is a time capsule: clothes hang in the closet, the inner tube that saved his life at sea hangs on the wall, Spiderman pajamas are laid out on the bed. And then there's the life-sized enlargement of the Pulitzer-prize-winning photograph of Elián hiding in the closet and being seized by federal border-patrol agents at gunpoint. The photo hangs right next to the real closet. Before you leave, you'll most likely be handed one of the eerie postcards piled by the front door. Sporting Elián's elfin face, it reads: 'Reward: Missing Child. Last seen 4/22/00 at 5:15am being removed forcibly by a woman and masked gunmen in a white utility vehicle…'

CUBAN MEMORIAL BOULEVARD
Map p255

The two blocks of SW 13th Ave south of Calle Ocho contain a series of monuments to Cuban patriots and freedom fighters (read: anti-Castro Cubans), including the **Eternal Torch in Honor of the 2506th Brigade** (the counterrevolutionaries who died during the botched Bay of Pigs invasion on April 17, 1961); a huge **brass map** of Cuba, dedicated to the 'ideals of people who will never forget the pledge of making their Fatherland free'; and a **bust of José Martí**. Bursting out of the island in the center of the wide boulevard, strong roots twisting up above the ground, is a massive ceiba tree, revered by followers of Santería.

LA PLAZA DE LA CUBANIDAD Map p255
W Flagler St at NW 17th Ave

This fountain and monument is a tribute both to the Cuban provinces and to the people who were drowned by Castro's forces while trying to escape from Cuba in 1994 on a ship, '13 de Mayo,' which was sunk just off the coast.

LATIN QUARTER CULTURAL CENTER OF MIAMI Map p255
☎ **305-649-9797; www.latinquarterculturalcenter .org; 1501 SW 8th St;** 🕑 **hours vary**

Stop inside this bright orange building for a jolt of culture – either through rotating exhibits in its light-filled art gallery or through one of its lectures, dance performances or theatre productions.

MÁXIMO GÓMEZ PARK Map p255
Domino Park; Calle Ocho at SW 15th Ave; 🕑 **9am-6pm**

Perhaps better known as 'Domino Park' because of the scores of elderly Cuban men playing dominoes, this is a highly sensory place to soak in the local scene. The clack-clack-clack sounds of hundreds of black-and-white dominos being slapped on cement tables is downright musical. If you're an adventurer who speaks a little Spanish, join in for yourself. The park's namesake, Máximo Gómez y Baez, was the Dominican-born general of the Cuban revolutionary forces in the late 1800s.

TOWER THEATER Map p255
☎ **305-649-2960; 1508 Calle Ocho**

This recently renovated 1926 landmark theatre has a proud deco facade and a newly done interior. This is thanks to a recent teaming up with Miami-Dade Community College that has brought the space back to life with frequent Spanish-language films and varied art exhibits in the lobby.

José Martí

Havana-born José Martí (1853–1895) was exiled to Spain in 1870 for 'opposition to Colonial rule.' He eventually made his way to North and South America, where his antiracist writings relentlessly extolled his vision of a free Cuba. He stirred up anti-Spanish sentiment wherever he could, including Florida. Although he was allowed to return to Cuba in 1878, he was quickly booted out by angry Spanish authorities. In 1895 Martí returned to Cuba again, this time to participate in the war for Cuban independence. Considered one of Cuba's leading writers and a hero of its independence, Martí was also one of the first to die in the conflict. **José Martí Park**, between the Miami River and Little Havana at 351 SW 4th St, was dedicated in his honor in 1950.

KEY BISCAYNE

Eating p105, Shopping p146, Sleeping p161

This city key is a fine example of Miami's juxtapositions, as it offers gorgeous stretches of sandy beaches and biking trails, yet the urban skyline hovers just across the bay and Downtown is only a quick causeway ride away. It's a perfect place for various outdoor pursuits, resort-style vacations and, more recently, some trendy dining. It's also the home of the legendary **Miami Seaquarium** (p68).

The Rickenbacker Causeway links the mainland with Key Biscayne via Virginia Key and provides a nice place to park, under the ironwoods at dusk, to watch the sunset. Virginia Key Beach, a lovely city park with picnic tables, barbecue grills and relative peace and quiet, is a perfect for families. Hobie Beach is great for windsurfing (p132). And after a long, hard day of playing, there are lots of waterfront restaurants boasting dramatic skyline views perfect for sunset drinks.

Orientation

The Rickenbacker Causeway, the eastern extension of 26th Rd, leads first to the small Virginia Key, and then over to Key Biscayne, an island that's just 7 miles long. It turns into Crandon Blvd, the key's only real main road, which runs all the way to the southernmost tip and the **Cape Florida Lighthouse** (below).

BILL BAGGS CAPE FLORIDA STATE RECREATION AREA Map p259

☎ 305-361-5811; www.floridastateparks.org/cape florida/; 1200 S Crandon Blvd; admission per person $2-4, on foot $1; ☉ 8am-sundown

This wildish 494-acre wetland park occupies the southern region of Key Biscayne. The barrier-island ecosystem is extensive, and there are plenty of walkways, boardwalks, bike trails, relatively secluded beaches, covered picnic areas and even a little café selling decent soups and sandwiches (watch for the roving raccoons who will try to steal your supper if you don't keep it close to your chest). A concession shack rents kayaks, bikes, in-line skates, beach chairs and umbrellas.

CAPE FLORIDA LIGHTHOUSE Map p259

☎ 305-361-8779; Bill Baggs Cape Florida State Recreation Area

At the park's southernmost tip, the 1845 brick Cape Florida Lighthouse, the oldest structure in Florida, replaced one that was severely damaged in 1836 by attacking Seminole Indians. You can tour it at 10am and 1pm (free). Tours are limited to about 12 people, so put your name on a sign-up list at least 30 minutes prior to the tour. The lighthouse also boasts an impressive first-order lens. What's that, you ask? French physicist Augustin Jean Fresnel (1788–1827) devised six different sizes of ingenious beehivelike reflecting lenses. The largest ones, of the first order, were

stationed on seacoasts and the smallest ones, of the sixth order, were used in harbors.

CRANDON PARK Map p259

Definitely worth a visit, this 1200-acre park boasts the **Marjory Stoneman Douglas Biscayne Nature Center** (p68) and Crandon Park Beach, a glorious but crowded white-sand beach that stretches for 3 miles. Much of the park consists of a dense coastal hammock and mangrove swamps.

JIMBO'S Map p259

☎ 305-361-7026; www.jimbosplace.com; Duck Lake Rd (at the end of Arthur Lamb Jr Rd), Virginia Key

Though it's just across the highway from the **Miami Seaquarium** (p68), this remote and scruffy spot feels worlds away. A collection of broken-down shacks on the edge of the bay, Jimbo's is technically an alfresco bar with cold beers, smoked fish and boccie ball matches, but its vibe is more private-trailer-park-bonfire-party. You might feel like a bit of an interloper when you first join the regulars who congregate here, but drink a brew, relax and be friendly;

Transportation

Bus B.
Car From the mainland, take the Rickenbacker Causeway, accessible from US Hwy 1 and I-95.

Stiltsville: Hanging in the Balance

'No one who chances on the phenomenon of Stiltsville for the first time will ever forget the sight of homes that hover above the waters, miles from any shore, like structures from a dream,' once penned Miami writer Les Standiford. It's true – but how long will it last? Stiltsville, a collection of seven houses that stands on pilings far out in the shallow water of Biscayne Bay, is a historic community that began in the early 1930s. That's when local fisherman 'Crawfish' Eddie Walker sold chowder from his shack, out on the mudflats, and soon gained neighbors who liked the idea of off-shore living. By the end of the '50s there were 27 houses on stilts. Over the years many have been destroyed by hurricanes, and eventually, the rich folk who began populating Key Biscayne complained that these bay 'squatters' would bring their property values down. Bay bottom leases were transferred from the state to the National Park. The unique community was a candidate for national landmark status, which would have protected it, but was ultimately denied such status because the houses were less than 50 years old. The houses, now a political hot potato, remain, but without leases; their removal has been mandated, but so far not enforced. Negotiations are ongoing, and an outcome may be days or years away.

you'll soon fit right in. You may even recognize the odd surroundings, which have been used for fashion photo shoots and various films and TV shows, including *Miami Vice* and *Flipper*.

MARJORY STONEMAN DOUGLAS BISCAYNE NATURE CENTER Map p259
☎ 305-361-6767; www.biscaynenaturecenter.org; Crandon Park, 6767 Crandon Blvd; admission free; ⏱ 10am-4pm
Especially fun for children, this namesake of a beloved environmental crusader can teach you all about its natural surroundings. There are weekend hands-on demonstrations and reef-ecology and sea-grass talks and walks, which let kids wade into the water with nets and catch sea horses, sponges, crabs, urchins and other marine life (which are released after a short lesson). Inside the center are ever-changing art and nature exhibits.

MIAMI SEAQUARIUM Map p259
☎ 305-361-5705; www.miamiseaquarium.com; 4400 Rickenbacker Causeway; adult/child $25.95/20.95; ⏱ 9:30am-6pm, last entry 4:30pm
This fine 38-acre marine life park excels in preserving, protecting and educating us about aquatic creatures and was one of the country's first places dedicated to sea life. There are dozens of shows and exhibits – easily a morning's worth – including a tropical reef; the Shark Channel, with feeding presentations; Faces of the Rainforest, with exotic birds and reptiles; and Discovery Bay, a natural mangrove habitat that serves as a refuge for rehabilitating rescued sea turtles. Check out the Pacific white-sided dolphins or visit the injured West Indian manatees being nursed back to health; some are released. Frequent shows put some particularly gorgeous animals on display for the audience's amusement, including a massive killer whale and some precious dolphins and sea lions. For an extra fee ($149 per person), you can participate in a swim-with-dolphins program.

STILTSVILLE Map p259
www.stiltsville.org
This collection of seven houses that stand on pilings out in Biscayne Bay has been around since the early '30s. You can view them, way out in the distance, from the southern shore of the **Bill Baggs park** (p67). Catch a glimpse while you can, as the future of this unique community is under constant political threat (above). The illustrious historian Dr Paul George offers occasional boat tours of Stiltsville (☎ 305-375-1621).

COCONUT GROVE
Eating p105, Shopping p146, Sleeping p161
If all you've heard about the Grove is that it's a groovy, bohemian village, you may be a bit disappointed when you arrive to find that its nucleus these days is a massive pair of outdoor malls, **CocoWalk** (opposite) and the **Streets of Mayfair** (opposite), which attract hordes of shoppers with all the standard chains, from Borders bookstore to the Gap. Steer clear of here, though, and you'll catch a glimpse of the town's charms that have longtime resi-

dents yearning for the heydays of the 1960s and '70s. Lush parkland lines S Bayshore Dr, museums and an excellent playhouse bring an infusion of culture and sweet little cottages sit nestled near multimillion-dollar mansions. Both Madonna and Sylvester Stallone have been among the celebs who have chosen Coconut Grove as home (one of several homes, at least).

Transportation

Train Metrorail to Coconut Grove or Vizcaya stations.
Bus 6, 22, 27, 37, 42, 48.
Car Follow S Dixie Hwy or 27th Ave into the heart of town.
Rickshaw Coconut Grove Rickshaw (☎ 305-669-9509) operates 10-minute rides ($5) through the village and 20-minute moonlight rides ($10) from 8pm-2am.

Orientation

The Grove unfolds along S Bayshore Dr (south of the Rickenbacker Causeway), which hugs the shoreline. South Bayshore Dr turns into the central village where it becomes McFarlane Rd and then Main Hwy, which eventually leads to Douglas Rd (SW 37th Ave), Ingraham Hwy, Old Cutler Rd and attractions in South Dade. The US Hwy 1 (S Dixie Hwy) acts as the northern boundary for the Grove.

BARNACLE STATE HISTORIC PARK
Map p258
☎ 305-448-9445; 3485 Main Hwy; admission $1;
☺ park 9am-4pm Fri-Mon, house tours 10am, 11:30am, 1pm & 2:30pm
In the center of the village, this 5-acre pioneer residence sits on its original foundations, which date back to 1891. Originally owned by homesteader Ralph Monroe, often called Miami's first snowbird (a nickname for Northerners who fly south for the winter), the house is open for guided tours, led by folks who are quite knowledgeable and enthusiastic about the park – which is, by the way, a lovely, shady oasis in which to stroll, especially

if you're seeking refuge from the consumerist madness across Main Hwy. The outdoor space also hosts frequent moonlight concerts, from jazz to classical.

COCOWALK/STREETS OF MAYFAIR
Map p258
☎ 305-444-0777, 305-448-1700; 3015 Grand Ave, 2911 Grand Ave
Credited for reviving Coconut Grove in the 1990s, this pair of alfresco malls of ubiquitous chain stores is perhaps (and inexplicably) the Grove's biggest tourist draw. See them for yourself if you must, but it's really just a big, bustling collection of the usual suspects.

Manatees' Biggest Threat

Manatees are shy and utterly peaceful mammals. Pollution is a problem, but their biggest killers are boaters, and of those, the worst offenders are pleasure boaters.

Manatees seek warm, shallow water and feed on vegetation. South Florida is surrounded by just such an environment, but it also has one of the highest concentrations of pleasure boats in the world. Despite pleas from environmental groups, wildlife advocates and the local, state and federal governments, which have declared many areas 'Manatee Zones,' some pleasure boaters routinely exceed speed limits and ignore simple practices that would help protect the species.

After grabbing a bite, manatees float up for air and often float just beneath the surface, chewing and hanging around. When speedboats zoom through the area, manatees are hit by the hulls and either knocked away or pushed under the boat, whose propeller then gashes the mammal as the boat passes overhead. Few manatees get through life without propeller scars, which leave slices in their bodies similar to the diagonal slices on a loaf of French bread.

There are several organizations throughout the state that rescue and rehabilitate injured manatees, but they're fighting what would appear to be a losing battle. One of the two largest is the **Miami Seaquarium** (opposite). There are only about 1700 (endangered) West Indian manatees left in the world, and the Seaquarium is dedicated to preserving their existence. Divers, animal experts and veterinarians of Seaquarium's Marine Mammal Rescue Team patrol South Florida waters, responding to reports of stranded manatees, dolphins and whales. While the Seaquarium's program has been very successful, pleasure boaters still threaten the manatees' survival.

Coconut Grove Rickshaws

To the tourists who love to shop at CocoWalk and gaze out at Biscayne Bay in the moonlight, the rickshaws here are a welcome sight. To many residents, though, the little red vehicles are law-breaking rebels. Many are not licensed or insured, say the city, and although so far they don't seem to be an annoyance that impedes traffic or causes accidents, folks around here are sticklers for rules and regulations. A recent news item in the *Coconut Grove Times* warned residents to report rebels to the Miami Parking Authority. You, though, may just want to sit back and enjoy the ride.

COCONUT GROVE PLAYHOUSE

Map p258
3500 Main Hwy
This Spanish-style theatre of the '50s, Miami's oldest playhouse, was originally built as a film house in the 1920s. It presented Samuel Beckett's *Waiting for Godot* in a spectacularly glitzy 1956 US premiere, and today hosts much-lauded shows that frequently move on to Broadway or the West End.

ERMITA DE LA CARIDAD Map pp244-5

☎ 305-854-2404; 3609 S Miami Ave
The Catholic Diocese purchased some of the bayfront land from Deering's **Villa Vizcaya** (right) estate and built a shrine here for its parishioners, displaced Cubans. Symbolizing a beacon, it faces the homeland, exactly 290 miles due south; note the mural that depicts Cuban history. After visiting the villa or the **Miami Museum of Science & Planetarium** (right), consider picnicking at this quiet sanctuary on the water's edge or at nearby Kennedy Park on S Bayshore Dr.

KAMPONG

4013 Douglas Rd; ⊗ **tours Mon-Fri by appointment only**
This is the historic former home of noted plant explorer David Fairchild (who also founded the **Fairchild Tropical Garden**, p72). In between world journeys in search of beautiful and economically viable plant life, Fairchild lived here with his wife Marian (daughter of inventor Alexander Graham Bell). The lush property was purchased in 1960 by Catherine Hauberg Sweeney, who later presented it as a gift to the Hawaii-based National Tropical Botanical Gardens. The Kampong is listed on the National Register of Historic Places.

MIAMI MUSEUM OF SCIENCE & PLANETARIUM Map pp244-5

☎ 305-646-4200; www.miamisci.org; 3280 S Miami Ave; adult/child/senior & student $10/6/8; ⊗ 10am-6pm
This Smithsonian-affiliated museum has great hands-on, creative exhibits: from turbulent weather phenomena and the mysterious universe to creepy-crawlies and coral-reef displays. The planetarium hosts various space lessons and telescope-viewing sessions, as well as the old-school laser shows, with trippy flashes set to the classic-rock of the Beatles and Pink Floyd. Kids especially love the outdoor Wildlife Center, which features dangerous animals of South Florida and exotic birds of prey.

PLYMOUTH CONGREGATIONAL CHURCH Map p258

☎ 305-444-6521; 3400 Devon Rd; ⊗ 8:30am-4:30pm Mon-Fri
This 1917 coral mission-style church is striking, from its solid masonry work to its hand-carved door, which originated at a Pyrenees monastery. Ask to take a peek inside during office hours. The church is set on a lush 11 acres – a popular spot for wedding photos and home to Dade County's first schoolhouse, a one-room wooden building that dates to 1887 and was moved here from its original site in 1970.

VIZCAYA MUSEUM & GARDENS

Map pp244-5
☎ 305-250-9133; www.vizcayamuseum.com; 3251 S Miami Ave; adult/child 6-12 yrs $12/5; museum ⊗ 9:30am-5pm, last admission 4:30pm; gardens ⊗ 9:30am-5:30pm
A magical seaside spot to stroll or sit – or get hitched, as many fanciful couples do – this

---

Coconut Grove/Coral Gables Top Five

- View the Italian opulence, inside and out, of **Vizcaya Museum** (above).
- The **Venetian Pool** (p73) is the best pool in Miami – and it's public.
- The **Biltmore Hotel** (opposite) is massive, grand and haunted.
- Trade the sun for afternoon stars at the **Miami Museum of Science & Planetarium** (above).
- A small, shady oasis, **Barnacle State Historic Park** (p69) is just feet from a bustling mall.

opulent Italian Renaissance–style villa was built for industrialist James Deering in 1916. Deering employed 1000 people (that was 10% of the local population at the time) for four years to fulfill his desire for a manse that looked centuries old. They did a great job. The villa itself is brimming with 15th- to 19th-century furniture, tapestries, paintings and decorative arts. And although the grounds, which once spread for 180 acres, have been reduced to a mere 30, they're a poetic 30 acres. They feature splendid gardens, beautiful fountains, sculptures, elegant pools, a charming gazebo, canals running everywhere and lots of trails. Fans of silly movies might recognize the palace, as it was the setting for the splendid dinner party in *Ace Ventura: Pet Detective,* while political junkies might recall this was the place where President Clinton hosted the Summit of the Americas, a historic gathering of 34 leaders of the Western Hemisphere. Savvy party promoters have also been known to use the place for lavish dance soirees. Be sure to take a tour (45 minutes) while you're here, as they are included with the price of admission.

CORAL GABLES

Eating p106, Shopping p147, Sleeping p162,

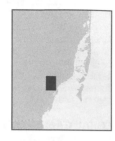

If there's any place that's the aural opposite of South Beach, it's this lovely, leafy 'City Beautiful,' which exudes opulence with a comforting quietude. Coral Gables is the vision of developer George Merrick, who took 1600 acres of inherited family land (planted with citrus and avocado trees), purchased 1400 more in 1921 and then went on an architect-hiring spree. His goal was simple: create a planned 'model suburb' with a decidedly Mediterranean theme, magnificent gateways, impressive plazas, fountains, ornate water towers and wide, tree-lined streets. The city was in full bloom a mere three years later, and by 1925 it was incorporated. Today, Coral Gables, while exciting to multinational corporations and resident diplomats, is a solid suburb with spreading banyan trees, fine restaurants, some very notable sites and an upscale arts scene. And trendiness – in the way of hoppin' new bars and eateries and shops – is rapidly paving over the staid traditions of the suburb, once known more for its plethora of bridal shops than its cool nightlife.

Orientation

The lovely Mediterranean-style city of Coral Gables is essentially bordered by Calle Ocho to the north, Sunset Dr (SW 72nd St/Hwy 986) to the south, Le Jeune Rd (SW 42nd Ave/Hwy 953) to the east and Red Rd (SW 57th Ave/Hwy 959) to the west. The US Hwy 1 slashes through at a 45-degree angle from northeast to southwest. The main campus of the University of Miami is located just south of the enormous Coral Gables Biltmore Golf Course, north of US Hwy 1 (S Dixie Hwy). Avenues here run east–west, while streets run north–south, the opposite of the rest of Miami.

BILTMORE HOTEL Map pp256-7
☎ 305-445-1926, 800-727-1926; www.biltmorehotel.com; 1200 Anastasia Ave
The city's crown jewel is the 16-story (315ft) tower of the Mediterranean revival Biltmore, modeled after the Giralda bell tower at the Cathedral of Seville in Spain and the brainchild of George Merrick. The history of the 1926

landmark hotel reads like an Agatha Christie novel on speed. Set against an old-world European-style backdrop, the subplots of murder and intrigue spar for attention with strong characters, famous gangsters and inquisitive detectives. Al Capone had a speakeasy here, and the Capone Suite is still haunted by the spirit of Fats Walsh, who was murdered here (for more ghost details, join in the weekly storytelling in the lobby, 7pm Thursday). In its heyday, imported gondolas transported guests around the property while celebrity guests ranged from Judy Garland to various Vanderbilts. More recently, the hotel hosted the 1994 Summit of the Americas and the

Transportation
Train Metrorail to Douglas Rd or University stations.
Trolley Once you're here, travel along Ponce de Leon Blvd or Miracle Mile.
Bus 24, 40, 42, 48, 56, 72.
Car US Hwy 1 takes you through the heart of town.

2002 wedding reception of *Sex and the City* star Kyle McLachlan. A sense of enormity is apparent throughout every nook and cranny of the hotel – especially out by the pool, which is the largest hotel pool in the continental USA. For a wonderful overview, whether you're staying here or not, check into one of the free guided tours run by the **Dade Heritage Trust** (☎ 305-445-1926; tours free; ◷ tours 1:30pm, 2:30pm & 3:30pm Sun).

CASA BACARDI Map pp256-7
☎ 305-284-2822; 1531 Brescia Ave; donation $5; ◷ 10am-5pm Mon-Fri
Housed at the Institute for Cuban and Cuban-American Studies at the University of Miami (and funded by *la familia* Bacardi), this interactive center highlights the cultures through a music pavilion, a cinema, rotating art exhibits and an impressive lecture series on subjects from Cuban cooking to the politics of Havana jails.

CORAL GABLES CITY HALL Map pp256-7
405 Biltmore Way
This grand building has housed city commission meetings ever since it opened in 1928. It's impressive from any angle, certainly befitting its importance as a central government building for the City Beautiful. Upstairs, there's a tiny display of Coral Gables Public Transport from the mid-20th century, plus rotating photograph and art exhibits. And check out Denman Fink's *Four Seasons* ceiling painting in the tower, as well as his framed, untitled painting of the underwater world on the 2nd-floor landing. Catch a small farmers' market on

Coral Gables Congregational Church (below)

the grounds here from 8am to 1pm January through March.

CORAL GABLES CONGREGATIONAL CHURCH Map pp256-7
☎ 305-448-7421; www.coralgablescongregational .org; 3010 DeSoto Blvd
George Merrick's father was a New England Congregational minister, so perhaps that accounts for him donating the land for the city's first church. Built in 1924 as a replica of a church in Costa Rica, the interior is graced with a beautiful but unboastful sanctuary and chapel, and its grounds are landscaped with stately palms.

FAIRCHILD TROPICAL GARDEN
Map pp244-5
☎ 305-667-1651; www.ftg.org; 10901 Old Cutler Rd; adult/child 3-12 yrs $10/5; ◷ 9:30am-4:30pm
The country's largest tropical botanical garden, the Fairchild covers 83 acres of lush rain-forest greenery. It has 11 lakes, streams, grottoes, waterfalls and hundreds of varieties of rare and exotic flowers. To simply think of it as a tourist attraction detracts from its serious purpose:

Singin' the Trolley Song

The newest word in Coral Gables transportation is trolley. The modern electric-hybrid vehicles with a decidedly old-time style rolled into town in late 2004, part of a new urban-improvement program that seeks to ease commuter traffic in what is essentially a driver-heavy Miami suburb. And, though many of the trolley's first riders were locals needing a way to get to work, it's the perfect way for a visitor to get a good look at the area. Choose from the north–south route on Ponce de Leon Blvd, running every 15 minutes from 7am to 7pm Monday to Thursday and until 10pm Friday, or the east–west Miracle Mile Twilight route, running 3pm until 7pm Monday to Thursday and 3pm until 10pm Friday. The best part? Rides are free!

the study of tropical flora by the garden's more than 6000 members. In addition to three easy-to-follow self-guided walking tours, there are good, free 40-minute tram tours of the entire park (on the hour 10am to 3pm) and a great bookstore – a delight to backyard botanists and amateur horticulturists.

LOWE ART MUSEUM Map pp256-7
☎ 305-284-3535; www.lowemuseum.org; 1301 Stanford Dr; adult/student $5/3; ☻ 10am-5pm Tue, Wed, Fri & Sat, noon-7pm Thu, noon-5pm Sun
On the University of Miami campus, the Lowe has one of Dade County's largest permanent collections (and a host of contemporary traveling shows). Works cover the spectrum, including Renaissance and Baroque art; Western sculpture from the 18th to the 20th centuries; European paintings by Gauguin, Picasso and Monet; Egyptian, Greek and Roman antiquities; African, pre-Columbian and Asian (textiles, paintings, ceramics) entries; and a collection of Southwestern weavings and Guatemalan textiles. The Central and South American collection includes material from Chile to Mexico in all media.

MATHESON HAMMOCK PARK
Map pp244-5
☎ 305-665-5475; 9610 Old Cutler Rd; admission per car $4; ☻ 6am-sunset
This 100-acre county park is the city's oldest and one of the most scenic. It offers good swimming for children in a closed tidal pool, lots of hungry raccoons, dense mangrove swamps, and crocodile spotting areas. There are leafy walking and biking trails, a nice picnic area at the front end of the park and a peaceful path edging Biscayne Bay.

MERRICK HOUSE Map pp256-7
☎ 305-460-5361; 907 Coral Way; admission $5; ☻ 1-4pm Sun & Wed
When George Merrick's father purchased this plot of land unseen for $1100 in 1899, it was a rocky plot with a rustic wooden cabin and some guava trees. George and his father certainly developed it, but Merrick's boyhood homestead does not have the same grand style that would later mark his adult vision. Today the modest family residence looks as it did in 1925, outfitted with family photos, furniture and artwork. While the house, recently restored, is primarily used for meetings and receptions, you can tour it and also see the well-maintained organic garden. King

Coral Gables Gallery Night
The fine art galleries of Wynwood and the Design District may get all the attention, but Coral Gables is home to more than 35 galleries – and on the first Friday of every month you can get a taste of them all, in the evening, as part of the 14-year-old tradition of Gallery Night. Showing a preponderance of Cuban and Latin artists, the galleries open their doors from 7pm to 10pm to the crowds of visitors who either walk, drive or take advantage of the minivan shuttle. Visitors are greeted with wine, cheese and, of course, paintings and sculptures. Just a few of the many galleries of note include **Cernuda Arte** (Map pp256-7; ☎ 305-461-1050; 3155 Ponce de Leon Blvd), featuring Cuban artists both alive and dead; **ArtSpace/Virginia Miller Galleries** (Map pp256-7; ☎ 305-444-4493; 169 Madeira Ave), with a more cutting-edge, modern perspective; and **Pop N' Art Gallery** (Map pp256-7; ☎ 305-445-4979; Village of Merrick Park), featuring, as you may have guessed, pop artists.

oranges, copperleaf, bamboo and other trees planted at the turn of the century are still thriving.

MIRACLE THEATER Map pp256-7
☎ 305-444-9293; 280 Miracle Mile
This beautifully renovated art-deco facility, a gleaming gem when it lights up the avenue at night, is home to the Actors' Playhouse. Acclaimed theatre works are produced in one of the three performance spaces – the 600-seat main-stage auditorium, a smaller children's theater and a black box for cutting-edge works – and the gleaming deco-style theatre is a lovely place to visit, whether you've got tickets or not.

VENETIAN POOL Map pp256-7
☎ 305-460-5306; 2701 DeSoto Blvd; adult/child Nov-Mar $6.25/3.25, Apr-Oct $9.50/5.25; ☻ generally 11am-5pm, call for details
As tons of earth and rock were taken for Merrick's building boom, a very large limestone quarry formed. Then a creative thinker thought: why not transform this eyesore by letting it fill with water and become an extraordinarily beautiful swimming hole? Now on the National Register of Historic Places, this 1924 spring-fed pool (with a capacity of 820,000 gallons) boasts coral rock caves, cascading waterfalls, a palm-fringed island, vine-covered loggias and

Venetian-style moorings. It was designed by Merrick's uncle, the ubiquitous muralist Denman Fink, and is large enough to accommodate a big waterfall, a kiddie area (note that toddlers must be over 38in tall or a parent must have proof that the toddler is at least three years old) and an adults' area for lap swimming. In fact, during its 1920s heyday, it hosted swimmer Esther Williams and Johnny 'Tarzan' Weismuller, both seen in historic photos at the pool. There's a decent snack bar (you can't bring in your own food) and locker rooms on the premises. And whether you want to swim in it or not, this pool is a site worth seeing.

ELSEWHERE IN MIAMI

In such a spread-out city, you're bound to have worthwhile sites in neighborhoods that aren't on any sort of trendy radar – yet. While some of the spots listed below are either way north or way south of the epicenters, some simply fall in between (Parrot Jungle Island, for example) due to the many waterways winding through the land.

NORTH

ANCIENT SPANISH MONASTERY

Map pp244-5

☎ 305-945-1461; www.spanishmonastery.com; 16711 W Dixie Hwy; adult/child $5/2; ☺ 9am-5pm Mon-Sat, 2-5pm Sun

The Episcopal Church of St Bernard de Clairvaux is a stunning early Gothic and Romanesque building. Constructed in 1141 in Segovia, Spain, it was converted to a granary 700 years later, and eventually bought by newspaper tycoon William Randolph Hearst. He dismantled it and shipped it to the USA in more than 10,000 crates, intending to reconstruct it at his sprawling estate near San Luis Obispo, California. But construction was never approved by the government, and the stones sat in boxes until 1954, when a group of Miami developers purchased the dismantled monastery from Hearst and reassembled it here. Now it's a lovely and popular (especially for weddings, so call before going) oasis that's allegedly the oldest building in the Western Hemisphere. There are nice garden walks around the cloisters, and inside the church sit rare lambskin parchment books and telescopic stained-glass windows. Church services are held Sunday at 8am, 10:30am and noon, and a healing service is held Wednesday at 10am.

BLACK HERITAGE MUSEUM

☎ 305-252-3535

This roving museum presents rotating exhibits in areas of Miami, Chapman and Deering. It's the brainchild of teachers Priscilla S Kruize, Dr Paul Cadby and Dr Earl Wells, who set out in 1987 to establish a center that celebrates the cultures of African Americans, Bahamians, Haitians and other Black cultures in Dade County.

DEERING ESTATE AT CUTLER

Map pp244-5

☎ 305-235-1668; www.deeringestate.org; 16701 SW 72nd Ave; adult/child 14 & under $7/5; ☺ 10am-5pm, last tickets sold 4pm

Charles, brother of James (of Vizcaya fame), created his own 150-acre winter estate, although it's a much more humble abode. The grounds, brimming with rare trees and other plant species, contain two houses, which you can tour (free with admission); they're also the place where an animal-fossil pit of bones dating back 50,000 years was discovered, as were prehistoric remains of Native Americans who lived here 2000 years ago, including a burial ground. Much of what is appropriate for display can be found at area museums, but some artifacts are on display at the estate. The offshore Chicken Key is also part of the estate, and you can take a three-hour guided canoe tour (per person $21; 10am Saturday and Sunday) out to the key, mangrove and marsh habitats. Naturalists will elucidate the difference between ibis and egrets, and red and black hammocks, and you can see turtles, sharks, a bird rookery and other seaside life.

HIALEAH PARK Map pp244-5

☎ 305-885-8000; 2200 E 4th Ave; ☺ 9am-5pm Mon-Fri

Slap-bang in the middle of Hialeah, a sprawling Cuban-American community that's west of Le Jeune Rd, is this former race track, laid out in 1925. It's quietly frozen in time now, as the horse racing stopped in 2001 and doesn't look like it'll resume any time soon. But the faded gem is worth a walk-through, if just to gaze at the grand staircases and stone fountains, walk among the swaying palm trees and pastel-painted concourse area, and close your eyes and listen for the long-stopped thunder of racing hooves.

LIBERTY CITY Map pp244-5

Liberty City, northwest of downtown, is a misnomer. Made infamous by the Liberty City Riots in 1980 (see Racial Tensions, p43), the area is very poor and crime is higher than in other parts of the city (see Safety, p224). And while plans exist to renovate the area by creating a village of cultural and tourist attractions, the prospects of that happening in the near future look doubtful. Whites, fearing 'Black encroachment' on their neighborhoods, actually went so far as to build a wall at the then-border of Liberty City – NW 12th Ave from NW 62nd to NW 67th Sts – to separate their neighborhoods. Part of the wall still stands, at NW 12th Ave between NW 63rd and 64th Sts.

For information on Liberty City, Overtown and other areas significant to Black history, contact the very helpful **Black Archives History & Research Center of South Florida** (Map pp244–5; ☎ 305-636-2390; 5400 NW 22nd Ave; ☻ 9am-5pm Mon-Fri, specific research projects 1-5pm) in the Caleb Center.

MUSEUM OF CONTEMPORARY ART

Map p251

MoCA; ☎ 305-893-6211; www.mocanomi.org; 770 NE 125th St; adult/senior & student $5/3; ☻ 11am-5pm Tue-Sat, noon-5pm Sun, 11am-5pm & 7-10pm last Fri of every month

Located in North Miami, a rapidly evolving neighborhood and real-estate magnet for hipsters (especially gay men) who have long since tired of the South Beach scene, MoCA has long been a reason to hike up here. Its galleries feature excellent rotating exhibitions of contemporary art done by local, national and international artists; recently featured creators have included Pablo Cano and his found-object marionettes, Louise Bourgeois's sculptures in fabric, and watercolors and sculptures from New York's Anne Chu.

OPA-LOCKA Map pp244-5

This poor and crime-ridden neighborhood is not the smartest place for a tour, but it should be noted that the area's architecture – envisioned by developer Glenn Curtiss as an Arabian-Oriental fantasy – does have its charms. Nowhere is it more apparent than at **Opa-Locka City Hall** (777 Sharazad Blvd), an explosion of domes, minarets and fanciful archways.

PELICAN ISLAND Map p251

On weekends you can take a short tootle over to itsy-bitsy Pelican Island on a free ferry from

Master Planner

George Merrick had a dream. He envisioned drawing people into a series of neighborhoods that felt 'old' (today the cynics among us might call it 'Disneyfication') from the start. He wanted to counter the sprawl that was already settling into Miami, with a perfectly designed Mediterranean-style city. So in 1921 he proceeded to hire a gaggle of professionals to realize his vision, including architects Phineas Paist and H George Fink (his cousin), landscaper Frank Button and artist Denman Fink (his uncle). Together they created several very distinct areas. If you were just driving around and stumbled upon them, you'd think you'd entered the twilight zone.

Look for the **Dutch South African Village** (6612, 6700, 6704 & 6710 SW 42nd Ave and 6705 San Vicente St) modeled after 17th-century Dutch colonists' farmhouses; a tiny **Chinese Village** (one block between San Sovino Ave, Castania Ave, Maggiore St and Riviera Dr); a **Florida Pioneer Village** (4320, 4409, 4515, 1520 & 4620 Santa Maria St), which looks a lot more like New Hampshire than Miami; the **Italian Village** (Altara Ave at Monserrate St); and the stunning **French Normandy Village** (on the block between SW 42nd Ave, Viscaya Court, Viscaya Ave and Alesio Ave).

Flush from his early successes, Merrick teamed up with magnate John McEntee Bowman in 1924 to build the $10-million Biltmore Hotel, with its trademark Giralda-style tower visible from anywhere in the city. The red-hot construction boom, though, began to cool in 1926, and a devastating no-name hurricane blew away any remaining embers of development. Merrick went broke in the subsequent real-estate crash brought on by the Depression and eventually died a poor man. The city of Coral Gables, only a year old in 1926, also went bankrupt. After the city's finances were sorted out, and it grew with Miami, Coral Gables always remained a bit aloof. It had the good fortune to attract more money and less attention.

Merrick's gorgeous 1925 **Colonnade Building** (169 Miracle Mile) served as the headquarters of his Coral Gables Corp. Note the central rotunda, arcades and a lavishly ornamental front entrance. Once the home of Colonnade Pictures, the building was combined with a new tower directly behind it in 1988, and has been converted into the **Omni-Colonnade Hotel** (☎ 305-441-2600, 180 Aragon Ave). It has shops and boutiques and also houses the **Coral Gables Chamber of Commerce**.

Because of Merrick's vision, Coral Gables is one of the few places in metropolitan Miami that's lovely for walking. Banyan trees shelter the winding streets and provide relief from the sun. It's also nice for a Sunday drive past the big, beautiful homes.

the JFK Causeway west of North Bay Village, which is about 2 miles west of 71st St in Miami Beach. It's a pleasant little place to unpack a picnic and peer at dozens of congregating pelicans, all with the long and lovely beach stretched before you.

SOUTH

FISHER ISLAND Map p250

One of Miami Beach's pioneering developers, Carl Fisher, purchased this glorious little island and planned on dying here. He even built a mausoleum. As is wont to happen, though, he soon got bored. When William K Vanderbilt II fell in love with the place, Fisher traded the island for Vanderbilt's 250ft yacht and its crew. Things were like that in those days. Vanderbilt proceeded to build a splendiferous Spanish-Mediterranean-style mansion, with guest houses, studios, tennis courts and a golf course.

Today, this exclusive resort is accessible only by air and private ferry. The condominiums that line the mile-long private beach range from $1-million hovels to the $7-plus-million pad President Clinton once borrowed. It is said that the sun shines over the island even when it's raining in Miami Beach. Perhaps when you play with nature by importing boatloads of sugary white sand from the Bahamas as they did on Fisher Island, you have some sway over the weather, too. Moneyed readers can overnight on Fisher Island at the **Inn at the Fisher Island Club** (p162). The island is usually open only to paying guests and residents, but you can arrange a tour if you're especially persistent. Ferries leave from the Fisher Island Ferry Terminal off the MacArthur Causeway. The air-conditioned ferries depart every 15 minutes around the clock and the trip takes 10 minutes.

FRUIT & SPICE PARK

☎ 305-247-5727; 24801 SW 187th Ave; adult/child $5/1.50; ☿ 10am-5pm

Set just on the edge of the Everglades, this 35-acre tropical public park has more than 100 varieties of citrus, 80 varieties of bananas, 40 types of grapes and a lot more exotic tropical fruits, plants and spices. Many of the plantings are organized by geography: from the Amazon River Basin to the Yucatán to Southeast Asia. In the heart of South Florida's agricultural district, it's the only place like it in the country. In fact, some of the species that grow here can't survive anywhere else. Best of all, while walking along the aromatic paths, you can take

anything that falls (naturally) to the ground. Barring that, you can buy the exotic offerings at the Redland Fruit Store. Try the pomelo, rambutan, lychee, breadfruit and tamarind. And don't forget to check out the poisonous plant area. Admission includes a free tour.

GOLD COAST RAILROAD MUSEUM

Map pp244-5

☎ 305-253-0063; www.goldcoast-railroad.org; 12450 SW 152nd St; adult/child 3-11 yrs $5/3; ☿ 11am-3pm Mon-Fri, 11am-4pm Sat & Sun

South Florida would still be a swamp today without the introduction of train services. Primarily of interest to serious train buffs (but also fun for kids), this museum was set up in the 1950s by the Miami Railroad Historical Society. It displays more than 30 antique railway cars, including the Ferdinand Magellan presidential car, which is featured prominently in a famous photograph of newly elected president Harry Truman. He's standing at the rear holding a newspaper bearing the famous erroneous headline 'Dewey Defeats Truman.' The car was also used by US presidents Franklin D Roosevelt, Eisenhower, and even Ronald Reagan (for whom it was outfitted with 3-inch-thick glass windows and armor plating). On weekends, a 2-mile, 15- to 20-minute train ride on the Edwin Link Railroad ($2) runs at 1pm and 3pm.

HIBISCUS, PALM & STAR ISLANDS

Map pp244-5

Hibiscus, Palm and Star Islands, though far less exclusive than Fisher Island, are little bastions of wealth. There aren't as many famous people living there now – just very rich ones – although Star Island is home to Miami's favorite star, Gloria Estefan. For a short time Al Capone lived (and died) on Palm Island; ironically, his house is now occupied by a Miami police officer. The islands' circular drives are guarded by a security booth and it's generally hard to get on them. But the islands' drives are also public, so if you ask politely and don't look like a hoodlum, you should be able to get in. Star Island consists of little more than one elliptical road lined with royal palms, sculpted 8ft ficus hedges and fancy gates guarding houses you can't see.

MIAMI CHILDREN'S MUSEUM Map pp244-5

☎ 305-373-5437; 980 MacArthur Causeway, Watson Island; admission $8; ☿ 10am-6pm

Miami's newest museum, located between South Beach and Downtown Miami (and across the causeway from **Parrot Jungle**, p78), isn't exactly a museum. It feels more like a glorified playhouse, with areas for kids to practice all sorts of adult activities – banking and food shopping (at models of corporate giants Bank of America and Publix, which probably paid good money to have their brands imprinted on the brains of the naïfs), caring for pets, reporting scoops as a TV news anchor in a studio, and acting as a local cop or fire fighter. And, to be fair, there are some educational displays about subjects ranging from Miami architecture to Brazilian culture. Be forewarned: this place is a zoo on rainy days.

MIAMI METROZOO Map pp244-5
☎ 305-251-0400; www.miamimetrozoo.com; 12400 SW 152nd St; adult/child $11.50/6.75; ⏱ 9:30am-5:30pm, last admission 4pm
This worthy zoo has 900 animals from more than 200 species. Look for Asian and African elephants, rare Bengal tigers, pygmy hippos, Andean condors, cute koalas, colobus monkeys, black rhinoceroses and a pair of Komodo dragons from Indonesia. Less than half of the 740 acres are developed, so you'll see plenty of natural habitats. Keep your eyes peeled for informative zookeeper talks in front of some exhibits. At the children's petting area, kids can play with potbellied pigs, sheep, ferrets, chickens, lizards and more. There are also good wildlife shows In the amphitheatre, and a historic carousel with hand-carved animals and chariots.

For a quick overview (and because the zoo is so big), hop on the Zoofari Monorail for a good orientation; it departs every 20 minutes. If you have time, take the Behind the Scenes Tram Tour ($2.50), a 45-minute ride that takes you past the veterinary hospital, quarantine pens and brooder and hatchery building.

A wonderful new addition to the far-reaching tour lineup are the Eco-Adventure guided bike and canoe trips ($20-30 per person), which are naturalist-led tours around the wild grounds.

MONKEY JUNGLE Map pp244-5
☎ 305-235-1611; www.monkeyjungle.com; 14805 SW 216th St; adult/child 4-12 yrs $17.95/11.95; ⏱ 9:30am-5pm, last admission 4pm
Monkey Jungle brochures have a tag line: 'Where humans are caged and monkeys run free.' And, indeed, you will be walking through screened-in trails, with primates swinging freely, screeching and chattering all around you. But it's not scary, just a bit odiferous, especially on warm days (well, most days).

In 1933 animal behaviorist Joseph du Mond released six monkeys into the wild. Today, their descendants live here with orangutans, chimpanzees and the lowland gorilla. The habitat, a tropical hardwood hammock that contains plants collected in South America, feels like the Amazonian ecosystem. The big show of the day (there are three actually) takes place at feeding time, when crab-eating monkeys and Southeast Asian macaques dive into the pool for fruit and other treats. Take note: this third-generation family-owned attraction is a long way to come from Miami and may be better combined with a trip to the Everglades.

NATIONAL HURRICANE CENTER
Map pp244-5
☎ 305-229-4404; www.nhc.noaa.gov; 11691 SW 17th St; ⏱ Jan 16-May 13 (hurricane off-season)
This fascinating center, which offers tours to the public by appointment only, documents the drama of hurricanes and elucidates the

Miami for Children
This is an excellent city for kids. First and foremost are the beaches – adventurous, sandy playgrounds no matter what your age. But attractions, either right in Miami or a short day trip away, abound. There's the **Miami Seaquarium** (p68), boasting a large collection of crocodiles, dolphins, sea lions and a killer whale, most of which perform. **Parrot Jungle Island** (p78) also puts on animal shows, but these from the feathered-friend sort of star; its new location, on a causeway right near Downtown, is convenient and well-maintained. Next door is the new **Miami Children's Museum** (opposite), an indoor playland where youngsters can try out the roles of TV anchor, banker and supermarket customer, among others. It's a slight hike, but worth it, to both **Miami Metrozoo** (above), a 740-acre zoo with plenty of natural habitats, and the **Gold Coast Railroad Museum** (opposite), which displays more than 30 antique railroad cars. Or try **Monkey Jungle** (above), an oasis of screeching primates, or the **Miami Museum of Science & Planetarium** (p70). Coral Gables draws water-wise kids to its way-fun, lagoonlike **Venetian Pool** (p73) – as does the **Fontainebleau Hilton** (p159). This, by the way, is an excellent place for families to bunk down. While many boutique hotels often shun little ones, several of the big guys – including **Loews Miami Beach** (p156) and the **Sonesta Beach Resort Key Biscayne** (p161) – run elaborate kids' programs.

intricacies of storm-tracking. The 40-minute tour includes a discussion of how the center works (including its technological tools such as satellite maps and radar) and a walkabout of the facility. It's located on the campus of Florida International University (FIU).

PARROT JUNGLE ISLAND Map pp244-5
☎ 305-666-7834; www.parrotjungle.com; 1111 Parrot Jungle Trail, off I-395/MacArthur Causeway, Watson Island; adult/child $24.95/19.95, plus parking $6; ☾ 10am-6pm

Parrot Jungle has been a kitschy attraction since 1936, but since a 2003 move to the much-more-accessible spit of land between South Beach and Downtown Miami, it's become a much sleeker spot to visit. Its new 18-acre waterfront facility, planted and lushly landscaped with a minimum of pesticides and solidified with 27,000 tons of structural fill, is now the proud home of parrots, macaws, flamingos and cockatoos in endless varieties, some caged but many flying in outdoor aviaries that simulate their natural environments. You can watch the birds, talk to them and feed them, or sit back and let them entertain you at one of the few stage areas (where trained birds chat with and, unfortunately, dance for audiences). Other creatures here include snakes, crocodiles, gibbons and orangutans, creating a minizoo that kids especially enjoy. The walkways are covered (from both rain and bird poop), and a indoor dining, game and shopping areas provide plenty of shelters from storms.

PINECREST GARDENS Map pp244-5
☎ 305-666-6942; www.pinecrest-fl.gov/gardens; 11000 SW 57th Ave; admission $5; ☾ 8am-sunset

When Parrot Jungle flew the coop for the big city, the village of Pinecrest, which is the community that hosted the Jungle's former location, purchased its lovely property in order to keep it as a municipal park. It's now a quiet oasis of gardens, playgrounds, and classrooms that offer a bevy of adult-ed culture and arts classes.

WINGS OVER MIAMI Map pp244-5
☎ 305-233-5197; www.wingsovermiami.com; Kendall-Tamiami Executive Airport, 14710 SW 128th St; adult/senior & child under 13 yrs $9.95/5.95; ☾ 10am-5:30pm Thu-Sun

Air and history buffs will be delighted at this Tamiami Airport museum, which chronicles the history of aviation. Highlights include a propeller collection, J47 jet engine, a Soviet bomber from Smolensk and the nose section of *Fertile Myrtle*. An impressive exhibit on the Tuskeegee Airmen features videos of the Black pilots telling their own stories. Historic bombers and other crafts drop in for occasional visits, so you can never be sure what you'll see.

Walking & Driving Tours

Walking & Driving Tours

Miami, huge and sprawling, and Miami Beach, long and lean, are not the most walkable places when taken as a whole. But break them down into little minitowns and you've got plenty of opportunities for hoofin' it. We've mapped out three specific walking tours – through parts of South Beach, the Design District and Little Havana – and thrown in a couple of other options just for good measure, including a drive in Coral Gables and a ride high over Downtown Miami, on the wacky Metromover.

ECLECTIC WALK: SOUTH BEACH

A huge part of South Beach's attraction is its supreme walkability – along with the ocean, the art-deco charm and the sexy scene, of course. This stroll offers a bit of it all.

Start at the famed Lincoln Rd, at its western end where it meets Alton Rd, where you'll see the beautiful, colored-glass walls of the **Regal South Beach Cinema** 1 (p125) – designed by Bernard Zyscovich in 1999 as a gateway for Lincoln Rd. For the next eight or so short blocks, you'll be strolling along the inimitable **Lincoln Road Mall** 2 (p55) – a bustling pedestrian pathway, designed in 1960 by Morris Lapidus, that's lined with chic shops, bars, eateries and galleries. A 1997 facelift made it *the* place to be, for everyone from clubbers to grandmas. At the southwest corner of the Meridian Ave–Lincoln Rd intersection you'll find the **ArtCenter/South Florida** 3 (p54), a maze of artists' open studios and a storefront gallery space that always has something unique on view. At the end of the pedestrian portion of the road you'll hit the refreshingly scruffy Washington Ave. Head south. If you've already worked up an appetite, pop into the decidedly untrendy **Flamingo Restaurant** 4 (p94), a small Nicaraguan-Cuban cafeteria serving authentic meals with fresh tamarind juice or coconut water in a homey atmosphere.

Continue south along Washington for half a block and you'll hit the edge of **Española Way Promenade** 5 (p52), two blocks above 14th Street between Collins and Jefferson Aves, so-named because of its Spanish-village Design, Which Dates From 1925. The cluster of Mediterranean facades began as an artists' colony and is now a tiny theme park of shops and eateries. Further south on Washington, you'll find architectural treasures: first, the **Post Office** 6 (p53), at 13th St, a curvy block of white deco in the 'stripped classic' style, the first restoration project for

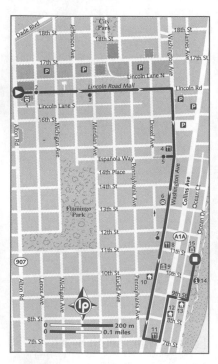

Walk Facts

Start Lincoln Rd at Alton Rd

End Casa Casuarina on Ocean Ave at 11th St

Time 1½ to two hours
Fuel Stop Puerto Sagua

South Beach's revitalization in the 1970s. Step inside to admire the Works Progress Administration project wall-mural, domed ceiling and marble stamp tables. The historic **Old City Hall 7** of Miami Beach, between 11th and 12th Sts, outgrew this beautiful Mediterranean tower, now an office building, by the '70s. Next look for the **11th Street Diner 8** (p94), a gleaming aluminum Pullman-car diner that was imported in 1992 from Wilkesbury, Pennsylvania; the imposing **Wolfsonian-FIU 9** (p54), an excellent museum of design that was formerly the Washington Storage Company, where wealthy snowbirds of the '30s safely stashed their pricey belongings before returning north; and the stunningly restored **Hotel Astor 10** (p152), designed in 1936 by T Hunter Henderson. Turn left on 7th St and walk one block to Collins Ave. At the corner is **Puerto Sagua 11** (p93), a traditional Cuban diner that has miraculously survived the influx of trendiness. It's a perfect place to stop and refuel before continuing along Collins, where you'll notice much more of a 'scene' than on Washington, fuelled by a crop of hipster hotels including the **Hotel 12** (p152), with an interior and roof deck designed by Todd Oldham. Originally called the Tiffany Hotel, it was designed with a proud deco spire in 1939 by L Murray Dixon.

Turn right on 9th St and go one block to Ocean Ave, where you'll spy nonstop deco beauties, such as the **Edison Hotel 13**, a 1935 creation of Henry Hohauser. The **Art Deco Welcome Center 14** (p51), an outpost of the Miami Design Preservation League, is on Ocean at 10th St. Step inside for a permanent exhibit on deco style, as well as to purchase deco souvenirs from the well-stocked gift shop (you can also join walking tours here). Finally, walk just one block north along colorful Ocean Ave to 11th Street, where you'll come to the famed **Casa Casuarina 15** (p52) – a Mediterranean edifice built in 1930, best known as the Versace Mansion; it's where designer Gianni Versace was gunned down in 1997 by stalker Andrew Cunanan. Gruesome as it may be, this is one of the most photographed spots on the tourist circuit.

METROMOVER RIDE: DOWNTOWN MIAMI

Downtown Miami's driverless Metromover – a one-car train that glides over the city in the area below NW 15 St – is a strange creature. But using it to see this part of the city feels safer than pounding the crumbling pavement along the abandoned, character-laden stretches. Plus, it's free!

Start at the **College/Bayside Station 1**, which is a short walk from the metered parking along Biscayne Blvd. Board the northbound Brickell Outer Loop and settle. You'll quickly notice that every other building seems to be under construction – cranes are everywhere, and there are plenty of half-toppled edifices, their eerie facades sometimes left standing, surrounded by only a flimsy chain-link fence. But there's plenty intact along the way, including the spectacularly ornate yellow **Freedom Tower 2** (p60), a Mediterranean Revival structure on Biscayne Blvd that was built in 1924 and inspired by the Giralda Tower in Seville, Spain. It housed the *Miami Daily News* for 32 years and became a processing station for Cuban exiles in the 1960s; it's currently being revamped into a Cuban museum. Just beyond it, in a strange architectural juxtaposition and perched on the edge of the bay, sits the sprawling **American Airlines Arena 3** (p59), home of the beloved Miami Heat basketball team. As the Metromover turns west, look south and you'll notice the **Miami-Dade Community College 4** (p61), which is not much to look at, and south of that the **Gesu Church 5**, which is a marvel to behold. Another example of Mediterranean Revival architecture, it's home to Miami's oldest Catholic parish, Holy Name, and dates from 1898; inside are stained-glass windows from Munich and an Italian-marble altar. Next door are the Neoclassic Revival **Capital Building 6** and the historic **Hahn Building 7**, both from 1925, as well as the **Old US Post Office 8** (p62), which was the first major federal building in Miami.

When the Metromover turns again to head south, check out both the **Miami-Dade Cultural Center 9**, home to the Miami Art Museum (p61) and the Historical Museum of Southern Florida (p60) as well as the imposing **Dade County Courthouse 10** (p60) built in 1928 by August Geiger and A Ten Eyck Brown. Keep your eyes peeled for a bit of kitschy history: the Concord Building and its famed neon **Coppertone sign 11**, which was preserved and brought here by the Dade Heritage Trust. It hung for 38 years on the now-demolished Parkleigh House on Biscayne Blvd. Next, in quick succession, is the site of the original **Burdines 12** (p143)

Start College/Bayside Metromover station

End Same as start, or else Bayfront Park station

Time About 40 minutes (minus lunch stop)

Fuel Stop Pasha's

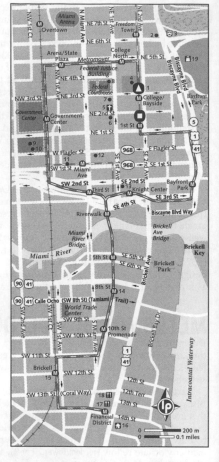

department store (remodeled into its current streamline look in 1936); and the **Bank of America Building** 13, whose spherical tower adds a beautiful blue glow to the night skyline. When you get to the **Eighth Street Station** 14, you may want to peer out when the doors open. It's one of eight stations that provide 'Art en Route' as a part of the city's widespread public-art project; this one is two-fold – a ceramic royal palm tree at the south end of the station and the *Portón de Sentimientos (Gate of Sentiments)* at the north, which features door handles of red tile to mark the gateway to Calle Ocho. The artist, local ceramicist Carlos Alves, works with found objects and broken tiles. It's also worth peering out at the **Brickell Station** 15, just a couple of stops away, where artist Connie Lloveras has created *Reaching for Miami Skies,* a concave ceiling mural of colorful, hand-formed ceramic tiles. The next and final stop (before the Metromover reverses direction) is a good place to catch a glimpse of the recently built **Conrad Miami** 16 (p160), a glimmering luxury high-rise hotel with a concave facade. It's also a good place to get out for something to eat – either at **Pasha's** 17 (p100), for a quick bite of healthy Mediterranean food, or next door at the new **Novocento** 18 (p99), a more upscale Latin-infused bistro. Your return trip will cover just a bit of new ground when you head east and then north to pass by the **Bayside Marketplace** 19 (p59), which may be worth a final stop if you're up for some serious tourist crowds and a major mall vibe. You can get off one stop before where you started, at the First Street Station.

ART WALK: DESIGN DISTRICT GALLERIES

Locally dubbed 'a mile of style,' this self-contained region is more like an *island* of style, floating, alone, off busy Biscayne Blvd and edged by stark landscapes of empty lots, construction sites and gas stations. The Design District itself has a distinctly industrial feel, brightened only by the sleek and pricey wares and colorful artworks behind the glass of storefront galleries and design boutiques. Just don't visit here on Sunday, when everything's closed.

Start at the corner of NE 2nd Ave and NE 40th St, where you'll notice the district's very own cool school, the **Design & Architecture Senior High School** 1 (DASH), where lucky teens get taught by leaders in their fields. Then duck into the **Melin Building** 2 (p64), a sort of mini-mall of showrooms and galleries. In the center lobby area stands Antoni

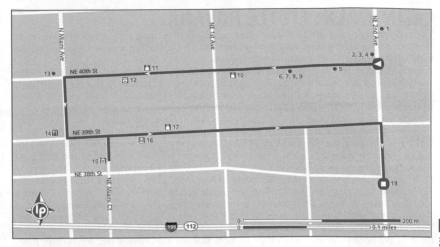

Miralda's **Gondola Shoe** 3, a story-high black glossy pump with a sexy red interior. Just off the lobby is **Coma's** 4 (p101), a bakery and café straight from Barcelona, which is a perfect place to pick up some strong java for the walk. Back out on NE 40th St, the strip with the most businesses, you'll find various galleries and shops. **Kartell** 5 (p144) is a showroom for plastic lovers, featuring furniture and housewares designed by

Walk Facts

Start NE 2nd Ave at NE 40th St

Finish NE 2nd Ave at NE 38th St

Time 45 minutes
Fuel Stop Coma's

none other than Philippe Starck, and Anna Castelli Ferrieri. The **Atlas Plaza** 6 (130 NE 40th St) has a variety of options in its courtyard: **Kuma Central** 7 (p145) sells whimsical, limited-edition toys based on the Japanese action-figure bear by Maria Samiento; **Casa Cielo** 8 offers a dizzying array of boldly colored tiles for anyone about to redo flooring in their home; and the **Artformz/Artists Space** 9 exhibits exciting group shows and sculptures made of string, wood and wire by owner Alette Simmons-Jimenez. Further west, **Artisan Antiques Art Deco** 10 (p144) is a gorgeous showroom of French art-deco lighting and furniture, with pieces from R Lalique, Sabino and De Gue. More stores follow on this simple path, offering everything from Persian carpets to modern chandeliers. Further along is **District** 11 (p101), a classy industrial indoor-outdoor eatery that's a fine place to stop and linger over lunch. Just across the street is this neighborhood's most sceney nightlife spot, **Grass Restaurant & Lounge** 12 (p113); the front gate will be pulled down during the day, but at night the velvet rope goes up and the outdoor lounge and grass-hut-topped dining tables hop with a see-and-be-seen crowd.

At the end of the block, across N Miami Ave, you'll spy a Design District landmark: the **Living Room** 13 (p64), by Rosario Marquardt and Roberto Behar, inhabiting a corner of a low-rise building that's currently vacant. The Argentine duo call it an 'urban intervention,' which cuts into the streetscape with an oversized replica of a room, wallpaper, couch, tall lamps and all. Grab lunch at the cute little **Secret Sandwich Co** 14 (p101). Turn onto NE Miami Ct for the unmissable **Barbara Gilman Gallery** 15 (3814 NE Miami Ct), run by a local pioneer who shows bigwigs from Andy Warhol to James Rosenquist. Return to 39th St and then peruse the galleries along NE 39th St, including **Chelsea Galleria** 16 (32 NE 39th St), specializing in fine art from the Caribbean and Americas, and the fine housewares boutique **World Resources** 17 (p145). Finish up back on NE 2nd Ave at **Holly Hunt** 18 (p144), a 22,000-sq-ft showroom of furniture and varied artworks. Whether you spend a dime or not, you'll certainly enjoy the parade of riches.

LATIN WALK: LITTLE HAVANA

The main artery of SW 8th St (Calle Ocho) and the surrounding side streets here are home to a diverse population that may have started out all Cuban but is now a mix of families from all over Latin America and the Caribbean.

Begin the stroll at the somber **Bay of Pigs Museum & Library 1** (p65), on SW 9th St at SW 18th Ave, which will provide a window into what drove so many families to this region to begin with. It's a quiet building that may look closed from the outside, but inside it's filled with remembrances of lives – those that were lost during the tragically failed invasion of 1961. Though the collection of photos and mementos is not too well organized, the talkative curator will gladly walk you through the place. Stroll east along SW 9th St for a block when you leave, savoring the quiet of this residential pocket before turning left onto SW 17th Ave and then right onto **Calle Ocho 2** (p65), which bustles with eateries, shops and traffic. As you walk, be sure to look down at the sidewalk occasionally to appreciate the local version of the **Walk of Fame 3**, with 23 stars honoring heroes from Celia Cruz to Gloria Estefan. To pay homage to current artists, step into the **Maxoly Art Cuba Gallery 4** (1600 SW 8th St), which features Cuban masters. Start shopping for souvenirs in the nearby **Old Cuba: The Collection 5** (p146), and settle into a big plate of oxtail and yucca at the pan-Latin **El Cristo 6** (p103). You can duck into **Botánica Mistica 7** (1512 SW 8th St) to get a sense of the Santeria religion through the books, candles and other artifacts that are sold here, then, for further proof that you're spoiled for choice when it comes to snacking, grab a shot of rocket-fuel Cuban coffee at **Exquisito Restaurant 8** (p104). You'll next notice the renovated **Tower Theater 9** (p125), which shows Spanish-language films, has a small art gallery and hosts occasional theatre performances and concerts. The **Latin Quarter Cultural Center of Miami 10** (p66), which is right nearby, is one of several wonderful galleries along this stretch; it's also home to theater and literature events, so be sure to peek at its schedule. Next, visit the tiny but hopping **Máximo Gómez Park 11** (p66), where the chatter of domino tiles is heard nonstop due to the groups of men (and the occasional woman) who gather round the shady game tables to play all day long.

Stock up on remembrances of the day at **Havana-to-go 12** (p145), or at **Moore & Bode Cigars 13** (1336 SW 8th St), which rolls fresh tobacco into fat stogies right before your eyes. Then, because it's been a full 20 minutes since you last imbibed something, grab a stool at the counter of **Los Pinareños Frutería 14**

Walk Facts

Start SW 9th St at SW 18th Ave
End SW 13th Ave (Cuban Memorial Blvd)
Time 45 minutes
Fuel Stop Los Pinareños Fruteria

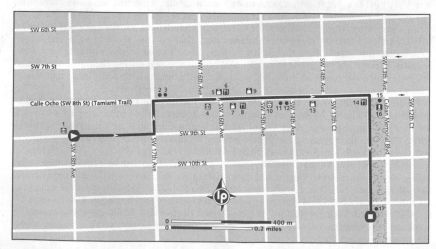

Miami skyline

(1334 SW 8th St), where you can slurp on refreshing shakes or juices of fruits from watermelon to manay.

Continuing east, you'll hit **Cuban Memorial Boulevard 15** (p66), or SW 13th Ave, which features the **Eternal Torch in Honor of the 2506th Brigade 16** (p66), a memorial to the Bay of Pigs casualties, at its entrance. Behind that are statues commemorating Jose Martí and Antonio Maceo, for leading Cuba out of Spanish rule, as well as a massive **ceiba tree 17**, sacred to followers of Santeria.

COMMUNITY DRIVE: CORAL GABLES TO COCONUT GROVE

Start your drive by entering Coral Gables via SW 37th Ave (Douglas Rd) going south. Take a right on Alhambra Circle at the **Alhambra Entrance 1** – one of three ornate, arched entryways to this, the **Country Club 2** region of Gables, which refers to the streets surrounding the **Granada Golf Course 3**. This is where you'll see some of the area's oldest constructions, featuring many of the Mediterranean-style homes developer George Merrick designed back in the early 1900s. When you cross Granada Blvd, take note of the **Granada Plaza 4**, a flourish of rock and brick pillars joined by a pair of reflecting pools. Follow the curve of Alhambra not far past here, to Ferdinand St, and you'll see the stylish **Alhambra Water Tower 5**, a 1924 Merrick project that once provided the drinking water here. When you hit Coral Way make a left, followed by a right onto Columbus Blvd, which will cut past some striking homes as well as the **Coral Gables Congregational Church 6 (p72)**, a Mediterranean Revival reproduction of a Costa Rican church, before leading you directly into the arms of the true-life fairy tale of the **Biltmore Hotel 7 (p71)**. Opened in 1926 and created by Merrick, the Moorish structure is partially a copy of Seville's Giralda bell tower, and the hotel is home to renovated grandeur, posh guests, Italian marble and goldleaf details.

From the hotel, zip up the diagonal of DeSoto Blvd, past the gurgling stone fountain of **DeSoto Plaza 8** and into the small, metered parking area for the **Venetian Pool 9 (p73)**, which is worth stepping out of your car for a look. The refreshing shock of fresh water at this public swimming hole is upstaged by both its grand history – Esther Williams and Johnny Weissmuller swam here – and its impossibly perfect landscaping, complete with waterfalls, palm trees and Spanish tiling. After gazing at the pool from behind its iron gate (nonpaying guests are only allowed in so far), you'll be backtracking just a bit by going west on Sevilla Ave until you hit Ferdinand St; make a left as it becomes Alhambra Circle to follow the street's southward curve around the edge of the Biltmore's golf course, being sure to enjoy the lovely homes and lush grounds you'll pass along the way. When you hit SW 40th St (Bird Rd) make a left, heading through the golf course, and when you get to Granada Blvd make a right, heading south. Keep following it, past Rte 1 (Ponce de Leon Blvd) until you come to a traffic circle; go almost all the way around it and get onto Ingraham Hwy. First

Drive Facts

Start SW 37th St at Alhambra Circle, Coral Gables

End Main Hwy, Coconut Grove

Time One hour

Fuel Stop Le Bouchon du Grove

hit Douglas Rd, then turn right onto Main Hwy. Soon you'll enter the community of Coconut Grove and notice, at the corner of Devon Rd, both the Byzantine **Bryan Memorial Church** 10, built as a memorial to the politician and attorney, and the Mission-style **Plymouth Congregational Church** 11 (p70), dating from 1917. Further along, at Charles Ave, is the **Coconut Grove Playhouse** 12 (p70), Miami's oldest, which often draws big names to its stage. Leafy parkland awaits you about a block further along Main Hwy in the form of the waterfront **Peacock Park** 13 and its **Barnacle State Historic Site** 14 (p69), the well-preserved original home of Ralph Munroe, one of the Grove's earliest pioneers. It's worth a stroll (you can also take a guided tour), so you should probably park at a metered spot along Main Hwy just past the park's entrance, by **CocoWalk** 15 (p69) and the **Streets of Mayfair** 16 (p146), two massive shopping complexes that make for a good walk after being cooped up in the car. Settle down on the edge of the shops for a lingering lunch at **Le Bouchon du Grove** 17 (p106), a French bistro that opens onto the street to offer people-watching with your salad nicoise.

Eating

Eating

In a country whose foodie movement is very of-the-moment, Miami, a city of the future, has found itself in a perpetually advantageous position. It's totally hot all over again – and especially in its dining scene. Finally, Miami's food has become as sultry as its weather, with top chefs, many from New York, jumping into the mix and enlivening everyone's search for the perfect night out. The cuisine here, as with every other cultural aspect, is infused with Latin influences – tropical vegetables and fruits, heady herbs and spices – and highlighted by fresh seafood that's plucked right from Miami's waters. It's also infused with a constantly festive vibe, with delicious cocktails, high-end wines, lounge-style seating, DJs, velvet ropes and beautiful people oftentimes blurring the line between 'restaurant' and 'nightclub' (see p91). For all the four-star posturing, though, you'll find plenty of down-to-earth eateries, where it's all about real food and real people. Old Cuban diners and Jewish delis sit proudly on trend-ridden blocks, still attracting a diverse mix of people who want to taste a bit of nostalgia in their meals. And if you venture out of South Beach to points north and south, you'll find high-end food with much less attitude. Whichever is more your style, do sample both. It would be a shame to leave here without having had glistening ceviche piled high with cumin-dusted plantain strips – and just as much of a shame to have not indulged in a corned-beef on rye.

Take Out & To Go

If you're a visitor more interested in creating your own ambience while you eat – whether on a beach picnic or on the terrace of your swanky hotel room – there are plenty of options to keep you sated. Number one on many Miamians' list is the **Epicure Market** (Map pp246–7; ☎ 305-672-1861; 1656 Alton Rd; dishes $7-10; ⏰10am-8pm Mon-Fri, 10am-7pm Sat, 10am-6pm Sun), a gourmet food shop just off Lincoln Rd in South Beach that has a beautiful selection of international cheeses and wines, fresh produce, baked goods and wonderful prepared dishes, from chicken noodle soup to lasagna. Many of the more than 25 Publix supermarkets throughout Miami are quite upscale, especially the Biscayne Blvd and 90th St **Publix** (☎ 305-751-4075; www.publix.com). They have a full range of produce, a bakery, wine and prepared items to choose from. The **Wild Oats Community Market** (Map pp248–9; ☎ 305-532-1707; 1020 Alton Rd; ⏰7am-11pm) is the biggest health-food store around, with an excellent produce department, pretty good deli of prepared meals and a so-so salad bar; its biggest draw is for vegetarians (not so well-catered-to in these parts) who are seeking a particular brand of soy milk or wheat-free pasta from its grocery aisles.

Finally, for the freshest, most delicious picnic items around, hit one of several **farmers' markets** (☎ 305-531-0038), alfresco cornucopias of produce, baked goods, flowers and even prepared salads or tacos. They hit various areas on different days. The one on Lincoln Rd, on Sundays, is perhaps the best known of these food fairs. But you'll find others on Española Way (Sunday), Normandy Village Fountain at 71st St (Saturday), the Aventura Mall (Saturday and Sunday), Downtown on Flagler St at Miami Ave (8am until 2pm Saturday), Coconut Grove on Grand Ave at Margaret St (Saturday) and Coral Gables City Hall (Saturday).

Also note that, in a recent development, many of Miami's favorite restaurants now deliver (especially Chinese and delis), catering more to the New Yorker–like needs here every day.

Opening Hours

Generally, restaurants serve breakfast from 6:30am to 11am; weekend brunch, on the other hand, won't usually start until 11am – especially in South Beach – and could last all day, or at least until 3pm or 4pm. Lunchtime is from about noon until 3pm, while dinner is served at about 6pm to 11pm. At restaurants doubling as nightclubs and lounges, however, dinner could be churned out until midnight, with special late-night menus available into the wee hours. Be aware that, in the off-season, many restaurants close on Mondays.

How Much?

On average, at midrange eateries, breakfast will cost you $6 to $10, lunch about $8 to $13 and dinner $15 and up. For high-end spots, dinner clocks in at about $25 to $35, with plenty of added-on costs depending on whether you order appetizers, cocktails, wine and dessert (plus tip). Note that main-dish prices given in our listings refer to dinner; lunch is generally much cheaper. Cheap Eats, for our purposes, refers to places where you can get a filling meal for under $10, including dinner. These tend to be very casual, mainly take-out spots or diners/delis.

Booking Tables

Reservations are essential at many of the top-end restaurants; call ahead, especially during high season or holidays. Some places don't accept reservations for parties of fewer than six – or at all. In these cases, show up early (by 7pm) or late (after 10pm) to reduce your wait.

Tipping

The standard formula for tips is to leave 18% of the total check; 15% if service wasn't great, 20% or more if it was excellent. The best way to calculate this is to figure out roughly 10% of the total and then double that; this is your tip amount (for example, if the check is $150, you would double $15 and leave $30). Be aware that many places – such as the **News Café** (p92) and other South Beach spots – include the tip automatically.

SOUTH BEACH

Though many other neighborhoods are gaining on South Beach, this is still pretty much the epicenter of eating – at least in its sheer number of choices. The influx of new eateries is astounding, as is the frequency of delicious meals, whether you're looking for Asian-fusion feasts or a plate of old-school rice and beans. At the top-end spots, do expect a festive scene, with folks dressed more like they're going to a party or dance club rather than to eat a plate of sushi – especially in the hotel restaurants, which are exclusive little worlds. Whatever you choose to eat, be prepared for some fun along with the food.

SOUTH OF 5TH STREET (SoFi)

BIG PINK Map p250   *American*
☎ 305-532-4700; 157 Collins Ave; dishes $8-20;
☺ breakfast, lunch, dinner & late night

Big Pink is big fun, '50s style. Here you'll find kitschy foods from burgers and buckets of fries to all-day breakfasts and a souped-up 'TV dinner' served on a compartmentalized steel tray. Eat in the cavernous, convivial dining room or at an equally fun sidewalk table. Or call for a delivery, which comes courtesy of a pink VW Beetle.

CHINA GRILL Map p250   *Chinese*
☎ 305-534-2211; 404 Washington Ave; mains $20-40;
☺ lunch & dinner

The southern outpost of Manhattan's famed grill, housed in a glitzy high-rise, sports the same flash and panache as its older sibling. Dishes are served family-style, in large bowls intended to be shared – the only way to eat Chinese. Try the dry-aged and grilled Szechuan beef, spicy sizzling whole fish, and lobster with ginger or curry and crispy spinach. And whatever you do, plan in advance: this is not an easy place to get into if you're not a model or VIP.

Top Five Eat Streets

- South Beach's **Lincoln Road Mall** (p55) really has it all – Cuban, fresh seafood, pan-Asian, eclectic American, Middle Eastern, and even a farmers' market.
- A bustling strip come nightfall, **Giralda Ave** (p106) in Coral Gables plays host to primped crowds seeking Italian, Latin, Vietnamese and more.
- A lovely Coconut Grove side street, **Commodore Plaza** (p105) is well versed in Japanese, barbecue, Indian, American and, best of all, people-watching.
- Rejuvenated after a long and shady past, **Biscayne Blvd** (p101) is bursting with trendy eats, from hot dogs to high-end Latin fusion feasts.
- The main artery of tiny Normandy Isle, **71st St** (p97) is becoming a dinner-destination spot. It has options that range from Greek to Thai.

JOE'S STONE CRAB RESTAURANT

Map p250 *American*

☎ 305-673-0365; 227 Biscayne St; mains $20-40;
✉ lunch & dinner mid-Oct–mid-May only

Joe's, established in 1913, is as close as Miami Beach gets to a world-famous restaurant. No reservations are accepted and the line is a mile long – so be prepared for a wait along with all the others whose mouths water at the thought of fresh stone crabs. Joe's is open only when these babies are in season. Folks who don't want to fiddle with the crustaceans can choose from the rest of the massive menu, which features juicy filet mignon or porterhouse steak, grilled swordfish and 10 types of potato dishes, from hashed to cottage fried. Avoid the crowds by ordering take out (☎ 305-673-4611) from the next-door shop, or even arrange for overnight air shipment (☎ 800-780-2722).

NEMO Map p250 *Asian Fusion*

☎ 305-532-4550; 100 Collins Ave; mains $25-35;
✉ lunch & dinner Mon-Fri, dinner Sat & Sun, brunch Sun

Settle into the stylishly warm dining room, accented by copper light sconces and wildly patterned banquettes, and go to town with treats such as nori-dusted tuna, Indian-spiced pork chops and crispy duck confit, which will have you ready to return on Sunday morning, when a killer brunch moves in.

PEARL RESTAURANT & CHAMPAGNE LOUNGE Map p250 *American*

☎ 305-538-1111; 1 Ocean Dr; mains $20-40;
✉ dinner Wed-Sun

This trendy eatery, attached to the even trendier nightclub **Nikki Beach Miami** (p115), is bathed in an orange glow. But its exquisite cuisine is no fly-by-night affair. Start with a bubbly in a molded chair around the showy champagne bar, or dip right into the food. You'll be pleased with the creative array of dishes, which include miso-marinated Chilean sea bass and celery-dusted scallops. And don't leave without at least a bite of someone's milk-chocolate marquise with coconut ice cream.

PRIME 112 Map p250 *Steakhouse*

☎ 305-532-8112; 112 Ocean Dr; dishes $30-40;
✉ dinner

This high-end, big-city steakhouse takes the idea of decadence to new levels, with seamless service, old-fashioned class and a modern aesthetic. Mobbed with a beautiful and sophisticated crowd from the minute it opened in 2004, Prime 112 serves up perfect steaks in any

Top Five South Beach Eats

- For old-school Cantonese, new-school hip try **Miss Yip** (p95).
- Pretty people and perfect steaks in historic environs at **Prime 112** (left).
- At **Nemo** (left) it's an Asian-fusion soiree, every night of the week.
- Meet **Talula** (p93), the new hotshot in town.
- The **Front Porch Café** (p92) is *the* place for brunch – morning, noon or night.

cut, plus a wicked $30 Kobe-beef burger that will spoil you forever. Appetizers run the gamut from oysters on the half-shell to seared foie gras, the wine list is massive and desserts like the bananas foster cheesecake will send you off happy. And it's all housed in Miami Beach's oldest inn, the beautiful 1915 Browns Hotel.

TAP TAP *Haitian*

☎ 305-672-2898; 819 5th St; dishes $9-20; ✉ dinner

Experience a taste of Haiti without going to Little Haiti at this vibrant, charming spot brimming with tasty specialities such as tropical fruit and veggie salads, and dishes such as stewed goat and pumpkin soup. It's also fun for a drink; sit among the colorful murals, enjoy frequent live music and try any cocktail containing the knock-your-socks-off Haitian Barbancourt rum, available in several grades (all strong).

TAVERNA OPA Map p250 *Greek*

☎ 305-673-6730; 36 Ocean Dr; mains $8-16;
✉ dinner & late night

Peer into this glass storefront at night, and you might think you've discovered an audience-participation theater performance. Step inside and take a seat, though, and you'll realize that it is indeed an eatery – serving big plates of meze and grilled meats and fish (plus some rice-based veggie dishes). Perhaps most important, though, is the ouzo that staff keep pouring; it fuels the nightly table-dancing by servers and the festive response of patrons.

NORTH OF 5TH STREET

1220 RESTAURANT

Map pp248-9 *American Creative*

☎ 305-604-5130; Tides Hotel, 1220 Ocean Dr;
mains $25-35; ✉ lunch & dinner

One of two eateries at the **Tides Hotel** (p157), this ultrachic dining room is a classy oasis that hovers over the cheesy stretch of Ocean Dr. Try for the wood-roasted tenderloin of beef or the citrus-glazed sea bass with plantain mash; the tastes, combined with the serene space and ocean views, will seem like heaven.

BED Map pp248-9   *Fusion*
☎ 305-532-9070; 929 Washington Ave; mains $15-35; ☽ seatings at 8-8:30pm & 10:30-11pm only (with same-day reservations)

If you can stand the restrictive reservations policy, off-putting 'fashionably chic and hip' dress code, and the fact that you'll have to eat while sprawled out on one of the eatery's big beds rather than in a simple chair, then you may just like this place, as the food is very good. The Chilean sea bass with vermouth cream sauce and the rack of lamb with mustard-tarragon sauce are standouts, and so are the rich desserts, such as the cappuccino crème brûlée. Plus, when you're done stuffing yourself, you can just lie back and rest.

BLUE DOOR Map pp246-7   *French Fusion*
☎ 305-674-6400; Delano Hotel, 1685 Collins Ave; mains $30-46; ☽ lunch & dinner

Madonna used to part own the chic main restaurant of the **Delano Hotel** (p155). But the Blue Door is so good it doesn't even need to use her name anymore – though it is notable that style guru Philippe Starck created the heavenly surroundings. You'll taste both Asian and Latin influences in creative French dishes such as cold chayote soup with pan-seared scallops and ragout of lobster in coconut-milk broth. A full dining experience.

BOND STREET Map pp246-7   *Japanese*
☎ 305-398-1806; Townhouse Hotel, 150 20th St; meals $20-30; ☽ dinner

This basement hotspot of white couches and round black tables turns into a trendy lounge scene late night (p110). But until then, it's a lauded sushi restaurant, serving up fresh big-eye tuna, yellowtail, Japanese amberjack and sashimi, spicy caviar *nigiri* (oval-shaped sushi), and sushi rolls such as avocado and scallop with spicy caviar sauce and sun-dried tomato with garlic *ponzu* (a soy-based sauce) and green-tea salt.

CASA TUA Map pp246-7   *Italian*
☎ 305-673-1010; 1700 James Ave; mains $25-40; ☽ dinner Mon-Sat

The most exclusive eatery in town (at press time, at least), this place is too cool to even have a sign out front. You'll know it by the oh-so-fabulous crowd streaming in, the hovering limos and what you can see of the beautiful building itself (much of it's hidden behind a high hedgerow). If you manage to get a table in the magnificent, 1925 Mediterranean-style villa, you can linger over high-priced (but delicious) lamb chops, steaks and pastas in one of several classy and gentlemanly quarters.

DAB HAUS Map pp248-9   *German*
☎ 305-534-9557; 852 Alton Rd; dishes $8-15; ☽ dinner

Behind the drab exterior lies a quick trip to Munich, with excellent German dishes such as bratwurst, currywurst, *knoblauchwurst* (beef garlic sausage), *sauerbraten* (sour roast) and pork and chicken schnitzel. You can also choose from crepes with mushrooms, potatoes, red cabbage and cheese. Don't miss the honey-garlic brie, which you can pair with a hearty Bavarian ale, preferably when there's live music and a lively crowd.

ESCOPAZZO Map pp248-9   *Italian*
☎ 305-674-9450; 1311 Washington Ave; mains $10-35; ☽ dinner Tue-Sun

This authentic Italian restaurant earns its loyal crowd and reputation nightly with delectable

---

Nightclub or Eatery?

You've made your dinner reservations, but arrive at the destination to find a velvet rope pulled across the entrance. You make it in, but are confused when you do step inside and take in the scene: denizens of the night are dancing with drinks in their hands, swaying to the sultry sounds of a DJ. The lighting is dramatic, seating options are couchlike, the crowd is dressed to kill. Is this a restaurant or a club? It's both, actually – representing the latest craze in fusion, which has nothing to do with cuisine. The nightclub-eatery marriage, which has been popular in cities such as New York and Los Angeles for a while now, seems to be at its peak in Miami. Find examples in the Design District at **Grass Lounge** (p113) and the **District** (p118), but mainly in South Beach. **Pearl Restaurant & Champagne Lounge** (opposite), **Rumi** (p93), **BED** (p112), **Bond Street** (above) and **Tantra** (p93) will all have you confused at first. But get into the spirit – chow down, sip a cocktail and groove to the music – and it'll all make sense soon enough.

dishes and friendly service. The homemade pasta and risotto dishes are exceptional. Reservations are a must – the dining room only seats 70 or so.

FRONT PORCH CAFÉ Map pp248-9   *Café*
☎ 305-531-8300; 1418 Ocean Dr; mains $18-15;
☺ breakfast, lunch & dinner

Since 1990 (eons by South Beach standards), the Front Porch has been noteworthy for its low-key, pleasant atmosphere and its good sampler salads and sandwiches. It tends to get mobbed for weekend brunches, but if you can wait it out, it's worth it. The big omelettes stuffed with fresh veggies and paired with juicy slices of ripe tomato are delicious, as are the fat pancakes, strong coffee and handsome servers.

GRILLFISH Map pp248-9   *Seafood*
☎ 305-538-9908; 1444 Collins Ave; mains $13-22;
☺ 6-11pm Sun-Thu, 6pm-midnight Fri & Sat

The wonderful atmosphere is hip but not seething with attitude, and the fish – Italian-inspired plates of trout over pasta, pan-seared grouper with pecans and grilled fresh catches – is sublime. The chicken, shellfish and pasta dishes are excellent, too.

JERRY'S FAMOUS DELI Map pp248-9   *Deli*
☎ 305-532-8030; 1450 Collins Ave; mains $7-15;
☺ 24 hr

Jerry's came along just in time to take over from the now-defunct Wolfie's, the deli legend that used to be just up the block. Housed in the massive space that used to be the Warsaw nightclub, this high-ceilinged Jewish deli has big booths and tables and an even bigger menu. Choose just about any traditional meal here – pastrami on rye, tuna salad, burgers and Reubens – and you'll be a happy camper.

Breakfasts are yummy and popular, too, as are the rich and creamy desserts. Jerry's also delivers, around the clock.

JOE ALLEN MIAMI BEACH
Map pp246-7   *American*
☎ 305-531-7007; 1787 Purdy Ave; mains $15-25;
☺ lunch & dinner

The South Beach outpost of Manhattan's famous Theater Row eatery is a gem hidden in an underdeveloped bayside neighborhood. Then again, judging from the crowds, it may not be so hidden. Diners keep coming for excellent steaks, fresh fish and salads, strong martinis and smooth service, and so will you.

LARIO'S ON THE BEACH
Map pp248-9   *Cuban*
☎ 305-532-9577; 820 Ocean Dr; dishes $10-30;
☺ 11am-3am

This Cuban-themed restaurant and salsa club, co-owned by singer Gloria Estefan, draws big tables of families and friends more for the party-all-the-time atmosphere than the food, though the eats are pretty good, too. Try the paella (for two people; it takes 45 minutes) or the well-spiced fish Creole. The live music will definitely put a smile on your face, too.

MARK'S SOUTH BEACH
Map pp248-9   *American Creative*
☎ 305-604-9050; Nash Hotel, 1120 Collins Ave;
mains $25-40; ☺ lunch & dinner

Chef-owner Mark Militello runs this innovative kitchen, preparing stunners such as Oregon black-truffle risotto with pappardelle, grapes, marsala and crisp pancetta and pistachio-crusted rack of lamb (though menu options change nightly). Desserts are as beautiful as the clientele. The subterranean dining room is cozy and elegant; staff is helpful and assured.

NEWS CAFÉ Map pp248-9   *American*
☎ 305-538-6397; 800 Ocean Dr; dishes $10-15;
☺ 24hr

It's worth spending part of an afternoon – at least for anthropological purposes – at this painfully trendy South Beach landmark, as the food almost rivals the street-side perch. It has terrific salads, plain omelettes and pasta dishes, but is perhaps more well known for its tangy tomato bruschetta. Pair it with an iced tea, sit back and watch the skaters wiggle and glide down Ocean Dr. (Note that a 15% tip is added to all checks.)

OSTERIA DEL TEATRO

Map pp248-9   *Italian*

☎ 305-538-7850; 1443 Washington Ave;
mains $16-42; ✆ dinner Mon-Sat

Considered Miami's best Italian restaurant by
many, Osteria offers upscale and very delicious
northern Italian meals with gracious service.
Ricotta-stuffed pastas, grilled tuna and salmon
in pink peppercorn-citrus sauce taste amazing
in this elegant dining room with a bustling
view of Washington Ave.

PUERTO SAGUA Map pp250   *Cuban*

☎ 305-673-1115; 700 Collins Ave; dishes $6-25;
✆ breakfast, lunch, dinner & late night

An anomaly on this stretch of Collins Ave – its
neighbors are the Gap and Benetton – this
authentic Cuban diner and restaurant survives
with gusto. It serves humongous portions of
tasty black-bean soup, arroz con pollo (rice
with chicken) or *ropa vieja* (shredded beef),
plus specialities such as *filete de pargo grillet*
(grilled red snapper), and excellent *café con
leche* (coffee with milk) in the authentic manner, with steamed milk in a separate cup.

RUMI Map pp246-7   *Fusion*

☎ 305-672-4353; 330 Lincoln Rd; dishes $25-30;
✆ dinner & late night

Named after the 13th-century spiritual poet,
this eatery-cum-nightclub strives for the Eastern, romantic, meditative vibe of its namesake.
And, keeping in mind that it's no temple or
mountaintop, it does a decent job with sumptuous banquettes, dark woods and soothing
lighting that soaks into mirrored walls. It's the
food, though, that will really help you reach nir-
vana: main dishes that include pan-roasted mahimahi with finger bananas and lime; ragout
of spiny lobster, fennel and wild mushrooms;
or orange and black-pepper dusted lamb loin.
Dessert options such as banana tiramisu and
flourless chocolate cake are sinfully good. After
dinner, move into the lounge area (p116), order
a cocktail and let the dance spirit move you.

SPIGA Map pp248-9   *Italian*

☎ 305-534-0079; Impala Hotel, 1228 Collins Ave;
mains $14-25; ✆ dinner

The lovely, intimate dining room is an oasis of
elegant tranquility on bustling Collins Ave. The
menu features homemade tagliolini pasta and
endive with a light Gorgonzola sauce, as well
as veal scallopini with prosciutto and sage in a
white-wine sauce. It's popular with the locals for
the high-quality meals that come sans attitude.

TALULA Map pp246-7   *American Creative*

☎ 305-672-0778; 210 23rd St; mains $25-35; ✆ dinner

This is a warm and intimate dining room that
has all sorts of coolios clamoring to get in.
And who can blame them? The cuisine here,
featuring a mix of Asian, Southwest and Italian influences, is quite stellar. Try the grilled-
shrimp tamale, grilled foie gras on blue-corn
cakes and soft-shell crabs served atop al
dente *papardelle* (long, flat ribbonlike noodles). Desserts and wines, by the way, are
just as excellent.

TANTRA Map pp248-9   *Seafood*

☎ 305-672-4765; 1445 Pennsylvania Ave; mains from
$32; ✆ dinner

Based on the premise that all senses are to
be awakened, Tantra delivers in the visual,
aural and taste departments. Large portions
of eclectic cuisine such as Thai spiced duck
confit with an orange-scented cucumber salad
share the stage with Moroccan mint-spiced
lamb and lobster Napoleon. The lobby features
freshly cut grass, while the bar pulses to tantric
music as sweet somethings wander around
offering aphrodisiac cocktails.

THAI TONI'S Map pp248-9   *Thai*

☎ 305-538-8424; 890 Washington Ave; dishes $10-20;
✆ dinner

Renowned for its chic clientele and a dramatically lit and understated open dining room,
Thai Toni's has indisputably very good Thai
food. Chicken or vegetable curries, the requisite pad Thai and a selection of grilled fish
specialities are standouts, as are the potent
cocktails. It's a touch of class on a slightly gritty
bit of Washington Ave.

TIGER OAK ROOM

Map pp246-7   *American*

☎ 305-534-6300; Raleigh Hotel, 1775 Collins Ave;
mains $18-35; ✆ breakfast & lunch Mon-Thu,
breakfast, lunch & dinner Fri-Sun

Lunch at the Raleigh Hotel's romantic New
American restaurant is a wonderful experience,
especially if you dine on the patio out back,
overlooking the lovely, elegant pool area. Try
roasted vegetables Provençal, a tuna burger
with ginger soy sauce, or grilled jumbo shrimp
gazpacho. Sunday brunch is a fun and chichi
affair; dine simply on a wild-mushroom omelette with fresh herbs and goat cheese. The
serene bar, if you haven't heard yet, makes one
of the best gin martinis on South Beach (it's
huge, dry and made with Bombay Sapphire).

Eating – South Beach

WISH Map pp248-9   *American*
☎ 305-531-2222; Hotel, 801 Collins Ave; mains $25-35;
🕑 7am-11pm Sun-Thu, 7am-midnight Fri & Sat

Put Wish on the top of your wish list for a quiet, romantic dinner spot. Within the Todd Oldham–designed hotel, highly acclaimed chef Michael Reidt takes contemporary French-Brazilian cuisine to the next level, emphasizing fresh fish, savory flesh and fancy fowl. Look for innovative mains such as marinated tuna served over a jicama-quinoa salad on spicy charred watermelon, or coriander-crusted lamb leg, smoked black-bean couscous, mint and pineapple. The elegantly understated dining room has Persian-inspired decor, and the adjoining candlelit courtyard may be Miami Beach's most romantic dining spot.

Cheap Eats
11TH STREET DINER
Map pp248-9   *Diner*
☎ 305-534-6373; 1065 Washington Ave; dishes $5-15;
🕑 24hr

This art-deco Pullman-car diner, trucked down from Wilkes-Barre, Pennsylvania, is a sleek and shiny sight. Plus it serves really good three-egg omelettes, sandwiches and down-home favorites such as fried chicken and meatloaf with leisurely but cheery service.

DAVID'S CAFE Map pp248-9   *Cuban*
☎ 305-534-8736; 1058 Collins Ave; dishes $3-6;
🕑 24hr

The round-the-clock *café con leche* market has been cornered by this storefront diner. It has counter service, OK Cuban food and breakfasts, and a colorful clutch of characters who linger and panhandle by the service window.

Restaurant Month: 'Miami Spice'

August is the hottest month to visit Miami – but not just in a bad way. For foodies on a budget, there's no better time because it's when the Greater Miami Convention & Visitors Bureau sponsors the annual Miami Restaurant Month, a chance for diners to eat out at one of more than 50 participating restaurants and pay a prix fixe of only $20.05 for lunch or $30.05 for dinner (in 2006 it'll be $20.06, and up, one cent at a time, from there). That's a 25% to 50% savings from the usual menu prices – and amazing opportunity to get your foot in the door at coveted dining spots from OLA to Talulah.

But when it comes to after-club hunger pangs or a midafternoon shot of coffee, this place is a downright institution.

FLAMINGO RESTAURANT
Map pp248-9   *Nicaraguan*
☎ 305-673-4302; 1454 Washington Ave; dishes $2.50-7; 🕑 breakfast, lunch & dinner Mon-Sat

A breath of fresh air in the form of a tiny, family-run, down-home storefront café, this is the place for Nicaraguan specialities such as hen soup, pepper chicken with rice and beans, fried grouper and a *tres leches* (milk cake) dessert. Also choose from a Cuban sandwich, fresh tamarind juice and the breakfast of two eggs, meat, potatoes, toast and coffee for $2.50!

LIME FRESH MEXICAN GRILL
Map pp248-9   *Mexican*
☎ 305-532-5436; 1439 Alton Rd; mains $5-9;
🕑 lunch & dinner

This bright new spot is just the kind of place South Beach needs more of – casual, affordable and delicious. Sit in either the tiny storefront or on the small outdoor patio and chow down on great tacos or burritos filled with chicken, beef, shrimp or veggies and gobs of homemade salsa and guacamole. You can also get chilly Mexican beers. Another affordable outpost, **Taste Bakery Café** (below), is further down Alton Rd.

PIZZA RUSTICA Map pp248-9   *Pizza*
☎ 305-538-6009; 1447 Washington Ave;
slices $2.50-3.50; 🕑 lunch

South Beach's favorite pizza place has three locations to satisfy the demand for Roman-style crusty/chewy slices topped with an array of exotic offerings. A slice is a meal unto itself. Mosey down to **863 Washington Ave** (Map pp248-9; ☎ 305-674-8244) or over to **667 Lincoln Rd** (Map pp246-7; 667 Lincoln Rd) to sample similar fare at the other Pizza Rustica braches.

TASTE BAKERY CAFÉ
Map pp248-9   *Café*
☎ 305-695-9930; 900 Alton Rd; mains $6-8; 🕑 lunch

Another great new spot from the folks who own **Lime Fresh Mexican Grill** (above). This mellow café doesn't mind if you linger – and it's got free WiFi to prove it. Order from an excellent selection of salads (caprese, Greek, Thai chicken), grilled panini sandwiches (chicken pesto, roasted eggplant and feta, turkey and salami) and wraps (mixed veggies, turkey and avocado). It's also got homemade baked goods, smoothies and a big selection of coffees and teas.

Nuevo Latino Trend

It was the so-called 'Mango Gang' – chefs Mark Militello (Mark's South Beach), Allen Susser (Chef Allen's), Douglas Rodriguez (first from Yuca and now at OLA) and Norman Van Aken (Norman's) – who were pioneers of the Nuevo Latino, or 'Floribbean,' cuisine movement in the '90s, back when South Beach's comeback was helping to rejuvenate the city. Only now, they are not alone. Nuevo Latino is a food trend that doesn't show signs of stopping because it's not only delicious but also logical. It's a way of cooking that fuses the tropical tastes of Latin American and Caribbean cuisine with traditional European cooking techniques, relying on regional produce, fish and spices that are easily accessible in Miami. Snapper, shrimp, conch and grouper may be playfully blended with fiery scotch bonnet peppers, sweet papaya or mango, tangy cilantro or lime – even yucca, hearts of palm or avocado. Look for hints of Nuevo Latino on Miami menus everywhere, whether you're at a diner or five-star dining room.

LINCOLN ROAD & AROUND

ALTAMAR Map pp246-7   *Seafood*
☎ 305-532-3061; 1223 Lincoln Rd; mains $16-25;
dinner

Located on the west side of Alton Rd – the stretch that most pedestrians miss in their haste to turn around and glide along the mall – this relative newcomer is an amazing and popular spot for fresh fish. Owner Claudio Giordano, of Coral Gables' Claudius fame, uses this tiny storefront space (with a tumble of tables that spill far along the sidewalk at night) to marry ultrafresh fish with spectacular flavors. The results range from his jumbo crab cake served with mustard sauce, soft-shell crab that has its meat marinated in lemon and herbs and then returned to the shell, and a tuna wasabi.

BALANS

Map pp246-7   *Mediterranean-Asian Fusion*
☎ 305-534-9191; 1022 Lincoln Rd; mains $10-20;
breakfast, lunch & dinner

This chic, British-owned, oh-so-Soho bistro has a modern-yet-comfortable atmosphere fueled by a bustling open-air seating area and very reasonable prices. The menu fuses Mediterranean and Asian cuisines, and the signature lobster club sandwich is a standout. Brunch is also *très* popular.

CAFÉ PAPILLON Map pp246-7   *French*
☎ 305-673-1139; 530 Lincoln Rd; dishes $8-25;
8:30am-11pm

Make a beeline here for elegant café meals of quiche, tartines (filled with marinated artichokes or peppers in pesto sauce), salads, crepes and other delicious French-bistro standards. Papillon has sidewalk tables and a casual, if small, French country dining room, plus newspapers for your perusal.

CAFETERIA Map pp246-7   *American*
☎ 305-672-3663; 546 Lincoln Rd; dishes $7-18;
24hr

Another South Beach outpost of a Manhattan favorite, this round-the-clock purveyor of comfort food doles out updated versions of diner classics to a hip crowd. Try the macaroni and cheese or meatloaf, plus a range of salads, pastas and burgers.

ICE BOX CAFÉ Map pp246-7   *American*
☎ 305-538-8448; 1657 Michigan Ave; items $7-20;
lunch & dinner

This small and sleek café serves beautifully prepared sandwiches, salads, pasta dishes and various specials, plus luscious desserts (try the jumbo s'mores) laid out in a massive glass display case. Lounge in the intimate storefront setting or on one of the several sidewalk tables, and don't forget the nice selection of wines.

MISS YIP Map pp246-7   *Chinese*
☎ 305-534-5488; 1661 Meridian Ave; dishes $12-25;
lunch & dinner

The newest star in the Lincoln Rd region is a nostalgia trip for folks old enough to remember when Cantonese was the only kind of Chinese cuisine you could find stateside. But it's also a full-on dining experience. Slide into one of the bright-red booths and soak up the classic Chinese teahouse vibe. Then choose from traditional favorites – fish filet in black-bean sauce, sweet and sour pork, Peking duck, *ma-po* tofu (a Szechuan dish of marinated pork, black beans and bean curd) – and discover that no matter what you choose, it's prepared flawlessly. You can also order a selection of dim sum, from chicken dumplings to egg custards, and a glass of sweet plum wine. It's like dining in New York's old-school Chinatown, but with hot, hip people and very cool environs.

PACIFIC TIME Map pp246-7 *Asian*
☎ 305-534-5979; 915 Lincoln Rd; mains $21-32;
🕑 dinner

Chef-owner Jonathan Eismann's time-tested favorite dazzles with Pacific Rim–inspired food served in a chic, bustling setting. The seafood dishes are dynamite – try any featuring locally caught mahimahi. The impressive wine list spans the world, and the service is top-notch.

SUSHI SAMBA Map pp246-7 *Asian Fusion*
☎ 305-673-5337; 600 Lincoln Rd; mains $18-30;
🕑 lunch & dinner

This sexy, loungelike eatery blends Japanese, Brazilian and Peruvian flavors in a mod setting that emphasizes the sensual rhythms of samba music. Try the sashimi ceviche; the one-of-a-kind sushi rolls; the *tiradito,* a Peruvian-inspired dish similar to ceviche; the blue-cornmeal-crusted calamari; and a saketini (martini with saki) or sakegria, made with plum sake.

VAN DYKE CAFÉ Map pp246-7 *American*
☎ 305-534-3600; 846 Lincoln Rd; dishes $6-15;
🕑 8am-2am

One of Lincoln Rd's most touristed spots, the Van Dyke is an institution, serving adequate food in a cool setting. It's usually packed to the rafters and takes over half the sidewalk. Service is very friendly, even efficient, and if you could just avoid the models preening and posing, it would be a far better place to enjoy the burgers, roast beef sandwiches and eggplant parmigiana. There's also nightly jazz upstairs.

YUCA Map pp246-7 *Cuban*
☎ 305-532-9822; 501 Lincoln Rd; dishes $22-40;
🕑 lunch & dinner

This pioneer Latin-fusion hotspot still attracts legions of fans for creative and well-executed dishes such as sugar-cane skewered guava shrimp, guava baby-back ribs and yucca shoestring fries. The vibe is fun and friendly, especially upstairs at the chic lounge, where you can enjoy a yummy *mojito* (Cuban rum-based cocktail).

Cheap Eats
DAVID'S CAFE II Map pp246-7 *Cuban*
☎ 305-672-8707; 1654 Meridian Ave; dishes $3-6, buffet lunch $7.50; 🕑 7am-11pm

Like the main outpost on Collins Ave, this café is where folks come for a shot of Cuban coffee. It's also popular for cheap breakfasts, taken at bar stools, and a bountiful lunch buffet, served in the dining room.

PANIZZA BISTRO Map pp246-7 *Italian*
☎ 305-695-8800; 1229 Lincoln Rd; mains $7-12;
🕑 breakfast, lunch & dinner

On the less-traveled west side of Alton Rd, this Argentine-run Italian bistro feels like you could be in any one of many Latin American or Mediterranean countries. The ordering, best done in Spanish, yields a delicious selection of quick, affordable, mostly Italian meals. Try the Spanish tortillas or plates of fresh lasagna, chicken parm or bean soup. Cheap red wine gets filled to the brim of your glass, and delicious Argentine pastries sit in bins for early-morning sweet treats. It's the perfect place for a quick pre-movie meal.

PASHA'S Map pp246-7 *Middle Eastern*
☎ 305-673-3919; 900 Lincoln Rd; meals $3-10;
🕑 lunch & dinner

Pasha is a serious self-promoter judging by this place, a sleek, two-level, healthy fast-food emporium that has his name everywhere you look. No matter; the food at Pasha's rocks. Satisfy your hunger with a quick and delicious *labneh* (thick yogurt) or grilled-vegetable wrap, a plate of tabbouleh and hummus or some grilled chicken served over rice. It's all good, and the interior feels as hip as a club. Other Pasha's locations are **Downtown** (pp252–3; 1414 Brickell Ave) and in the **Design District** (Map p254; 3801 N Miami Ave).

MIAMI BEACH

It *seems* like all the restaurants cluster at the southern end of the beach, but head north and you'll find a diverse selection, from old-time gangster steakhouses to up-to-the-minute dining lounges, plus plenty of ethnic cuisines. Eateries are spread out along this route. The only real collection of places is on Normandy Isle, in a burgeoning village area where you can browse menus and dining rooms until you find what you like.

MID-BEACH
ARNIE & RICHIE'S
Map p251 *Delicatessen*
☎ 305-531-7691; 525 41st St; dishes $4-24;
🕑 breakfast, lunch & dinner Mon-Fri, breakfast & lunch Sat & Sun

Smoked whitefish, corned beef on rye, matzoball soup and other Jewish deli staples rule the roost at this authentic deli, where ex–New

Yorkers crowd in to big tastes of what they left back home.

FORGE Map p251   *Steakhouse*
☎ 305-538-8533; 432 41st St; mains $25-42; Ⓥ dinner Mon-Sat, brunch & dinner Sun

An over-the-top statement of decadence for more than 30 years, this legend is best known for its reputation as a former gangster hangout – and for the nostalgia-loving pop stars (Britney Spears among them) who dine there today. Folks stream in to enjoy the ornate stained-glass, antiques and chandeliers; to dine on succulent cuts of steak or options of fish and chicken; and to gawk at (or make special arrangements to dine in) the famous wine cellar, which holds 300,000 bottles.

NORMAN'S TAVERN Map p251   *Steakhouse*
☎ 305-868-9248; 6770 Collins Ave; mains $15-25; Ⓥ lunch & dinner

Perched behind a glass front that overlooks a bustling strip of Collins, Norman's is a less-glitzy alternative to Miami Beach's other steak spots, attracting locals who love the lean cuts of meat, the international soccer matches shown on bar TVs and the popular pool table.

TAMARIND Map p251   *Thai*
☎ 305-861-6222; 946 Normandy Dr; mains $12-20; Ⓥ lunch & dinner

A brand-new addition to the isle, Tamarind is a mellow, cozy spot with outdoor tables that provide a perfect view of the rest of this hoppin' little village. It has all your favorite Thai classics, from green papaya salad and spicy tom yum soup to rich pad Thai and red-curry chicken. The menu, in a special nod to vegetarians, denotes each of its meat-free options with a little 'V'.

Cheap Eats

OASIS CAFE Map p251   *Middle Eastern*
☎ 305-674-7676; 976 41st St; lunch dishes $7-10, dinner mains $7-16; Ⓥ lunch & dinner Mon-Sat, dinner Sun

Vegetarians who are desperately seeking salads will love it here; a Mediterranean café serving fresh dolmas (stuffed grape leaves), eggplant salad, hummus, grilled tofu and mixed greens. Try the grilled fish on focaccia, vegetable lasagna or grilled turkey for more substance.

TASTI CAFÉ Map p251   *Café*
☎ 305-673-5483; 4041 Royal Palm Ave; mains $4-9; Ⓥ breakfast, lunch & dinner Mon-Thu, breakfast & lunch Fri & Sun, closed Sat

This Israeli-run, kosher café is always bustling, and for good reason. All of its reasonably priced dishes are fresh and delicious, and they run the gamut from light, veggie entrees to hearty pastas and sandwiches (and sinful homemade desserts). Try the grilled zucchini and fresh-tomato sandwich on challah, the soy chicken burger on a bagel, spicy sesame linguini or generous salad Niçoise. A drive-through take-out window is great for coffee or picnic luncheons on the run.

NORTH BEACH TO SUNNY ISLES

CAFÉ PRIMA PASTA Map p251   *Italian*
☎ 305-867-0106; 414 71st St; dishes $10-20; Ⓥ lunch & dinner Mon-Fri, dinner Sat & Sun

This Argentine-Italian spot serves homemade pastas and other specialties – crab-stuffed ravioli, seafood-smothered fettuccine, fresh fish and salads – that draw serious crowds who must often queue up outside for a table. Join them for a delicious meal at an excellent price.

LEMON TWIST Map p251   *Mediterranean*
☎ 305-868-2075; 908 71st St; dishes $10-20; Ⓥ dinner Tue-Sun

This is a warm, unpretentious little bistro in the heart of Normandy Isle. The hosts whet your appetite immediately by treating you to bowls of spicy olives and baskets of warm, fresh bread. It gets better when you order, choosing from well-executed options including Moroccan chicken and pumpkin ravioli. The portion size of starters and desserts – such as the cheese and dried-fruit plate and homemade crème brûlée – are generous, as are the gratis lemon-drop shots served by the owner (who was new in 2004) at the end of a meal.

OUZO'S Map p251 *Greek*
☎ 305-864-9848; 940 71st St; mains $10-18; ☺ dinner Mon-Thu, lunch & dinner Fri-Sun

It's always a party at this authentic Greek taverna in Normandy Isle, where chatty crowds pack the small storefront and spill out onto the sidewalk sitting at outdoor tables, dining on grilled meats and fish, lamb chops, meatballs, spinach pies and cool shots of – what else? – ouzo. The frequent live music and belly dancers really rile up the fans.

ROGER'S Map p251 *American*
☎ 305-866-7111; 1601 79th St Causeway; mains $9-16; ☺ dinner

This causeway is blessed with remarkable views of Biscayne Bay and the city, but always lacked a great dining option at which to enjoy them. Enter Roger's, a casual and delicious eatery that came on the scene in 2004. It's all about the waterfront deck (though the vast dining room is atmospheric, too), where seats at an alfresco bar or serene tables let you gaze over the bay, and actually hear it lapping against the patio as you chow down on simple but well-prepared steaks, grilled fish and pasta dishes. It's a popular spot for sunset cocktails.

TIMO'S Map pp244-5 *American*
☎ 305-936-1008; 17,624 Collins Ave; mains $15-40; ☺ lunch & dinner

When chef Tim Andriola left Mark's South Beach in 2003, he opened this classy bistro, much to the delight of the North Beach crowd. He's been creating a buzz ever since by turning out stellar dishes like rock-shrimp and artichoke gnocchi, wood-burning stove pizzas and chicken-and-parmesan dumplings in truffle-infused broth, all served in a sprawling and elegant space.

Cheap Eats

PATACÓN Map pp244-5 *Colombian*
☎ 305-931-3001; 18,230 Collins Ave at 182nd St; dishes $5-10; ☺ lunch & dinner

Part of a small local chain, Patacón is named in honor of a popular Colombian dish of fried plantains often topped with extras like beans, shrimp or shredded beef. You can sample it here, of course, along with cheap and delicious empanadas stuffed with beef and potatoes or a hearty stew made of hen, tripe and corn.

WOLFIE COHEN'S RASCAL HOUSE
Map pp244-5 *American*
☎ 305-947-4581; 17,190 Collins Ave; dishes $7-15; ☺ 24hr

Wolfie Cohen's nostalgic 1954 Miami eatery has sassy service, classic swivel stools at the counter and Naugahyde booths. It bustles with older patrons, Northeastern snowbirds and curious tourists who relish roast brisket, latkes, blintzes, Reuben sandwiches, borscht and Lake Erie whitefish salad. Everything is homemade and it's all available for take-out. Expect to wait, though the packed queues move efficiently.

DOWNTOWN MIAMI

Downtown has a cornucopia of choices – quick bites from around the globe that cater to on-the-go government employees, characterful riverfront fish eateries, tourist traps on the bay, and now, a full range of high-end options that sit housed in the luxury high-rise hotels along Brickell Ave. Whatever your pleasure, you'll find it here.

ACQUA Map pp252-3 *American Creative*
☎ 305-358-3535; Four Seasons Hotel, 1435 Brickell Ave; mains $20-40; ☺ lunch & dinner

Posh and pricey, the dining establishment of the new **Four Seasons Miami** (p160) is every bit as over-the-top and amazing as you'd expect it to be. Choose one of the separate dining areas – the pool terrace, more casual Galleria and sprawling main space – and pore over succulent dishes such as tuna carpaccio, grilled striped bass and rich risotto. Lunch, at a fixed price of $23 to $27, is a surprising deal.

AZUL Map pp252-3 *Fusion*
☎ 305-913-8288; Mandarin Oriental, 500 Brickell Key Dr; mains $20-40; ☺ dinner daily, lunch Sun-Fri

Located within the luxe **Mandarin Oriental Miami** (p160) on Brickell Key, this is the fancier of the two on-site eateries. It's a fine choice for a special night out, as delights such as rich bouilla baisse, prawns in orange-anise sauce and slippery foie gras are served with a flourish, in an elegant space and by a seriously doting staff.

BIG FISH Map pp252-3 *Seafood*
☎ 305-373-1770; 55 SW Miami Ave; mains $10-30; ☺ lunch & dinner

It's got riverfront competition, but the big fish on the block grills some tasty denizens of the deep. (Some dependable Italian dishes grace the menu, too.) Waiting at the congenial bar for a table with dramatic skyline views and a funky atmosphere won't be difficult, but you'll have to do it. You may recognize the back patio as the spot where Alec Baldwin impersonated a policeman in the '80s cult flick *Miami Blues*.

BLUE WATER CAFÉ Map pp252-3 *Seafood*
☎ 305-577-1000; Intercontinental Hotel, 100 Chopin Plaza; mains $10-16; ⏲ lunch & dinner
For a Downtown perspective of the sublime Biscayne Bay, skip the tourist traps at the Bayside Market and make a beeline to this aptly named pool café, graced with amazing views, delightful breezes and an eclectic menu. Try the refreshing watermelon, goat cheese and fresh-mint salad; the Vietnamese-style fresh-fish stir-fry; or the hearty sandwich of fresh mozzarella, ham and beefsteak tomatoes served on *ciabatta* (Italian bread). Vegetarians will find plenty of options, to boot.

CAFÉ SAMBAL Map pp252-3 *Pan-Asian*
☎ 305-913-8251; Mandarin Oriental, 500 Brickell Key Dr; lunch mains $12-20, dinner mains $18-30; ⏲ 6:30am-11pm
Located within the luxe **Mandarin Oriental Miami** (p160) on Brickell Key, this more casual eatery is a nouveau Asian bistro, pairing exceptional food such as rich crab cakes, super-fresh sushi and creative noodle dishes with a skyline view that deserves to be savored.

CAPITAL GRILLE Map pp252-3 *Steakhouse*
☎ 305-374-4500; 444 Brickell Ave; mains $15-30; ⏲ lunch & dinner Mon-Fri, dinner Sat & Sun
This posh carnivore's paradise boasts steak, steak and more steak. Service is hushed and reverent, catering to the suited expense-accounters who appreciate the chandeliers, marble floors and dark wood paneling as much as the meat. The bar is equally hush-hush and handsome, the perfect perch for a secret rendezvous and a dry martini.

FISHBONE GRILLE Map pp252-3 *Seafood*
☎ 305-530-1915; 650 S Miami Ave; mains $10-25; ⏲ lunch & dinner Mon-Fri, dinner Sat
One of Miami's stellar fish houses, this casual place with an open, tiled kitchen features grilled, blackened, sautéed, baked or Française seafood preparations. Prices fluctuate with the market; check the long chalkboard list for the prime catches-of-the-day. Highlights include the seafood gumbo, rich jalapeño

cornbread, mouth-watering pizzas and a reasonably priced wine list.

GARCIA'S Map pp252-3 *Seafood*
☎ 305-375-0765; 398 NW N River Dr; dishes $11-market price; ⏲ lunch
Another reliable choice for inexpensive, fresh seafood on the banks of the seedy Miami River, Garcia's is a hit for power lunches among suit-wearing Cuban professionals. Snag a coveted table out back on the river or just pop a squat at the front counter; either way, the incredibly fresh and simple menu – jumbo shrimp, conch steak, dolphin fillet, grilled lobster, whole fried yellowtail – will have you hooked. Buy some to cook at home at the on-site fish market.

NOVOCENTO Map pp252-3 *Eclectic*
☎ 305-403-0900; 1414 Brickell Ave; dishes $10-19; ⏲ lunch & dinner
It's original South Beach outpost (1080 Alton Rd) is already a big hit. And now Downtowners can get in on the delicious scene, too. New to the area in late 2004, the airy classy space is anchored by an inviting, round bar that sits proudly in the middle. Choose from creative, tasty and reasonable options including crab ravioli in creamy saffron sauce, grilled rib-eye steak, breaded veal topped with a fried egg or one of several freshly made pizza options.

PORÇAO Map pp252-3 *Brazilian*
☎ 305-373-2777; 801 Brickell Bay Dr; per person $33; ⏲ noon-midnight
You'd better come with an appetite. This excellent Brazilian *churrascaria* (restaurant that serves meat) features an elaborate *rodízio*, a traditional endless feast of skewered, flame-broiled meats. Waiters circulate with the flaming skewers and describe exactly what's what. You won't be able to stop saying 'OK, more.' Plus, there are endless salad options at the

Eating –Downtown Miami

Top Five Downtown Eats

- Top service, posh surroundings and outstanding cuisine at **Azul** (opposite) in the Mandarin Oriental.
- Bay views and breezes sans touristy mobs at **Blue Water Café** (left).
- At **Garcia's** (above) enjoy the hustle and bustle, riverfront seating and fresh catches.
- There's something for everyone at **Jamaica International Café** (p100), a global spot.
- **Mini Healthy Deli** (p100) is a tiny surprise in the midst of urban grit.

buffet. The name is appropriate, as you'll definitely feel a bit like a stuffed pig by the time you leave.

CHEAP EATS

GRANNY FEELGOOD'S

Map pp252-3   *Vegetarian*
☎ 305-377-9600; 25 W Flagler St; mains $4-12;
☾ breakfast & lunch Mon-Fri

A neighborhood staple since the mid-1970s, this health-food emporium has good, simple vegetarian dishes such as tofu sandwiches, veggie burgers and spinach lasagna, plus healthy food for carnivores such as turkey burgers and shrimp stir-fry.

JAMAICA INTERNATIONAL CAFÉ

Map pp252-3   *International*
☎ 305-400-6694; 119 SE 1st Ave; dishes $5-11;
☾ breakfast, lunch & dinner

This bright spot on a drab strip is a friendly, eclectic spot, serving a truly mind-boggling range of global dishes. Choose from a Mexican quesadilla, Italian vegetable lasagna, Cuban sandwich or Greek-style pizza. But the way to go here is Jamaican, via the curry lobster, stewed peas with pork, jerk chicken or vegetable curry (one of several veggie options here). Traditional breakfasts include eggs or akee served with boiled bananas and fried dumplings, and dessert spoils you rotten with sweet-potato pudding.

MINI HEALTHY DELI

Map pp252-3   *Latin Café*
☎ 305-523-2244; Station Mall, 48 E Flagler St;
dishes $4-6; ☾ lunch

Tucked into an obscure corner of a half-vacant mini-mall is this tiny gem, where chef and manager Carlos Bedoya works solo behind his counter to churn out remarkably fresh and delicious daily specials, such as grilled tilapia served with fresh salad and rice and beans. Plates are a super value, and you'll find only two little tables. But it's worth waiting – or standing while you eat.

PASHA'S Map pp252-3   *Middle Eastern*
☎ 305-416-5116; 1414 Brickell Ave; dishes $4-10;
☾ lunch & dinner

A smaller, newer location than the Lincoln Rd flagship, this branch of Pasha's offers healthy, heavily veggie options in a slick and casual spot, which is a welcome sight in this glitzy, high-rise 'hood. Try a kebab or veggie wrap, Mediterranean pizza or tabbouleh-hummus platter. It's all good.

WYNWOOD, THE DESIGN DISTRICT & NORTH BISCAYNE BOULEVARD

The biggest explosion of eateries in the past few years has been in this area of Miami – mainly in the Design District, where several trendy spots have helped put the 'hood on the map, and north of there, along the formerly seedy Biscayne Blvd on the edge of the residential Morningside, where you'll now find a barrage of cute little cafés and hip cheap eats.

WYNWOOD

Cheap Eats

ENRIQUETA'S Map p254   *Latin Diner*
☎ 305-573-4681; 186 NE 29th St; dishes $4-7;
☾ breakfast & lunch Mon-Sat

From the outside, it looks like a shady roadhouse. But step inside and you'll quickly discover why the parking lot is perpetually full: good, cheap, filling basics, served with old-fashioned charm at either the luncheonette counter or one of about a dozen booths. There are egg sandwiches, steak with ham and eggs, grilled chicken and tuna salad – plus shots of Cuban coffee, which you can order and slug down at an outdoor service window.

S&S RESTAURANT Map p254   *American*
☎ 305-373-4291; 1757 NE 2nd Ave; dishes $4-10;
☾ breakfast & lunch

Step back into the past at this classic '40s-style diner (located right across the street from a historic cemetery, by the way). It has downright sassy service ('Keep yer shirt on, hon!') and great old-fashioned, comfort-food choices such as burgers, meatloaf and baked macaroni and cheese, plus more adventurous entries like shrimp Creole. The small horseshoe-shaped linoleum lunch counter is always bustling, especially, it seems, with cops.

TREE OF ZION Map p254   *Vegetarian & Raw*
☎ 305-573-5874; 2426 NE 2nd Ave; dishes $5-10;
☾ lunch & dinner Mon-Sat

Angela, a native Miamian, and her boyfriend Sebastian, were dismayed by the lack of vegetarian eateries in town. So what did they do?

They opened their own place in 2004. Now it's a sort of hippie haven, a raw space with mismatched furniture and a small vintage-clothing boutique in the back, where all sorts file in for items hard to find in these parts. Choose from raw entrées, such as pizza (made with almond 'cheese' on a bed of sprouts), almond paté, and a Reuben (walnut jerky on flax bread with homemade sauerkraut and almond cheese); cooked vegan specials including Jamaican soy patties and a teriyaki tofu sandwich; and smoothies, fresh juices and vegan desserts. Some nights feature live music and readings.

THE DESIGN DISTRICT

DISTRICT Map p254 *American Creative*
☎ 305-576-7242; 35 NE 40th St; dishes $12-20;
☾ lunch & dinner Tue-Sat

Miami's hottest neighborhood nightspot, the District packs in hipsters for twists on classic dishes such as skirt steak with chipotle chilies and pan-seared scallops in citrus vinaigrette. But the big draw to the relaxed space – which features an intimate dining room with high-backed chairs that's fronted by an interior courtyard for dining under the stars – is the happy hour, sometimes featuring lounge or jazz singers, and always offering tasty cocktail specials.

GRASS RESTAURANT & LOUNGE

Map p254 *Asian Fusion*
☎ 305-573-3355; 28 NE 40th St; dishes $16-30;
☾ dinner Mon-Sat

This trendy spot could be seen as a lounge – a fabulous one, where model-gorgeous folks get let in through a velvet rope – but it does, in fact, have quite a good menu. The whole place is alfresco, and has a combo of open-air

lounging banquettes and tiki huts, on elevated platforms, for more intimate dinners. The menu is drawn from all over Asia, with entrées such as Szechuan tuna and Sumatran chicken beef tenderloin taking center stage – next to the exquisite patrons, that is.

Cheap Eats

CANE Á SUCRE Map p254 *Café*
☎ 305-572-0111; 3535 NE 2nd Ave; mains $4-7;
☾ breakfast & lunch Mon-Sat

A funky French café housed in what looks like a former gas station, this neighborhood favorite is the perfect place to start your day with coffee and a croissant. You could also choose from a wonderful array of fresh sandwiches and salads – fire-roasted chicken breast with smoked mozzarella and caramelized onions on a baguette, a buttery *croque monsieur* (French ham-and-cheese sandwich), roasted plum tomatoes with avocado and fresh mozzarella served over greens. The vibe is sweet and the rich desserts are sweeter.

COMA'S Map p254 *Café & Bakery*
☎ 305-576-8109; 3930 NE 2nd Ave; dishes $3-10;
☾ lunch

This small café and bakery is the perfect place for a pit stop during a gallery hop. Daily specials range from linguini with garlic sauce to stuffed chicken with mustard sauce, and you can also choose from light pastries, salads and strong coffee concoctions.

SECRET SANDWICH CO Map p254 *Deli*
☎ 305-571-9990; 3918 N Miami Ave; meals $5-8;
☾ lunch Mon-Fri

A cute little place on the edge of the gallery streets, you'll come across plenty of covert finds in here, mainly sandwiches with clever names: Bay of Pig (thin-sliced roast pork with onion and mojo marinade), Mata Hari (lime-marinated grilled chicken breast with fresh greens, caramelized onions and cilantro dressing) and Offshore (blackened mahimahi with greens and garlic dressing). Also choose from half-pound burgers (turkey, beef or Portobello) and a couple of very fresh salads.

NORTH BISCAYNE BOULEVARD

ANDIAMO! Map p254 *Pizza*
☎ 305-762-5751; 5600 Biscayne Blvd; pizzas $8-15;
☾ lunch & dinner

Andiamo! has won local pizza awards for its pies, which come topped with goodies ranging

Eating – Wynwood, the Design District & North Biscayne Boulevard from Italian sausage and fresh spinach to goat cheese and white tuna. But it's just as beloved for its fun setting – in a former garage that still has an operational (and very popular) car wash attached. Where else can you see your vehicle get scrubbed while you clean your plate?

CHEZ ROSIE Map p251 _Caribbean_
☎ 305-756-9881; 7015 Biscayne Blvd; mains $5-20;
🕑 breakfast, lunch & dinner
Rosie's has got it all: breakfast of codfish with steamed plantains, lunch and dinner options including Greek salad, shrimp Creole, fried goat or vegetable stew. The miniscule kitchen and 'dining area' will make you wonder how she does it, but one bite and you won't question that she does it well.

DOGMA GRILL Map p251 _Hot Dogs_
☎ 305-759-3433; 7030 Biscayne Blvd; dogs $3-4;
🕑 lunch & dinner
This hip roadside stand has what it calls 'a frank philosophy': dogs, dogs and more dogs. Get them in beef, Polish sausage or pure-veggie soy, and smothered in toppings from bacon and chili to cucumber and kalamata olives. The rolls are delicious, too – fresh and soft, and coated with poppy seeds. Folks against dogmatic menus can choose from options such as a grilled chicken sandwich, pastrami Reuben or Greek salad.

OLA Map p254 _Café_
☎ 305-758-9195; 5061 Biscayne Blvd; dishes $20-35;
🕑 dinner Tue-Sat
After kicking off the Cuban-fusion craze in 1980s Miami by opening **Yuca** (p96), and then making a splash with it in New York City at Patria, chef-restaurateur Douglas Rodriguez returned, promptly making another name for

himself with OLA (Of Latin America). It's a very chichi spot with high style and a hyper-foodie following, serving sophisticated fusion meals such as empanadas stuffed with foie gras and figs, plantain crusted mahimahi, and a ceviche crafted from _hamachi_ (young yellowtail tuna), blood-orange, watermelon and radish. Enjoy a _mojito_ by the cascading waterfall, or hunker down at a table for some serious wining and dining.

SOYKA Map p254 _American Creative_
☎ 305-759-3117; 5556 NE 4th Ct; mains $8-15;
🕑 lunch & dinner Mon-Sun, brunch Sun
Mark Soyka is one smart dude. His first move was cornering the South Beach casual-food market with **News Café** (p92) and **Van Dyke Café** (p117), then he became a pioneer in this neck of the woods, opening Soyka to instant success. Housed in a massive, raw space with high ceilings, terrazzo flooring, an open kitchen and huge, cushy brown banquettes, this place is fun, delicious and free of oppressive attitude. The menu is eclectic and large, with burgers, pastas, pizzas and main dishes such as pan-seared mahimahi, _steak au poivre_ (steak with peppercorns) and sesame-seared salmon. Sunday brunch here is a particular treat – no crazy waiting and a great menu of eggs benedict and the like.

SUSHI SIAM Map p254 _Japanese_
☎ 305-751-7818; 5582 NE 4th Ct; mains $8-20;
🕑 dinner
Sandwiched between **Soyka** (above) and **Andiamo!** (p101) is this loungelike sushi den, with low lighting, a view of the bustling streetscape and lots of healthy dining options from chef Yuth Knattangcome. You'll find usual appetizers like _edamame_ (green vegetable soybean)

Where's the Un-beef?

In a city with access to some of the freshest, most delicious produce in the country, you'd expect the vegetarian scene to be as hoppin' as it is in, say, San Francisco – or at least New York. But, unfortunately, you'd be wrong. Herbivores will definitely not go hungry. In fact, they're damn well catered for at any one of the many Middle Eastern or Asian (especially Thai and Chinese) eateries, and can, more often than not, find a veggie option on any menu. Still, don't expect to be overwhelmed by the amount of restaurants that make vegetarianism their philosophy. They do exist, however – though you will often have to go out of your way to get to them. The newest and most radical is **Tree of Zion** (p100) in Wynwood, where the food is at least vegan and at most raw. Then there are **Granny Feelgood's** (p100), a tiny café in Downtown Miami; **Honeytree** (Map p62; 5138 Biscayne Blvd), a small health-food store featuring a prepared-food deli counter; and, way up in Aventura, **Artichoke's** (p108), specializing in eclectic vegan dishes. If you'd rather just cook up your own tofu treats, hit the shelves at **Wild Oats Community Market** (Map pp248–9; 1020 Alton Rd) or **Whole Foods** (Map pp244–5; 21105 Biscayne Blvd), in Aventura.

and pork *gyoza* (fried dumpling), unusual sushi-bar specials such as Tiger's Eye (squid stuffed with salmon and asparagus) and Green Mussels Sakamushi (steamed green mussels with sake, served chilled with *ponzu* sauce), and fresh sushi and sashimi.

Cheap Eats
JIMMY'S EAST SIDE DINER

Map p251   *Diner*
☎ 305-754-3692; 7201 Biscayne Blvd; mains $5-9;
😊 breakfast & lunch

Come to Jimmy's, a classic greasy spoon, for big, cheap breakfasts of omelettes, pancakes or French toast, and for turkey clubs and burgers later in the day. It's 'your friendly neighborhood eatery,' and gay-friendly, too, judging by the big rainbow flag that hangs out front.

UVA 69 Map pp244-5   *Café*
☎ 305-754-9022; 6900 Biscayne Blvd; mains $4-9;
😊 breakfast & lunch

After cultivating so many fans with **Cane á Sucre** (p101), the owners recently branched out with this second outpost offering casual, outdoor seating and a menu that's similarly fresh and light but different in flavor. Try a breakfast burrito, roasted plum-tomato soup, cobb salad, pressed roast-beef sandwich or savory quiche of the day. It's also a wine bar, with a great choice of vinos by the glass.

LITTLE HAVANA

No longer strictly Cuban, Little Havana is the place to be for just about any sort of Latin cuisine, from Nicaraguan and Mexican to Spanish and Argentine. Though you'll have a major advantage if you speak Spanish or at least have a Spanish-English dictionary on hand, most places do offer English-language menus or at least have someone on staff who can help you translate before you order. For a different sort of big night out, plan a visit to one of the neighborhood's many supper clubs, where kitsch and cabaret come with the meal.

CASA JUANCHO Map p255   *Spanish*
☎ 305-446-4914; 2436 SW 8th St; mains $19-36;
😊 lunch, dinner & late night

A massive, upscale, traditional Spanish tavern that's a bit out of the bustling fray, this is the place to go for a special occasion or pull-out-all-the-stops evening. Join the festive mover-and-shaker crowd for updated takes on standards, including pan-seared salmon in creamy saffron-almond sauce, baby lamb chops and filet mignon stuffed with goat cheese and peppers. There's no shortage of tapas, Spanish wines, heavenly desserts – or entertainment, as balladeers stroll around and serenade you as you dine.

CASA PANZA Map p255   *Spanish*
☎ 305-643-5343; 1620 SW 8th St; mains $12-18;
😊 lunch, dinner & late night

Dark and cozy and more than a little kitschy, Casa Panza serves authentically prepared and presented dishes of Spain, along with live flamenco music and dance shows. Order a glass of sherry and start with *caldo gallego* (white-bean soup with pork sausage), graze all night on tapas like a *tortilla de patatas* (potato tortilla), *gambas al ajillo* (shrimp in garlic sauce) and *boquerones in vinagre* (fresh anchovies in vinaigrette). End your meal with the sweet and silky *crema catalana* (Spanish custard).

EL CRISTO Map p255   *Latin Diner*
☎ 305-261-2947; 1543 SW 8th St; mains $5-15;
😊 breakfast, lunch & dinner

A popular locals' hang, the down-to-earth El Cristo has options from all over the Spanish-speaking world. Try Argentine empanadas, Bolivian *salteñas* (beef or chicken pies), Galician soup, shrimp Creole or Cuban-style pork chops, strip steak or seafood casseroles. There is also a range of fruit shakes and juices, and cheap ($2.50) breakfasts of eggs, grits and potatoes.

LA CARRETA   *Cuban*
☎ 305-444-7501; 3632 SW 8th St; dishes $5-20;
😊 24hr

The original link in a Cuban chain, La Carreta features all the traditional Cuban dishes you'll find at **Versailles** (below). The decor is a little less glaring and in-your-face, though no less kitschy in its country-farmhouse way. Open around the clock, it's popular for *medianoches* (Cuban-style grilled ham-and-cheese sandwiches) and *café cubano*. If you just need a caffeine and sugar fix, order from the take-out window in the back.

VERSAILLES   *Cuban*
☎ 305-444-0240; 3555 SW 8th St; mains $8-15;
😊 breakfast, lunch, dinner & late night

Don't be fooled by the name; the cavernous and gaudy-glitzy Versailles (pronounced ver-sigh-yay) is not French but thoroughly Cuban, and a landmark to boot. The massive diner menu has plenty of solid choices – from plates of roast chicken with rice and beans to grilled fish with yucca – but the real reason worth making a trip here is the scene. It's a favorite with celebrating families, ladies who lunch, power-brokering businessmen, tourists and, in the wee hours, bug-eyed night-clubbers and showy drag queens. It's a trip to see all types eating in harmony. The adjoining bakery has little snacks, *mucho* pastries and shorter waits.

CHEAP EATS
CHIMICHURRI

Map p255   *Cuban & Argentine*
☎ 786-2878-3027; 1390 SW 8th St; mains $3-11;
☾ breakfast, lunch & dinner Mon-Sat
One of the newer stool-and-counter luncheonettes fronting Calle Ocho is this pan-Latin favorite, with various takes on the classic Cuban sandwich, Argentine steak and chicken dinners, plus big salads and hearty egg breakfasts.

EXQUISITO RESTAURANT Map p255 *Café*
☎ 305-643-0227; 1510 SW 8th St; dishes under $7;
☾ 7am-midnight
For cheap coffee, casual atmosphere and home-style food, this place is exquisite. Order any combination of steak, french fries, sausage, ham, eggs, toast and *café con leche* for under $4. The full breakfast *(desayuno)* will keep you going all day.

GUAYACAN Map p255   *Nicaraguan*
☎ 305-649-2015; 1933 SW 8th St; dishes $7-15;
☾ lunch & dinner
Nicaraguan meals served by friendly folks in a pleasantly homey atmosphere is what it's all about. Along with the hearty specialty soups, you could make a meal of the *antojitos* (snacks)

Top Five Little Havana Eats

- **Casa Juancho** (p103) is a no-holds-barred Spanish tavern.
- Sample Latin food from the world over at **El Cristo** (p103).
- No Little Havana jaunt is complete without a stop at **Versailles** (p103).
- Restaurant Crowds head to **Hy Vong Vietnamese** (right) for cheap, delicious fare.
- For rice-and-beans relief try the crepes and salads at **I Love Calle Ocho** (right).

---

such as *chorizo de cerdo* (pork sausages) and Nicaraguan tamales. You could also order the house special: *pescado a la Tipitapa* (whole red snapper, de-boned and deep fried, served with a zingy pepper-and-onion sauce). All specials come loaded with sides: salad, rice and beans, plantains, french fries, corn tortillas, bread.

HY VONG VIETNAMESE RESTAURANT   *Vietnamese*
☎ 305-446-3674; 3458 SW 8th; dishes $8-15;
☾ dinner Tue-Sun, closed mid–late Aug
Little Havana's culinary anomaly rocks Miami's food world. Hy Vong really does serve some of the best Vietnamese food in the USA. Favorites include *bun* – thin sliced meat with vermicelli – and the squid salad marinated in lime juice and onions. Most dishes are quite spicy and portions are generous. Just get to the tiny storefront eatery early; it may look like a dive, but it's no secret.

I LOVE CALLE OCHO Map p255   *Café*
☎ 305-643-3737; 1547 SW 8th St; dishes $5-12;
☾ breakfast & lunch
Can't take another plate of rice and beans? Check out this new little eclectic café, which has a range of menu items including bagels and omelettes for breakfast and fresh green salads, chicken-salad wraps, and a range of crepes (including the unique guava and cream cheese option) for lunch. A rainbow sticker on the door indicates that it's gay-friendly, a bit of a rare pronouncement in these parts.

ISLAS CANARIAS   *Cuban*
☎ 305-649-0440; 285 NW 27th Ave; dishes $8-10;
☾ breakfast, lunch & dinner
Many Cubans think Islas Canarias has Miami's best Cuban food. Bring a hearty appetite and order one of the daily specials, such as *ropa vieja* (shredded beef stew) or *bacalao* (salted codfish). It's located in a strip mall and the decor is strictly Formica, but the service is friendly.

TAQUERÍAS EL MEXICANO   *Mexican*
☎ 305-858-1160; 521 SW 8th St; dishes $5-10;
☾ 9am-11pm
This casual, friendly joint serves tasty and authentic Mexican food from enchiladas to *chilaquile*s – a breakfast dish that consists of tortilla chips simmered in green sauce mixed with scrambled eggs and covered with cheese and sour cream, served with rice and beans. Wash your dinner down with a Mexican beer like Bohemia or Negra Modelo.

KEY BISCAYNE

You won't be overwhelmed with options here (and probably not inspired enough to make a trip here just for eating) but after a long day in the sun or an afternoon of dolphin shows at the **Seaquarium** (p68), you will find plenty to please your palate. Sunset drinks and meals are particularly well provided for.

ARIA Map p259 *American*
☎ 305-365-4500; Ritz-Carlton, 455 Grand Bay Dr; mains $15-25; ☺ lunch & dinner

A lovely outdoor patio connected to a grand dining room and open kitchen give you plenty of seating options, while the high-end and creative menu will have you agonizing over which meal to choose. Braised veal cheeks with langoustines and rich lentil ragout, or warm lobster salad and asparagus 'cappuccino' soup? Whatever your pleasure, you can't really go wrong.

LE CROISIC Map p259 *French Bistro*
☎ 305-361-5888; 180 Crandon Blvd; dishes $10-20; ☺ dinner

This relatively new and cheery bistro actually *is* worth driving over the bridge for, say some Miami locals. Named after a region in Brittany that's known for its crepes, this cozy storefront is following suit with similar fare. In addition to juicy filet mignon and specials such as salmon in red-wine sauce you can get delicate crepes, with fillings from savory asparagus and parmesan to sweet chocolate and Calvados.

RUSTY PELICAN Map p259 *American*
☎ 305-361-3818; 3201 Rickenbacker Causeway; mains $10-20; ☺ lunch & dinner

More than the fare itself, it's the panoramic skyline views, among the best in Miami, that draw the faithful and romantic to this airy, tropical restaurant. If you do come for a drink, the fresh air could certainly seduce you into sampling the surf-and-turf menu, which is good enough, considering the setting and lack of options.

STEFANO'S Map p259 *Italian*
☎ 305-361-7007; 24 Crandon Blvd; mains $11-29; ☺ dinner

Surf-and-turf, pastas and good Italian specialties lead the menu, but Stefano's also has a wackiness about it that adds a whole other layer of flavor – if you don't mind hopping into a time machine and going back to the 1980s, courtesy of nightly time-warped DJs and a loyal older following. This place does have staying power.

Building a Cuban Sandwich

The traditional Cuban sandwich, also known as a *sandwich mixto*, is not some slapdash creation. It's a craft best left to the experts – but here's some insight on how they do it. Starting with the correct bread is crucial – it should be Cuban white bread: fresh, soft and easy to press (which comes at the end). The insides of the bread, both sides, should be buttered, then layered, in this order, with the main ingredients: sliced pickles, slices of roast Cuban pork, ham (preferably sweet-cured) and baby Swiss cheese. Then it all gets pressed in a very hot *plancha* (sandwich press) until the cheese melts. Mmmm!

CHEAP EATS

OASIS Map p259 *Cuban*
☎ 305-361-5709; 19 Harbor Dr; dishes $4-10; ☺ breakfast, lunch & dinner

From blue-collar workers to blue-blood politicians, socioeconomic barriers come tumbling down at this Cuban coffee oasis. More aptly described as a hole-in-the-wall with a take-out coffee window, Oasis serves cheap and delicious dishes such as sandwiches, paella and plates of roasted chicken. At least stop in for a 50c thimbleful of high-octane Cuban coffee.

COCONUT GROVE

Though it's become a tad chain-heavy, especially in the area around **CocoWalk** (p69), the Grove can still satisfy practically any culinary craving, from top-notch Indian to down-home Southern.

ANOKHA Map p258 *Indian*
☎ 786-552-1030; 3195 Commodore Plaza; mains $11-18; ☺ lunch & dinner

Touted as one of Miami's best Indian restaurants, this family-run phenom goes beyond excellent vindaloos, curries and tandooris with unique specials such as the shrimp cooked in mustard sauce and the chicken with spinach and cilantro. It's small in size but big in legend.

BERRIES RESTAURANT
Map p258 *American Creative*
☎ 305-448-2111; 2884 SW 27th Ave; dishes $11-20; ☺ lunch & dinner

Relying on a food-prep philosophy that leans on seasonal produce and fresh ingredients, the menu at this open-air café is brimming with clean-livin' options. Try the pan-fried crab cakes on a bed of greens, pumpkin-and-lobster ravioli, grilled mahimahi or sesame-crusted tofu with veggie, rice and cashews. Vegetarians are well cared for here.

LE BOUCHON DU GROVE
Map p258 *French*
☎ 305-448-6060; 3430 Main Hwy; mains $12-25; ☽ breakfast, lunch & dinner
The atmosphere here is authentic – tables crammed close together and walls laden with antique signs – and the staff is friendly and heavily accented. It's a cozy respite from the mall scene, and meal options, such as the beef filet in peppercorn sauce, light crepes or traditional onion soup are all scrumptious.

MR MOE'S
Map p258 *Southern Barbecue*
☎ 305-442-1114; 3131 Commodore Plaza; mains $6-20; ☽ lunch, dinner & late night
A Grove newcomer, this Southern-barbecue theme eatery features log swingsets at outdoor tables, and an interior, with taxidermy projects lining the walls, that feels like honest Abe's first home. Chow down on a range of big-food options, including pizzas, big burgers (with a buffalo-meat option), slow-smoked pork, barbecued baby back ribs or chicken, country fried steak or fat slabs of T-bone or New York strip. Things get rowdy after midnight, when crowds hang to throw down until 5am.

PAULO LUIGI'S Map p258 *Italian*
☎ 305-445-9000; 3324 Virginia St; mains $8-30; ☽ lunch & dinner
Practically obliterated by CocoWalk, this now-hidden, family-friendly Italian restaurant has been a local favorite since the mid-1970s. Why? It offers decent pizza and creative pasta

---

Top Five Coconut Grove & Coral Gables Eats

- For curry flavors and more, visit **Anokha** (p105).
- The fresh, seasonal cooking at **Berries Restaurant** (p105) will make you feel good.
- **Miss Saigon** (opposite) serves Vietnamese classics in style.
- **Norman's** is an institution (opposite).
- Go to the Caribbean at **Ortanique on the Mile** (opposite) – without leaving the mainland.

---

dishes for reasonable prices in a homey environment. It's no wonder it's here to stay.

SOMOTO Map p258 *Japanese*
☎ 305-448-9017; 3190 Commodore Plaza; mains $12-24; ☽ lunch & dinner Mon-Sat, dinner Sun
At the quiet end of the plaza, this tiny storefront is bursting with fresh sashimi and quirky sushi rolls, from the spider (soft-shell crab, masago, asparagus and scallion) to the kinky eel (salmon, crab, cream cheese, avocado and masago). Non-sushi items include *donburi* (rice bowls), noodle plates, teriyakis and tempura.

CHEAP EATS
DAILY BREAD MARKETPLACE Map p258
Middle Eastern
☎ 305-856-5893; 2400 SW 27th St; dishes $3-6; ☽ breakfast & lunch
Essentially a small grocery store with tables (a few outdoors), this family-run Middle Eastern deli has superb lentil soup, lamb kebabs, spanakopita, falafel and gyro sandwiches. Otherwise, assemble a picnic with olives, baba ghanoush, baklava and homemade pita bread.

GREEN STREET CAFE
Map p258 *American*
☎ 305-567-066; 3110 Commodore Plaza; mains $5-17; ☽ breakfast, lunch & dinner
A landmark-favorite, you can order anything from elaborate pastas and grilled fresh fish dishes to fresh salads and hearty breakfasts from its eclectic range of offerings. But it's people-watching that takes precedence, as crowds queue up round-the-clock to elbow their way to a coveted sidewalk table.

CORAL GABLES
You'll find that this community is a bit of a goldmine for foodies, as it boasts an ample supply of international, eclectic and high-end dining options. Many Coral Gables restaurants are clustered on or near 'Restaurant Row,' on Giralda Ave between Ponce de León Blvd and Le Jeune Rd, but that is far from the only game in town.

CAFFE ABBRACCI Map pp256-7 *Italian*
☎ 305-441-0700; 318 Aragon Ave; mains $14-24; ☽ lunch & dinner
Abbracci embraces you warmly from the time you make a reservation to the moment you're

walking out the door a satisfied customer. This dark, elegant and upscale eatery is decidedly trendy, but it serves some of the best northern Italian food in the city. Pastas are fresh, antipasto plentiful, veal a speciality and the tiramisu a delight. Following the crowd, in this case, is a smart idea.

MISS SAIGON BISTRO

Map pp256-7   *Vietnamese*

☎ 305-446-8006; 148 Giralda Ave; mains $12-18; ☻ lunch & dinner

Enjoy Vietnamese classics – *bun,* curries and summer rolls, for starters – in an elegant and festive yet relaxed atmosphere that packs 'em in and always has folks waiting. It's worth it.

NORMAN'S Map pp256-7   *International*

☎ 305-446-6767; 21 Almeria Ave; mains $20-40; ☻ dinner Mon-Sat

The word about chef-owner Norman Van Aken's restaurant – that it's the best restaurant in Miami and perhaps in southeastern USA – isn't hyperbole. If you're gong to splurge, this is the place to do it (just make sure you have a reservation). With gracious service, handsome surroundings, an open kitchen serving creative New World cuisine that fuses Caribbean, Asian, Latin and North American, Norman's delights the senses. Look for delectable dishes such as pecan-crusted Louisiana catfish with fried green tomatoes and mashed sweet potatoes. The wine pairing is exceptional.

ORTANIQUE ON THE MILE

Map pp256-7   *Caribbean*

☎ 305-446-7710; 278 Miracle Mile; mains $13-30; ☻ lunch & dinner Mon-Fri, dinner Sat & Sun

Named after a rare tropical fruit, this contemporary and upscale Caribbean restaurant puts an adventurous, French twist on standards, turning out lovingly prepared dishes such as chunky pumpkin soup, jerk foie gras and conch ceviche. It's both laid back and festive, and will bring you to an island getaway, at least in your mind and on your palate.

RESTAURANT ST MICHEL

Map pp256-7   *International*

☎ 305-446-6572; 162 Alcazar Ave; mains $10-30; ☻ lunch & dinner daily, brunch Sun

A romantic European storefront, you'll find low lighting, excellent service and eclectic international cuisine at this hotel bistro. The menu offers hearty and lighter dishes. Try the Australian

lamb, aged meats, wild game, sauteéd Florida Keys yellowtail with a citrus *beurre blanc* (butter sauce), or filet mignon in cabernet sauce with caramelized red-onion marmalade and chipotle mashed potatoes. The desserts are superb, too. Slip into the adjoining cocktail lounge for a postmeal glass of port.

THAI ORCHID Map pp256-7   *Thai*

☎ 305-443-6364; 317 Miracle Mile; lunch mains $10-18; ☻ lunch & dinner

Find excellent takes on pad Thai, red chicken curry, basil duck and sweet-and-sour fish, head to this popular and casual Thai palace, overlooking the bustling Mile.

CHEAP EATS
ALLEN'S DRUG STORE

Map pp256-7   *American*

☎ 305-665-6964; 4000 Red Rd; dishes $3-8; ☻ breakfast, lunch & dinner

For drugstore chic and retro cheesiness, Allen's boasts cheap and reliably good burgers, meatloaf, diner specials and a cool jukebox. Since the actual drugstore caters to elderly patrons, you'll be chowing down next to walkers and other paraphernalia that aid seniors.

ALTA TABERNA CARLO

Map pp256-7   *Spanish Tapas*

☎ 305-442-4525; 2312 Ponce de León Blvd; tapas $4-10; ☻ dinner & late night

Step into this brand-new tapas joint on the boulevard and you'll think you've landed in Barcelona. It's intimate and warm, with a big wood bar and small tables with stools, and the tapas menu has all your favorites, from tortillas and fried yucca to marinated octopus. Pair your nibbles with Spanish red wine and you'll have a lovely evening here, guaranteed.

LATIN AMERICAN   *American*

☎ 305-448-6809; 2940 Coral Way; dishes $3-8; ☻ breakfast, lunch & dinner

This down-home minichain has three locations. Here local Latins perch on stools around a massive, u-shaped counter, while families choose tables on the porch for big Sunday brunches. The food is straight-up Cuban – black beans, Cuban sandwiches, shredded steak – and the coffee, with milk served properly separated, is delicious. You'll find the other braches in **Coconut Grove** (Map p258; 2740 SW 27th Ave) and **Hialeah** (1750 W 68th St).

ELSEWHERE IN MIAMI

No, you've no shortage of options in the already-covered neighborhoods. But in case you're near any of these other spots, visiting your Aunt Helen at her gated community or feeling hungry after a visit to the **Museum of Contemporary Art** (p75) – or simply feel like taking a drive – here are just a few more suggestions.

NORTH

ARTICHOKE'S Map pp244-5 *Vegetarian*
☎ 305-945-7576; 3055 NE 163rd St; mains $15-25;
☺ dinner

Seems crazy to go this far for a restaurant dedicated to good herbivore grub, but that's Miami for you. The menu ranges from conservative dishes such as broccoli pasta and veggie burgers to more exciting options such as stuffed artichokes and macrobiotic tempeh plate.

CHEF ALLEN'S Map pp244-5 *American*
☎ 305-935-2900; 19,088 NE 29th Ave; mains $26-40;
☺ dinner

It's been more than 10 years since Chef Allen was dubbed 'Best American Chef' in the southeast by the esteemed James Beard Foundation, but legions of fans say he could've won every year since. Master of his universe (which clearly reaches far beyond this Aventura neighborhood), he reigns with New World-Floribbean cuisine, which pairs fresh local ingredients with tantalizing global flavors. A special trek here will reward you with a bellyful of memories.

HANNA'S GOURMET DINER
Map p251 *American*
☎ 305-947-2255; 13,951 Biscayne Blvd; mains $26-40;
☺ brunch, lunch & dinner

A very eclectic take on classic diner fare, Hanna serves up specialities such as grilled snapper, rack of lamb and chicken chaseur (in a wine and mushroom sauce) on interesting silver railroad-track-like structures that stand in for plates. Don't miss her fruit tarts, worth a trip all on their own. Sunday brunches are popular and delicious, sans the South Beach crush.

NORTH 110 Map p251 *American*
☎ 305-893-4211; 1152 Biscayne Blvd; mains $17-25;
☺ dinner

New in mid-2004, the creative American fare here keeps all tastes in mind. Grilled local fish, salads that explode with flavor and even a vegetarian option that incorporates grilled tofu are all well executed. A good wine list and scrumptious desserts top you off nicely.

SOUTH

SHORTY'S BBQ Map pp244-5 *American*
☎ 305-670-7732; 9200 S Dixie Hwy; dishes $6-16;
☺ lunch & dinner

This South Dade institution has been famous since the early '50s, long before deco became de rigueur, and will probably still be dishing out sweet baby back ribs, corn, barbecued spare ribs and tender chicken on its picnic tables long after the vibe settles over South Beach. Look for another branch at **11575 SW 40th St** (Map pp244-5; ☎ 305-227-3196) when you're heading back into the city from the Everglades.

Miami's Neuvo Latino (p95) cuisine has its own take on seafood

Nightlife

Nightlife

Miami is a city that comes alive at night. And that's not only because of its shimmering skyline and neon-kissed deco facades, but because it's a city that knows its audience – fun-loving, pleasure-seeking creatures of the night. Fittingly, Miami Beach, with clubs and lounges that take decor to a high-art level and attract scores of celebs in the process, is one of the most stylish nightclub spots in the country – and parts of mainland Miami are catching up fast. But going out at night doesn't always mean drinking and dancing. Whether you prefer hard-rock or symphonies, you'll find that Miami really is a sound machine, and host to a growing clutch of musical talents. The same goes for the rich worlds of local theater and dance – valued so highly, along with music, that the city has been throwing money at a long-time-coming **Performing Arts Center** (p121), which folks are banking on to turn around grungy Downtown. So pick your poison – martinis on the bay or soliloquies in the Grove or anything in between. Chances are high that you'll find exactly what you're looking for.

DRINKING

Cocktails and Miami vacations go hand in hand – and hotels and restaurants clearly know this, as they bend over backward to entice sippers with gimmicks such as neon bars, long lists of 'specialty' cocktails, two-for-one hours and extras such as poolside drink service, outdoor beds to sprawl across and lounges bathed in flowing, gossamer fabrics. Whatever your scene, you'll find it in one of the endless lounges, hotel lobbies, pubs and dives. But cool your jets, college freshmen: the drinking age, 21, is strictly enforced in Florida. Most bars stay open till at least 2am, some until 4am or 5am.

HOTELS

BAHIA Map pp252-3
☎ 305-358-3535; Four Seasons Hotel, 1435 Brickell Ave, Downtown
Perched high up on the 7th floor of the **Four Seasons Miami** (p160), this Downtown terrace bar is hip enough to lure a South Beach crowd – at least on Fridays. The alfresco bar and lounge, on the edge of the pool area and edged by a light-up waterfall wall, draws a sexy Latino crowd with its tasty *mojitos* (Cuban rum-based cocktails), beers from Argentina and the Dominican Republic and occasional live Cuban bands.

BOND STREET LOUNGE Map pp246-7
☎ 305-398-1806; Townhouse Hotel, 150 20th St, South Beach
After the sushi eaters go home, a new crowd rolls in – one that prefers litchitinis over yellowtail. Throw yourself over a white couch or cylindrical white ottoman and order up, then sip. You may be in a hotel's basement, but this sleek hangout is no rec room.

CIRCA 39 Map pp251
☎ 305-538-3900, 3900 Collins Ave, Mid-Beach
Tucked off to the back of this new hotel's moody front lobby, its bar has a very warm, welcoming feel to it. Definitely stop in for a cosmopolitan if you're up this way, before sauntering across the street and checking out the nighttime ocean.

CLEVELANDER BAR Map pp248-9
☎ 305-531-3485; Clevelander Hotel, 1020 Ocean Dr, South Beach
This open-air glass and neon bar, adjacent to a wet T-shirt kind of pool and overlooking the Ocean Dr tourist parade, is a crowded, tropical-drink-guzzling, Spring Break sort of scene where hard drinking begins way before the sun goes down. So is the inside sports bar, which is just a bit more muted because of the lack of air.

CHESTERFIELD HOTEL Map pp248-9
☎ 305-531-5831; 855 Collins Ave, South Beach
The small lobby of this hotel relies on the same formula as other South Beach Group hotels – a free happy hour (for guests) of a specific cocktail that changes nightly, and a mellow hangout for passers-by who like lobby life. This bar has a striped-animal, safari kind of look.

HOTEL ASTOR Map pp248-9
☎ 305-531-8081; 956 Washington Ave, South Beach
The side patio, alfresco lounge of this classy inn has become so popular with Saturday-night

Top Five Hotel Bars

- The **Bahia** (opposite) is sky high.
- Visit the **Rose Bar** (right) and join the swanky, sipping beauties.
- Sip martinis while gazing out over Biscayne Bay at the Mandarin Oriental's **M Bar** (below).
- The **Raleigh Hotel** (right) is classy, handsome and intimate.
- Choose between Moroccan-themed al fresco lounging or red-bathed hip-hop posing at **Skybar** (right).

clubbers that management has indefinitely covered over the property's pool in order to make room for the revelers. It's a swank yet intimate spot to imbibe.

HOTEL CHELSEA Map pp248-9

☎ 305-534-4069; 944 Washington Ave, South Beach
This is a quiet, dark little den with a sleek black bar and one long banquette. You'll find hotel guests drinking free happy-hour cocktails early in the evening, followed by mellow locals who like the live DJs and friendly 'tenders.

HOTEL PLACE ST MICHEL Map pp256-7

☎ 305-444-1666; 162 Alcazar Ave, Coral Gables
Located on a quiet street in Coral Gables and attached to the very European, antique-filled boutique hotel, this lounge is the kind of place where you'd find a cigar-chomping sugar daddy buying rounds for his young lady as sophisticated hotel guests and quiet-seeking locals bend elbows nearby. It's hushed, unsleek and friendly.

M BAR Map pp252-3

☎ 305-913-8288, Mandarin Oriental, 500 Brickell Key Dr, Downtown
The high-class lobby bar here may be tiny, but its martini menu – over 250 strong – really isn't. And neither is the sweeping view, high up over shimmering Biscayne Bay.

MARLIN HOTEL Map pp248-9

☎ 305-604-5000; 1200 Collins Ave, South Beach
Island Records founder and former Marlin owner Chris Blackwell may have moved on from this favorite hotel, but the beautiful bar, bathed as heavily as ever in futuristic steel decor, is as hot as ever. Enjoy strong martinis, DJs and an atmosphere that's *trés* chic indeed.

NOIR Map pp252-3

☎ 305-503-6500; Conrad Hotel, 1395 Brickell Ave, Downtown
On the 18th floor of this sleek downtown high-rise you'll find this new beauty. It's a dark and sexy lounge, all black except for splashes of orange and red, which come courtesy of the geometric candles perched on low coffee tables and along the bar. Be sure to saunter out into the lobby after a few drinks, where you can peer out over the bay and into the night sky through one of two high-powered telescopes.

RALEIGH HOTEL Map pp246-7

☎ 305-534-6300; 1775 Collins Ave, South Beach
Martinis are the drink of choice in this intimate little bar that has a handsome, old-world charm and sits just off the landmark deco lobby.

ROSE BAR AT THE DELANO Map pp246-7

☎ 305-672-2000; Delano Hotel, 1685 Collins Ave, South Beach
The ultrachic Rose Bar at this elegant Ian Schrager original is a watering hole for beautiful creatures (or at least those with a healthy ego). Get ready to pay up for the privilege – but also prepare to enjoy it. The setting is an absolute stunner.

SAGAMORE Map pp246-7

☎ 305-535-8088; 1671 Collins Ave, South Beach
The small lobby bar is like the elegant iceberg of this white and shiny space, which doubles as an impressive art gallery. But the service is quite warm. It's a good and quiet respite from the madness at the **Delano Hotel** (p155) next door.

SKYBAR Map pp246-7

☎ 305-695-3900; Shore Club, 1901 Collins Ave, South Beach
This three-part stunner – and current fave among the most beautiful, most fabulous, most A-list hipsters in South Beach – is a bit full of itself. However, if you're lucky enough to get granted entrance past the velvet rope, you'll soon see why: a massive alfresco lounge and lush, upstairs garden is overflowing with delicious Moroccan cushions, firm beds and billowing curtains, while the inside Red Room has a more dancey, hip-hop posture.

STANDARD Map pp244-5

☎ 305-673-1717; 40 Island Ave, South Beach/Downtown
Not quite open yet at press time, this high-style bar and lounge brings respite and

Nightlife – Drinking

Shaken or Stirred?

Miami bars serve the standard cocktails you'd find anywhere. But the specialities are quirky and colorful tropical concoctions, often made with fresh fruit juice, muddled berries or chopped herbs – and top-shelf liquors, of course. Expect a fancy glass, a precious garnish and a big sticker price. Most bartenders have a signature drink; be sure to ask for a suggestion if you're up for a tasting adventure.

Many of the usual Miami drinks are Latin-infused – you could sample, perhaps, a Cuba Libre, rum with Coke and a splash of lime, served on the rocks; or a daiquiri, made with rum, lime and sugar, flavored with anything from mango to strawberry, and served on the rocks or frozen (beware of brain freeze). Margaritas, made with tequila, triple sec and fresh lime juice, can also be flavored (prickly pear, pineapple, papaya) and served on the rocks or frozen. A *mojito* (Cuban rum-based cocktail) is a very popular Cuban drink made with rum, club soda, lime juice and fresh mint leaves muddled with sugar, while the similar *caipirinha*, from Brazil, is a mix of *cachaça* (a Brazilian liquor similar to rum), fresh lime juice and sugar, served on the rocks. But the reigning elixir is still the martini – either a classic, made of chilled vermouth and vodka or gin, topped with an olive or lemon twist, or one of the many flavored versions, such as the cosmopolitan (with cranberry and grapefruit juices) or the Asian-themed litchitini (with litchi-nut juice). To sample to your heart's content, pay a visit to **M Bar** (p111), where the bar menu boasts more than 250 martini versions.

good-natured fun to the folks who stay here for the yoga, massages and various healing rituals. It may be a spa hotel, but it's not an alcohol-free one. Everyone appreciates that – especially, in fact, nonguests, who now have a perfectly good excuse to come and gaze upon the beautiful new hotel and its stunning waterfront locale.

BARS & PUBS

ABBEY BREWERY Map pp246-7
☎ 305-538-8110; 1115 16th St, South Beach
Abbey Brewery makes really good beer, including Abbey Brown, Oatmeal Stout, Porter Christmas and India Pale Ale (all are $4.25 a pint). But it also has some dozen more beers on tap and a little pub grub. Its atmosphere is unpretentious and relaxed.

BOY BAR Map pp251
☎ 305-864-2697; 1220 Normandy Dr (71st St),
Mid-Beach
The newest gay bar in town, from the owner of Score (p116) on Lincoln Rd, is this small little bare-bones watering hole. It's a friendly neighborhood type of place, complete with a pool table, cute bartenders and a festive back-patio area that's surrounded by hedges.

IRISH HOUSE BAR & GRILL Map p50
☎ 305-534-5667; 1430 Alton Rd, South Beach
This comfy bar is a local fave, featuring half-price weekday happy hours, cheap pitchers, pool tables, video games, dart boards and a jukebox. Definitely not your usual South Beach haunt.

MAC'S CLUB DEUCE BAR Map p50
☎ 305-673-9537; 222 14th St, South Beach
The oldest bar in Miami Beach (established in 1926), the Deuce is a real neighborhood bar and hype-free zone. It's just straight-up seediness, which, depending on your outlook, can actually be quite refreshing. Plan to see everyone from transgendered ladies to construction workers and hipsters to bikers.

SEVEN SEAS
☎ 305-266-6071; 2200 SW 57th Ave, Coral Gables
This funky, wood-paneled watering hole, designed to look like a sailors' haven, is a magnet for everyone from blue-collar regulars and old men to pool sharks and plain ol' beer drinkers. Enjoy the backyard patio, stack of three televisions (all tuned to something different) and bric-a-brac decor, which includes a suit of armor and women's shoes hanging from the ceiling.

TOBACCO ROAD Map pp252-3
☎ 305-374-1198; 626 S Miami Ave, Downtown
Miami's oldest bar has been on the scene since the 1920s. Though it's primarily loved for being a blues and jazz joint, it offers a generous happy hour and a complete cast of characters with which to share a pint, music or not.

LOUNGES

BED Map pp248-9
☎ 305-532-9070; 929 Washington Ave, South Beach;
🕑 Wed-Sun
In addition to serving some of the most succulent gourmet meals around (p91), BED is

far from sleepy once dinner hour ends. Everything but dancing is done here while comfortably ensconced on an actual bed, so take off your shoes and stay a while. The DJs, highly watchable crowd and occasional floor shows will have you lazing about for hours.

BUCK 15 Map pp246-7
☎ 305-538-3815; 707 Lincoln Ln (upstairs from Miss Yip), South Beach
Opened by the owner of **Miss Yip**, p95), this upstairs lounge differs from anything else you'll find in South Beach – maybe even the whole of Miami. It feels more Brooklyn-hipster, actually, with its spread of couches and low tables, rotating DJs and live bands, and its cool graffiti-art murals and a quirky display of pieces from Jennie Yip's Japanese-toy collection.

CAFETERIA Map pp246-7
☎ 305-672-3663; 546 Lincoln Rd, South Beach
This slick eatery (p95) likes to serve up healthy portions of lounging and DJ beats along with its mac 'n' cheese. Plot a course onto one of the odd egg-shaped chairs or do a little dancing; especially popular are Open House Fridays and Intimate Saturdays (with complimentary drinks from 10pm to 11pm), with rotating DJs.

FAVELA CHIC Map pp251
☎ 305-861-6707; 928 71st St, Mid-Beach
This Brazilian party in Normandy Isle is a restaurant and lounge that fuels its rhythmic patrons with strong *caipirinhas* (a Brazilian rumlike cocktail) and a potent mix of house, samba, salsa and hip-hop from the DJ owner.

GRASS RESTAURANT & LOUNGE Map pp254
☎ 305-573-3355; www.grasslounge.com; 28 NE 40th St, Design District; ☽ Tue-Sat
This Design District restaurant-cum-lounge is a special space indeed – intimate, yet alfresco, and thus open to all the heavens. Dress your best and head to the velvet-roped entrance. Inside, you can either dine on cool Asian-fusion dishes (p101) or simply posture and dance and watch the door (like everyone else here).

PEARL RESTAURANT & CHAMPAGNE LOUNGE Map p250
☎ 305-538-1111; www.penrods.com; 1 Ocean Dr, South Beach; ☽ 7pm-5am
The ultramod lounge, bathed in an otherworldly orange glow, caters to those who favor bubbly and caviar over beer and chips. Recline

in fur-trimmed chairs and enjoy the mellow sounds of various DJs. See also p90 for details on the food served here.

SOFI LOUNGE Map pp250
☎ 305-532-4444; www.sofilounge.com; 423 Washington Ave, South Beach
Not long after its arrival, the Sofi Lounge was touted in a *Miami Herald* article as being 'an oasis for skateboarders, surfers, models, club promoters and others disenchanted with the increasingly glutted and pretentious South Beach club scene.' So if you count yourself among them, head here – a dark and narrow space with DJs, live music and special events.

TANTRA Map pp248-9
☎ 305-672-4765; www.tantrarestaurant.com; 1445 Pennsylvania Ave, South Beach
This exotic restaurant (p93) is one of those eatery-nightlife blends, where guest DJs spin music to complement the sensual, candlelit ambience and aphrodisiac cocktails.

BILLIARDS & BOWLING

FELT Map pp248-9
☎ 305-531-2114; 1242 Washington Ave, South Beach
Boasting 10 pool tables is one way to stand out from the crowd in these parts, and it seems to be working. Grab a drink and a cue and enjoy the come-one-come-all attitude here.

LAUNDRY BAR Map pp246-7
☎ 305-531-7700; www.laundrybar.com; 721 Lincoln Ln N, South Beach
This bar/billiards parlor/coin laundromat is a hoot. As they say, 'get sloshed while you wash.' The place has a decidedly gay vibe, but it's relaxed and welcomes all. In addition to two-for-one drinks daily until 9pm, this cool place offers nightly specials and themes, including discounted laundry services on Tuesdays.

STRIKE MIAMI Map pp244-5
☎ 305-594-0200; www.strikemiami.com; Dolphin Mall, 11401 NW 12th St, Greater Miami; per game $23-30
This brand-new, 37,000-sq-ft space is a lot more than a place to throw strikes. In addition to its 34-lane bowling alley (which ends at a massive, and distracting, video wall), it's got three bars, a multimedia sports bar, private VIP rooms and Cuban cuisine. So play a couple of games – or not – and then take in the swirling scene.

CLUBBING

There are few things you can count on in life – and the state of clubs in Miami is certainly not one of them. Like in most cosmopolitan cities, what's cool one week does not mean it's what will be cool (or even open) the next. It's not for lack of trying, though. Club promoters cater to celebs, hoping that their regal presence will draw the media, and that the hipster crowds will follow. But Britney and J Lo and Usher get bored, too, and they will all eventually move on, taking the followers with them.

Still, one thing that's constant is the sheer number of options, as well as the range of scenes. You'll find hip-hop mobs, electronica soirees, rock bashes and sultry lounges, most serving a mixed gay-and-lesbian crowd but many also catering to a predominantly gay-only scene (we'll note which is which below). Though our listings represent the hottest parties as of press time, we urge you to do some follow-up research when you arrive: talk to friends, your concierge and, most importantly, pick up a copy of one of the local arts weeklies, namely *Miami New Times* or *Street News*, or a free monthly like *Miami Living Magazine* or the pint-sized *Ego Miami Magazine*. Also note that partying here comes with a price – a door charge that's usually at least $20, though all vary slightly.

TAT THE BOULEVARD Map pp251
☎ 305-756-7770; www.boulevardnightclub.com; 7770 Biscayne Blvd, North Miami
Before the arrival of Boulevard – which, to the delight of the neighborhood, took over the space of a former XXX theater at the end of 2004 – most of the serious gay party boys in town made the drive to Fort Lauderdale, where **Coliseum** (p213) offered the best fun within a 60-mile radius. Now they've got this place, located in an area known as the Upper East Side. Though it's not quite glitzy or exclusive enough for a true Circuit-boy crowd (it's a bit gritty and hustler-ish for that), it's got a fun vibe, plenty of go-go boys, occasional drags shows and an elegant smoking patio out front. It's definitely not lesbian-friendly, though, as evidenced by the lack of doors on the toilet stalls.

CROBAR Map pp248-9
☎ 305-531-5027; www.crobarmiami.com; 1445 Washington Ave, South Beach; cover $25; ☾ Thu-Sun
This South Beach version of the three-city megaclub (there are also Crobars in Chicago and New York) is housed in the renovated art-deco Cameo Theatre. Now the massive, carpeted dance floor gets mobbed with some of the most hardcore scenesters in town. Sunday night's mostly-gay Backdoor Bambi party is as quirky and eclectic as it gets.

I/O Map pp252-3
☎ 305-358-8007; www.iolounge.com; 30 NE 14th St, Downtown
Britpop nights and a loyal, international following has made this downtown joint the indie-alternative of choice for anyone turned off by the wannabes who flock to South Beach. There's plenty of space for lounging, sipping and listening, both to DJs and occasional Latin, electronica and rock bands.

JAZID Map pp248-9
☎ 305-673-9372; 1342 Washington Ave, South Beach
While the downstairs caters to folks seeking a mellow, candlelit spot to hear live jazz, soul

LGBT Nightlife

It was gay men, many will claim, who truly put the new South Beach on the map. But, though they still have a massive presence here, it's become a bit watered down of late, as the boys, always on a quest for the next cool thing, have relocated to other, more up-and-coming parts of Miami: Morningside, the Upper East Side, Wynwood, North Miami. Many still come to party, though, as evidenced by the always-swarming clubs **Score** (p116), **Laundry Bar** (p113) and **Twist** (p116), and the roving gay nights that pack places such as **Mansion** (opposite), **Crobar** (above) and **Jade Lounge** (Map pp246–7; ☎ 305-695-0000; 1766 Bay Rd, South Beach), which has a popular Euphoria Fridays bash. New spots keep popping up, too, namely **At the Boulevard** (above) and **Boy Bar** (p112), which have had no trouble at all finding audiences.

Lesbians, though, should take note: since Ingrid Cesares made her Sapphic mark with Liquid in the '90s, there hasn't been a visible lesbian in the nightlife world. There is not a single bar or club dedicated to lesbians and, at press time, just one ongoing party – the L-Lounge, Thursdays at **Six2Six** (Map pp246–7; 626 Lincoln Rd, South Beach), which attracts a glammy, LA-type – though it could have ended by now. Come to town in November during **White Party Week** (p19) or in May for **Aqua Girl Weekend** (p117) though, and you'll have endless lesbionic action to choose from.

For up-to-date club and event listings, check out the weekly *Express* or *Wire* newspapers.

and funk bands, the upstairs lounge has DJs spinning soul, funk and hip-hop to a cool, multiculti crowd. By being cool and not trying to be, this place has remained popular while places all around it have come and gone.

MANSION Map pp248-9
☎ 305-532-1525; www.mansionmiami.com; 1235 Washington Ave, South Beach
The newest megaclub addition, from the owners of **Opium Garden & Privé** (below), is awash in elegance, with ceiling murals, red velvet couches, dark-wood bars, leather club chairs and a blend of massive and intimate spaces to move among. Too bad its typical crowd – guys in baggy pants – isn't as classy. Come late on a weekend for a spiffier, even celeb-laced, scene. Sundays host the popular gay party Anthem, formerly held at **Crobar** (opposite).

MYNT Map pp246-7
☎ 786-276-6132; 1921 Collins Ave, South Beach
Join (or at least try to join) the celebrities who favor this mint-green, mint-scented space – Justin Timberlake, Vin Diesel, Britney Spears and plenty of others. Once you're in, order a *mojito* and try not to go green with envy while drinking in all the beautiful people.

NIKKI BEACH MIAMI Map pp250
☎ 305-538-1111; www.penrods.com; 1 Ocean Dr, South Beach
Shenanigans along this exclusive stretch of sand include open-air movie screenings, thong-clad partiers, outdoor beds for lounging and seaside teepees for snuggling (or whatever). Various DJs and themes, such as bonfires and free bubbly, keep everyone interested.

OPIUM GARDEN & PRIVÉ Map pp250
☎ 305-531-5535; 136 Collins Ave, South Beach
This outdoor garden and its 2nd-floor A-list counterpart, Privé, are not for the faint-of-ego. Crowds clamor at the velvet ropes as if they were starving folks at a bread line, and act cool as cucumbers once they make it in. The only night that really brings in the big names, though, is Friday; Thursdays are especially wannabe-ish. The DJ sound tends to be hip-hop heavy, and the sound system is surprisingly muddled.

OXYGEN LOUNGE Map p258
☎ 305-476-0202; Streets of Mayfair, 2911 Grand Ave, Coconut Grove
This is the mall underground – literally – of Coconut Grove. It's a rather elegant, sprawling

Top Five Nightclubs
- When the freaks come out at night, they congregate at **Crobar** (opposite).
- The **Mansion** (left) is a sumptuous space with a rotating vibe.
- For sleazy-chic, sample the **Pawn Shop** (below) in the Design District.
- Cruise and booze at **Score** (p116), right on Lincoln Rd.
- **Space** (p116) is a megaclub that lives up to its name.

club and lounge that doubles as sushi restaurant. Mondays are for hip-hop, Thursdays and Fridays for Latin sounds and, though the place gets points for having a gay night on Sundays, it loses them for dubbing it 'alternative-lifestyle night.' Please get with it, people.

PAWN SHOP Map pp252-3
☎ 305-373-3511; www.thepawnshoplounge.com; 1222 NE 2nd Ave, Downtown
Home of the popular Revolver party on Fridays, this new den of hipness still has its original pawn shop facade, with signs announcing 'We buy diamonds' and 'We buy gold.' It's all about true (but glamorous) grit here – and

Nikki Beach Miami (left), South Beach

'I'm on the list'

It's all a bit high school, trying to gain nightclub entry. You don your coolest outfit, do your hair and approach the crowd with a collection of your hippest pals. And then you do whatever you need to do – change your personality, show a little skin, shed every ounce of self-respect – to get the popular football player (or the mean and handsome doorman, rather) to like you. Sound like fun? Then here are some tips to make your acceptance a bit less of a struggle:

- **Be polite** Don't be skittish, but don't act like you're J Lo, either. And whatever you do, don't yell at the doorman – or touch him or yank on his clothing – to try to get his attention. And for heaven's sake, don't dare touch the velvet rope.
- **Try to get yourself guest-listed** Ask the concierge at your hotel to help you out, or simply call the club and leave your name; it's often this simple.
- **Remain confidently aloof** Instead of watching the doorman with pleading eyes, look elsewhere – but look hot doing it. Make him wonder who you are.
- **Be aggressive** If there's a clamoring crowd, standing at the back of it and hoping it'll soon part is about as effective as being meek when you need a seat on the New York subway. Push your way through to the front.
- **Dress correctly** Look hip and hot – but not slutty. For women, showing a teasing, sophisticated amount of skin is effective.
- **Get there early** Do you want to be cool, or do you want to get in? Hitting up the doorman when he's bored is always a good strategy.
- **Don't name drop** No one will be impressed. Plus, people who really know Sam the manager wouldn't need to be clamoring with the masses.
- **If you're a man, bring a woman** A man alone is not worth much (unless you're at a gay club, natch); up your value by having a beautiful woman – or two or three – on your arm.

varying DJs who spin funky, edgy electronica. The club's concept is the brainchild of nightlife vet Kurt VanNostrand, formerly of **Bed** (p112) and other hotspots.

RUMI Map pp246-7
☎ 305-672-4353; 330 Lincoln Rd, South Beach
Named for the 13th-century Sufi mystic whose poetry is currently in vogue (one can only cringe at the idea of what he'd think of it all), Rumi is like a scene out of *Arabian Nights*. Its numerous dining rooms (p93), decorated in dark, rich red and earth tones, are transformed into intimate lounges and dance areas by midnight.

SCORE Map pp246-7
☎ 305-535-1111; 727 Lincoln Rd, South Beach
It's hard not to stare when you saunter by this place – but only because all the men who drape themselves at tables at its outdoor lounge are so damn gorgeous. Go inside for the best time, though. The only gay club that's right on Lincoln Rd, Score is a multilevel affair with drinking, dancing and everything in between.

SOHO LOUNGE Map pp254
☎ 305-576-1988; 175 NE 36th St, Design District
Located in the heart of the Design District, Soho is the antithesis of the nearby **Grass Lounge** (p113). Here it's all about electronica, indie-cool and '80s worship – especially by folks

too young to even remember how much the decade sucked.

SPACE Map pp252-3
☎ 305-375-0001; www.clubspace.com; 142 NE 11th St, Downtown
This multilevel warehouse is one of the current late-night/early-morning clubs of choice. With 30,000 sq ft to fill, dancers have room to strut their stuff. An around-the-clock liquor license redefines the concept of after-hours. DJs usually pump each floor with a different sound – hip-hop, Latin, heavy trance – while the infamous rooftop lounge is the place to be for sunrise. Theme nights vary, with a gay night taking over most Sundays.

TWIST Map pp248-9
☎ 305-538-9478; 1057 Washington Ave, South Beach
Never a cover, always a groove. This two-story gay hangout has serious staying power and a little bit of something for everyone: six different bars, including a rooftop patio; go-go dancers; drag shows; lounging areas; and a small dance floor.

LIVE MUSIC

When most people think about the live-music scene in Miami, they'll start hearing one of two sounds: Latin or hip-hop. And while it's true that these are still the beats that rule this town, there's much more than that going on here. Electronica rules at more and more Design District and downtown clubs, lovely jazz spots are not hard to find, and an exploding indie-rock scene in recent years has infused music venues and their fans with a real sense of on-the-verge excitement.

JAZZ & BLUES

JAZID Map pp248-9
☎ 305-673-9372; 1342 Washington Ave, South Beach
While the upstairs lounge relies on DJs for its following, the candlelit downstairs gets its own fans with quality jazz, soul and funk bands. It's very un-South Beach (in the best of ways).

LES DEUX FONTAINES Map pp248-9
☎ 305-672-7878; www.lesdeuxfontaines.com; 1230 Ocean Dr, South Beach
This lively French restaurant and bar offers nightly jazz, Dixieland and swing that'll make you feel like you've landed in New Orleans.

TOBACCO ROAD Map pp252-3
☎ 305-374-1198; www.tobacco-road.com; 626 S Miami Ave, Downtown
This venerable 1912 bar and live-music venue presents loud and gritty blues, jazz and jam bands nightly.

VAN DYKE CAFÉ Map pp246-7
☎ 305-534-3600; www.thevandyke.com; 846 Lincoln Rd, South Beach; cover $5
Local and nationally known jazz musicians play to a sophisticated crowd nightly in this intimate 2nd-floor restaurant lounge overlooking the jumpin' Lincoln Road Mall. See also p96.

WALLFLOWER GALLERY Map pp252-3
☎ 305-579-0069; www.wallflowergallery.com; 10 NE 3rd St, Downtown
This gallery hosts an eclectic lineup, from the pop stylings of The Avenging Lawnmowers of Justice to the jazzy Gabe Nixon Band.

LATIN

BONGOS CUBAN CAFÉ Map pp252-3
☎ 786-777-2100; www.bongoscubancafé.com; 601 Biscayne Blvd, Downtown; cover $10-20
Gloria and Emilio Estefan's Disneyfied Cuban restaurant and salsa club, set under a massive pineapple motif on the edge of the Biscayne Bay, gives a lively and popular show to a packed house that makes good use of the expansive dance floor.

CASA PANZA Map pp255
☎ 305-643-5343; 1620 SW 8th St, Little Havana
This atmospheric Spanish taverna (p103) hosts lively and popular flamenco music and dance

Circuit City

One of the many subcultures of gay life is the circuit scene – a nonstop series of massive, decadent, drug- and DJ-fueled dance parties that bring hordes of beautiful, shirtless men to cities including Philadelphia, New York, Montreal and Ibiza for colorfully named soirees such as the Blue Ball, the Black Party and the Red Party. Miami, of course, is one of these three-ring-circuit destinations – once in November, for the **White Party** (p19), again in March, for the **Winter Party Week** (p18), and yet again in May, when one of the country's rare lesbian soirees, Aqua Girl Weekend, comes to town.

The White Party is a lavish 10-day spectacle held at **Vizcaya Museum & Gardens** (p70), which brings in upwards of 10,000 people who party with a purpose: to raise money for Care Resource, South Florida's oldest and largest HIV/AIDS service organization. Now in its 25th year, it's gained a reputation within some circles for being a bit 'old-school', but while it does not have quite the same cache as the Winter Party, it certainly has no problem drawing a crowd.

Many of the White Party's events, held at various local venues, are specifically geared to women – a welcome treat for lesbians in a city whose gay scene is heavily skewed to the boys. Which makes **Aqua Girl Weekend** (www.aquagirl .org) a hot event, too. Now in its sixth year, the weekend also benefits the Women's Community Fund, a South Florida organization for LGBT (lesbian, gay, bisexual and transgender) women; it features a slew of cocktail soirees, dance parties, performances and sporting events that draw more than 2000 women to various venues around Miami.

The hipper-than-thou Winter Party Festival, meanwhile, is the main event for well-sculpted, well-heeled men from around the globe. It features top circuit DJs, the Miami Light Project show, tea dances, film festivals and on-the-beach dance blowouts held under dramatically billowing scrims, with the sea creating the perfect background scene. This party, which benefits various LGBT organizations around Miami-Dade as well as the National Lesbian and Gay Task Force, draws about 5000 men, most of whom stay in South Beach and transform the seaside community into a gay-male paradise that rivals scenes of Greek-god mythologies. Whichever party is your scene, you won't be disappointed.

Winter Music Conference

Anyone who's anyone in the dance-music industry, from DJs to promoters to straight-up fans, can be found in Miami come the end of March. That's when the **Winter Music Conference** (WMC; p17) comes to town, bringing with it dance parties, performances, seminars, workshops and the International Dance Music Awards ceremony for the attending crowd of about 40,000 enthusiasts and professionals from all over the globe. Now in its 21st year and stationed in South Beach, the WMC has something for everyone who loves music you can move to. There are networking parties for DJs who want to share tips about the latest sounds, showcases for DJs who want to strut their spinning stuff, seminars on marketing strategies and artist management, workshops on new-media technology and parties galore for folks who just want to get their groove on. Some say the WMC is all about the parties and not much else, others go for some serious learning. Either way, do stay out of Miami if none of this is of any interest to you, because the conference is a really big deal – and an extremely crowded affair.

Nightlife – Live Music

shows, including mellow Spanish guitarists on weekends. If you are so inspired, you too can dance around dinner tables with the other patrons.

CLUB TROPIGALA Map pp251
☎ 305-541-2631; 4441 Collins Ave, Mid-Beach; cover $25
The Fontainebleau Hotel houses this '50s era, kitschy Cubano supper club (think: Desi Arnaz), which features highly-produced dance shows that cater to tourists nightly.

GIL'S CAFÉ Map p251
☎ 305-867-0779; 216 71st St, Mid-Beach; cover after 8pm $5
Live Brazilian jazz, R&B, Latin, reggae and blues are on tap here Wednesday to Sunday, while a gospel brunch praises the Almighty on Sunday. Catch group salsa lessons on Tuesday.

HOY COMO AYER Map p255
☎ 305-541-2631; 2212 SW 8th St, Little Havana; cover $8-25
This Cuban hot spot – with authentic music, unstylish wood paneling and a small dance floor – is enhanced by cigar smoke and a house packed with Havana transplants. Stop in nightly

for *son* (a salsa-like dance that originated in Oriente, Cuba), *boleros* (a Spanish dance in triple meter) and modern Cuban beats.

MANGO'S TROPICAL CAFÉ Map pp248-9
☎ 305-673-4422; 900 Ocean Dr, South Beach; cover $10-20
You can play it safe by simply joining the curious crowd gathering around the entrance at Mango's, beloved by tourists. Or you can shed your inhibitions, make your way into the packed courtyard and join the bumping, grinding and booty-shaking. Live bands play salsa, reggae and merengue into the early morning hours.

PACO'S TAVERN Map pp251
☎ 305-673-5888; 3425 Collins Ave, Mid-Beach; ☾ Tue-Sat
Old-school Miami is alive and well at Paco's, a slightly cheesy but fully spirited little place where anyone from Flamenco guitarists to Latin rockers take center stage under the fake-vine decor. It's a great place for a night fuelled by red wine and pure fun.

ROCK, HIP-HOP & INDIE

AUTOMATIC SLIMS Map pp248-9
☎ 305-675-0795; 1216 Washington Ave, South Beach
One of South Beach's few authentic rock 'n' roll bars, those into the gritty scene cram into this tiny space to hear totally loud rock, punk, '80s and metallic sounds. Look for the Harley parked out front.

CHURCHILL'S HIDEAWAY Map p254
☎ 305-757-1807; www.churchillspub.com; 5501 NE 2nd Ave, Little Haiti; cover $10-15; ☾ 11am-3am Mon-Sat, noon-3am Sun
The self-dubbed 'cradle of indie music,' Churchill's Hideaway has been around since the 1950s and is as popular as ever. It's an authentic English bar that also broadcasts UK football and rugby matches. But its main draw is music, from the Monday night jazz jams to other nightly sounds such as indie rock, retro metal and punk.

DISTRICT Map p254
☎ 305-576-7242; 35 NE 40th St, Design District
Formerly Picadilly Garden, which was home to the very popular Pop Life indie-rock party, the District restaurant and lounge still has an ear for music. It's owned by the tune-loving proprietors of I/O (p114), and features rotating sets of

DJs and live performers in the courtyard who bring you indie rock, pop and electro (Thursday); '80s, rock and hip-hop (Fri); and sexy house or jazz (Saturday) along with your meal (p101).

I/O Map pp252-3
☎ 305-358-8007; www.iolounge.com; 30 NE 14th St, Downtown
Britpop nights and a loyal international following has made this Downtown joint the indie-alternative of choice for anyone turned off by the wannabes who flock to South Beach. There's plenty of space for lounging, sipping and listening to DJs and the frequent Latin, electronica and rock bands. Don't miss the wildly infamous Pop Life Saturdays, which host indie poppers from around the globe.

POLISH AMERICAN CLUB Map pp254
☎ 305-635-2240; 1250 NW 22nd St, Wynwood
No, it's not the most glamorous Miami nightspot, but the backpack-wearing youngsters who flock here for all-age indie shows don't seem to mind. The riverside reception hall has recently been host to on-the-edge bands including the Faint and TV on the Radio.

PURDY LOUNGE Map pp246-7
☎ 305-531-4622; 1811 Purdy Ave, South Beach
Tucked out of the South Beach fray, this little club-lounge hybrid is a great spot to check out sounds that range from hip-hop to rock.

PERFORMING ARTS
The various performance houses around Miami serve multiple purposes, hosting shows of dance, theater, music and sometimes even film and art thrown in for good measure. They'll remain this way, most likely, until the Performing Arts Center (p121) finally opens its doors downtown, providing a central spot – and a good looking one, to boot – for all manner of artists to perform, and all types of audiences to be satiated. For now, though, it's still a mixed bag.

CLASSICAL MUSIC & OPERA
For fans of classical, a solid collection of chamber orchestras and symphonies are always imbuing one theater or another with beautiful, classic sounds. Though formerly the home of three opera companies, Miami has just one now – but it's far from lowly.

CHOPIN FOUNDATION OF THE UNITED STATES Map p251
☎ 305-868-0624; www.chopin.org; 1440 79th St Causeway, Mid-Beach
This national organization hosts a treasure trove of performances for Chopin fans – the Chopin Festival, a series of free monthly concerts and the less frequent National Chopin Piano Competition, an international contest held in Miami every five years (next scheduled for 2010).

CONCERT ASSOCIATION OF FLORIDA Map pp246-7
☎ 305-532-3491; www.concertfla.org; 555 17th St, South Beach
Founded in 1967, this nonprofit association is run by dedicated folks who bring world-class music (and occasional dance) to various venues in Miami. Past events have included the Boston Pops symphony, Itzhak Perlman, a Flamenco Festival, the Deutsche Philharmonie and Luciano Pavarotti on the beach.

FLORIDA GRAND OPERA Map pp244-5
☎ 800-741-1010; www.fgo.org; 1200 Coral Way, Coconut Grove
Founded in the 1940s, this highly respected opera, now based in Coconut Grove, performs five nights a week in both Miami (at the Miami-Dade County Auditorium, p121) and Fort Lauderdale. Operas include stagings of *Madame Butterfly*, *The Magic Flute*, *Don Giovanni* and many others.

MIAMI CHAMBER SYMPHONY Map pp256-7
☎ 305-858-3500; Gusman Concert Hall, 1314 Miller Dr, Coral Gables; tickets $15-30; ☺ performances Nov-May
Its yearly series features world-renowned soloists at shows held at the University of Miami's Gusman Concert Hall, which is not to be confused with the downtown Gusman Center for the Performing Arts (p60).

NEW WORLD SYMPHONY Map pp246-7
NWS; ☎ 305-673-3331; www.nws.org; tickets $20-70; ☺ performances Oct-May
This deservedly heralded NWS serves as a three- to four-year preparatory program for very talented musicians who've already graduated from prestigious music schools. Founded in 1987, the NWS is led by artistic director Michael Tilson Thomas, who still conducts performances for 12 weeks a year despite his national fame and fortune. There are an

astonishing number of inspiring and original performances (many of which are free), held at the **Lincoln Theatre** (opposite).

UNIVERSITY OF MIAMI SCHOOL OF MUSIC

☎ 305-284-6477; www.music.miami.edu;
⊙ performances Oct-May

Also held at the **Gusman Concert Hall** (Map pp256–7; 1314 Miller Dr, Coral Gables), as well as **Clark Recital Hall** (5501 San Amaro Dr, University of Miami, Coral Gables), these free concerts highlighting university students are a bargain. Seek out the long-running international **Festival Miami** (☎ 305-284-4940), late September to late October, featuring symphonies, chamber music and jazz.

DANCE

World-class ballet, and modern and international dance scenes can all be found in Miami, where many new companies have formed over the past decade.

BLACK DOOR DANCE ENSEMBLE

☎ 305-380-6233; www.blackdoordance.org

Established by the Miami-Dade Community College dance department director, Karen Stewart, Miami's premiere African-American dance company performs modern, neoclassical ballet, traditional African pieces and Afro-Caribbean works at various city venues, usually the **Colony Theater** (right) on Lincoln Rd.

BRAZARTE DANCE COMPANY

☎ 305-441-0372; www.brazilskindo.com; Coral Gables

The first Brazilian dance company in Florida, based in Coral Gables, presents lavish, Carmen-Mirandaesque shows of Brazilian dance in many styles – folkloric, *capoeira* (An Afro-Brazilian dance that incorporates self-defense moves), lambada and samba. Call for show schedules and venues.

IFÉ-ILÉ AFRO-CUBAN DANCE

☎ 305-476-0388; www.ife-ile.org

A nonprofit organization, Ifé-Ilé promotes cultural understanding through dance, and performs in a range of styles – traditional Afro-Cuban, mambo, rumba, conga, *chancleta* (a Latin dance in which rhythms are amplified by the dancers' wooden shoes), *son*, salsa and ritual pieces. Live musical accompaniment comes courtesy of bongos, piano, timbales

and trumpets. Please call or visit the website for performance schedule and venues.

LA ROSA FLAMENCO THEATRE Map p251

☎ 305-899-7729; www.larosaflamencotheatre.com; 13126 NW Dixie Hwy, North Miami

This professional flamenco, salsa and merengue dance company blends flamenco styles with tap, Middle Eastern and Indian movement, and also offers a full range of classes and educational programs.

MAXIMUM DANCE COMPANY

☎ 305-259-9775; www.maximumdancecompany.com

Founded by former Miami City Ballet dancers in 1997, this contemporary ballet troupe holds unique world premieres, often using hip musical scores that have included the likes of Stuart Copland, U2 and Dave Brubeck. Check the website or call for the performance schedule.

MIAMI CITY BALLET

☎ 305-929-7010, 877-929-7010;
www.miamicityballet.org

Formed in 1985, this troupe is guided by artistic director Edward Villella, who studied under the great George Balanchine at the NYC Ballet. So it's no surprise Balanchine works dominate the repertoire, with shows held at the **Jackie Gleason Theater** (opposite). Its three-story headquarters, designed by the famed local architectural firm Arquitectonica, allows you to watch the dancers rehearsing through big picture windows if you've come by to purchase tickets.

MIAMI HISPANIC BALLET

☎ 305-549-7711; www.miamihispanicballet.com

Directed by the Cuban-trained Pedro Pablo Peña, this troupe presents mainly classical ballets; its main event is the annual International Ballet Festival of Miami, in September.

MOMENTUM DANCE COMPANY

☎ 305-858-7002; www.momentumdance.com

Performing original, modern dance programs at rotating venues for more than 25 years, this small troupe has a focus on education and children's performances.

PERFORMING ARTS VENUES

COLONY THEATRE Map pp246-7

☎ 305-674-1026; 1040 Lincoln Rd, South Beach

A stunning deco showpiece, this small 1934 performing arts center has 465-seats with

Performing Arts Center Drama

Call it a case of performance anxiety. After being eagerly anticipated since its approval in 2001 as the great hope for Downtown Miami, the Performing Arts Center (PAC) has been a $400-million-plus project plagued by contractor bickering, budget shortfalls and other sundry headaches. Originally scheduled to open in late 2004 or early 2005, planners at press time were warning excited factions not to expect the PAC to be running until 'sometime' in 2006. It wasn't always so unpromising. Conceived as the answer to revitalizing Downtown and giving it (safe) life after dark, when everything usually shuts tight, the PAC is meant to be an architectural landmark. Designed by Cesar Pelli, the form taking shape is indeed grand – slate, stone, stainless steel and glass flourishes built on a limestone construction that's using the deco Sears Tower as its base. It'll be the home of cultural groups including the Florida Grand Opera, Miami City Ballet and the Florida Philharmonic, and provide several large auditoriums. And it's all been part of a larger plan that seeks to spruce up the shores of the Miami River, develop an entire 'entertainment district,' revitalize nearby areas such as Overtown and woo developers of high-rise luxury condos. While the condo part definitely seems to be working out, the rest of the plan is still a bit shaky. You can check for the updates at www.pacfmiami.org.

great acoustics. It's a treasure. And it hosts everything from movies and an occasional musical to theatrical dramas, ballet and off-Broadway productions.

CORAL GABLES CONGREGATIONAL CHURCH Map pp256-7

☎ 305-448-7421; www.coralgablescongregational .org; 3010 DeSoto Blvd, Coral Gables; tickets $20-30
In addition to its impressive choirs, this church hosts various concert series, from jazz to classical, all of which draw regional crowds to its beautiful Mediterranean setting.

GUSMAN CENTER FOR THE PERFORMING ARTS Map pp252-3

☎ 305-374-2444; www.gusmancenter.org; 174 E Flagler St, Downtown
This ornate venue, within an elegantly renovated 1920s movie palace, services a huge variety of performing arts – film festivals, symphonies, ballet and touring shows. The acoustics are excellent and the fresco ceiling is covered in twinkling stars and clouds.

JACKIE GLEASON THEATER OF THE PERFORMING ARTS Map pp246-7

☎ 305-673-7300; www.gleasontheater.com; 1700 Washington Ave, South Beach
Built in 1951, the Miami Beach's premiere showcase for touring Broadway shows, orchestras and other big musical productions has 2700 seats and excellent acoustics. Jackie Gleason chose to make the theater his home for the long-running 1960s TV show, but now you'll find an eclectic lineup of shows – Elvis Costello or Albita one night, the Dutch Philharmonic or over-the-top musical the next.

LINCOLN THEATRE Map pp246-7

☎ 305-531-3442; 555 Lincoln Rd, South Beach
Miami Beach's theatrical jewel, an intimate house with great acoustics and a perfect location, hosts a wide variety of performances from local groups to visiting artists. It's also the home of the **New World Symphony** (p119).

MIAMI-DADE COUNTY AUDITORIUM Map pp244-5

☎ 305-547-5414; 2901 W Flagler St, Little Havana
On the western edge of Little Havana, this 2500-seat venue with excellent acoustics hosts opera and classical music, many arranged by the Concert Association of Florida.

LIGHT BOX THEATRE/MIAMI LIGHT PROJECT Map p254

☎ 305-576-4350; www.miamilightproject.com; 3000 Biscayne Blvd, Wynwood
The Miami Light Project is a nonprofit cultural foundation that represents innovative shows from theater troupes and performance artists from around the world; recent shows have included Laurie Anderson, Beethova Obas of Haiti and the Rinko-Gun Theater Company of Japan. The Project is housed at the Light Box Theatre, which also runs an impressive and diverse performing-arts program that includes the Mad Cat Theatre original production company, Dolla Jams open-mic series, the D Projects hip-hop theater troupe, and the Miami Hip Hop Exchange performance and education program.

THEATER

You'll find ample evidence of a community that loves theater here, whether it's classic,

Spanish-language or avant-garde. There are options in a variety of neighborhoods, from Coral Gables to South Beach, many housed in lovely, stylish playhouses that evoke a long-ago, more splendorous time.

ACTORS' PLAYHOUSE Map pp256-7
☎ 305-444-9293; www.actorsplayhouse.org; 280 Miracle Mile, Coral Gables; tickets $30-40
Housed within the 1948 deco Miracle Theater, this three-theater venue stages well-known musicals and comedies, children's theater on its kids stage and more avant-garde productions in its small experimental black-box space. Recent productions have included *Aida*, a lyrical revue and *Cinderella* for the little ones.

COCONUT GROVE PLAYHOUSE Map p258
☎ 305-442-4000; www.cgplayhouse.com; 3500 Main Hwy; adult $40-45, youth under 24 yrs $15
This lovely state-owned theater, anchoring the Grove since 1956, gained fame from the moment it opened by premiering Samuel Beckett's *Waiting for Godot*. The main stage, with 1100 seats, features highly regarded earnest and experimental productions by local and international playwrights. The smaller Encore Room features theater-in-the-round cabaret.

GABLESTAGE Map pp256-7
☎ 305-445-1119; www.gablestage.org; 1200 Anastasia Ave, Coral Gables; tickets $15-35
Founded as the Florida Shakespeare Theatre in 1979 and now housed on the property of the Biltmore Hotel after several moves, this company still performs an occasional Shakespeare play, but mostly presents contemporary and classical

pieces; recent productions have included *Frozen, Bug* and *The Retreat From Moscow*.

JERRY HERMAN RING THEATRE Map pp256-7
☎ 305-284-3355; www.miami.edu/ring; 1321 Miller Dr, Coral Gables; tickets $15
This University of Miami troupe stages musicals, dramas and comedies, with recent productions including *Falsettos* and *Baby*. Alumni actors include Sylvester Stallone, Steven Bauer, Saundra Santiago and Ray Liotta.

NEW THEATRE Map pp256-7
☎ 305-443-5909; www.new-theatre.org; 4120 Laguna St, Coral Gables; tickets $20-25
This strong Coral Gables company performs an eclectic mix of contemporary pieces and modern classics that fall squarely between the conventional and alternative. You'll be up close and personal with the actors since there are only 70 seats in the house.

READINGS & SPOKEN WORD
Poetry readings abound in Miami, especially among the young hip set that flocks to the type of multipurpose spaces taking over areas like the Design District. They're far from stuffy affairs, usually blending some hip-hop, lounge music and cocktail-swilling into the mix. To hear well-known authors read from new works, stick to renowned bookshops such as **Books & Books** (below).

BOOK ADDICTION Map p258
☎ 305-476-8191; 3805 Grand Ave, Coconut Grove
A cozy Coconut Grove bookshop with small café tables, this space is poetry central on Fridays, when the 'Release Yourself Fridays' open-mic series takes over.

BOOKS & BOOKS Map pp246-7
☎ 305-532-3222; www.booksandbooks.com; 933 Lincoln Rd, South Beach
Both this location of this well-stocked and popular book seller and its branch in **Coral Gables** (Map pp256–7; ☎ 305-442-4408; 265 Aragon Ave, Coral Gables) feature frequent solo readings from famous (and not so famous) local authors, as well as group readings on a particular theme (science fiction, Tibetan culture, Brazil) and various book-discussion groups.

Arts Festivals

In addition to the many entertainment options at any regularly scheduled moment, Miami gets frequent injections of culture from its many annual festivals, from the famous to the specific and obscure. Below is a just a sampling of what happens when.

Dance

Annual Tango Fantasy Festival (http://totango.net/USTC) The largest tango festival in the world outside Argentina takes place in late May and features performances and workshops that span nine days.

Florida Dance Festival (p18; www.FLDance.org) Choreographers, performers, teachers and students from around the world gather for two weeks in June for learning and performing.

Baila USA (www.ife-ile.org) Anchored by dance, this Afro-Cuban festival also features music, films, art and readings in October via Miami-Dade Community College.

International Ballet Festival of Miami (www.miamihispanicballet.com) Held in September, the week of events features showcases of America's biggest modern, ballet, jazz and ballroom dance companies.

Music

FIU Music Festival (www.fiu.edu) Featuring everything from chamber music to blues shows, this world-class fest hits every October.

JVC Jazz Festival Miami Beach (www.festivalproductions.net/jvc/miami) Held in various venues in early May, the jazz fest, like its other incarnations in places including New York and Newport, attracts top performers in the genre.

Miami Ultra Music Festival (www.ultramusicfestival.us) Held in March each year at Bayfront Park, this massive festival is an enormous electronica showcase. Recent artists to take part include Paul Van Dyk, Tiesto, Carl Cox and Goldie.

Miami Reggae Festival (☎ 305-891-2944) This mega-concert, held every July for more than 20 years, brings big-name lineups to Bayfront Park.

Theater

International Hispanic Theater Festival (www.teatroavante.com) A city-wide festival, held in the first two weeks of June, features performances in Spanish, Portuguese, and English from companies all over the world.

Here & Now Festival (www.miamilightproject.com) An annual favorite of the Miami Light Project, this is a March showcase of cutting-edge works-in-progress from local dramatists.

City Theatre's Summer Shorts (www.citytheatre.com) This annual series of one-act plays, held in June, features works from both local and global playwrights.

Film

Miami International Film Festival (p17; www.miamifilmfestival.com) The 23-year-old happening, held in February, has a focus on Ibero-American cinema and documentaries. It's launched careers of filmmakers including Pedro Almodóvar and Atom Egoyan.

Miami Latin Film Festival (www.hispanicfilm.com) The April event, held in South Beach theaters, features films from and about any Latin country.

Miami Gay & Lesbian Film Festival (p18; www.mglff.com) Joining a series of LGBT film fests held in cities across America, this April fest, now in its eighth year, brings queer features, shorts and docs to the big screen.

Brazilian Film Festival of Miami (www.brazilianfilmfestival.com) Held at the **Colony Theater** (p120) in June before traveling to NYC in July, this dynamic cultural fest was founded in 1997.

DQ BOOKSTORE Map p258
☎ 305-441-7103; www.dqbookstore.com; 3162 Commodore Plaza, Coconut Grove

This adorable bookstore/café presents a full schedule of events, including wine and poetry nights, author readings and book signings, and frequent storytelling events for children.

LITERARY CAFÉ Map pp244-5
☎ 786-234-7638; 12325 NE Sixth Ave, North Miami

Saturday nights here at the Literary Café are awash with a winning combination of culture and cool – trippy DJ music combined with poetry readings and a bohemian vibe.

MEZA FINE ART GALLERY & CAFÉ Map pp256-7

☎ 305-461-2733; 275 Giralda Ave, Coral Gables

This lively gallery of contemporary Latin American art also hosts frequent and eclectic readings, mainly of poetry and prose.

POWER STUDIOS Map p254

☎ 305-576-1336; 3701 NE 2nd Ave, Design District

This cutting-edge Design District space is all things to all (creative) people: art gallery, restaurant, recording studio and film house. It's the home of the Poet's Café, a popular slam and open-mic (first Thursday of each month) that rewards winners with big cash prizes.

WALLFLOWER GALLERY Map pp252-3

☎ 305-579-0069; www.wallflowergallery.com; 10 NE 3rd St, Downtown

In addition to offering a well-rounded lineup of music, dance and film, the gallery features poetry readings, spoken-word artists and open-mic poetry nights.

Nightlife – Comedy

COMEDY

Though it may not be the most popular nightlife event of choice, a night of laughing your ass off while getting constant fuel for the fire in the form of potent, overpriced cocktails, is a pretty universal way to have fun. And Miami, though not bursting at the seams with options, is no exception. There's more here than meets the eye.

4400 CLUB LIVE COMEDY Map p254

☎ 786-230-6561; 4400 NW 7th Ave, Wynwood

You'll find a variety of comedy series here, from improv shows and open-mic nights to big-name specials that get filmed for TV networks.

IMPROMEDY Map pp244-5

☎ 305-226-0030; Roxy Performing Arts Center; 1645 SW 107th Ave, Greater Miami; tickets $10

An improvisational comedy troupe formed at Florida International University in 1997, you can catch their shows on weekends at the Roxy west of Coral Gables in Sweetwater.

JUST THE FUNNY Map pp244-5

☎ 305-693-8669; www.justthefunny.com; Miami Museum of Science & Planetarium, 3280 S Miami Ave, Coconut Grove; tickets $5-12

This interactive sketch comedy draws a crowd to the museum auditorium each Saturday.

LAUGHING GAS

☎ 305-461-1161; www.laughinggasimprov.com; venues vary; tickets $12

This long-running, wacky improv and comedy-sketch troupe brings its costumed craziness to venues around town, usually in Coral Gables and nearby Miami Lakes. Check the website for information.

MIAMI IMPROV Map p258

☎ 305-441-8200; www.miamiimprov.com; 3390 Mary St, Coconut Grove; tickets $10-70

Part of a national chain, this 3rd-floor club has all the usual club-circuit suspects – Jeff Garcia, Gary Owens, Mo'Nique – plus monthly Miami Comics, open-mic shows and Urban Nights, which features stars from *Showtime* on Comedy Central, HBO's *Def Comedy Jam* and BET's *Comic View*.

CINEMAS

In addition to the many standard megaplexes that play Hollywood fare, there are various art-film and indie houses that draw folks from the excellent film community in Miami.

ABSINTHE HOUSE CINEMATHEQUE Map pp256-7

☎ 305-446-7144; 235 Alcazar Ave, Coral Gables

This art house is a blend of old-fashioned and mod – it has only one screen for independent and foreign films, but a cool lounge serving as an atmospheric snack bar.

BILL COSFORD CINEMA Map pp256-7

☎ 305-284-4861; www.miami.edu/cosford; Memorial Classroom Bldg, off University Dr, Coral Gables

On the University of Miami campus, this renovated art house was launched in memory of the *Miami Herald* film critic. They do him justice, too, with a great lineup of first-run indie and foreign movies, plus presentations from visiting filmmakers.

IMAX Map pp256-7

☎ 305-663-4629; www.IMAX.com; Shops at Sunset Place, 5701 Sunset Pl, Coral Gables

This virtual-reality screen, which is way larger than real life, comes with surround sound shows and dramatic, sometimes educational footage that takes advantage of its size; also catch fun stuff best viewed through 3-D glasses.

Clevelander Bar (p110), South Beach

MIAMI BEACH CINEMATHEQUE

Map pp248-9

☎ 305-673-4567; www.mbcinema.com; 512 Española Way, South Beach

This new addition to the film scene is a great one, as it features a wonderfully curated program of smart documentaries, kitschy classics, holiday-timed screeners, speaking events and film-themed art exhibits. A recent sampling of eclectic programs includes a Russ Meyer tribute, Italian shorts, dance films and Judaica on film.

REGAL SOUTH BEACH CINEMA

Map pp246-7

☎ 305-674-6766; 1100 Lincoln Rd, South Beach

This mod, state-of-the-art, 21-screen theater anchors the western end of Lincoln Rd by being both an architectural delight and a filmgoers' paradise. It shows a good blend of foreign, independent, and critically acclaimed Hollywood stuff.

TOWER THEATER Map p255

☎ 305-644-3307; www.thetowertheater.com; 1508 Calle Ocho, Little Havana

This 1926 renovated city-owned movie theater, on the National Register of Historic Places, shows Spanish-language films and dubbed English-language films, plus also hosts music performances and art exhibits in its lobby.

GAMBLING

It's no Las Vegas, but Miami does have its fair share of options if you want to participate in the vice of chance. For starters, head to a *jai alai* match or a horse-racing track, where you can also drop your money into slot machines thanks to an initiative that was passed overwhelmingly by Miami voters in a special March 2005 election. You can also hop on a gambling boat at the bay or take a day trip to the **Miccosukee Resort** (p198).

ATLANTIC CASINO MIAMI Map p250

☎ 305-532-2111; Miami Beach Marina, Alton Rd at 5th St, South Beach; cruise $20

This gaming cruise offers a plethora of slots, video gambling, poker, roulette and blackjack tables, plus an observation deck and full bars.

CASINO PRINCESA Map pp252-3

☎ 305-379-5825; www.casinoprincesa.com; 100 S Biscayne Blvd, Downtown; cruise $9.95

Docked adjacent to the Hard Rock Café in the **Bayside Marketplace** (p59), the Casino Princesa is a large, upscale yacht that departs on 4½-hour voyages that head 3 miles offshore. The boat has two decks of gaming tables (blackjack and craps are big), slot machines and bars.

GULFSTREAM PARK

☎ 954-454-7000; www.gulfstreampark.com; 901 S Federal Hwy, Hallandale

Located in Hallandale, which is north of Miami, toward Hollywood, this 60-plus-year-old horse-racing track features almost-daily live racing and nationwide simulcasting. So if you have a hankering for a wager...

MIAMI JAI ALAI Map pp244-5

☎ 305-633-6400; www.fla-gaming.com; 3500 NW 37th Ave, Greater Miami

The ball game, which came to Miami from Spain via Cuba, combines elements of polo and soccer (but is extremely fast and unique and hard to explain). You can bet on games. For more information on jai alai, see p130.

Sports, Health & Fitness

Sports, Health & Fitness

Most Miamians, being Americans, are quite into sports. Many are also vain and body obsessed – hence the interest in working out, whether it's lifting weights at the gym, running along the ocean, rollerblading in South Beach or *om*-ing through a beachfront yoga class.

For the voyeurs of the city, it's all about football – the Miami Dolphins, whose fans never stop hoping for a repeat of the 1972 Don Shula–led Super Bowl glory – and basketball's Miami Heat, which got a fresh infusion of excitement in 2004 with the addition of the 7ft 1in superstar Shaquille O'Neal. For participants, there is no shortage of activities or locations, with everything from rock-climbing walls and running paths to rental bikes and canoes at your disposal. So pick your game, and go play.

WATCHING SPORTS

Whenever you visit Miami, you're sure to find something worth watching. Catch football in fall, basketball in winter, baseball in spring and jai alai pretty much anytime in between.

FOOTBALL
MIAMI DOLPHINS
☎ 305-620-2578; www.miamidolphins.com; Pro Player Stadium, 2269 NW 199th St, North Dade; admission $20-54; ☾ season Aug-Dec

Attending an American football game may be one of the most intense experiences in spectator sports, and 'Dol-fans' get more than a little crazy when it comes to their team. Even though a Super Bowl showing has evaded them since 1985, and the 1972–3 glory days of coach Don Shula taking his team to 17-0 are long since over (it's still an National Football League record, though), games are wildly popular and the team normally successful – raising fans' hopes but so far not taking them all the way.

Top Five Sporting Moments

- Watching Shaquille O'Neal barrel down the court at a **Miami Heat** (right) home game on the bay.
- Betting on the best pelota handler at a high-speed match of **jai alai** (p130).
- **Sailing** (p132) across Biscayne Bay in a chartered boat.
- **Bicycling** (p131) along the shady paths of Coral Gables.
- Taking a scenic sunset **run** (p131) along the Mid-Beach boardwalk.

If you're a real football fanatic, you can watch preseason practices near Fort Lauderdale. Take I-95 or Florida's Turnpike to I-595 west to the University Dr exit. Turn left at SW 30th St and make another left. The training facility is half a mile down on the right.

UNIVERSITY OF MIAMI HURRICANES
☎ 800-462-2637; www.hurricanesports.com; admission $25-45

The UM Hurricanes dominates college area sports, especially the game of football. Watch them play at the famed **Orange Bowl Stadium** (Map pp244–5; 1145 NW 11th St, Greater Miami), always hoping to make it into the Orange Bowl (which brings a frenzy of excitement to town each January). Their last such win was in 2004.

BASKETBALL
MIAMI HEAT
☎ 786-777-4328; www.nba.com/heat; American Airlines Arena, 601 Biscayne Blvd, Downtown; admission $33-100; ☾ season Nov-Apr

When Stan Van Gundy stepped in for celebrity coach Pat Riley in 2003, the team was in trouble. But with Lamar Odom and Dwayne Wade leading the way, Gundy soon became the first Heat coach to win his first playoff game in his first coaching season. Now all hopes are on Shaquille O'Neal, traded to the Heat for Odom in 2004 after leading the LA Lakers to three consecutive National Basketball Association (NBA) titles.

UNIVERSITY OF MIAMI HURRICANES
☎ 800-462-2637; www.hurricanesports.com; Miami Arena, Miami Ave, Downtown; admission $20

Catch the beloved college Hurricanes shooting hoops at the Miami Arena (Map pp252–3).

BASEBALL

FLORIDA MARLINS

☎ 305-626-7400; www.marlins.mlb.com; Pro Player Stadium, 2269 NW 199th St, Opa-Locka; admission $4-55; ⊙ season May-Sep

Founded in 1993, the Florida Marlins are the fastest franchise in the history of baseball to win a World Series (1997). The triumph disgusted baseball purists, who loudly shouted that their hallowed series had been bought – a reference to the team's then outlandish payroll. As if to prove them right, the owner sold the star players immediately after winning the World Series. They eventually did have a comeback, miraculously winning again in 2003, getting everyone very excited once again and finally making progress on funding for their oft-dreamed-of Downtown baseball stadium.

UNIVERSITY OF MIAMI HURRICANES

☎ 800-462-2637; www.hurricanesports.com; Mark Light Stadium, University of Miami, 6201 San Amaro Dr, Coral Gables; admission $7-15

Hurricane's un-pro baseball can often please when the Marlins disappoint.

HOCKEY

FLORIDA PANTHERS

☎ 954-835-8000; www.floridapanthers.com; Office Depot Center, 1 Panther Pkwy, Sunrise; admission $14-67; ⊙ season mid-Oct–mid-Apr

Since thrilling Miamians by reaching for the Stanley Cup in 1996, the Panthers have gone steadily downhill, becoming one of the worst teams in the National Hockey League (NHL). The bitter, destructive owners' lockout and players' strike cost the NHL its entire 2004–05 season, and jeopardized the league itself. Still, watching a game at least gets you out of the heat. And they could always have a comeback, right?

AUTO RACING

HIALEAH SPEEDWAY Map pp244-5

☎ 305-821-6644; www.hialeahspeedway.com; 3300 W Okeechobee Rd, Hialeah

Catch the Saturday-night races at this 50-year-old track, featuring limited late-model, street-stock, ministock and cyclone cars. Special events include a demolition derby and Pro Cup Challenge.

HOMESTEAD MIAMI SPEEDWAY

☎ 305-230-7223; www.homesteadmiamispeedway .com; 1 Speedway Blvd, Homestead

This $50-million racing center built in 1995 hosts National Association for Stock Car Auto Racing (Nascar) and Winston Cup races. The *New York Times* once quipped that it would be hard to imagine anyone in Homestead wanting to see something coming at them at 200mph after Hurricane Andrew, but people do. Go figure.

HORSE RACING

CALDER RACE COURSE

☎ 305-625-1311; www.calderracecourse.com; 21001 NW 27th Ave; admission $2

With live races from May to December, this 1971 track, up toward Hollywood, hosts the Festival of the Sun Derby and always has simulcasts (TV broadcasts) of national races.

GULFSTREAM PARK

☎ 954-454-7000; www.gulfstreampark.com; 901 S Federal Hwy, Hallandale; admission $2-4

Catch live races and simulcasts at this classic track.

OUTDOOR ACTIVITIES

Doin' it yourself is a great way to ensure you stay in shape on what is bound to be a gastronomically fulfilling vacation. Work up a sweat, burn some calories and take in some local scenery while you're at it – whether running oceanside or pumping iron among the hottie bodybuilders at the gym.

EQUIPMENT RENTAL

Bicycles & Skates

FRITZ'S SKATE SHOP Map pp246-7

☎ 305-532-1954; 730 Lincoln Rd, South Beach; per hr/day $7.50/22; ⊙ 10am-10pm

For in-line skate rentals, roll over here. Fritz gives free lessons on Sunday morning at 10:30am – just about the only time there's ever room on the mall anymore.

MANGROVE CYCLES Map p259

☎ 305-361-5555; 260 Crandon Blvd, Key Biscayne; per 2 hr/day/week $15/20/65; ⊙ 9am-6pm Tue-Sat, 10am-5pm Sun

Key Biscayne is a perfect place to bike; Mangrove has basic, luxury and children's bicycles.

Miami Jai Alai

Jai alai (pronounced 'high aligh'), which roughly translates from Spanish as 'merry festival,' is a fascinating and dangerous game. Something of a cross between racquetball and lacrosse, it originated in the Basque region of the Pyrenees in the 17th century, and was introduced to Miami in 1924. The fronton (arena) where the games are held is the oldest in the States, having been built just two years after the game was introduced. How is it played? Well, players hurl a pelota (a small ball of virgin rubber that's wrapped in goat skin and so powerful it can shatter bullet-proof glass) at more than 170mph to their opponents, who try to catch it with the cesta – a woven basket that's custom-made from Spanish chestnut and reeds from the Pyrenees – that's attached to their glove. The game is held in a round robin, and the object is to toss the pelota against the front wall of the court with so much speed that the opposition cannot catch it or return it in the fly or first bounce. Audiences wager on the lightning fast games, said to be the speediest sport on earth.

Catch the action for yourself at **Miami Jai Alai** (Map pp244–5; ☎ 305-633-6400; 3500 NW 37th Ave; admission $1-5; ☽ matches noon-5pm Wed-Mon, 7pm-midnight Mon, Fri & Sat). It's great fun to watch these guys whack around their pelota at lightning speed – and even more exciting to wager bets on who will win.

MIAMI BEACH BICYCLE CENTER
Map p250

☎ 305-674-0150; 601 5th St, South Beach; per hr/day/week $8/20/70; ☽ 10am-7pm Mon-Sat, 10am-5pm Sun

Rent Treks, Raleighs and Cannondales at this friendly neighborhood bike shop, right in the southern heart of South Beach.

TWO WHEEL DRIVE Map pp248-9

☎ 305-534-2177; 1260 Washington Ave; per hr/day/week $6/15/45; ☽ 10am-7pm Mon-Fri, 10am-6pm Sat, 11am-4pm Sun

Another South Beach spot, this one has great prices.

Water Vessels & Gear

DIVERS PARADISE Map p259

☎ 305-361-3483; Crandon Marina, 4000 Crandon Blvd, Key Biscayne; for certification $375-450

Rent what you need – and learn how to use it if you're a beginner. Just know that the best spot around is in Key Largo (p165), and worth driving to if you're serious about underwater exploration.

FANTASY WATER SPORTS Map pp244-5

☎ 305-940-2628; 100 Sunny Isles Blvd, Sunny Isles; rates vary

Head to Fantasy to rent kayaks and small boats – as well as loud and dreadful jet skis, power boats and wave runners – which, by the way, kill manatees and fish, rip up sea plants and protected sea grass, scare swimmers, annoy locals and result in several deaths a year. Hint, hint.

FLORIDA YACHT CHARTERS Map p250

☎ 305-532-8600, 800-537-0050; 1290 5th St, South Beach; ☽ 9am-5:30pm

Wanna buzz down to the Keys, or, say, float over to the Bahamas? This place, at the Miami Beach Marina, rents yachts with and without captains (as long as you pass a little practical test).

SAILBOARDS MIAMI Map p259

☎ 305-361-7245; 1 Rickenbacker Causeway, Key Biscayne; s/tandem per hr $15/20

Also rents kayaks. You can also purchase a 10-hour card for $90. To get some exercise for your lower body, you could try renting water bikes, which sit in a kayak-type boat and rent for the same prices as the kayaks. In either case, if you're goal-oriented and need a destination, head for the little offshore sandbar.

SAILBOATS OF KEY BISCAYNE Map p259

☎ 305-361-0328; 4000 Crandon Blvd, Key Biscayne; 22ft Catalina rentals per hr/half-day/day $35/110/170

If you're a bona fide seaworthy sailor, this place will rent you a vessel.

URBAN TRAILS KAYAK RENTALS
Map pp244-5

☎ 305-947-0302; 3400 NE 163rd St, Bal Harbour

Rent a canoe or kayak for solo exploration, or join in on one of the company's excellent guided expeditions of the Oleta River or the Everglades.

X-ISLE SURF SHOP Map p250

☎ 305-673-5900; 437 Washington Ave, South Beach; per hr/day $10/30

Rent foam boards and buy used boards for about $120 to $275. New ones start at $400.

BICYCLING

The **Miami-Dade County Parks & Recreation Department**
(☎ 305-755-7800; www.co.miami-dade.fl
.us/parks/bike_paths.asp) is helpful when it
comes to cycling around the city. It leads
frequent eco bike tours through parklands
and along waterfront paths, and offers a list
of traffic-free cycling paths on its website. Try
the Old Cutler Bike Path, which starts at the
end of Sunset Dr in Coral Gables and leads
to Matheson Hammock Park and Fairchild
Tropical Garden, or the Rickenbacker Causeway, taking you up and over the bridge to
Key Biscayne for an excellent workout combined with gorgeous water views. Pedaling to
the end of the Key is a lovely way to spend the
afternoon. Oleta River State Park has a chal-
lenging dirt trail with hills for off-road adventures. For less strenuous rides, try the side
roads of South Beach or the shady streets of
Coral Gables and Coconut Grove, but you'll
have to rent your bike elsewhere and drive it
over; all of the Gables/Grove bike shops have
stopped doing rentals due to an increase in
lawsuits by clumsy tourists. Shame.

IN-LINE SKATING

In-line skating used to be the most popular form of South Beach transportation. It
seemed that everyone had a pair of skates,
and most streets were excellent for it – until
the serious crowds came along, turning
sidewalks and promenades into obstacle
courses for anyone crazy enough to strap
on a pair of blades. That doesn't mean it
doesn't happen, of course. But leave the
crowded strips to the experts and try the
ocean side of Ocean Ave, for starters, or
Lincoln Rd early in the morning, before the
shoppers descend.

TENNIS & GOLF

Key Biscayne's Tennis Center at **Crandon Park**
(Map p259; ☎ 305-365-2300; 6702 Crandon
Blvd, Key Biscayne) is best-known for its annual 10-day Nasdaq 100 Tennis Open, which
draws star players each March. But you too
can play here; choose from two grass, eight
clay and 17 hard courts. The **Flamingo Tennis
Center** (Map pp248–9; ☎ 305-673-7761; 1000
12th St, South Beach) has 19 clay courts that
are open to the public; but beware of the zoolike crowds on evenings and weekends. Two
other great options are the **Salvadore Park Tennis
Center** (Map pp256–7; ☎ 305-460-5333; 1120

Andalusia Ave, Coral Gables) and the **Tropical
Park Tennis Center** (☎ 305-223-8710; 7900 SW
40th St, Coral Gables).

Golfers also have many options. Check
out the lovely 1925 **Biltmore Golf Course** (Map
pp256–7; ☎ 305-445-8066; 1210 Anastasia
Ave, Coral Gables), which boasts the company of the Biltmore Hotel. **Doral Golf Course**
(Map p251; ☎ 305-592-2000; 4400 NW 87th
Ave) is highly rated, which may explain why
it's difficult to get in and also why it's the
home of the PGA Ford Championship. For
easier access, try the **Crandon Golf Course** (Map
p259; ☎ 305-361-9129; 6700 Crandon Blvd,
Key Biscayne), overlooking the bay from its
perch on Key Biscayne, or the **Haulover Golf
Course** (Map p259; ☎ 305-940-6719; 10,800
Collins Ave, Haulover), a 9-hole, par-3
course that's great for beginners.

KAYAKING & CANOEING

Kayaking through mangroves is magical,
and you can do it at Haulover Beach Park
or Key Biscayne, at the Bill Baggs Florida
State Park, where you can paddle along the
shoreline for views of the Atlantic, sandy
beaches and the historic lighthouse. Equipment rental is cheap, and you won't even
need lessons to make the boat go where
you want it to. Also check out Oleta River
State Park (Map p251), with various grove
channels of the Intracoastal Waterway that
are perfect for a kayak or paddleboat (both
of which are available for rental here).

Canoeing around the **10,000 Islands** (p200),
or on the **Wilderness Waterway** (see the boxed
text, p200) between Everglades City and
Flamingo, is one of the most fascinating
ways to get away into nature.

RUNNING

Running is quite popular, and the beach
is very good for jogging, as it's flat, wide
and hard-packed. The **Promenade** (p53) is
the stylish place for both, as is the **Boardwalk**
(p55), which shoots north from 21st St and
offers great people-watching and scenery as
you move along. But more serious runners
may appreciate the Flamingo Park running
track, just east of Alton Rd between 11th
and 12th Sts; the entrance is on the 12th St
side at the east end of the fence. Elsewhere
around the city, running is good along S
Bayshore Dr in Coconut Grove, around
the Riviera Country Club in Coral Gables

and anywhere on Key Biscayne. Or try the jogging path that runs along the beach in Bal Harbour, made of hard-packed sand and gravel and stretching from the southern boundary of town to the Haulover Cut passageway. A great resource for races, special events and other locations is the **Miami Runners Club** (☎ 305-227-1500).

SURFING & WINDSURFING

We can't say it enough: offshore Miami bears no resemblance to the Banzai Pipeline. So don't get too excited. But on the Beach, the best surfing is just north of South Pointe Park, with 2ft to 5ft waves and a nice, sandy bottom. Unfortunately, there are a few drawbacks: it's usually closer to 2ft than to 5ft (except, of course, before storms); it can get a little mushy (so longboards are the way to go); and it's swamped with weekend swimmers and surfers. It's better further north near Haulover Beach Park (Map p251) or anywhere north of, say, 70th St. Sunny Isles Beach, at the Sunny Isles Causeway, is also favored by surfers. Call the recorded **surf report** (☎ 305-534-7873) for daily conditions or check in with the popular **Bird's Surf Shop** (Map p251; ☎ 305-940-0929; 250 Sunny Isles Blvd). For windsurfing, make a beeline to Hobie Beach(Map p259), between the mainland and Virginia Key, which features a long and lovely strip of bay that's perfect for catching a breeze in your sail. Other good spots include the waters at 1st St, north of the Government Cut, and at 21st St.

SAILING

Key Biscayne sailing is a pure joy (get outfitted at **Sailboats of Key Biscayne**, p130), as is gliding along the waters just about anywhere else off of Miami. Good starting points include the **Miami Beach Marina** (Map p250; ☎ 305-673-6000; MacArthur Causeway, 300 Alton Rd), which has 400 slips and all sorts of rentals; **Haulover Marine Center** (Map p251; ☎ 305-945-3934; 15000 Collins Ave), a down-to-earth sort of spot; and **Monty's Marina** (Map p258; ☎ 305-854-7997; 2640 S Bayshore Dr, Coconut Grove), which is perfect if you have your own boat.

DIVING & SNORKELING

Miami is not known for great diving, but between offshore wrecks and the introduc-

tion of artificial coral reefs, there's plenty to look at if you can part the waters and scratch beneath the surface. Go on a calm day with a group; try **Bubbles Dive Center** (Map p258; ☎ 305-856-0565; 2671 SW 27th Ave, Coconut Grove), which has divers head out on weekends, or **Divers Paradise** (p130) of Key Biscayne. **South Beach Divers** (Map pp248–9; ☎ 305-531-6110; www.southbeachdivers. com; 850 Washington Ave, South Beach) runs regular excursions to Key Largo (again, worth the trip) and around Miami, plus offers three-day classes. Or make the very worthy drive to **Biscayne National Park** (www.nps.gov /bisc, p201), in the southeastern corner of the county, a huge park that contains the northern tip of the world's third-longest coral reef. Of the park's 173,000 acres, about 95% of them are underwater.

FISHING

Locals have always fished these bountiful waters and you can, too. Rent a pricey charter (around $800 per day), hop aboard a 'head boat' with 100 or so other fisherfolk (boats are rarely full, and it's only about $30), or cast a line off numerous piers or bridges. You don't need a license if you're fishing from shore or from a bridge or pier (just check for signs, which declare some bridges off-limits). On your own, drop a line at **South Pointe Park** (Map p250), off the **Rickenbacker Causeway** or any Key Biscayne beach or from **Haulover Beach Park** (Map p251). To go for the fishing charter boat, try **Crandon Park Marina** (Map p259; ☎ 305-361-1281; 4000 Crandon Blvd, Key Biscayne) or **Blue Waters Sport Fishing Charters** (Map pp252–3; ☎ 305-373-5016; Bayside Marketplace, 401 Biscayne Blvd, Downtown). Or catch a group-fishing party boat with either the **Kelley Fleet** (Map p251; ☎ 305-945-3801 at Haulover Beach Park, 10,800 Collins Ave, North Beach) or **Reward/Reward Won** (☎ 305-372-9470; Dock A, Miami Beach Marina, 300 Alton Rd, South Beach).

ULTRALIGHTS & SKYDIVING

Miami is an aviation center, and the skies are filled on a daily basis with hundreds of small planes – including ultralights, which are regulated small aircraft that you don't need a pilot's license to fly (scarily enough). Get a good taste of the ultralight experience at the **Homestead General Aviation Airport** (☎ 305-247-4883; 28,700 SW 217th Ave), not quite in Miami, but close enough if you're really jazzed about getting up in the air. It's a field specifically for these tiny planes; call for rates, which vary. Or try **Tony's Ultralight Adventures** (Map p259; ☎ 305-361-3909; Rickenbacker Causeway, Key Biscayne), where you can get lessons or a sightseeing flight. If you'd rather someone else fly the plane while you just jump out of it, head to **Skydive Miami** (☎ 305-759-3483; www.skydivemiami.com; Homestead General Aviation Airport, 28,700 SW 217th Ave), where you can pay $175 to get pushed out of a plane or head out in tandem (attached to an experienced diver).

ROCK CLIMBING

It's unlikely that you've come to Miami to go rock climbing, but still. If the urge hits, your best bet is to head over to **X-Treme Rock Climbing** (Map pp244–5; ☎ 305-233-6623; 13972 SW 139th Ct, North Miami; per day $15), where you'll find more than 11,000ft of climbing surfaces, including beginning routes and expert roof overhangs. You can take classes by appointment only. Then there's the Spa of Eden at **Eden Roc Resort** (p159), which has a very good indoor climbing wall. You can use this even if you're not a spa member or resort guest. But it'll cost you – $50 for just one day.

SWIMMING

Some folks in Miami *actually* swim in the gorgeous pools around town, usually just serving as backdrops for the cocktail swilling set – or as quick cool-downs for vacationing sunbathers. If a bit of freestyle or breaststroke is how you like to get your workout, fear not: there are places for you, even if you're not lucky enough to be staying at a hotel with an excellent swimming hole (among the best of these are the **Delano Hotel**, p155; **Shore Club**, p157; **Biltmore Hotel**, p162; **Raleigh Hotel**, p157; and **Fontainebleau Hilton Hotel & Resort**, p159). In Coral Gables, the famous **Venetian Pool** (p73), known more as a pretty place at which to play and float and gawk, has lap swimming hours several times a week; call for details, which change often. Other options include the **Flamingo Park Swimming Pool** (Map pp248–9; ☎ 305-673-7750; 999 11th St, South Beach), which has a swimming pool with lap lanes, and the public **Bright Park Pool** (☎ 305-696-0605; 760

35th St, Hialeah), which also has specific lap-swimming hours.

HEALTH & FITNESS

Before you can allow your body to worship the sun, you must sculpt it – at least that's what countless shape-obsessed Miamians believe, judging from the amount of gyms and sundry exercise classes available here. Though indoor workouts in a city with such beautiful weather may seem criminal to visitors, it's clearly no crime here. Take your pick – from grunt-heavy lifting sessions to clear-your-mind yoga classes.

GYMS

CRUNCH Map pp248-9
☎ 305-674-8222; 1259 Washington Ave, South Beach; per day/week $21/88
This offshoot of the New York City fave has great workout equipment, a cool attitude and a slew of unique classes, from Cardio Striptease to Belly Moves. Work those abs, people.

DAVID BARTON GYM Map pp246-7
☎ 305-672-2000; Delano Hotel, 1685 Collins Ave, South Beach; per day/week $20/75, 10-visit pass $150
Another NYC branch, this is the nightclub of health clubs, where striking poses with your already-in-shape bod is the hottest activity of all. It has top-notch equipment, loud club music and dim (and flattering) lighting. Your workout pass gets you into the pool.

GOLD'S GYM SOUTH BEACH Map pp248-9
☎ 305-538-4653; www.miamibeach411.com/Sports /golds.html; 1400 Alton Rd, South Beach; per day/week $20/90
This outpost of the world's largest gym chain is a 20,000-sq-ft 'super-fitness complex,' featuring cardio machines, free weights, an outdoor patio deck and classes in spinning, boxing, kickboxing, cardio step and lots more. It's South Beach's newest (and biggest) gym.

IDOL'S GYM Map pp246-7
☎ 305-532-0089; 715 Lincoln Ln N, South Beach; per 3 days/week $25/50
Just off Meridian Ave, this small but hip and hottie-filled workout den is best suited for exhibitionists, as the entire space is walled with a glass store front, giving Lincoln Rd passers-by plenty to gawk at.

X-Games Miami

Swimming, running and cycling are good enough activities for most folks in Miami. But for the wildest and craziest enthusiasts, those who just can't seem to get enough adrenaline from such pedestrian workouts, there are extreme sports. Perhaps the most popular (though all are pretty much underground) are wakeboarding and kiteboarding, both of which can be witnessed in the late afternoon on Biscayne Bay, off Key Biscayne. Wakeboarding is to water skiing what snowboarding is to skiing – that is, instead of being on two skis as you're pulled along by a motorboat, you're wearing bindings that attach to a short, wide single board. Then, while moving at an average speed of 20mph, wakeboarders do all sorts of tricks that make them look like on-water skateboarders. The biggest name in wakeboarding these days is Tom Finn, a Floridian who provides commentary for televised competitions and who also runs a Wakeboarder Camp out of Claremont, Florida.

Take that all one step further and you get kiteboarding, which replaces the speeding boat with a massive, parachute-like kite that pulls the boarder along the water's surface at up to 25mph. Kiteboarders often become airborne – up to 20ft or more – before landing and being lifted again and again. Watch these guys fly up and down with unbelievable grace and ease on the glassy bay. For lessons or equipment, try **Miami Kiteboarding** (☎ 305-345-9974; www .miamikiteboarding.com).

Then there's Red Bull Flugtag – more of a wacky stunt than an adventure, but extreme-sport athletes often count it among their interests. It involves creating a handmade flying machine (often Wright Brothers–type airplane wings), strapping it on your back, running along a dock or other 'runway' and hoping to fly a few feet before plunging into the waters below. Miami flugtag contests have taken place off Bayfront Park, but have not yet become regularly organized events. The craziest, not yet with a major foothold in Miami, is BASE Jumping, which is an acronym for the list of places that these folks hurl themselves from – buildings, antenna, span (bridge) and earth. Enthusiasts strongly recommend taking classes in how to leap properly, but only after the beginner has done at least 250 skydives, in order to get comfortable with the feeling of falling. Wakeboarding is sounding better and better all the time...

SOUTH BEACH IRONWORKS

Map pp246-7

☎ 305-531-4743; 1676 Alton Rd, South Beach; per day/3 days/week $15/25/56

Popular with locals, this gym offers lots of yoga and aerobics classes and a super array of workout equipment.

DAY SPAS

On the luxurious side, **Brownes Beauty** (☎ 888-276-9637; www.brownesbeauty.com; 841 Lincoln Rd), Agua Spa at the **Delano** (Map pp246–7; ☎ 305-673-2900; 1685 Collins Ave, South Beach) and Splash Spa at the **Four Seasons** (Map pp252–3; ☎ 305-358-3535; 1435 Brickell Ave; Downtown) will pamper you from head to toe with massages, facials, body wraps and more. **Russian & Turkish Baths** (☎ 305-867-8316; Castillo del Mar, 5445 Collins Ave, Mid-Beach) is less glamorous and very popular because of it.

YOGA & PILATES STUDIOS

MIAMI YOGASHALA Map pp246-7

☎ 305-538-4059; www.miamiyoga.com; 210 23rd St, South Beach

You'll find classes in guided *ashtanga, vinyasa* and power yoga here, plus private sessions, a yoga boutique selling yogic items and frequent workshops.

PILATES MIAMI Map p254

☎ 305-573-4430; 3936 N Miami Ave, Design District; s/semi-private/mat $68/41/15

This Design District loft space offers machine training sessions as well as group classes using mats.

PRANA YOGA CENTER Map pp256-7

☎ 305-567-9812; www.pranayogamiami.com; 247 Malaga Ave, Coral Gables; s/5-class $16/70

In Coral Gables, this multifaceted studio offers classes in *ashtanga, prana, vinyasa, hatha, kundalini* and guided meditation.

SYNERGY CENTER FOR YOGA & THE HEALING ARTS Map pp248-9

☎ 305-538-1244; www.synergyyoga.org; 435 Española Way, South Beach; beach/studio $5/14

Check in here for fabulous on-the-beach yoga classes, plus studio sessions in *ashtanga,* basic, gentle, *iyengar, jivamukti* and pilates.

YOGA GROVE Map p258

☎ 305-448-3332; www.yogagrove.com; 3100 S Dixie Hwy, Coconut Grove; s/5-class $15/65

Located in Coconut Grove, this studio is dedicated to the *ashtanga-vinyasa* system made popular in Mysore, India. Other classes include power yoga and the new afroyoga, a blend of yoga and African dance.

Shopping

Shopping

Americans love to consume, and Miamians are certainly no exception. Whether they're bored, depressed, rich or actually in need of some new clothes or shoes or housewares, you'll find a seemingly endless supply of shoppers who have money burning holes in their pockets. Oh, and you'll quickly join them – whether you're a fan of leisurely shopping or not – because the pickings are so damn fat. Pick a 'hood, any 'hood, and you'll be bombarded by cute boutiques, strips of art galleries, and sexy shops that have such cool music, lighting and vibes that you'll be lured inside, soon dropping cash for the privilege of taking home your new-found love – whether it be a pair of jeans, a piece of jewelry or a simple antique postcard. Mall rats won't have any trouble finding a place to feel at home, as most every region of Miami has a sprawling mega-center, either glitzy or basic, at this point. As for quirkiness and indie shops, stick to the Design District, Little Havana, hotel lobbies, museums and South Beach (though South Beach has had a major influx of major chains of late). Whatever your spending pleasure, you'll find it here.

Top Five Shopping Strips

- At **Collins Ave south of 9th St** Find A/X, Barney's, Sephora and more of the coolest chains ever.
- Mall-store lovers will be in heaven in the **Grand Ave** area of Coconut Grove – and it's alfresco, to boot.
- For boutiques, cafés and people-watching opportunities, visit **Lincoln Road Mall** – there's no better place to shop.
- For home decorators, there's no better spot than **NE 40th St** in the Design District.
- **Bal Harbour Shops** (p142) is the Rodeo Drive of Miami (but inside, of course)

Shopping Areas

Practically every part of Miami has a shopping 'area,' but to simplify matters, and make your beeline to spend simpler, we'll give you the most clear-cut, basic destinations, starting with South Beach, the best place for fashion hunting. There are two main strips in this neighborhood – Lincoln Road Mall, the pedestrian road between Washington Ave and Alton Rd, which is lined with a great mix of indie shops and chain stores, and the southern end of Collins Ave, below 9th St. Here you'll find mostly chains, but high-end ones, such as A/X, Ralph Lauren and Barney's Co-op. Shooting way north of here, you'll find two extremely popular shopping malls: the Aventura Mall (p142), a mainstream collection including JC Penney and Bloomingdale's, and the chichi Bal Harbour Shops (p142), a classy scene boasting Prada, Gucci, Chanel and Saks Fifth Avenue outposts.

Move over to the mainland for more options; the hippest being the Design District, where you'll find a glut of design, art and housewares showrooms and just a sprinkling of clothing and accessories hawkers. Also, just south of here, along NW 6th Ave between 23rd and 29th Sts, is the less fashionable Fashion District (in Wynwood proper), with outlets for about 30 of the 500 or so garment manufactures in the Miami area. From holes-in-the-wall with handbags to a few chic boutiques, patient shoppers will enjoy the adrenaline rush that comes with finding a bargain. You'll have an easier time, though, at the touristy, chain-store-drenched Bayside Marketplace (p143), on the shores of Downtown Miami. Find more outdoor malls in Coconut Grove, at the ever-popular CocoWalk (p146) and adjacent Streets of Mayfair (p146). Coral Gables, meanwhile, has the brand-new Village of Merrick Park (p147), anchored by the classy department stores Neiman Marcus and Nordstrom.

Opening Hours

In areas where creatures of the night are bopping around and ready to spend right up until the moment they hit the restaurants or nightclubs – namely South Beach…and South Beach – expect to find the majority of stores open by 10am and staying open till 9pm or 10pm.

More standard hours of operation, such as in malls and in more staid parts of town, are typically 9am or 10am until 7pm or 8pm. Note that almost all Design District businesses are closed on Sundays and Mondays.

Sales, Taxes & Bargaining

Typically, fashion retail shops around Miami have sales in between seasons – but those seasons are shorter than nonfashionistas would think. Just when you're getting used to it being winter, for example (January), is when winter merchandise will start to get marked down – with savings as high as 60% off – to make way for the new spring duds. Look for summer sales starting in July. If you're lucky and have a keen eye, you can often come across special sale events as well. In the Design District, for example, major sample sales – showcases either for floor samples, surplus stock from the ending season or brand-new introductions from designers – happen a few times a year. Check www.designmiami.com/events for updates. Sales tax in Florida is 6.5%. As for bargaining: this is Miami, people, not India. Unless you're shopping for a used car or a piece of real estate, be prepared to pay what's on the price tag – or forget it.

SOUTH BEACH

Just as it's a winner in most other categories – sleeping, eating, clubbing, sun worshiping – South Beach will not disappoint even the most picky shopper, especially if it's a new wardrobe you're after. You can explore the plethora of stores along Lincoln Road Mall, the long pedestrian-only byway, bursting with boutiques for clothing, gifts, accessories, housewares and food, not to mention a collection of cafés, galleries and even frequent outdoor-market stands hawking produce, plants and antiques. Collins Ave between 6th and 9th Sts, meanwhile, is a less self-contained shopping strip; you'll find an ever-changing crop of trendy retailers, mixed in among boutique hotels and restaurants, and standing within just a block of the beach and its bustling Ocean Dr. Washington Ave is a mixed bag, catering mostly to bargain hunters who forgot to pack sunblock or a beach towel; Alton Rd caters to needs revolving around gourmet food and drink.

ABSOLUTELY SUITABLE

Map pp246-7   *Swimsuits*
☎ 305-604-5281; 1560 Collins Ave
For looking your best on the beach and by the pool, peruse these fine racks for bikinis and swimsuits, in all sizes and shapes imaginable, plus swim trunks, flip-flops and sun hats.

ALEXA & JACK

Map pp246-7   *Children's Clothing & Toys*
☎ 305-534-9300; 635 Lincoln Rd
Can't they just stay little till their Moschinos wear out? This popular Lincoln Rd stop hawks minifashions from the Italian designer, plus D&G Junior and Juicy Couture. Also find quality toys, gifts and accessories.

ART DECO WELCOME CENTER

Map pp248-9   *Collectibles & Gifts*
☎ 305-531-3484; 1001 Ocean Dr
You could get lost in this quirky gift shop – despite the fact that it's teeny. The retail outlet of this information center has shelves stocked with books, jewelry, accessories such as sunglasses and parasols, vintage postcards, posters, souvenir T-shirts and cool little knick-knacks, from table lamps to soap dishes.

ARTCENTER/SOUTH FLORIDA

Map pp246-7   *Art*
☎ 305-538-7887; 800 Lincoln Rd
If you're in the market for painting, sculpture and any other medium by young, up-and-coming artists, this dynamic space, featuring open studios and gallery exhibits, is a good place to start.

A/X ARMANI EXCHANGE

Map pp248-9   *Clothing*
☎ 305-531-5900; 760 Collins Ave
The 'affordable' retail branch of Armani, A/X, is well stocked with all manner of sporty-chic pants, sweaters, jackets, button-downs and dresses.

BARNEY'S NEW YORK CO-OP

Map pp248-9   *Clothing*
☎ 305-421-2010; 832 Collins Ave
The Miami outpost of New York City's hip den of style, this always bustling shop has a little

of everything to satiate label whores – Seven Jeans, Marc by Marc Jacobs trousers, Manolo Blahnik shoes and Khiel's skin balms.

BASE

Map pp246-7   *Clothing, Accessories & Music*
☎ 305-531-4982; www.baseworld.com; 939 Lincoln Rd
Quite likely the coolest new shop on Lincoln Rd, this hip-hop groovy outlet has everything you need to be a good clubber – the latest Puma sneaker styles, funky streetwear, designer baseball caps, men's shaving and skincare products from gourmet labels, and a whole range of CDs (techno, electronica and hip-hop), available for sampling at storefront listening stations.

BASS MUSEUM SHOP

Map pp246-7   *Giftware*
☎ 305-673-7530; 2121 Park Ave
The small, well-curated shop inside this excellent art museum has art, photography and architecture books, unique gift items, postcards, educational toys, and affordable original works of art and jewelry made by local artisans.

Clothing Sizes
Measurements approximate only, try before you buy

Women's Clothing

Aus/UK	8	10	12	14	16	18
Europe	36	38	40	42	44	46
Japan	5	7	9	11	13	15
USA	6	8	10	12	14	16

Women's Shoes

Aus/USA	5	6	7	8	9	10
Europe	35	36	37	38	39	40
France only	35	36	38	39	40	42
Japan	22	23	24	25	26	27
UK	3½	4½	5½	6½	7½	8½

Men's Clothing

Aus	92	96	100	104	108	112
Europe	46	48	50	52	54	56
Japan	S		M	M		L
UK/USA	35	36	37	38	39	40

Men's Shirts (Collar Sizes)

Aus/Japan	38	39	40	41	42	43
Europe	38	39	40	41	42	43
UK/USA	15	15½	16	16½	17	17½

Men's Shoes

Aus/UK	7	8	9	10	11	12
Europe	41	42	43	44½	46	47
Japan	26	27	27½	28	29	30
USA	7½	8½	9½	10½	11½	12½

BEATNIX
Map pp248-9   *Collectibles & Gifts*
☎ 305-532-8733; 1149 Washington Ave;
☷ noon-midnight
This shop has a monstrous collection of kitsch, including clothes such as vinyl dresses, '70s tracksuits and platform heels, plus stuff such as coasters, postcards, glasses and wacky wigs.

BOOKS & BOOKS Map pp246-7   *Books*
☎ 305-532-3222; 933 Lincoln Rd
Like its branch in **Coral Gables** (p147), this indie bookstore has an excellent array of titles, especially when it comes to Floridian and Miamian history, photography, coffee-table tomes, and literature by local authors from Edna Buchanan to Carl Hiaasen. Also catch poetry readings and author book signings.

BROWNES & CO APOTHECARY
Map pp246-7   *Grooming Products*
☎ 305-532-8703; 841 Lincoln Rd
This casually chic shop has the best selection of soaps, cosmetics and beauty and skin products from around the world, from labels including Acca Kappa, Agent Provocateur, Bliss, Bumble & Bumble and Dr Hauschka. The expert staffers also analyze skin and hair problems and offer makeup lessons and a range of salon and spa services.

BURDINES-MACY'S
Map pp246-7   *Department Store*
☎ 305-674-6311; 1675 Meridian Ave
A grand Southern department store, this one-stop-shopping spot, hovering at the edge of Lincoln Rd, is an old-school sort of experience where you'll join retired snowbirds (Northerners who fly south during winter) and hipsters alike, all looking for some sort of dress-lipstick-towel-pillow-sham collection of goods.

CHROMA Map pp246-7   *Women's Clothing*
☎ 305-695-8808; 920 Lincoln Rd
This little gem of an indie boutique, a locals' favorite, features mostly one-of-a-kind pieces from up-and-coming designers. The style is fashionable and edgy, but not so trendy that what you buy won't outlast a couple of seasons.

CLUB MONACO Map p250   *Clothing*
☎ 305-674-7446; 624 Collins Ave
The funky chain boutique has slick and affordable streetwear with a European vibe, for both men and women.

COMPASS MARKET

Map pp248-9   *Essentials*

☎ 305-673-2906; Waldorf Towers Hotel, 860 Ocean Dr
This basement market is packed to the gills with anything you'd ever need while on a relaxing beach vacation: cheap sandals, umbrellas, deli items, cigars, wine and newspapers. And it's got a funky vibe to boot.

DASZIGN NEW YORK

Map p250   *Women's Clothing*

☎ 305-531-5531; www.daszign.com; Ritz-Carlton South Beach, 1663 Collins Ave
Move over, **Scoop** (p141). This new boutique is hot, bursting with labels including Rebecca Taylor, Juicy Couture, 2 B Free, and denim from Seven, Paper Denim & Cloth, Joe's, Hudson and more. Unique accessories and footwear from New York designers are also on full display.

DECO DENIM Map p250   *Clothing*

☎ 305-532-6986; 645 Collins Ave
For basic casualwear, this is your place, especially if you're looking to pick up some classic American Levi's in any form – from 501 button fly and super-low 518s to boot cuts and cargo pants.

EN AVANCE Map pp246-7   *Clothing*

☎ 305-534-0337; 734 Lincoln Rd
Want your shopping experience to be as chic as your nightclubbing? Then by all means head here, where you'll be greeted by a velvet rope and a hot collection of high fashion once inside. The friendly staff will help you negotiate through the Rebecca Taylor, Juicy Couture, Tse and more. You'll also find Defile makeup and even designer styles for infants. Don't be surprised if you rub elbows with a celeb or two.

EPICURE MARKET

Map pp246-7   *Gourmet Food & Wine*

☎ 305-672-1861; 1656 Alton Rd
Whether you have cooking facilities in your inn or just want to shop for a fancy beach picnic, this is the place. You'll find an outstanding array of fresh produce, sinful baked goods, fresh flowers, premade meals (including matzo-ball soup, lasagna and salads), imported treats such as jams and tapenades, and an excellent selection of fine, global wines.

ETE Map pp246-7   *Clothing & Accessories*

☎ 305-672-3265; 530 Lincoln Rd
A little fashion treasure trove, this den of funky casualwear includes items from Paul Frank and

similarly fresh, youthful styles. The backpack set will be thrilled with the selection of babydoll tees, quirky socks and hoodies.

INTERMIX Map pp246-7   *Women's Clothing*

☎ 305-531-5950; 1634 Collins Ave
A funky fresh purveyor of stylish basics, also with outposts in New York and Los Angeles, this is the perfect place to find the perfect tee, skirt or sweater.

JEWISH MUSEUM OF FLORIDA GIFT SHOP Map p250   *Judaica*

☎ 305-672-5044; www.jewishmuseum.com; 301 Washington Ave
The gift shop in the front lobby of this museum is tiny, but it has a lovely little selection of Judaica, including menorahs, Sabbath-candle holders, mezuzahs and prayer books.

JOYELLA

Map pp246-7   *Women's Clothing & Accessories*

☎ 305-531-5338; www.joyella.com; 841 Lincoln Rd
A new boutique, Joyella boasts a superb array of clothing from local and global designers, from a Lucy Barnes hand-beaded velvet skirt to swimwear from Miami's Red Carter.

KAFKA INC Map pp248-9   *Books*

☎ 305-673-9669; 1464 Washington Ave
Kafka is one-stop shopping for word lovers: you'll find thousands of used books, a terrific magazine and newspaper selection, Internet access on 24 computer terminals and a café.

KIEHL'S Map pp246-7   *Grooming Products*

☎ 305-531-0404; www.kiehls.com; 832 Lincoln Rd
Since 1851, when this old-fashioned apothecary got its start in NYC's East Village, this

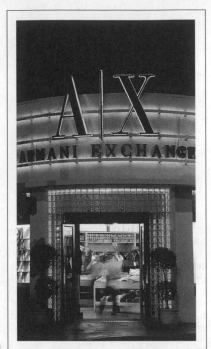

A/X Armani Exchange (p137), South Beach

simple-label, simple-formula line of products has had many ardent fans. This sleek South Beach emporium is now just one of many locations across the country hawking the high-quality lip balms, skin moisturizers, shampoos, soaps, hair-styling lotions and shaving products.

LILIBLUE PARIS

Map p250 *Jewelry & Accessories*
☎ 305-538-7431; 760 Ocean Dr
Born in Cannes and now expanded to NYC, West Palm Beach and right here on Ocean Dr, this sophisticated shop sells lovely bags, scarves and jewelry from France and Italy.

MAC Map p250 *Cosmetics*
☎ 305-604-9040; 650 Collins Ave
Join the fabulous folks who have, at one point or another, been spokesmodels for this *trés* hip makeup shop: RuPaul, KD Lang, Linda Evangelista and Diana Ross. You'll be ready to do a testimonial, too, once you fall in love with the cosmetics' sleek packaging, fab hues,

subtle fragrance and great staying power – as well as the shop's policy to donate all sales profits from its Viva Glam lipstick to the Mac AIDS Fund.

ME & RO Map pp246-7 *Jewelry*
☎ 305-672-3566; Shore Club, 1901 Collins Ave
If it's in the Shore Club, it has got to be good. Right? Join in-the-know bauble mavens (including Julia Roberts) who shop for these bracelets, rings and earrings in silver and gold, crafted with Asian accents by celebrity jewelers Robin Renzi and Michele Quan.

MISS SIXTY Map pp246-7 *Women's Clothing*
☎ 305-538-3547; 845 Lincoln Rd
This is one seriously hot Italian label, boasting an array of jeans, dresses, jackets and sweaters for the cool, skinny, model-beautiful gals among us.

NEO ACCESSARIO

Map pp246-7 *Accessories*
☎ 305-674-1317; 710 Lincoln Rd
Why do celebs including J Lo and Gloria Estefan flock here to buy bags and belts? Come see for yourself, and find a superior selection of accessories, including lots of lavish leather, from a range of top-end designers.

NEO SCARPA Map pp246-7 *Shoes*
☎ 305-535-5633; 817 Lincoln Rd
Owned by the same folks who own **Neo Accessario** (above), this shoe addict's heaven is on fire. Find slick (and pricey) styles for your dogs from Miu Miu, Prada, Enrico Fantini and many more.

NEWS CAFÉ STORE

Map pp248-9 *Periodicals*
☎ 305-538-6397; 800 Ocean Dr
Look for the separate 24-hour newsstand between the **News Café** (p92) bar and restaurant. It has a good selection of international and domestic papers.

NICOLE MILLER

Map p250 *Women's Clothing*
☎ 305-535-2200; www.nicolemiller.com; 656 Collins Ave
Think Hamptons-chic at this boutique: home to perfect little halter tops, skirts, cocktail dresses and blouses.

POP Map pp248-9 *Collectibles & Gifts*
☎ 305-604-9604; 1151 Washington Ave
Find the collectible kitsch of your dreams at this pop-culture purveyor. From George Jet-

son and his nuclear family to Ken and Barbie, the traditional household unit is covered.

RECYCLED BLUES

Map pp246-7   *Used Clothing*
☎ 305-538-0656; 1507 Washington Ave
Got budgetary blues? This place makes South Beach a great nabe for used clothing. Find Levi's for $15, shorts for $10 and jackets for $20.

RITCHIE SWIMWEAR

Map pp248-9   *Swimwear*
☎ 305-538-0201; 106 8th St
Mix-n-match bikini tops and bottoms make a big-busted, tiny-hinied (or flat-chested, big-bootied) gal feel at home. This place is heavy on string-comprised, minimum-coverage styles.

SAGE APOTHECARY

Map p250   *Grooming Products*
☎ 305-674-8591; 425 Washington Ave
This hot newcomer is a cool place to stock up on Nyakio coffee-and-sugar body scrub, Glow shea-butter bath truffles, Belli skincare for expectant moms, coconut-scented South Beach Lip Shine by Tinte Cosmetics, and just about any other feel-good product you need, from nail polish to face moisturizer.

SCOOP Map pp246-7   *Clothing*
☎ 305-532-5929; Shore Club, 1901 Collins Ave
Located off the billowy **Shore Club** (p157) lobby, this is the spot to scoop up hot-ticket fashion items for men and women, from both its own label and others, including Juicy Couture, Paul Smith and Theory.

SEE Map pp246-7   *Eyewear*
☎ 305-672-6622; 921 Lincoln Rd
Find high-style eyeglass frames from clunky electroclash-DJ to wireframe bookish-babe, straight from manufacturers used by big-name labels, all available at reasonable prices.

SENZATEMPO

Map pp246-7   *Housewares & Gifts*
☎ 305-534-5588; 1655 Meridian Ave
This retro gallery shop has an array of decorative pieces and 20th-century designer furniture plus plenty of clocks and watches.

SEPHORA Map p250   *Cosmetics & Fragrances*
☎ 305-532-0904; 721 Collins Ave
This massive makeup chain emporium has every conceivable line of cosmetics and skin products – Clinique, Hamadi, Clarins, Toni &

Tina, Hard Candy, Nars, Estée Lauder, Paula Dorf, Korres and much, much more.

SOBE SHOE COMPANY

Map pp246-7   *Shoes*
☎ 305-695-9585; 829 Lincoln Rd
Behind the slightly intimidating, ever-so-fashionable facade is actually a very cool collection of hip styles at even cooler bargain prices.

SPEC'S MUSIC Map p250   *Music*
☎ 305-534-3667; 501 Collins Ave
Spec's, the Tower Records of Miami, has almost 20 supershops around town (for a list, check www.fye.com). This two-story location has a café, lots of listening booths and a so-so selection of CDs, DVDs and videos that leans toward the mainstream.

UNCLE SAM'S MUSIC Map pp248-9   *Music*
☎ 305-532-0973; 1141 Washington Ave
Join the hipper-than-thou skate rats and club kids who dig through piles of the coolest new (and used) trance, hip-hop and trip-hop, as well as stickers, clubwear, incense and the like.

VERSACE JEANS COUTURE

Map pp248-9   *Clothing*
☎ 305-532-5993; 755 Washington Ave
Creepily located just a couple of blocks from where Versace himself was gunned down by a stalker, the big spenders milling about among the racks of jeans, shirts and jackets don't seem the least bit fazed by the irony. And once you get hypnotized by the sexy collection here, you may not be either.

Top Five Local Designers

- The creator of the Raiza clothing and accessories line, **Theresa Turchin**, won the 2004 GenArt's Fresh Faces Award.
- **Red Carter** is a South Beach–based bikini designer; fans love the removable bust pads, double lining and signature red-beach-bag packaging. Styles have local names such as 'the Shore Club' and 'the Española Way.'
- Based in Coral Gables, **Eileen Christine** makes signature handbags from Cuban cigar boxes, adding semiprecious handles.
- **Julian Chang**'s couture is graceful and chic yet tailored.
- The popular Krelwear line of **Karelle Levy** is based on brightly colored, clingy knit pieces.

WHITTALL & SHON

Map pp248-9   *Menswear*

☎ 305-538-2606; 1319 Washington Ave

The disco beat here gets your adrenaline going while you flip through racks of way-gay muscle tees, tank tops and sundry other clingy tops, some sporting cruisey phrases like 'caliente!,' '69' or 'coach.' Teensy, bubble-butt-squeezing swim trunks are also on display.

WILD OATS NATURAL MARKETPLACE

Map pp248-9   *Health Food & Groceries*

☎ 305-532-1707; 1020 Alton Rd

This natural-food grocery store has a great array of organic produce, packaged products from cereals to soaps, bulk items, prepared meals and an OK salad bar. You'll also find a good range of wines, beers and fresh elixirs squeezed at the juice bar. Come here for a coffee too.

WOLFSONIAN-FIU GIFT SHOP

Map pp248-9   *Giftwares*

☎ 305-531-1001; Wolfsonian-FIU,
1001 Washington Ave

The small gift shop housed in this quirky and wonderful museum of design has one of the most unique collections of eclectic items around. You'll find sleek business-card holders, oddly shaped water pitchers and glassware, technofied bags and notebooks, excellent art and design books, cool wallets and more.

MIAMI BEACH TO AVENTURA

This northern stretch Miami Beach – that is, the entire swath above South Beach, which ends around 21st St – is known for its preponderance of malls, namely those of **Aventura** (below) and **Bal Harbour Shops** (right), all of which are stuffed with pretty outstanding shops of every genre (despite being airless, Muzak-spewing, fake environment…well… *malls*). Various little independent shops are always popping up too, so keep your eyes open for fun stops en route to the megamall of your choice.

AVENTURA MALL

                                    Mall

☎ 305-935-1110; www.shopaventuramall.com; 19501 Biscayne Blvd

This mainstream granddaddy of a mall attracts families with its enormous indoor playground, and shoppers with its Macy's, Lord & Taylor, Burdines and Bloomingdale's department stores, plus smaller boutiques of every genre (including the forthcoming Anthropologie clothing shop and Tumi luggage emporium). There is also a scarily massive 24-screen movie theater with stadium seating, as well as hotel shuttles that make it a cinch even for South Beach visitors to haul themselves up here.

BAL HARBOUR SHOPS Map p251   *Mall*

☎ 305-866-0311; www.balharbourshops.com; 9700 Collins Ave

This exclusive, Rodeo Drive–like Bal Harbour Shops mall (opposite) boasts tony shops such as Chanel and Hermés, plus has a parking garage and outdoor cafés and sitting areas. The anchor department stores are Saks Fifth Avenue and Neiman Marcus.

BCBG MAXAZRIA

                                    Clothing

☎ 305-936-9227; Aventura Mall, 19501 Biscayne Blvd

This clothier has the signature fashions of the BCBG label, from sexy power suits to cocktail dresses and slimming trousers and jackets.

BETSEY JOHNSON

                                    Clothing

☎ 305-673-0023; Aventura Mall, 19501 Biscayne Blvd

The bright, quirky and thoroughly eclectic line from the bright-eyed Betsey specializes in fun and sexy skirts and dresses, with funkified frilly blouses and hose thrown in for good measure.

KOKO & PALENKI SHOES

                                  Shoes

☎ 305-792-9299; Aventura Mall, 19501 Biscayne Blvd

Get excited over the addiction-inspiring collection here, with styles from D&G, Guess, Charles Jourdan and more.

LALIQUE Map p251   *Giftware*

☎ 305-861-5211; Bal Harbour Shops, 9700 Collins Ave

The French makers of fine gifts present their awe-inspiring collection of crystal vases, fine stemware, leather bags, silk scarves, porcelain dishware and high-end watches and jewelry. It's the perfect place to shop for a high-class bride.

LA PERLA Map p251   *Lingerie*

☎ 305-864-2070; Bal Harbour Shops, 9700 Collins Ave

This fine and sexy lingerie collection, in silk and lace, is the perfect object of splurging if you want to make a particular impression in the boudoir.

Bal Harbour Shops: Must You *Really* Call It a Mall?

For anyone used to malls and all their mainstream cheese – food courts, Gaps and Payless Shoes, roving packs of teens – you're in for a shock at the Bal Harbour Shops. Visited by some of the poshest mavens in Miami, this is the place for consumers with lots of class and even more cash. It was rated the number-one shopping mall in the country by *Women's Wear Daily*, boasts super-lovely plantings and landscaping, and has a roster of stores that reads like a Beverly Hills who's who: Bulgari, Brooks Brothers, Cartier, Dolce & Gabbana, Emporio Armani, Fendi, Gucci, Lacoste, Marc Jacobs, Prada, Tiffany & Co, Yves Saint Laurent and much, much more. And don't worry, normal-income folks: you'll find Banana Republic, Gap and Ann Taylor, too.

MIKE'S CIGARS

Map p251 *Collectibles & Gifts*
☎ 305-866-2277; 1030 Kane Concourse, off 96th St;
☯ 8am-6:30pm Mon-Fri
Although Little Havana hosts the bulk of Miami's cigar shops, Mike's offers sweet tobacco from Jamaica, Honduras and the Dominican Republic.

MINI OXYGENE

Map p251 *Children's Clothing*
☎ 305-868-4499; Bal Harbour Shops, 9700 Collins Ave
Clothe your baby or toddler in fine French fashions. Isn't the mini-you worth it?

TARGET *Discount Superstore*
☎ 305-933-4616; 21265 Biscayne Blvd, Aventura
☎ 305-668-0262; 8350 S Dixie Hwy, South Miami
☎ 305-944-5341; 14075 Biscayne Blvd, N Miami Beach
☎ 305-386-1244; 15005 SW 8th St, Kendall
It's the discount-store of the moment in US cities, with good reason. Where else can you find Isaac Mizrahi fashions, high-threadcount sheets, a new set of flatware, a digital camera, shoes, Michael Graves–designed housewares, toys, shower curtains and a bag of potato chips all under one roof? Prices are incredibly cheap, too.

TIFFANY & CO Map p251 *Gifts & Jewelry*
☎ 305-864-1801; Bal Harbour Shops, 9700 Collins Ave
Tiffany is home of the famed little blue box and was forever immortalized by Audrey Hepburn. This Miami outpost means you now don't need to go to New York's Fifth Ave to have the same remarkable array of gift items – from Elsa Peretti silver-heart necklaces and Tiffany jazz diamonds to china dinnerware and Atlas watches.

WHOLE FOODS MARKET

Map pp244-5 *Natural-Foods Grocery*
☎ 305-933-1543; 21105 Biscayne Blvd
If you're up in this neck of the woods, come here to marvel at the massive, well-stocked shelves of picture-perfect exotic produce, hormone-free meats and poultry, gourmet chocolates, imported olives, fine wines and aisles upon aisles of natural or organic food and health-and-beauty products.

DOWNTOWN MIAMI

The heart of Downtown, especially along Flagler St, is crammed with dozens upon dozens of shops selling export-ready electronics, primarily to Latin American visitors. You'll also see countless storefronts hawking cheap luggage, watches, cameras (without warranties) and leather items, mainly to the folks who pile off cruise ships day after day at the nearby port. Then, of course, there's the Mall of America–ish **Bayside Marketplace** (below), with enough mainstream chain stores to make your head spin.

BAYSIDE MARKETPLACE

Map pp252-3 *Outdoor Mall*
☎ 305-577-3344; www.baysidemarketplace.com; 401 Biscayne Blvd
This touristy bayfront mall has entertainment, restaurants, bars, tour-boat docks, push-cart vendors and name-brand shops. A sampling of usual suspects includes the Disney Store, Victoria's Secret, Sunglass Hut, Bath & Body Works, Gap, Express, Skechers and, of course, Starbucks. There are no surprises, except for the nice views.

BURDINES-MACY'S

Map pp252-3 *Department Store*
☎ 305-577-2312; 22 E Flagler St
This is the Downtown branch of Burdines, a grand Southern department store offering everything from clothing for women, men and children; housewares for the bath and bedroom; jewelry and watches; shoes and more.

GOTTA HAVE IT!
COLLECTIBLES
Collectibles

☎ 305-446-5757; 4231 SW 71st Ave

For autograph hounds who've just 'gotta have it,' these folks can make sure you get it. From signed team jerseys and JFK paraphernalia to the estate of Marilyn Monroe and Beatles album jackets, they've seen and sold it all.

HISTORICAL MUSEUM OF SOUTHERN FLORIDA GIFT SHOP

Map pp252-3 *Collectibles & Gifts*

☎ 305-375-1492; 101 W Flagler St

The gift shop at the **Historical Museum of Southern Florida** (p60) thrives on Florida, Florida and more Florida: think faux alligators and tacky postcards, plus a fine array of Seminole arts, eclectic souvenirs and Miami books.

SEYBOLD BUILDING Map pp252-3 *Accessories*

☎ 305-374-7922; 36 NE 1st St; 🕑 9am-5:30pm Mon-Sat

Upwards of 300 independent stores in this sort of mini-mall offer a lively array of glittery diamonds, gold pendants, rings and other trinkets.

WALLFLOWER GALLERY Map pp252-3 *Art*

☎ 305-579-0069; 10 NE 3rd St

Put this funky, cool gallery on your short list of places to check out. Between performance pieces, live music and 'regular' art shows featuring local talent, this cultural oasis boasts plenty of artwork worth splurging for.

WYNWOOD, THE DESIGN DISTRICT & LITTLE HAITI

You'll find mighty eclectic offerings in these parts – from the design-heavy boutiques and showrooms that cluster around the square mile of the Design District to the random fashion, book and art shops that pop up both north and south of the area. Still, if art and design are what you feel like throwing cash at, you are the ones who will be most pleased with the pickings in these parts.

ANNABELLA BUCHELI COLLECTION

Map p254 *Interior Design*

☎ 305-573-0605; 4100 NE 2nd Ave

This 7000-sq-ft Design District showroom features exclusive designs and furniture, wood

Top Five Indie Clothing Boutiques

- **Base** (p138) mixes up clubwear with footwear, skin products and CDs – with plenty for the boys.
- It's new; it's chic; it's in the Ritz-Carlton. It's **Daszign New York** (p139).
- Join in-the-know locals who love the fashion basics at **Chroma** (p138).
- Local designers are on full display at **Joyella** (p139) – including Red Carter's on-fire bikinis.
- With **Soye** (opposite), two Colombian brothers brought their fashion genius to the Little Haiti region.

flooring and custom upholstery for all your interior-design needs.

ARTISAN ANTIQUES ART DECO

Map p254 *Furniture & Home Design*

☎ 305-573-5619; 110 NE 40th St

Here you'll find the Design District's largest selection of French art-deco lighting, furniture and accessories, including unique pieces by LaliqueSabino and De Gue.

BARBARA GILLMAN GALLERY

Map p254 *Art*

☎ 305-759-9155; 3814 NE Miami Ct

From unknown local painters to Rauschenberg and Warhol, to a tried-and-true collection of black-and-white jazz photography by Herman Leonard, this gallery has the lot. It also has staying power and plenty of art-collecting fans.

HOLLY HUNT

Map p254 *Furniture & Home Design*

☎ 305-571-2012; www.hollyhunt.com; 3833 NE 2nd Ave

This spectacular 22,000-sq-ft showroom has a massive selection of furniture, textiles, lighting, art and decorative accessories. Featured designers include Holly Hunt, Christian Liaigre, Rose Tarlow and Kevin Kiley.

KARTELL Map p254 *Home Design*

☎ 305-573-4010; 170 NE 40th St

This large storefront is filled with a pretty panoply of plastics – all finely sculpted in to bona fide works of art (in the form of chairs, shelving units and tables) by designers including Philippe Starck, Giulio Polvara and Anna Castelli Ferrieri.

KUMA CENTRAL Map p254 *Art Toys*
☎ 305-573-4486; 130 NE 40th St

A small and funky limited-edition toy shop, Kuma Central features various little action-figure bears based on a sleek and cartoonish Japanese design. Choose from unique offerings, including small figurines, plush toys, T-shirts, baseball caps, art toys and prints.

LAMBDA PASSAGE
Map p251 *Books & Videos*
☎ 305-754-6900; 7545 Biscayne Blvd

Since the mid-1980s, this bookstore has been a fixture and meeting place for gays and lesbians, and a seller of coming-out books, gay literature, rainbow paraphernalia, magazines and films; it also has a special back-room for queer porn.

LIBRERI MAPOU Map p254 *Books & Music*
☎ 305-757-9922; 5919 NE 2nd Ave

For a good taste of Haitian culture, peruse the shelves at this bookstore, bursting with 3000 titles (including periodicals) in English, French and Creole, as well as items such as crafts and recorded music.

LUXE Map p254 *Lighting*
☎ 305-576-6639; 1 NE 40th St

Light up your life – and your home, wherever it may be – with some of the classiest, trendiest designer lighting accessories ever. Choose among chandeliers, wall sconces, table lamps, floor lamps, halogen lighting and lighting controls.

M-80 Map p254 *Clubwear*
☎ 305-573-2122; 21 NW 36th St

Club kids can get well outfitted here. There are hip clothing styles, artsy plush toys and electronic music, which you're free to test out at the small collection of in-store turntables.

SOYE
Map p254 *Women's Clothing & Accessories*
☎ 305-757-8577; 5580 NE 4th Ct (Biscayne Blvd at 55th St)

This tiny little storefront, located just next door to the restaurant **Sokya** (p102), is a fashion boutique owned by two enterprising brothers from Colombia, Alberto and Robert Chehebar. It's name is derived from Colombian slang meaning 'a mind-altering experience.' The designers make only five of each piece, each of which is funky, elegant and on the cutting edge of style.

TREE OF ZION
Map p254 *Used Clothing & Accessories*
☎ 305-573-5874; 2426 NE 2nd Ave

This new little vegan and raw-foods hippie eatery has a small shop in back, where the owners hawk used dresses, tees, shoes, scarves, bags, belts and whatever else they can rustle up. You never know what treasure you'll unearth.

WORLD RESOURCES
Map p254 *Gifts & Housewares*
☎ 305-576-8799; www.worldresources.com; 45 NE 39th St

An excellent boutique, World Resources has a truly unique collection of furniture and objects d'art from India and Indonesia, as well as beautiful pillows, candles and the like.

LITTLE HAVANA

It should come as no surprise that this is the 'hood to hit if you're in the market for some tasty, fresh-rolled cigars. You'll also find great selections of Latin music, kitschy souvenirs, Spanish-language books and authentic Cuban clothing.

CERVANTES BOOK STORE
Map p255 *Books*
☎ 305-642-5222; 1898 SW 8th St

Find all sorts of titles, from timeless classics to crappy romances, all *en español*.

DO RE MI MUSIC CENTER
Map p255 *Music*
☎ 305-541-3374; 1820 SW 8th St

It's Latin music in all forms – CDs, vinyl, cassettes and even a range of instruments for you to bust out on by yourself.

EL CRÉDITO CIGARS Map p255 *Cigars*
☎ 305-858-4162; 1106 SW 8th St

Owner Ernest Curillo and friends hand roll some damn tasty stogies here – for purchase in bulk or singles.

HAVANA-TO-GO Map p255 *Souvenirs*
☎ 305-857-9720; www.littlehavanatogo.com; 1442 SW 8th St

This is Little Havana's official souvenir store, and it has some pretty cool items, from Cuban-pride T-shirts to posters, flags, paintings, photo books, cigar-box purses and authentic clothing.

LA TRADICIÓN CUBANA Map p255 *Cigars*
☎ 305-643-4005; 1895 SW 8th St
Watch workers roll your cigars before you buy them at this little rolling factory.

OLD CUBA: THE COLLECTION
Map p255 *Souvenirs*
☎ 305-643-6269; www.oldcubathecollection.com; 1561 SW 8th St
Here you can get your hands on just about any sort of Cuba-themed souvenir that you desire. Whether it's Team Habana baseball hats and T-shirts, rhinestone 'Cubanita' belt buckles, straw hats, Lucy & Ricky cigar-box purses, coffee-table books, or even bottles of Havana cola – they're all here.

POWER RECORDS Map p255 *Music*
☎ 305-285-2212; 1419 SW 8th St
Comb the racks for your favorites from a huge selection of Cuban, salsa, rumba, South American and Latin sounds.

KEY BISCAYNE
It's certainly not a shopping destination, but if you find yourself on this fantasy island and need something (well, shorts, toys or some gourmet food), you'll be pleasantly surprised with the few worthy options.

PALM PRODUCE RESORTWEAR
Map p259 *Clothing*
☎ 305-361-6999; 328 Crandon Blvd
Buy all your swimsuits, flip-flops, sun hats and flowered, draw-string, loungey resort-getups, especially from that classic Jams label, at this mellow beach boutique.

STEFANO'S Map p259 *Italian Grocery*
☎ 305-361-7007; 24 Crandon Blvd
If you find yourself in sudden need of olive oil, biscotti, ground coffee, imported pasta or canned tomatoes, the small Italian grocery attached to this popular surf-n-turf restaurant is there for you.

TOY TOWN Map p259 *Toys*
☎ 305-361-5501; 260 Crandon Blvd
This adorable kids' shop has all the distractions you'll need, from Beanie Babies and Barbies to sand toys, model cars, stuffed animals, tricycles and dress-up costumes.

COCONUT GROVE
With a few exceptions, individual shops have given way to those two infamous outdoor malls. Still, it's worth hunting around for the examples of funky, old-time Coconut Grove.

ARCHITECTURAL ANTIQUES
Map pp258 *Antiques*
☎ 305-285-1330; 2500 SW 28th Ln
Since much of the merchandise in this warehouse comes from mansions, there's treasure in these serious piles of furniture, paintings and other household items. Get ready for a scavenger hunt.

COCOWALK Map p258 *Mall*
☎ 305-444-0777; 3015 Grand Ave
In the heart of a formerly charming neighborhood, this open-air mall has a Gap, Victoria's Secret, Banana Republic and all the other usual suspects – plus a 16-screen AMC movie theatre.

STREETS OF MAYFAIR Map p258 *Mall*
☎ 305-448-1700; 2911 Grand Ave
Sitting adjacent to CocoWalk, the Streets of Mayfair shopping mall offers a whole other range of chain stores – Borders bookstore, Banana Republic, Bath & Body Works – plus some cute indie boutiques and a few restaurants and galleries.

Top Five Ethical Buys
- All profits from Viva Glam lipstick sold at **Mac** (p140) benefit the Mac AIDS Fund.
- Support local growers – especially those who shun pesticides – by buying organic avocados at the **farmers' market** (p88).
- Purchase an antique clock from Coconut Grove's **Antique & Jewelry Show** (opposite). You could also choose a vintage bracelet or lamp or anything else. Either way, your purchase benefits Coconut Grove Cares, a social-service organization that runs various youth programs.
- Drinking fair-trade coffee at **Wild Oats Natural Marketplace** (p142) will allow you to support the fair-trade label and get some good, organic beans while you're at it.
- Among other ethical items in the gift shop at **Lowe Art Museum** (p73) are the beautiful Claude Monet cards, printed on 100% recycled paper and assembled by disabled US veterans.

Outdoor Markets

Sure, shopping is fun. The thing is, with Miami's beautiful sunny, breezy days, who wants to be cooped up inside stores or malls all day long? The city's range of outdoor markets – from flea markets to green markets – is the perfect indoor-shopping antidote, often boasting some of the most unique merchandise around. Antique lovers will want to make it a point to check out the **Antiques & Collectibles Market** (☎ 305-673-4991; Lincoln Rd, South Beach), held on the second and fourth Sunday of each month, and the **Antique & Jewelry Show** (☎ 305-444-8454; S Bayshore Dr, Coconut Grove). Held on the third weekend of each month, the proceeds here benefit Coconut Grove Cares, which funds after-school and summer-job youth programs. For various crafts, artworks, clothing, global foods and jewelry, check out the hippie-style Española Way Market, between Washington and Drexel Aves in South Beach, every weekend. And, a bit out of the way at the **Opa-Locka/Hialeah Flea Market** (Map pp244–5; ☎ 305-688-8080; 12705 NW 42nd Ave), you're sure to find what you want, as the daily blowout boasts about 1200 vendors, hawking everything from jeans and carpets to jewelry and antiques. (For a rundown of area farmers' markets, where you can buy fresh produce, plants and flowers, see p88).

CORAL GABLES

Miracle Mile is a broad and shady street that runs from dowdy discount shops to an unusually large selection of bridal shops, with a constantly changing mall that's being led by Starbucks, Barnes & Noble and the like. The biggest shopping news in these parts, though, has been the recent and much-heralded arrival of **Village of Merrick Park** (right), which is – what else? – a mall.

ARTEMIDE Map pp256-7 *Lighting Design*
☎ 305-444-5800; www.artemide.com; 277 Giralda Ave
This Italian company features cutting-edge lamp and lighting styles from international designers.

BOOKS & BOOKS Map pp256-7 *Books*
☎ 305-442-4408, 296 Aragon Ave
Long live the independents! The best locally owned bookstores, Books & Books hosts visiting authors, discussions and poetry readings and has an excellent selection of materials, much like its other branch in **South Beach** (p138).

LOWE ART MUSEUM GIFT SHOP
Map pp256-7 *Gifts*
☎ 305-284-3535; www.lowemuseum.org;
1301 Stanford Dr
On the University of Miami campus, the Lowe has one of Dade County's largest permanent collections – as well as a great little gift shop filled with unique finds, from excellent art books to global crafts and jewelry.

MIAMI TWICE *Collectibles & Gifts*
☎ 305-666-0127; 6562 SW 40th St
Collectibles, accessories, jewelry and clothes… it's all here at a veritable retro department store where you'll find everything from Bakelite jewelry and fiestawear to leather jackets and furniture from throughout the decades.

MODERNISM GALLERY
Map pp256-7 *Furniture & Design*
☎ 305-442-8743; 1622 Ponce de León Blvd
If you're serious about vintage and retro interior design, then look no further than this renowned dealer of deco furniture and accessories, plus a range of items from designers including Gilbert Rohde and Paul Frank.

VILLAGE OF MERRICK PARK
Map pp256-7 *Mall*
☎ 305-529-0200; www.villageofmerrickpark.com;
358 San Lorenzo Ave
Anchored by Nordstrom and Neiman Marcus department stores, this upscale newcomer boasts boutiques including Burberry, Gucci, Etro, Anthropologie, Betsey Johnson, Ann Taylor and Jimmy Choo.

ELSEWHERE IN MIAMI

Beyond the usual borders is where you'll find even more malls, not to mention some discount superstores.

DADELAND MALL Map pp244-5 *Mall*
☎ 305-665-6226; www.shopsimon.com; 7535 N Kendall Dr
In addition to 175 or so other stores, this massive Kendall mall boasts Florida's first and largest Burdines department store, plus another Burdines solely devoted to home furnishings. Also find Lord & Taylor, Saks Fifth Avenue, a two-story Express and the unexpectedly cool Arango, a local, independent housewares store.

DOLPHIN MALL Map pp244-5 *Mall*

☎ 305-365-7446; www.shopdolphinmall.com; Florida's Turnpike & Dolphin Expressway, 11401 NW 12th St, Greater Miami

This mall boasts Saks Fifth Avenue, Marshall's Megastore, Mikasa, BCBG and Burlington Coat Factory, plus a 28-screen cinema, huge food court, rollercoaster and bowling alley (p113).

YESTERDAY & TODAY *Music*

☎ 305-468-0311; 7902 NW 36th St

This being DJ-saturated Miami, Yesterday & Today has that comforting, old-school medium known as vinyl, as well as every other recorded-music format. The very helpful and knowledgeable staff specialize in '50s, '60s and '70s tunes, and even have a selection of 45s (singles).

Sleeping

Sleeping

When it comes to cool hotels, Miami may very well be the world capital. This is the town that has elevated sleeping nooks to a high art form – especially in South Beach, where gem-like art-deco buildings, usually two- to four-stories high, have received stunning makeovers inside and out. Meanwhile, new neighbors have moved in, and all are upping the ante on each other by offering over-the-top treats such as frothy waterfalls and soft-sand beaches – indoors – and alfresco lounges sprawling across rooftops and poolsides. North Beach and Downtown dens have also stepped up their offerings, upscale chains included, as everyone seems locked in a spiraling frenzy to lure the most beautiful and fabulous guests around. Because of their talents, hoteliers – especially bed king Ian Schrager (**Shore Club**, p157; **Delano**, p155) and design guru André Balazs (**Raleigh**, p157; **Standard**, p162) – are seen as rock stars. Even locals clamor to get inside their places, anxious to sip cocktails and strike poses with the best of 'em. And nostalgia seekers, beware: Key Biscayne's classic **Sonesta Beach Resort** (p161), the area's preeminent property for more than 36 years, is to be no more. Struggling among glitzier competition, the resort will be torn down and replaced with a five-star hotel. It will include, of course, plenty of condo-hotel units.

Don't be too intimidated by the glamour, though. Because Miami hotels just won't stop coming (there are more than 500 and counting), proprietors can't sleep on the job; instead, they must do all they can to ensure a steady flow of customers, and in many cases, that means offering rates competitive enough to let just about anyone join the party. Plus, there is a fair share of quality budget boutiques – check out the offerings from the clever South Beach Group (see the **Chesterfield**, opposite) and a couple of hostels scattered among the glitter, where their short walks to the beach and hoppin' lobby bars make it easy to forget you're not at the hottest place in town.

Price Ranges

Accommodations costs range wildly, depending on the place, the name, the location and the season. (In Florida 'high season' is defined as running between December and April.) Generally, a budget hotel costs less than $100 a night during the low season, while the most expensive places start at $300 and rise steeply from there; hostel beds (in shared rooms) can be had for as low as $15 a night. Hotels that front the ocean are almost always the most expensive – but beware that you may pay even more in the form of sleep, as the throbbing beat of music and chatting along South Beach's Ocean Dr could keep you up all night. No matter where you stay, you'll have to pay the 12.5% room tax. A few places even tack on an obligatory 15% service charge.

And parking is always going to cost you, no matter which option you choose: there are meter lots, which are just $1 an hour but require you to feed in your quarters every three

---

The Rate Stuff

When you're booking a room in Miami, it can pay – in savings of up to 50% – to not make your reservations with the hotel directly. That's because the published rates, known in the biz as 'rack rates,' are always the highest when quoted by the hotel directly. Instead, do what all savvy travelers know to do: use an Internet search engine to help track down the lowest possible rates. Some of the best sites include **Orbitz** (www.orbitz.com), **Go Travel** (www.gotravel.com), and **Expedia** (www.expedia.com), which also offer discounts on air travel and car rentals, and sometimes packages of all three. Other sites, such as **Priceline** (www.priceline.com) and **Hotwire** (www.hotwire.com), let you enter a bid for the type of hotel you're interested in, and then either accept or reject it. That comes with risks, however, as you don't know where you'll end up until your bid is already locked in and you've been automatically charged. Also, check the individual hotel's website: many offer deals if you book through the Internet, rather than on the phone.

hours; garages, which are about $8 to $10 a day but don't include in-and-out privileges; and hotel valet parking, which is about $15 per day but does allow you in-and-out movement.

Reservations

Just because this city has many beds doesn't mean you shouldn't reserve a room – especially if there's a particular place you've got your eye on – because there's no shortage of visitors, either. Check-in time is most often 3pm, with checkout set for either 11am or noon. Many Miami properties have a three-night minimum in high season; ask before making a reservation.

SOUTH BEACH (1st TO 11th ST)

AVALON MAJESTIC HOTEL

Map p250   *Hotel*

☎ 305-538-0133, 800-933-3306; www.southbeach hotels.com; 700 Ocean Dr; r low season $95-220, late Dec-Mar $165-260

In a classic and streamline 1941 building, this hotel is perhaps known more for its trademark white-and-yellow 1955 Lincoln convertible parked out front than for its 64 rooms, which are simple and pleasant and, thanks to a 2004 decor update, slightly more stylish than in the past (with puffy white duvets and clean-lined Ikea-style furniture). The crowds of young folk love the location and price, which includes a Continental breakfast buffet.

BEACON HOTEL Map p250   *Hotel*

☎ 305-674-8200; www.beacon-hotel.com; 720 Ocean Dr; r low season $145-215, Nov-May $190-315

This nicely restored deco hotel has a grand lobby and 79 truly spic-and-span rooms, with warm wood furnishings, white bedspreads and shiny marble floors and plush carpeting. Just know that the small courtyard rooms, which overlook an outside hallway rather than the ocean or any greenery, are the least fabulous. The place has wheelchair-accessible rooms, valet parking and free wireless Internet connection.

BENTLEY BEACH HOTEL

Map p250   *Boutique Hotel*

☎ 305-938-4600; www.bentleybeachhotel.com; 101 Ocean Dr; $TBD

Just opened in mid-2005, this swank addition to SoFi (the region south of 5th St in South Beach) is an all-suite beachfront haven, with requisite white outdoor couches, a luxe health club and spa and endless amenities. The hotel was in a 'soft open' phase at press time; check the website for updated information.

CASA GRANDE HOTEL Map pp248-9 *Hotel*

☎ 305-531-8800, 800-688-7678; www.casagrande hotel.com; 834 Ocean Dr; ste & 1-bedrooms low season $200-350, Oct-May $325-475

Set back from the street, off a lobby redolent with flowery incense, the Casa Grande offers respite from the standard deco look with its own sort of earthy glamour. Its lobby flaunts Mexican touches, such as colorful tiles and bright ochre walls, while the suites (both one-bedrooms and studios) have more of an Asian flair with dark, carved-wood furniture and four-poster beds set against stark white walls and tiled floors. Service is refined, with plenty of perks such as a nightly turndown service and flowers on your pillow.

CENTURY HOTEL Map p250   *Hotel*

☎ 305-674-8855, 888-982-3688; www.centurysouth beach.com; 140 Ocean Dr; r $95-215, ste $190-350

The 31-room Century is one of the best pre-served deco spots on the strip, gleaming like a polished white gem at the far-south, quiet end of Ocean Dr. Rooms in the 1939 building are the perfect balance of sleekness and warmth, with hardwood floors, all-white bedding, marble bathrooms and dark-wood accents to offset the pure white walls. And the attached alfresco restaurant Joia, with its billowing fabric and excellent Mediterranean fare, is pure joy.

CHESTERFIELD HOTEL

Map p250   *Boutique Hotel*

☎ 305-531-5831, 800-244-6088; www.southbeach group.com; 855 Collins Ave; r $95-215, ste $190-350

The Chesterfield is part of the ubiquitous South Beach Group – along with the **Hotel Chelsea** (p154), **Lily Leon Hotel** (p153), Mercury Resort, Hotel Shelley and **Whitelaw Hotel** (p153). It's a smart company, SBG, as its philosophy seems to be hip, hot style that's totally affordable. It keeps costs down by employing Ikea-like furniture and decor that can look flimsy if closely inspected – but the big picture is sleek and beautiful. The biggest lures seem to be the happening lobby bars (with free-drink happy hour for guests), complete with DJs who blast loungey hip-hop, and SBG's promise to get you on the guest list of your favorite nightclub. The theme of the Chesterfield's rooms lean toward jungle, with pumpkin-orange walls, hanging African masks and animal-print fabrics. There's a lovely front porch for people-watching.

CLEVELANDER HOTEL Map pp248-9 _Hotel_
☎ 305-531-3485; www.clevelander.com; 1020 Ocean Dr; r low season $80-160, Jan-May $99-199
The fact that the Clevelander is known more for its neon deco facade and its party-hearty glass-and-neon beachside bar speaks volumes – loud volumes – about how much of a cozy sleep pad this is. The rooms are basic but fine, with jazzy Caribbean-print bed spreads and dark tiled floors rather than the sleek white-ness you may expect. But it's the noise of the shiny happy people living it up until all hours that should give you pause (unless you're one of them, of course).

CLINTON HOTEL
Map pp248-9 _Boutique Hotel_
☎ 305-938-4040; www.clintonsouthbeach.com; 825 Washington Ave; r $189-800
Renovated and reopened in 2004, this outpost of hip jazzes up an otherwise quiet stretch of Washington with a sultry lobby filled with blue velveteen banquettes and modern metallic ceiling fans. Inside, rooms are as simple and stark as all the others in this town, with high-thread-count white linens, earth-toned furniture and tiny sun porches, perfect for breakfast or a sunset cocktail. Other features include a small pool, plus some rooms with Jacuzzis and flat-screen TVs. An Asian-fusion dining room is warm and relaxing, though the folks at the lobby's reception desk have a major attitude, which only serves as a buzzkill here.

ESSEX HOUSE HOTEL
Map pp248-9 _Boutique Hotel_
☎ 305-534-2700, 800-553-7739; www.essexhotel.com; 1001 Collins Ave; r/ste low season $140/185, Nov-Apr $175/265
The lovingly restored Essex, with its ever-so-authentic deco lobby, is a friendly place with a helpful staff, a small pool and large rooms furnished with soft, subdued colors. The side veranda, filled with rattan furnishings, is a par-ticularly pleasant place to people-watch. A Continental breakfast is included with the 58 rooms and 18 suites.

HOTEL Map pp248-9 _Boutique Hotel_
☎ 305-531-2222; 801 Collins Ave; r/ste low season $255-295/395, Jan-May $275-325/425
This place is stylin' – and why shouldn't it be, with Todd Oldham as the designer behind the boldly beautiful rooms here? Inspired by the colors of the 'sand, sea and sky,' the finely stitched bedding adds a classy dash of eye candy, as do the bright mosaic doorknobs and shower stalls, tie-dyed robes, brushed-steel sinks and wood furnishings. The Hotel boasts the best rooftop pool in South Beach, with cabanas, a fitness facility and showers – plus a brand-new lounge in the sky, which Oldham designed for the 2004 opening. It's overshad-owed only by the lovely deco spire. Yes, the spire says 'Tiffany,' and that's because it's what the place was named before the blue-box jew-elry place threatened a lawsuit.

HOTEL ASTOR Map pp248-9 _Hotel_
☎ 305-531-8081, 800-270-4981; www.hotelastor .com; 956 Washington Ave; r/ste low season $110-230/220-600, Jan-Mar $195-290/390-900
A classic favorite, these 40 oh-so-inviting rooms with classy beige carpeting are done in soothing earth tones, all padded from the noise on Washington St below by windows made of special double-pane glass. The Astor has covered over its small pool to make room for the trendy crowd of clubgoers who come to drink and bop to DJs on the lovely back-patio lounge. The intimate lobby is classic, with a paddle-fan ceiling, terrazzo floors and overstuffed chairs.

HOTEL ST AUGUSTINE
Map p250 _Boutique Hotel_
☎ 305-532-0570, 800-310-7717; www.hotelstaugus tine.com; 347 Washington Ave; r $205-245
A lovely recent addition to SoFi, this gem of a find is housed in a white deco building on a quiet block that's still a quick walk from party central. Rooms are sleek yet warm, thanks to quilted bedspreads, natural wood details and soothing lighting – and especially thanks to the fabulous glass-enclosed showers, which turn into personal steam rooms with the flick of a switch.

JEFFERSON HOUSE BED & BREAKFAST Map pp248-9 _B&B_
☎ 305-534-5247, 877-599-5247; 1018 Jefferson Ave; r $99-205
Located on a quiet residential block that's just a short walk from the bustling beach area, this

gay inn, recently under new ownership, caters to folks who want personal service and an all-gay scene (although all are actually welcome here). The small but lovely rooms in the 1928 main house and larger suites in a building edging the private and lush pool area are furnished with eclectic antiques and have wood floors. Folks converge for breakfast in an alfresco dining area, and again for a super-friendly happy hour nightly.

LILY LEON HOTEL Map pp248-9 *Hotel*
☎ 305-673-3767; www.lilyleonhotel.com; 841 Collins Ave; ste low season $95-195, high season $140-275
Ending a fierce competition, the owners of the excellent Leon recently sold out to the South Beach Group, which owned the lovely Lily next door. All rooms here are suites, and they are impeccably decorated – not only with the requisite white linens but with splashes of soft color, modern art works, shiny wood floors and high ceilings. And you will find not only the SBG's usual lobby bar, but also a nice garden café out back. Even pets are welcome.

LOFT HOTEL Map pp248-9 *Boutique Hotel*
☎ 305-534-2244; www.thelofthotel.com; 952 Collins Ave; r & ste $99-159
A recently renovated darling, the Loft seduces you with its tranquil signage on Collins. It has a quiet, tiny lobby that's big enough for reception only, but big rooms. They are subtly elegant, motel-like quarters that have been transformed into boutique chic with sheer white scrims, firm new beds with wrought-iron headboards and cute kitchenettes.

PARK CENTRAL Map p250 *Boutique Hotel*
☎ 305-538-1611, 800-727-5236; www.theparkcentral.com; 640 Ocean Dr; r/ste low season $95-165/145-195, Nov-Apr $185-250/295-350
This 1937 art-deco classic, designed by deco master Henry Hohauser, is a legendary SoBe (South Beach) hot spot; its pool is fabulous (if small) and it has a lovely rooftop deck. The 127 guest rooms and bathrooms are small but first-rate. The Vampire Lestat Room (No 419), described in Anne Rice's *Tale of the Body Thief* as the one the vampire stayed in, is heavily booked, though it isn't any more expensive than similar rooms. To reach the roof, walk past reception, take the elevator to the top floor and walk out to the right. Go around 4pm, when cruise ships chug down Government Cut, or on any weekend night for a great view of the Drive's action.

PELICAN HOTEL
Map pp248-9 *Boutique Hotel*
☎ 305-673-3373, 800-773-5422; www.pelicanhotel.com; 826 Ocean Dr; r low season $135-310, high season $170-440
Finally, something different! Theme rooms rule here like nowhere else on Miami Beach. When the owners of Diesel jeans purchased the hotel in 1999, they scoured garage sales looking for just the right stuff. They found it. From the 'Me Tarzan, You Vain' jungle motif and warm 'Cubarean Islands' lovefest to the oddly cold 'With Drill,' all 30 rooms are completely different and fun (though all have beautiful recycled-oak floors). Hotel amenities include complimentary wireless Internet and beach chairs.

ROYAL HOTEL Map pp248-9 *Boutique Hotel*
☎ 305-673-9009, 888-394-6835; www.royalhotelsouthbeach.com; 763 Pennsylvania Ave $119-200
The Royal is time-warp central, but it's unclear whether its traveled to the past or the future. Though 'futuristic' is the way the Royal likes to describe itself, it's in the old-fashioned way – the Jetsons' way. Now it just feels, well, current. The 42 renovated rooms have oddly shaped molded-plastic end tables and beds (with cup holders), plus ultrawhite bedding, lavender and lime walls, shag throw rugs, refrigerators and modern tiled bathrooms. Note that the front door is on Washington Ave.

WALDORF TOWERS HOTEL
Map pp248-9 *Boutique Hotel*
☎ 305-531-7684, 800-933-2322; www.waldorftowers.com; 860 Ocean Dr; r low season $89-199, Nov-Apr $139-249
The Waldorf was renovated in early 2002. Though it may not be regarded as the hottest spot around, it's certainly underappreciated. The 42 crisp but warm rooms are comparable to most boutiques on the strip and feature blonde hardwoods, shellacked floors, platform beds, silver ceiling fans and big windows.

WHITELAW HOTEL
Map pp248-9 *Boutique Hotel*
☎ 305-398-7000; www.whitelawhotel.com; 808 Collins Ave; r low season $95, Nov-Apr $195
The brochure promises 'clean sheets, hot water, stiff drinks,' but the 49-room Whitelaw goes beyond that. The crisp bedding is Belgian, the bathrooms marble, and the alcohol complimentary from 8pm to 10pm at the hotel's new 808 martini bar. After white sheets, white robes,

billowy white curtains and white floors, the sea-blue bathrooms come as a welcome shock. (To be fair, the blinds are chrome.) Airport pick-up and Continental breakfast are included.

CHEAP SLEEPS
HOTEL CHELSEA

Map pp248-9   *Boutique Hotel*
☎ 305-534-4069; 944 Washington Ave; r $95-195

Right next door to Hotel Astor, Chelsea, of the South Beach Group, is another great option for style seekers with small budgets. Rooms are sleek and spare, with low futonlike beds, beige faux-wood floors, a funky lobby where DJs spin (loudly) on weekends and a fun little front patio, nicely sheltered from the busy avenue with a privet hedge and wide umbrellas. The free nightly cocktail isn't too bad, either.

MIAMI BEACH INTERNATIONAL TRAVELERS HOSTEL Map pp248-9 *Hostel*
☎ 305-534-0268, 800-978-6787; www.sobehostel .com; 236 9th St; dm year-round $13-15, r low season $32-59, r Jan-Apr $49-89

This 9th St hostel, not an HI member, has a little less of everything than the competition, but that applies to the digits on the prices as well. Rooms are a tad worn and quite drab, but security is good, the staff friendly and the lobby cheerful. Half the 100 rooms are private; dorms have four beds. The kitchen is big, the video-rental library decent and the Internet access speedy. Strictly speaking, you'll need an

out-of-state university ID, HI card, US or foreign passport with a recent entry stamp, or an on-ward ticket to get a room, but these rules are only enforced when it's crowded.

SOUTH BEACH (11th TO 23rd ST)

ALBION Map pp246-7   *Boutique Hotel*
☎ 305-535-8606, 877-782-3557; www.rubellhotels .com; 1650 James Ave; r/ste low season $155-220/200-265, high season $245-265/320-390

This sexy, sleek hotel, designed by Carlos Zapata, bills itself as the nexus of cutting-edge design and deco, where the role models are Vincent Gallo and Martha Graham and the best minibar items are condoms and Red Bull. That's about right. The vibe is cool at the pool, too. As for the 96 rooms, they feature white bedding, gray carpeting, blond-wood furnishings and stainless steel accoutrements.

AQUA HOTEL Map pp246-7   *Boutique Hotel*
☎ 305-538-4361; www.aquamiami.com; 1530 Collins Ave; r & ste low season $95-395, Nov-May $125-600

Recently renovated, this hip inn has taken over the shell of a former motel – the kind whose rooms, on two levels, all open to the outside and are set around a pool? That old-school vibe barely survives, with the sleek design that includes muted-aqua doors, alfresco lounging areas with fountains, giant palms, teak furnishings, a hot tub and even a bed. Rooms have wood and concrete flooring, firm beds, quirky pieces of furniture such as a sumptuous chair made of spotted cowhide, and marble and stainless steel in the bathrooms. A front desk made of a shiny surfboard sets the mellow, hipster tone. Pets are welcome.

BEACHCOMBER HOTEL
Map pp248-9   *Boutique Hotel*
☎ 305-531-3755, 888-305-4683; www.beachcomber miami.com; 1340 Collins Ave; r $110-140

The deco classic with a green-banana-colored facade and a happy starfish in its logo has just been renovated, making it a serious competitor to others on this stretch of Collins. The front lobby has a soothing, mint-green glow, between a green-flecked terrazzo floor, seafoam-green couches and a chartreuse bar, all floating beneath sleek aluminum ceiling fans and framed, large-format photos of fruits. The rooms, while not quite as seductive as the entrance, have lovely wood floors and are basic, cozy and clean, though they could use firmer beds.

CARDOZO HOTEL

Map pp248-9   *Boutique Hotel*
☎ 305-535-6500, 800-782-6500; www.cardozohotel
.com; 1300 Ocean Dr; r & ste low season $150-400,
Nov-May $195-450

The leopard-patterned hallway carpet sets the tone for singer Gloria Estefan's hotel, which looks just as fabulous as she does. Many of its 43 large rooms and four suites have dark hardwood floors, handmade furniture, beds with billowing canopies and settees upholstered in more of that leopard pattern. Triple sheeting is but one of the typically luxurious amenities. The small bathrooms are outfitted with glass, marble and cool porcelain sinks.

CAVALIER HOTEL

Map pp248-9   *Boutique Hotel*
☎ 305-531-3555, 800-688-7678; www.cavaliermiami
.com; 1320 Ocean Dr; r/ste low season $130-160/250-
275, Oct-May $175-210/350-395

Got deco-overdose jitters? The Cavalier has earthy touches in its rooms, batik fabrics in tones of brown and beige, warm wood furniture and lightweight white bedspreads. The gorgeous facade may be familiar to you, as it's often the backdrop for fashion shoots.

CREST HOTEL SUITES

Map pp246-7   *Boutique Hotel*
☎ 305-531-0321, 800-531-3880; www.cresthotel
.com; 1670 James Ave; r/ste low season $115-140/
145-195, high season $155/195-235

This family-owned place, with 61 rooms in two buildings, is an excellent choice. Stylish studios and one-bedroom suites – with whiteclad beds, plush furniture and wood floors – feature custom galley-kitchens, combo living/dining areas, modern bathrooms and small work spaces. Don't overlook the added value of a pool and rooftop solarium.

DELANO HOTEL

Map pp246-7   *Boutique Hotel*
☎ 305-672-2000, 800-555-5001; 1685 Collins Ave;
r low season $205-475, Jan-Apr $325-575

To enter this fashionable Ian Schrager sanctum, you must confidently stride past two hyper-tanned doormen into the architectural wonder of a sweeping lobby; collect yourself after this visual feast, then head up to one of the 208 slick and sparse rooms. Though it's no

longer quite the white-hot-spot it once was (Schrager's **Shore Club**, p157, has quickly taken over, thank you very much), its stellar legacy – namely that Madonna once had a birthday party here and used to own the **Blue Door** (p91) restaurant downstairs – makes rooms here still very much in demand. A theater-set designer clearly worked the lobby: a Euro dance beat pulses, and floor-to-outrageously-high-ceiling curtains billow around enormously round pillars. And the pool scene is pure decadence, ringed with private cabanas, outdoor beds, towering palms and private curtain-rimmed nooks.

GREENVIEW Map pp246-7   *Boutique Hotel*
☎ 305-531-6588, 877-782-3557; www.rubellhotels
.com; 1671 Washington Ave; r/ste low season
$95-150/175-230, high season $160/260

With only 40 rooms, this delightful find is at once homey and elegant. Furnishings are spare, with sisal rugs and bamboo lamps, plus black-and-white photos on the walls. A Continental breakfast is included, as are the pool facilities at its sister hotel, the **Albion** (opposite).

HOTEL IMPALA

Map pp248-9   *Boutique Hotel*
☎ 305-673-2021, 800-646-7252; www.hotelimpala
miamibeach.com; 1228 Collins Ave; r & ste low season
$145-325, Oct-May $185-400

Accessed through its lush, fountain-graced courtyard and set back off Collins, this lovely European-style hotel features a warm, intimate lobby and 17 rooms with oversized marble bathtubs, big firm beds and full entertainment systems. The friendly staff has managed to create atmospheric elegance without arrogance. Rates include a Continental breakfast.

HOTEL NASH Map pp248-9   *Boutique Hotel*
☎ 305-674-7800; www.hotelnash.com; 1120 Collins
Ave; s/d $155-300, ste $495-1400

A quiet, elegant inn, the expansive marble lobby leads to 54 rooms that are plush but a bit lacking in character, with tons of shiny blond wood, beige-and-grey checked carpeting and furniture tucked into white slipcovers. The outdoor lounge is peaceful, and features three small spa pools.

HOTEL OCEAN Map pp248-9   *Boutique Hotel*
☎ 305-672-2579; www.hotelocean.com; 1230 Ocean
Dr; r & ste low season $225-540, high season $260-645

This intimate, Mediterranean-style hotel isn't pompous or exclusive, but the renovated waterfront suites (expensive but not outlandish when you consider what you get) have every right to be. Most of the hotel's 27 large rooms have ocean views and lots of light streaming in; some have a private terrace, and all have brightly tiled bathrooms and colorfully painted walls. You'll also enjoy fine fabrics, finer furnishings and the finest aesthetics.

HOTEL VICTOR

Map pp248-9   Boutique Hotel
☎ 305-428-1234; www.hotelvictorsouthbeach.com; 1144 Ocean Dr; r & ste $405-1400
A snazzy addition to the scene that opened in January 2005, this is a boutique property with a secret: it's part of the Hyatt Hotels & Resorts conglomerate. Still, you'd never know it by the indie-chic decor – rooms have beaded lamps (resembling jellyfish, a popular symbol here), potted orchids, and rich textiles and bedding – and the property features a rimless pool, a massive fitness club and the VIX restaurant and VUE bar. It's in the center of all the action, with ocean views from many of the 91 rooms.

KENT HOTEL Map pp248-9   Boutique Hotel
☎ 305-531-6771, 800-688-7678; www.thekenthotel .com; 1131 Collins Ave; r low season $130-350, Oct-May $145-350
Renovation is one thing, but jazzy modernism that clashes with classic deco is quite another. Still, young party types will probably get a kick out of the decor: a lobby filled with fuchsia and electric-orange geometric furniture plus bright Lucite toy blocks is an aggressively playful welcome, while individual rooms are decked out in lilac bedding, furniture and walls. The special Lucite Suite is almost entirely constructed of the see-through material, giving it an icy playground feel. Take refuge in a side garden with Indonesian-style tables, bamboo and hammocks, or at the beach, which is just a block away.

LOEWS MIAMI BEACH

Map pp246-7   Luxury Chain Resort
☎ 305-604-1601, 800-235-6397; www.loewshotels .com; 1601 Collins Ave; r low season $249-399, mid-Sep–May $339-499, ste up to $4000
New in late 1998 and geared toward conventioneers, this monstrous monolith boasts an incredible 800 rooms and 20 butler-serviced oceanfront cabanas. The palatial marble lobby sets a tone that suggests you could be in any metropolitan locale. Expect all the high-end amenities of a convention hotel: fitness center,

a beautiful pool, private beachfront, six restaurants (including the popular Emeril's) and endless meeting rooms. Luckily the restored deco St Moritz Hotel is attached to the property, too.

MARLIN HOTEL

Map pp248-9   Boutique Hotel
☎ 305-604-5000, 800-688-7678; www.marlinhotel .com; 1200 Collins Ave; r & ste $325-895
Known for its star power under former owner Chris Blackwell, whose on-site Island Records studios brought in folks from Aerosmith to U2, the Marlin was recently purchased (for a whopping $7.5 million!) by the new Palm Resorts Group, made up of young hotshots from New York City. The Marlin is still home to the Elite Modeling Agency, so don't expect the number of gorgeous skinny minnies to go down much. And you'll still find 12 top-class suites, each with different decor themes ranging from dark-wood floors and safari bedspreads to a round bed, claw-foot tub and white-tiled kitchen. Small dogs are welcome as long as they're willing to cede control to resident poodle-in-charge Goose, whose slate-grey fur matches the stainless-steel madness in the futuristic lobby.

NASSAU SUITE HOTEL

Map pp248-9   Boutique Hotel
☎ 305-532-0043, 866-859-4177; www.nassausuite .com; 1414 Collins Ave; ste low season $175-280, Nov-May $190-300
All of these 22 homey, contemporary pads feature shellacked hardwood floors, walls painted in earthy tones, white slipcovered furniture, comfy pull-out sofas, fully equipped kitchens and walk-in closets. The rooms also have DSL connections and entertainment centers. You could easily imagine living here a while.

NATIONAL HOTEL

Map pp246-7   Boutique Hotel
☎ 305-532-2311, 800-327-8370; www.nationalhotel .com; 1677 Collins Ave; r low season $275-375, Oct-May $350-495
This deco landmark, renovated in 2003, doubles as a super-chic South Beach hangout. The rooms aren't as stylish as the lobby – more blond-wood and beige accents and checked carpeting – but they're comfortable and immaculate. About a quarter of the 152 guest rooms in this midrise have balconies overlooking the tropical grounds and the unique swimming arrangement: one spectacular 250ft-long palm-lined pool leads to another, which in turn leads to a beachside tiki bar.

RALEIGH HOTEL

Map pp246-7   *Boutique Hotel*

☎ 305-534-6300, 800-848-1775; www.raleighhotel
.com; 1775 Collins Ave; r low season $209-359,
Oct-May $319-499

This fave just got even better. Always a high-style deco star, the property was purchased in 2004 by celebrity hotelier André Balazs, who's got the Midas touch right now. Upon stepping in, he promptly added 6ft of sand around the pool to give his guests a better ocean-viewing perch; and that's only the beginning of the pampering services you'll find at the new Raleigh. The bar is excellent; the pricey dining room is romantic; the fitness equipment is alfresco; pets are permitted; and the closets are cedar-lined. The 107 rooms have contemporary amenities such as three separate phone lines. Low platform beds make rolling out of bed in the morning very easy. And the stunning pool? It's got Esther-Williams-swam-here cachet.

REGENT SOUTH BEACH

Map pp248-9   *Boutique Hotel*

☎ 305-672-4554; www.theregentsouthbeach.com;
1458 Ocean Dr; $TBD

Another hotel-condo hits the oceanfront, this one featuring penthouses with exclusive rooftop gardens, amazing views, a full-service spa and the restaurant Table 8 – a local branch of Govind Armstrong's famous LA eatery. At press time the Regent was still being constructed, with a projected opening date of July 2005.

RITZ-CARLTON SOUTH BEACH

Map pp246-7   *Luxury Chain Hotel*

☎ 786-276-4000; www.ritzcarlton.com; 1 Lincoln Rd
at Collins Ave; s & d $399-599, ste $479-3000

This luxurious behemoth has 376 rooms, many set around a lovely oceanfront pool. The rooms are upscale if a tad bland, and amenities are endless, from three restaurants and a spa to personal shoppers and babysitting services. Various butlers – bath, pool and 'tanning' – are ready to serve you, and water ballet performers bring drama to the pool every Saturday at sunset. You'll be hard-pressed to find anything lacking at the Ritz.

SAGAMORE Map pp246-7   *Boutique Hotel*

☎ 305-535-8088; www.sagamorehotel.com; 1671
Collins Ave; r & ste low season $215-595,
high season $355-1050

Just next door to the **Delano** (p155) sits this unshowy gem, which has the distinction of having its rooms double as art galleries, thanks to its talented curator and impressive roster of artists. Quarters are white and plush, with tile and marble floors and whirlpool bath-showers; its beachfront lounge area has a lovely infinity pool and its guests are somehow more low-key than the next-door neighbor's. A spa-fitness center is on its way.

SETAI Map pp246-7   *Boutique Hotel*

☎ 305-672-7900; www.setai.com; 101 20th St;
r & ste $2000-6000

It's the most expensive sleep in Miami. This brand-new luxury hotel, comprising eight floors of a high-rise residence and a restored art-deco building across Collins Ave, has Mao-collared hosts greet you in an intimate lobby that has a hushed vibe splashed with the color of whole oranges that sit in glass votives. The Setai offers massive quarters with a sumptuous, Asia-meets-deco style that relies on teak floors, silk-upholstered sofas and black granite bathtubs, with features including Dux beds, a Bose sound system, iPods and Aqua di Parma bath products. A top-end spa offers body wraps and foot massages (also available right in your room), while the resort grounds boast three oceanfront pools, teak cabanas and lushly tropical landscaping.

SHORE CLUB Map pp246-7   *Boutique Hotel*

☎ 305-535-8088; www.shoreclub.com; 1901 Collins
Ave; r & ste $345-2200

Ian Schrager's latest addition to the scene has taken over from the **Delano** (p155) as the place to be – whether you choose one of its David Chipperfield–designed rooms or suites, a duplex bungalow, an in-house restaurant such as Nobu's high-end Japanese or the Tuscan Ago, the Moroccan-themed lounge **Skybar** (p111) or the 8000-sq-ft rooftop spa. This, my friends, is the SoBe of your dreams.

TIDES Map pp248-9   *Boutique Hotel*

☎ 305-604-5070, 800-688-7678; www.thetideshotel
.com; 1220 Ocean Dr; r/ste low season $475/575,
mid-Dec–May $525/625, penthouses up to $3000

Everything's chic and chichi at the Tides, where service is ultracool but surprisingly gracious. The lobby is awash in Latin jazz, soft lighting and overstuffed couches. Guest rooms – all 45 of which face the ocean – are soothing, decorated in a rich palette of beige, cream and a paler shade of white. They all have telescopes for planetary or Hollywood stargazing. The excellent pool is open around the clock.

TOWNHOUSE HOTEL

Map pp246-7   *Boutique Hotel*

☎ 305-534-3800, 800-688-7678; www.townhouse
hotel.com; 150 20th St at Collins Ave; r $135-395
Jonathan Morr – known for creating the **Blue Door**
(p91) restaurant at the **Delano** (p155) – opened
Townhouse in 2000. An affordable-chic den of
starkness, Townhouse features all-white, igloo-
like rooms with random scarlet accents, plus a
breezy rooftop lounge furnished with red umbrellas and waterbeds, all designed by fashion
guru India Mahdavi. The basement **Bond Street
Lounge** (p110), serving sushi and fab cocktails,
is a new in-spot among night owls.

CHEAP SLEEPS

ABBEY HOTEL Map pp246-7   *Boutique Hotel*

☎ 305-531-0031; www.abbeyhotel.com; 300 21st St;
r/studios high season $79-195/$99-225
Insulated from the partying throngs, these
50 rooms manage to make timeless deco
feel contemporary and warm. For the price,
they're very good value. Renovated in 1999,
bedrooms and studios feature touches of bur-
nished chrome, platform beds and an earth-
toned color scheme. There's no pool, but there
is a nice garden and a fitness room. (A rooftop
solarium has been in the works for a while.)

BRIGHAM GARDENS GUESTHOUSE

Map pp248-9   *Guest House*

☎ 305-531-1331; www.brighamgardens.com; 1411
Collins Ave; r low season $70-110, mid-Nov–May $100-145
This charming guest house, built around a lush
garden that attracts tropical birds, is a sanctuary
from the neon madness. Perhaps it's the bamboo, hammocks, fountains, patio chairs or the
attentive hosts. Choose from among 23 large
and airy guest rooms (most with kitchens and
bathrooms), studios and apartments. Some have
convertible futon sofas; all rooms have tropical
colors and a home-away-from-home vibe. There
are also laundry facilities and a barbecue area,
plus weekly discounts. Pets are welcome.

CLAY HOTEL & MIAMI BEACH INTER-
NATIONAL HOSTEL Map pp248-9   *Hostel*

☎ 305-534-2988, 800-379-2529; www.clayhotel.com;
1438 Washington Ave; dm $15-18, s/d low season$40-
54/42-60, high season $42-64/46-76
Perhaps the country's most beautiful HI hostel, this 100-year-old Spanish-style villa is also
Miami Beach's most established. The Clay has
an array of clean and comfortable rooms, from

single-sex dorms with four to eight beds and
spacious VIP rooms with balconies, to family rooms and decent private rooms with TV,
phone, bath and air con. Many are located in
a medina-like maze of adjacent buildings. The
excellent kitchen is large, but very warm in
summer. While the staff might be a little harassed due to sheer volume, they're friendly and
helpful. Internet access is readily available.

CREEK HOTEL Map pp246-7   *Budget Hotel*

☎ 305-538-1951, 800-746-7835; www.thecreeksouth
beach.com; 2360 Collins Ave; r $49-159
Formerly the rundown Banana Bungalow, this
hip, low-key bargain has been renamed and
remade. It's still geared toward young partiers,
though, as evidenced by the pool's underwater speakers, and the nubile crowd lounging
about around the pool and outdoor bar. The
signature rooms, designed by local artists, have
the most panache; they feature visual treats
such as purple floors, wall murals and brightly
colored bedspreads and fixtures. For $5 a day
you can use the fitness facility at the Roney
Palace hotel across the street; daily parking is
also $5 a day. The cool lobby is enclosed in a
freestanding triangle building of glass.

TROPICS HOTEL & HOSTEL

Map pp246-7   *Hostel*

☎ 305-531-0361; www.tropicshotel.com; 1550 Collins
Ave; dm $19-24, r $50-125
The surprisingly nice Tropics sports an Olympic-
sized swimming pool, a spacious brick patio,
a barbecue area and a full kitchen. Its clean
dorms have four beds and an attached bath,
while the extremely basic private rooms have

Top Five Rooftops

- Todd Oldham designed the cool pool-shower-bar
  combo at **Hotel** (p152), with an ocean view.
- Lined with sun-worshiping lounges, the **Park
  Central** (p153) is quiet, despite the madness
  down below.
- Red outdoor couches and a happening nightlife
  scene after sunset make the **Townhouse** (left)
  the breeziest nightclub in South Beach.
- The swank vibe continues all the way to the roof
  of the **Tides** (p157), where a sophisticated pool
  and lounge area awaits.
- The rooftop of **Aqua Hotel** (p154) isn't high up,
  but the cool alfresco lounge area overlooks all the
  action on Collins.

firm mattresses, TV and phone. Some have great views of the pool. Lockers and Internet access ($1 per five minutes) are available.

MIAMI BEACH

ALEXANDER Map p251 *Resort*
☎ 305-865-6500, 800-327-6121; www.alexanderhotel .com; 5225 Collins Ave; ste $269-639

This oceanfront, all-suites behemoth attracts a more mature crowd – AARP (American Association of Retired Persons) members, mainly – who want luxury without trendy trappings. The grounds feature lush gardens and lovely pools, and rooms offer kitchens, balconies, paintings and sculptures. It also has a massive spa, as well as the popular Shula's Steak House.

BEACH HOUSE BAL HARBOUR
Map p251 *Boutique Hotel*
☎ 305-535-8600, 877-782-3557; www.thebeach househotel.com; 9449 Collins Ave; r $105-267

The Beach House is one of the loveliest stays up in this neck of the woods. It's a down-to-earth inn with a beachy feel, complete with wainscoting, conch shells and fresh-looking sheets with blue ticking in every room. But the Bal Harbour Shops across the street will keep you anchored in Miami-glitz reality.

CIRCA 39 Map p251 *Boutique Hotel*
☎ 305-538-3900, 877-824-7223; www.circa39.com; 3900 Collins Ave; r $109-279

Another new addition, this is a bit north of the South Beach fray (though it likes to say it's in South Beach). Built in 1939, and formerly called the Copley Plaza, this 86-roomer reopened in 2004 with a fresh new look. Its vibe is a combo of youthful hip and cool families (the website pictures kids in its pool – a rarity!), and the decor is Ikea-minimalist, with white bedspreads, ice-blue curtains and pillows, white furniture and not much else (though some of the pale carpeting has unfortunate stains). The hallways glow with sexy red lighting.

CLARIDGE HOTEL
Map p251 *Boutique Hotel*
☎ 305-604-8485, 888-422-9111; www.claridgefl.com; 3500 Collins Ave; r low season $129-285, high season $149-385

This bright-yellow beauty, a 1928 Mediterranean palace recently reopened after a gorgeous renovation, sports frescoed walls, gleaming stone floors, rich paintings and a wonderfully European atrium. The large rooms have an old-world feel, with lots of earth tones, and tile and wood accents. It's run by Clarion, but the Claridge tries hard to achieve an indie vibe.

EDEN ROC RESORT Map p251 *Resort*
☎ 305-531-0000, 800-327-8337; www.edenrocresort .com; 4525 Collins Ave; r low season from $200, high season $275

The gloriously renovated Eden Roc Resort, a grand dame standing right next to its main competitor, **Fontainebleau Hilton** (below), has enough amenities to keep you within its confines during your entire Miami stay. With 349 rooms (featuring walk-in closets and balconies overlooking the ocean) and extras such as an indoor rock-climbing complex, an Olympic-sized pool and an oceanfront spa and health club, it's a great place to get away if you like the resort scene.

FONTAINEBLEAU HILTON HOTEL & RESORT Map p251 *Resort*
☎ 305-538-2000, 800-548-8886; www.fontainebleau .hilton.com; 4441 Collins Ave; r low season from $189, late Dec-May $239

Probably Miami Beach's most recognizable landmark, the 1200-room Fontainebleau opened in 1954, when it became a destination for a slew of glamorous celebrities and the set for many a Hollywood production (including *Goldfinger*, *The Bellboy* and *Scarface*). It was purchased by Hilton in 1978 and received a much-needed renovation in 2003. The hotel has got every conceivable amenity, including restaurants and bars galore, beachside cabanas, seven tennis courts, a kids' activity program, grand ballroom, business center, marina, shopping mall and an ab-fab swimming pool. But all of that wasn't enough, apparently: now the 18-acre property also includes the brand-new, sold-out Fontainebleau II, a 36-story condominium-hotel that opened at the end of 2004 and sold units for prices ranging from $435,000 to $1.8 million; construction has also begun on the Fontainebleau III, another condominium-hotel that'll rise 18 stories on the property. One thing is for certain: this hot property is rolling in dough.

PALMS SOUTH BEACH
Map p251 *Boutique Hotel*
☎ 305-534-0505, 800-550-0505; www.thepalmshotel .com; 3025 Collins Ave; r & ste $179-399

Technically it's north of South Beach, but the decor is just as cool as SoBe – lots of palm trees, a white-columned lobby, tile floors, beige rooms with wicker furniture and killer ocean views, a massive pool with thatched-roof gazebos and a swanky dining room. It's Downtown style, uptown.

CHEAP SLEEPS

BAY HARBOR INN & SUITES

Map p251 *Inn*
☎ 305-868-4141; www.bayharborinn.com; 9660 E Bay Harbor Dr; r low season $89-99, high season $119-139
Operated by earnest Johnson & Wales University students as an integral part of their hands-on hospitality training, this upscale small hotel has a warmer, more country feel than the sleek spaces you get used to seeing in Miami. Friendly service keeps this place from being too stuffy. A complimentary Continental breakfast is served on the waterfront deck.

INDIAN CREEK HOTEL
Map p251 *Hotel*
☎ 305-531-2727, 800-491-2772; www.indiancreek hotel.com; 2727 Indian Creek Dr; r $69-260
The rustically civilized lobby and tropical courtyard here are delightfully serene places to while away a few hours. Mix in a friendly staff, a cool pool and a location just far enough from the madness, and you've got a recipe for a restful retreat. The 61 deco-style rooms are a tad dark, but the quirky character makes up for that.

DOWNTOWN MIAMI

CONRAD MIAMI
Map pp252-3 *Luxury Hotel*
☎ 305-503-6500; www.conradhotels.com; 1395 Brickell Ave; r & ste $200-450
This new, 36-story glass-and-steel tower, featuring a sublimely concave facade, adds to the image of Miami's skyline – as well as to the formerly paltry offerings in this part of town. Conrad, a luxury line of Hilton, has every upscale amenity you could ask for, from massive suites and a rooftop pool to excellent eateries and a 25th-floor sky lobby with sweeping views of the ocean and Downtown. The vibe here is more wealthy businessman than celebrity fabulous.

FOUR SEASONS MIAMI
Map pp252-3 *Luxury Hotel*
☎ 305-358-3535; www.fourseasons.com/miami; 1435 Brickell Ave; r & ste $275-1150
Another new addition to the skyline, this 70-story high-rise is a palace. Witness its luxe rooms overlooking Biscayne Bay, marble common areas that double as modern-art-gallery spaces, a massive spa and various on-site eateries. Most fabulous of all, though, is the 7th-floor terrace bar, **Bahia** (p110), which is pure *mojito*-laced, Latin-loved swankiness.

MANDARIN ORIENTAL MIAMI
Map pp252-3 *Luxury Hotel*
☎ 305-913-8288, 866-888-6780; www.mandarin oriental.com; 500 Brickell Key Dr; r & ste $300-1250
This premier Asian hotelier always takes top honors in most parts of the world, and this exclusive, extravagant Miami location is no exception. Prepare for marble bathrooms, in-room balconies facing either the ocean or the bay, a massive spa and a swank private urban sand beach. The lobby's **M Bar** (p111) lets you choose from more than 250 martinis, best sipped while staring out over the glassy Biscayne Bay.

MIAMI RIVER INN
Map pp252-3 *B&B*
☎ 305-325-0045, 800-468-3589; www.miamiriverinn .com; 119 SW South River Dr; r $69-1249
This historic B&B, sitting in the middle of a colorful nowhere, has charming New England–style rooms with wicker, brass and antiques. In addition to friendly service, wicker furniture and fluffy comforters, you'll enjoy the landscaped pool and Continental breakfast. There are 40 rooms, including a couple of apartments, in four wooden buildings from the early 20th century. Check out the treasure trove of Miami books in the guest library.

Sleeping – Downtown Miami

KEY BISCAYNE

RITZ-CARLTON KEY BISCAYNE

Map p259   *Luxury Hotel*

☎ 305-365-4500, 800-241-3333; www.ritzcarlton.com; 455 Grand Bay Dr; r & ste $300-1200

A sprawling, bright-yellow oceanfront resort, this is one of three Miami Ritz-Carltons. Here you'll find lushly landscaped oceanfront grounds, an 11-court tennis area, full kids' program (centered in a Ritz Kids beach pavilion) and large rooms with ocean or bay views.

SILVER SANDS BEACH RESORT

Map p259   *Resort*

☎ 305-361-5441; www.silversandsmiami.com; 301 Ocean Dr; r/cottages low season $129-149/279, mid-Dec–late Apr $169-189/329

Hidden in a quiet neighborhood just steps from the beach, this 60-room single-story motel is a subtle gem. The simple rooms, half of which spill out onto a garden courtyard (they're worth the extra bucks), have clean bathrooms, tiles rather than carpeting, firm mattresses and minikitchens. And there is, of course, a pool.

SONESTA BEACH RESORT KEY BISCAYNE Map p259   *Resort*

☎ 305-361-2021, 800-766-3782; www.sonesta.com; 350 Ocean Dr; r $169-399, ste $629-1099

On a wide stretch of powdery sand, this 295-room midrise hotel works hard and successfully to make you never want to leave the property. It's a really fine place to relax, and boasts an oceanfront pool, a kids' activity program, bicycle rentals, plenty of bars and restaurants, contemporary rooms, tennis courts and a fitness center.

COCONUT GROVE

COCONUT GROVE BED & BREAKFAST   *B&B*

☎ 305-665-2274, 800-339-9430; www.kwflorida .com/coconut.html, Douglas Rd; r low season $115-175, high season $135-210

Highly recommended, this two-story house has only three rooms (The Garden, The Palm and The Banyan), but they're nicely decorated with the pottery, textiles and paintings of owner Annette Rawlings. Her family has been in South Grove for decades, and was among a legendary group of starving artists who set out to make names for themselves in the late '60s – and did. Rates include a spectacular homemade breakfast. Ann doesn't take walk-ins and prefers not to be on our map, so you'll have to get directions when making reservations.

GROVE ISLE CLUB & RESORT

Map p258   *Resort Hotel*

☎ 305-858-8300, 800-884-7683; www.groveisle.com; 4 Grove Isle Dr; r low season $200-500, high season $300-600

Hiding on its own little island just off the coast of Coconut Grove is this stunner – a boutique hotel with colonial elegance, lush tropical gardens and sunset views over Biscayne Bay. The large rooms feel very Key West, with terra-cotta floors, colorful kilims, wicker furniture and modern four-poster beds. A classy restaurant, Baleen, and brand-new Indonesian-style spa, Spa Terre, satisfy all your other needs.

MAYFAIR HOUSE Map p258   *Hotel*

☎ 305-441-0000, 800-433-4555; www.mayfairhouse hotel.com; 3000 Florida Ave; r low season $169-209, high season $289-329

Tucked behind the **Streets of Mayfair** (p146), this exclusive all-suite hotel has 179 units overlooking a courtyard. The large Mayfair, Executive and Deluxe suites feature Japanese hot tubs, marble bathrooms, separate sitting areas and private terraces. Get ready for chintz, leopard prints and tones of salmon and coral in the quarters.

MUTINY HOTEL Map p258   *Hotel*

☎ 305-441-2100, 888-868-8469; www.mutinyhotel .com; 2951 S Bayshore Dr; ste $199-1500

This small luxury bayfront hotel, with 120 one- and two-bedroom suites, featuring balconies, boasts an indulgent staff, luxe bedding, gracious appointments, fine amenities and a small heated pool. Although it's on a busy street, you won't hear the traffic once inside.

RITZ-CARLTON COCONUT GROVE

Map p258   *Luxury Hotel*

☎ 305-644-4680, 800-241-3333; www.ritzcarlton .com; 3300 SW 27th Ave; r & ste $300-1200

The third of a power troika of Ritz-Carlton's in Miami, this one overlooks the bay, has totally luxe rooms and offers butlers for every need, from shopping and web surfing to dog walking and bathing. The massive spa is stupendous.

SONESTA HOTEL & SUITES COCONUT GROVE Map p258   *Hotel*

☎ 305-529-2828; 2889 McFarlane Rd; r $165-500

Opened in March 2002, this 300-room hotel is the excellent sister property to the one on **Key Biscayne** (left).

CORAL GABLES

BILTMORE HOTEL Map pp256-7 *Hotel*
☎ 305-445-1926, 800-727-1926; www.biltmorehotel
.com; 1200 Anastasia Ave; d Jan-Mar from $359 (4
seasonal price changes throughout the year), ste a
heck of a lot more

The brochure buzzwords here are apt: splendor, glamour, opulence, bygone era, exquisite style, pampered luxury. You get the idea. This 1926 National Historic Landmark, built in a Mediterranean style, also has the largest hotel pool in the country. Promise to stop by even if you haven't packed in high-style; you can catch weekly tours as well as evening ghost stories in the lobby on most Tuesdays.

HOTEL PLACE ST MICHEL

Map pp256-7 *Hotel*
☎ 305-444-1666; www.hotelplacestmichel.com;
162 Alcazar Ave; r $125-225

The first things you'll notice at this charming old-world, European-style hotel is the fact that you've left the land of stark deco. Enjoy vaulted ceilings, fancy tile work, plush furnishings and inlaid wood floors. With only 27 rooms, though, the hotel's hallmark is excellent service. You can also expect amenities such as Continental breakfast, a morning newspaper and an evening turndown service. There is a lovely restaurant and a cool bar/lounge downstairs, too.

OUTER NEIGHBORHOODS

INN AT THE FISHER ISLAND CLUB
Map pp244-5 *Resort*
☎ 305-535-6080, 800-537-3708; www.fisherisland
.com; r low season $325-1135, Oct-May $395-1735

If you're not one of its super-rich residents (a recent five-bedroom condo sale went to the tune of $8.7 million), then the only way to glimpse exclusive Fisher Island is to stay at this luxurious resort. Whether in 'simple' rooms or Vanderbilt-era cottages, your money will be well spent. Spa packages include two Swedish massages or aromatherapy treatments, one fitness assessment or seaweed body wrap, two island salt-glow or aromatherapy herbal wraps, a hydromassage or target massage, one deep pore cleansing facial and one manicure.

STANDARD Map pp244-5 *Boutique Hotel*
☎ 305-673-1717; 40 Island Ave; r & ste $150-750

Another André Balazs palace – this one of his own making – this was set to make its Miami debut in mid-2005. Not quite in South Beach and not quite Downtown, but on a lovely little island in between, this new spot follows the already successful formulas of his two Standards in Los Angeles (a third just opened in New York City); it's a sort of urban spa-by-the-sea. The '50s-motel-type building, housed in what was the legendary Lido, has divine amenities: hydrotherapy treatments available in your room, an outdoor pool sporting various water-massage features, a massive 'wall of sound' shower with sound and light effects, and the amazing group *hamam* (Turkish bath) with a heated marble floor, based on the traditional bath houses of Istanbul. Rooms are precious dens, with outdoor bathtubs, futonlike mattresses and flat-screen TVs that you can cover up with a cozy if you'd prefer to keep your head in the clouds.

TRUMP INTERNATIONAL SONESTA
BEACH RESORT Map pp244-5 *Resort*
☎ 305-692-5600, 800-766-3782; www.trumpsonesta
.com; 18001 Collins Ave; r & ste $169-700

Located up in Sunny Isles, Trump's take on Miami is just as you might expect it to be: 32 stories of ocean views, a ballroom and luxury rooms, along with a spa and extensive kids' program. The lagoon pool is full of waterfalls and palm trees and there are four on-site restaurants.

The Florida Keys & Key West

The Florida Keys & Key West

This long line of islands, stretching south of Miami like an alligator's tail, has long captivated visitors. And, just as you'd be careful while trekking through gator territory, exploring the Keys today demands a certain amount of caution. No, there are no real dangers here (although the crass consumerism comes close). But there are real highs and real lows. And because there is so much joy to be had from the highs – stunning tropical fish, unparalleled views of the sea, scrumptious dining adventures – it's best to not waste any time with the lows of T-shirt shopping or cheesy hotel stays.

The 45-island chain, held together by a 113-mile roadway, has a pace of life that becomes more mellow and islandlike the further you get from Miami. Surroundings also turn more beautiful as you travel south, and your experience will peak in all ways as soon as you settle into the most southern point in the lineup, Key West. But don't make the mistake of flying by all that rests in between the big city and Margaritaville; while much of US Hwy 1 (the only road that takes you through) is lined by fortresses of strip malls that block any views of the gleaming shores, it's worth turning off the highway, breaking through the barrier and enjoying what lies in wait. Key Largo's John Pennekamp Coral Reef State Park, Grassy Key's Dolphin Research Center, Marathon's kayaking tours and the surprisingly delicious Cuban food tucked away in Big Pine Key are just a few of the pleasures.

Orientation

The many tiny islands are strung from northeast to southwest and connected by US Hwy 1. Also called the Overseas Hwy, US Hwy 1 is a combination of highways and causeways built on the foundations of the FEC Railway, which was destroyed by a hurricane in 1935. It's the main road through the Keys. The most southern point, Key West, is about a three- or four-hour drive from Miami, depending on the season.

Getting There & Around

The most direct and convenient way to travel the Keys is by car (Key West is 160 miles from Miami), though traffic along the one major route, US Hwy 1, can be maddening during the high season of winter. **Greyhound** (☎ 800-229-9424) buses serve all Key destinations along US Hwy 1, departing from Downtown Miami and Key West; you can pick up a bus along the way by standing on the Overseas Hwy and flagging one down, Mexico-style. If you fly into Fort Lauderdale or Miami, the **Keys Shuttle** (☎ 888-765-9997) provides door-to-door service to most of the Keys – for a price (fees start at around $80 for two). Reserve at least a day in advance.

You can fly into one of two airports. **Key West International Airport** (EYW) has frequent flights from major cities – some direct, but most going through Miami – and **Marathon Airport** (☎ 305-743-2155) has less frequent, more expensive flights.

Top Five Experiences

Most elusive nature sighting
This would have to be the key deer (p175). You have to be strategic – and lucky – to catch a glimpse of these little furry fellas.

Worthiest tourist trap
Jump aboard Key West's Conch Tour Train (p183). The guides have great stories, and the breezy ride is delightful. It's touristy, sure. But you can always wear a disguise.

Best bar for meeting (really cool) Key West locals
Yes, upstairs La Te Da (p187) is packed with queen-gawking tourists. But downstairs, outside, it's refreshingly real.

Top luxury splurge
At $800 a night, Little Palm Island Resort & Spa (p176) is over the rainbow. You can only get there by boat or plane.

Most surprising hidden gem
Seascape Ocean Resort (p173) in Marathon is paradise – off a highway and at the end of a cul-de-sac.

UPPER KEYS

The Upper Keys stretch from Key Largo south to Long Key. Most visitors head down US Hwy 1 from Florida City, but you could also take the less trafficked FL 997 and Card Sound Rd to FL 905 (toll $1), which passes the very colorful Alabama Jack's (p169).

KEY LARGO & TAVERNIER

Key Largo may have been immortalized by John Huston's 1948 blockbuster of the same name, starring power couple Humphrey Bogart and Lauren Bacall, but its most beloved feature today is its concentration of dive sites – the largest in the Keys. The most alluring of these sites are at John Pennekamp Coral Reef State Park, the most accessible place to see the Florida reef. You will also find some of the best eats between Key West and Miami, with abundant sunset-cocktail spots. Tavernier, just south of Key Largo, is a small town with some interesting architecture and a wonderful bird sanctuary.

Orientation

Key Largo is the name of the island, at 33 miles the longest in the Keys, and the town, which stretches from about MM 106 to MM 97. Tavernier is at MM 93.

Information

Key Largo Chamber of Commerce (☎ 305-451-1414, 800-822-1088; www.keylargo.org; MM 106 bayside; ☾ 9am-6pm) Helpful office; has area-wide information.

Key Largo post office (MM 100 bayside)

Mariner Hospital (☎ 305-852-4418; Tavernier, MM 91.5 bayside)

Tavernier post office (MM 91.5 bayside)

Sights & Activities

JOHN PENNEKAMP CORAL REEF STATE PARK

If you make just one stop in Key Largo, make sure that it's **Pennekamp** (☎ 305-451-1202; www.pennekamppark.com; MM 102.5 oceanside; 1 person $3.50, 2 people $6, each additional person 50¢; ☾ 8am-sunset), the first underwater park in the USA. Its amazing geography covers 75 sq miles of ocean containing living coral

reef, plus 170 acres of land with walking trails, which include the **Wild Tamarind Nature Trail**, home to air plants, gumbo-limbo, wild bamboo, Jamaica dogwood, crabwood and, of course, wild tamarind.

The best feature, though, is the full program of ranger-led activities, with a range of options for exploring the Florida reef. You can take a **glass-bottom boat or snorkel-sailing tour** (p168); go on straight-up **snorkeling trips** (adult/child $27.95/22.95) or **diving excursions** ($41); or **rent canoes or kayaks** (☎ 305-451-1621; per hr $12) to journey through a 3-mile network of canoe trails. Or you can rent power-boats, starting at $200 per day. If getting on or in the water is not for you, get a taste of what's out there at the visitor center, which has an excellent 30,000-gallon aquarium showcasing living coral and tropical fish and plant life, plus a theater showing continuous nature videos. The park offers great programs, including nature walks through mangrove and hardwood hammocks, a campfire program, a lecture series and campsites.

FLORIDA KEYS WILD BIRD REHABILITATION CENTER

A labor of love, courtesy of a local veterinarian, this is a sort of alfresco **hospital** (☎ 305-852-4486; www.fkwbc.org; 93,600 Overseas Hwy, MM 93.6; donation suggested; ☾ 8am-6:30pm) opened in 1984 to care for sick and injured wild birds. But it also operates as an educational center in an attempt to prevent fishers, children and motorists from carelessly hurting the feathered friends in dumb accidents (most of the injured birds here swallowed discarded fishing hooks, were shot with BB guns or got hit by cars). Visit with turkey vultures, barred owls, cooper's hawks, great blue herons, great white herons and a slew of extremely brown pelicans, who get fed with great fanfare at 3:30pm. Just beware of serious mosquitoes and zoolike smells on particularly hot days.

DIVING

There are dozens of dive shops in Key Largo, most of which are located within Pennekamp Park. Two other recommended options are the **Silent World Dive Center** (☎ 305-451-3252, 800-966-3483; MM 103.2 bayside) and **Amoray Dive Resort** (☎ 305-451-3595, 800-426-6729; MM 104.2 bayside), which also features villalike accommodations.

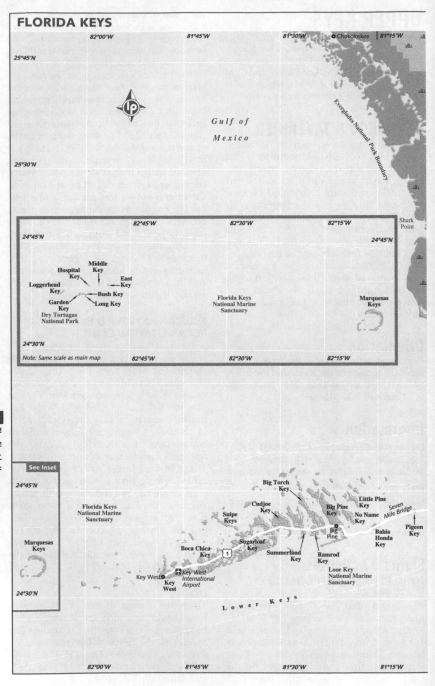

FLORIDA KEYS

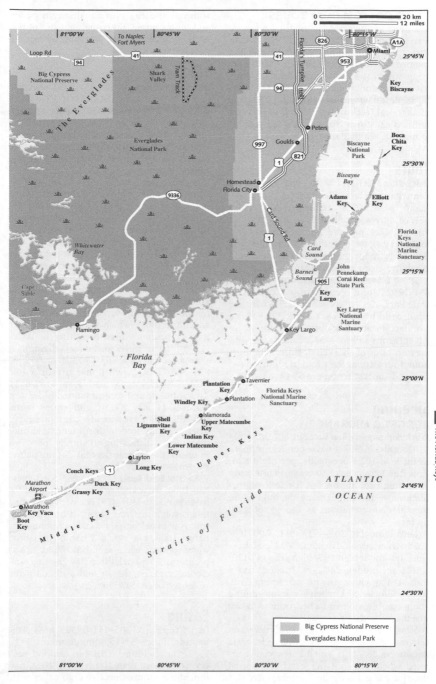

0 _____ 20 km
0 _____ 12 miles

81°00'W   80°45'W   80°30'W   80°15'W

To Naples;
Fort Myers

Loop Rd   94   41   41   826   A1A

Big Cypress   Shark   953   Miami
National Preserve   Valley   25°45'N

The Everglades   Tram Track   Key
                                                                            Biscayne

                                                        94

                        Everglades
                        National Park   997   Boca
                                                                            Chita
The Everglades   Goulds   Biscayne   Key
                                        821   1   National
                                                           Park   25°30'N
                                        Homestead
                        9336   Florida City   Biscayne
                                                           Bay
                                                           Adams   Elliott
                                                           Key   Key

                                        1   Card   Florida
Whitewater   Sound Rd   Keys
Bay   National
                                        1   Card   Marine
                                                Sound   Sanctuary
                                                                           25°15'N
                                                Barnes
Cape   Sound   John
Sable   905   Pennekamp
                                                Key   Coral Reef
                                                Largo   State Park

Flamingo   Key Largo Key Largo
                                                           National
                                                           Marine
                                                           Santuary
Florida
Bay
                                                                           25°00'N
                        Plantation   Tavernier
                        Key
                                      Plantation Florida Keys
                        Windley Key   National Marine
                                      Islamorada Sanctuary
                        Shell
                Lignumvitae   Upper Matecumbe
                Key   Key
                        Indian Key
                        Lower Matecumbe
                        Key   24°45'N
                Layton   Upper Keys
        Conch Keys 1   Long Key   ATLANTIC
Marathon
Airport   Duck Key   OCEAN
                    Grassy Key
Marathon
Key Vaca   Straits of Florida
Boot
Key   Middle Keys

                                                                           24°30'N

                                        Big Cypress National Preserve
                                        Everglades National Park

81°00'W   80°45'W   80°30'W   80°15'W

GLASS-BOTTOM-BOAT TOURS

The most popular **tour**, lasting for 2½ hours, leaves from Pennekamp Coral Reef State Park (p165) and heads out to **Molasses Reef** (named for a wrecked Jamaican ship carrying sugarcane molasses), which extends from Fort Lauderdale through the Dry Tortugas. You'll be wowed by the filigreed flaps of soft coral, Technicolor schools of fish and brilliant creatures from creepy barracudas to massive sea turtles.

Tours

Glass Bottom Boat Tours (☎ 305-451-1202; John Pennekamp Coral Reef State Park, Key Largo, MM 102.5 oceanside; adult/child $21/14) gives excellent 2½-hour tours at 9:15am, 12:15pm and 3pm. Stand on top for breezy views, or gather around the glass floors inside for guided tours of billowing coral and electric-blue creatures.

Sailing & Snorkeling Catamaran Tours (☎ 305-451-1202; John Pennekamp Coral Reef State Park, Key Largo, MM 102.5 oceanside; adult/child under 18 yrs $33.95/28.95) is a wonderful state-park option, combining an adventurous sail on a 38ft catamaran with over an hour of snorkeling time. The four-hour tours are at 9am and 1:30pm; mask, fins and snorkel rental are $2 each extra.

Sleeping

BUDGET & MIDRANGE

John Pennekamp Coral Reef State Park (☎ 305-451-1202, 800-326-3521; www.pennekamppark.com; MM 102.5 oceanside; per night $26) You don't even have to leave Pennekamp at closing time if you opt for tent or recreational-vehicle (RV) camping, but be sure to make a reservation, as the 46 sites fill up fast.

Largo Lodge (☎ 305-451-0424, 800-468-4378; www.largolodge.com; MM 102 bayside; apt low season $95, high season $125) These six hidden cottages, tucked into a lush setting with a private swimming cove, feature efficiency kitchens, a living-dining room combination and a bedroom with two queen-size beds.

Sunset Cove Resort (☎ 877-451-0705; www.sunsetcoveflorida.com; MM 99.5 bayside; r, ste & cottages $85-140) You'll know you've arrived when you spot the kitschy oversized dino guarding this family-friendly place. This good value resort offers 20 tidy rooms (some with full kitchen), plus an Airstream trailer and motor home. Everyone's got use of the barbecue grills, a beach area and canoes and paddleboats.

TOP END

Jules' Undersea Lodge (☎ 305-451-2353; www.jul.com; 51 Shoreland Dr, MM 103.2 oceanside; per person $295-595) Permanently anchored 30ft beneath the water's surface, Jules' Undersea Lodge can accommodate six guests. But is it safe? Well, it was designed for scientists who lived onboard for long periods of time. Even if all the backup generators and systems failed, there would still be about 12 hours of breathing time inside the hotel. Staff are on duty 24 hours a day. In addition to two fairly luxurious private guest rooms, there are two common rooms, including a fully stocked kitchen/dining room and a wet room with hot showers and gear storage. Telephones and an intercom connect guests with the surface. Guests must be at least 10 years old; smoking and alcohol aren't permitted. If you just want to visit the hotel, sign up for a three-hour mini-adventure ($60), which also gives access to its facilities and three breathing hookahs (120ft-long air hoses for tankless diving).

Kona Kai Resort & Gallery (☎ 305-852-7200, 800-365-7829; www.konakairesort.com; MM 97.8 bayside; r $152-293, ste $189-841) This intimate and recommended hideaway features 11 airy rooms and suites (with full kitchens), all warmly contemporary. There's plenty to do – from tennis, kayaking and paddleboating to simply lounging in one of the hammocks that dot the palm-strewn, white-sand beach.

Sheraton Beach Resort (☎ 305-852-5553, 800-826-1006; www.keylargoresort.com; MM 97 bayside; r & ste $109-479) Formerly a Westin, this is still a first-rate resort. It has 200 airy rooms with balconies, two main restaurants, nature trails, two pools, a bar, a myriad of water sports, a white-sand beach and a kids' program. A special three-day package includes breakfast, dinner and a discount on water activities ($470 to $590).

Eating

Crack'd Conch (☎ 305-451-0732; MM 105 bayside; lunch $9-15, dinner mains $11-25; ☯ noon-10pm) This fun seafood eatery, with more than 100 types of beer, has lunchtime sandwiches like crab cakes with bacon and cheddar. The dinnertime mixed seafood platter is an appetite buster and a wallet killer, but well worth it.

Mrs Mac's Kitchen (☎ 305-451-3722; MM 99.4 bayside; breakfast & lunch $4-5, dinner $6-12; ⊗ 7:30am-9:30pm Mon-Sat) Serving home-style cooking by and for locals, this low-key diner has walls plastered with license plates and a menu bursting with meat and potatoes, stuffed pita pockets, steak sandwiches, Cajun shrimp baskets and burgers. It's a nice cheap stop for breakfast, too.

Num Thai Restaurant & Sushi Bar (☎ 305-451-5955; 103,200 Overseas Hwy; lunch dishes $6-9, dinner mains $8-17; ⊗ 11:30am-3pm & 5-10:30pm Mon-Fri, 5-10:30pm Sat-Sun) An Asian oasis in a sterile strip mall, the cozy Num Thai has fresh sushi and excellent Pad Thai and red-curry chicken.

Snook's Bayside Restaurant (☎ 305-453-3799; www.snooks.com; MM 99.9 bayside; mains $10-27, ⊗ 11:30am-3:30pm & 5-9:30pm, brunch 10am-3pm0 Sun) Snuggled against the bay, with an expansive outdoor dining area that lets you chow down in the warm glow of sunset, Snook's has something for everyone, from a fresh catch of the day served in one of nine ways (including blackened, grilled or almondine) to grilled asparagus on its extensive tapas menu. Knock back a kick-ass cocktail at the waterfront bar along with the locals who belly up here.

Tugboat Restaurant (☎ 305-453-9010; 2 Seagate Blvd; mains $10-22) East of the MM 100

traffic light, this locals' favorite, set alongside a marina, lets you choose from tables in its dark bar, screened-in porch or back patio. The seafood dishes rock – especially the lobster dinner and nut-crusted snook.

Drinking & Entertainment

Alabama Jack's (58,000 Card Sound Rd; dishes $10-16) This funky joint, on the banks of a mangrove swamp on the back road between Florida City and Key Largo, is a trip. More bar than eatery, it attracts everyone from Harley Davidson riders and pickup drivers to boaters and rich folks in stretch limos.

Fish House Encore (☎ 305-451-0650; www .fishhouse.com; MM 102.3) A recent, funky-upscale addition to the Key Largo eatery the Fish House, this piano lounge offers a nightly, festive karaoke blow-out (as well as the seafood and steaks of the Fish House, served on a lovely outdoor patio).

Sushi Nami (☎ 305-453-9798; MM 99.5 bayside) In addition to delicious sushi dinners served with a flourish on the bay, weekend evenings offer live music.

Tavernier Towne Cinemas (☎ 305-853-7003; www.taverniercinemas.com; MM 92) This new five-plex, showing new releases, is the perfect rainy-day solution.

Getting There & Around

Greyhound stops at MM 99.6 oceanside.

Swimming with Dolphins

Experts say 'structured' programs – in which staff accompany swimmers in controlled areas for swims with dolphins that are accustomed to human contact – are safer and more humane than 'unstructured' ones. There are three swim-with-dolphins programs on the Keys.

Theater of the Sea (☎ 305-664-2431; www.theaterofthesea.com; Islamorada, MM 84.5 bayside; adult/child 3-12 yrs $18/11; ⊗ 9:30am-4pm) might look cheesy, but it has been here since 1946. Structured dolphin swims and sea lion programs include 30 minutes of instruction and 30 minutes of supervised swim. The swims ($135/95 for the dolphin/sea lion program) are by reservation only at 9:30am, noon and 2pm. They run some other nice programs, including continuous dolphin and sea lion shows; a marine exhibit with sharks, stingrays and tropical fish; a living shell exhibit; and a five-minute boat ride in their dolphin lagoon.

Near Marathon on Grassy Key, **Dolphin Research Center** (☎ 305-289-1121; www.dolphins.org; MM 59 bayside; adult/child 4-12 yrs/senior $15/10/12.50; ⊗ 9am-4pm) is an open-lagoon, nonprofit educational center dedicated to spreading understanding about dolphins. You can join a Dolphin Encounter program, in which you'll learn about and then swim with their dolphins for $135. Dolphin Splash programs, during which you'll stand on a submerged platform while a dolphin comes up to meet you, include 10 minutes in the water and 20 minutes spent preparing for it.

Dolphins Plus (☎ 305-451-1993, 866-860-7946; www.dolphinsplus.com; off MM 99.5 bayside; adult/child 7-17 yrs $10/7), a Key Largo center, specializes in recreational and educational unstructured swims. They expect you to already know a good deal before embarking upon the swim, even though a classroom session is included. Daily 30-minute natural swims ($100) are held at 9am and 1:45pm. Structured swims ($160), with a classroom session and hands-on interaction, are offered at 8:30am, 12:45am and 3pm.

ISLAMORADA

Islamorada (eye-luh-murr-*ah*-da) is actually a collection of smaller islands, with names just as fanciful – Plantation, Upper and Lower Matcumbe, Shell Lignumvitae. It's one of the best stretches to drive along, as you can see water on both sides of the road for much of the way, and there are several lovely ocean-beach nooks providing for scenic rest stops. Islamorada is known for fishing and, as a result, some of the best seafood dining in the Keys.

Orientation & Information

Islamorada comprises more than 20 miles of land, running from MM 90 to MM 74. The Islamorada Chamber of Commerce (☎ 305-664-4503, 800-322-5397; www.fla-keys.com; MM 82.5 bayside; ⊙ 9am-5pm Mon-Fri, 10am-3pm Sat & Sun) is located in an old caboose. Find the post office an MM 82.9 oceanside.

Sights & Activities

LIGNUMVITAE KEY STATE BOTANICAL SITE

Only accessible by boat, this site (☎ 305-664-2540), pronounced lignum-*vite*-ee, encompasses a 280-acre island of virgin tropical forest (bring mosquito repellent!). The simple attraction is the 1919 Matheson House, with its windmill and cistern. The forest features strangler fig, mastic, gumbo-limbo and poisonwood trees, as well as native lignumvitae trees, known for their extremely hard wood.

On the island, 1¼-hour guided walking tours are given at 10am and 2pm Thursday to Monday, but you can only visit by boat. From Robbie's Marina (right), boats depart for the 15-minute trip (adult/child $15/10) about 30 minutes prior to each tour; reservations are highly recommended.

INDIAN KEY STATE HISTORIC SITE

Also accessible only by boat, this 23-acre historic island (☎ 305-664-2540) has an interesting history. In 1831 renegade wrecker Jacob Housman bought the island and opened his own wrecker station after falling out with Key West wreckers. Housman developed it into a thriving little city, complete with a warehouse, docks, streets, a hotel and about 40 to 50 permanent residents. By 1836 Indian Key was the seat of Dade County. But Housman eventually lost his wrecker's license and in 1840 he lost the entire island after an attack during the Second Seminole War.

There's not much here today – just foundation remains, some cisterns, Housman's grave and lots of plant life. But there are trails and an observation tower. Free 1½-hour ranger-led tours (9am and 1pm Thursday to Monday) detail the fascinating history, not just of the wrecking operation, but also of the island's geological and natural history. There's a catch, though: you need to have a boat or take a 10-minute shuttle ($15/10 adult/child) from – you guessed it – Robbie's Marina (below).

ROBBIE'S MARINA

Robbie's (☎ 305-664-9814; www.robbies.com, MM 77.5 bayside; ⊙ 8am-6pm) All sorts of boats can be rented here. Rates for a 16ft boat start at $70 for half a day and, depending on the boat size and number of people, rise briskly from there. You can also feed tarpon right from the dock here ($1 to $2 per bucket of fish food); the best time is midmorning.

DIVING

Area dive shops include Holiday Isle Dive Shop (☎ 305-664-3483, 800-327-7070; www.diveholidayisle.com; MM 84.5 oceanside), with dive and snorkel tours departing at 9am and 1pm, plus a full range of equipment for rent or sale, and Ocean Quest (☎ 305-664-4401, 800-356-8798; MM 88.5), a training facility located at the Smugglers Cove Resort.

Sleeping

BUDGET & MIDRANGE

Long Key State Recreation Area (☎ 305-664-4815, reservations 800-326-3521; www.reserve america.çom; MM 67.5 oceanside; sites without/with electricity $24/26) Make reservations right this minute: it's tough to get one of these 60 sites, but once you do, you'll never want to leave. Most of the waterfront sites offer decent wooded privacy between one another.

Ragged Edge Resort (☎ 305-852-5389; www .ragged-edge.com; 243 Treasure Harbor Rd; units $69-209) This low-key and popular efficiency and apartment complex, far from the maddening traffic jams, has 10 quiet units and friendly hosts. The larger studios have screened-in porches. There's no beach, but you can swim off the dock and at the pool.

TOP END

Casa Morada (☎ 305-664-0044, 888-881-3030; www.casamorada.com; 136 Madeira Rd, off MM 82.2; ste low season $229-539, mid-Dec–mid-May $229-649) This hidden, romantic enclave of 16 contemporary suites, recently remodeled, has an upscale boutique-hotel feel to it. You'll find lots of white linens, potted orchids and oversized hammocks (plus Jacuzzis and sea views in the most expensive quarters).

Cheeca Lodge & Spa (☎ 305-664-4651, 800-327-2888; www.cheeca.com; MM 82 ocean-side; low season $199-1200, r high season $225-2200) This chichi conference-style Rockresort, recently converted into a partial condo-hotel property, is for those who like to be pampered. The 203 upscale rooms are located in the main hotel or outlying villas; some are oceanfront, most have balconies. Their dive shop arranges all sorts of trips, or you can just wander the nature trails, rent a bike or kayak, laze by the seductive pool or enjoy a full treatment at the recently added spa.

White Gate Court (☎ 305-664-4136, 800-645-4283; www.whitegatecourt.com; MM 76 bayside; units low season $126-239, high season $165-298) With only seven studios and villas, all recently renovated, these family-friendly places go fast – with good reason. Each well-equipped unit has a full kitchen, a laundry, free local calls, a barbecue grill and a nice garden area with torch lights. Guests have free use of paddleboats, snorkeling gear and bicycles. You can swim off the dock.

Eating

Manny & Isa's Kitchen (☎ 305-664-5019; MM 81.6 oceanside; lunch $5-8, dinner mains $11-18; 🕙 11am-9pm Wed-Mon) This Spanish/American, value-packed, no-frills joint has good daily specials, lobster enchiladas, *ropa vieja* (shredded beef) and chili con carne. The Key lime pie rules.

Mile Marker 88 (☎ 305-852-9315; MM 88 bayside; mains $15-24; 🕙 5-9pm Tue-Sun) Touted for years as the best of the Keys, this chef-owned institution serves creative seafood preparations, from lobster to delectable stone crabs.

Morada Bay (☎ 305-664-0604; MM 81.6 bayside; lunch $9-16, dinner mains $21-27; 🕙 11:30am-10pm) If you can ignore the overwhelmed service, there's no more

Key Lime Pie

Many places claim to serve the original Key lime pie, but no one knows who discovered the tart treat. Types of crust vary, and whether or not the pie should be topped with meringue is debated. However, the color of Key lime pie is not open to question. Beware of places serving green Key lime pie: Key limes are yellow, not green. Restaurants that add green food coloring say that tourists expect it to be green. Steer clear.

atmospheric and romantic beachfront place on the Keys. Enjoy the laid-back Caribbean setting, complete with Conch architecture, an imported powder-white sandy beach and nighttime torches, along with your tapas or fresh seafood dishes.

Pierre's (☎ 305-664-3225; MM 81.6 bayside; mains $25-30; 🕙 5:30-10pm) Ready to spend? Then by all means do it here. This two-story waterfront plantation house, owned by the adjacent Morada Bay, specializes in creative seafood dishes. At the very least, treat yourself to a cocktail out on the veranda; you'll feel like royalty.

Time Out Barbecue (☎ 305-664-8911; MM 81.5 oceanside; lunch $5-6, dinner $10-14; 🕙 11am-10pm) This low-brow eatery with linoleum floors dishes up killer barbecue with a smoky aroma that wafts into your car the moment you pull up to the front door.

Drinking & Entertainment

Loreli Restaurant & Cabana Bar (☎ 305-664-4656; MM 82) Join the crowds of youngsters for watered-down cocktails, live music and sunset raucousness fuelled by happy-hour specials from 4pm to 6pm.

Morada Bay (☎ 305-664-0604; MM 81.6 bayside) In addition to its excellent food (left) and wine menu, Morada hosts live bands on weekends and extremely popular full-moon parties monthly.

Papa Joe's (☎ 305-664-8109; MM 79.7 bayside) Though it's been *the* place for down-home eats since mid-1930s, this rustic, nautical landmark is perhaps more popular for its rockin' outdoor tiki-style raw bar, which draws crowds for sunset happy hours.

Woody's (☎ 305-664-4335; MM 82 bayside) It's seamy, it's raunchy, it's got pizza. This odd combination of strip-club, restaurant and house of comedy is also home to a

The Florida Keys – Upper Keys

double-entendre-obsessed band, Big Dick & the Extenders. You must be at least 21 – and willing to shed your dignity – to enter.

Getting There & Around

Greyhound stops at the Burger King at MM 82.5 oceanside.

LONG KEY

LONG KEY RECREATION AREA

This 965-acre **recreation area** (☎ 305-664-4815; MM 67.5 oceanside; admission per car $4, plus per person 50¢) takes up much of Long Key. It's about 30 minutes south of Islamorada and is filled with gumbo-limbo, crabwood and poisonwood trees, and lots of wading birds in the mangroves. Two short nature trails head through distinct plant communities. In addition to ranger-led programs a couple of times a week, Friday evening campfire programs and a two-hour guided nature walk on Wednesday morning (10am), the park also has a 1½-mile canoe trail through a saltwater tidal lagoon and rents canoes (hourly $5, daily $12).

MIDDLE KEYS

The Middle Keys run from Long Key (MM 67.5) to Pigeon Key, which explores the building of the Overseas Hwy (the lifeline of the Florida Keys), and the famed Old Seven Mile Bridge (MM 46.5 to MM 40). In between are tiny Conch Keys (MM 63 to MM 61), Duck Key (MM 63 to MM 61), Grassy Key (MM 60 to MM 57), and Key Vaca (MM 54 to MM 47), on which Marathon is located.

MARATHON & GRASSY KEY

Marathon, the second largest Keys town after Key West, is located on Key Vaca. Here, as well as on the neighboring Grassy Key, it's all about fishing – with hiking, beaches, seedy bars and hotels, over-developed strip malls and turtle-loving thrown in for good measure (for proof, take a tour of the Turtle Hospital, right). It's also an ideal place for a kayak trip through the mangroves (right).

Orientation

Marathon sits right on the halfway point between Key Largo and Key West, and is a good place to stop on a lazy road trip from one to the other.

Information

Fisherman's Hospital (☎ 305-743-5533; MM 48.7 oceanside) Has a major emergency room.

Food for Thought (☎ 305-743-3297; Gulfside Village Shopping Center, MM 51 bayside) A combination bookstore/health-food shop.

Marathon Visitors Center Chamber of Commerce (☎ 305-743-5417, 800-262-7284; www.floridakeys marathon.com; MM 53.5 bayside; ☼ 9am-5pm) Has a mother lode of information and sells Greyhound tickets.

Sights & Activities

MUSEUMS OF CRANE POINT HAMMOCK

This lush, 63-acre hardwood hammock **complex** (☎ 305-743-9100; www.cranepoint.org; MM 50.5 bayside; adult/student or child over 6 yrs/senior $7.50/4/6; ☼ 9am-5pm Mon-Sat, noon-5pm Sun) includes the Museum of Natural History of the Florida Keys and the Children's Museum of the Florida Keys, plus a vast system of nature trails, mangroves, a raised boardwalk, an early-20th-century Bahamian-style house, exhibits on pirates and wrecking, a walk-through coral reef tunnel and a bird sanctuary that houses injured wild birds. It's a lovely dose of nature on an unremarkable highway.

TURTLE HOSPITAL

This amphibian **safe haven** (☎ 305-743-6509; www.theturtlehospital.org; 2396 Overseas Hwy; ☼ appointment only) is a small place with a big mission: to rescue, rehabilitate and release injured sea turtles. It aims to teach humans about what causes the amputations and intestinal impactions – from fishing lines to discarded plastic bags – by letting you see the sweet loggerheads and other species up close.

SOMBRERO BEACH

Tucked away down a residential side street, this ocean beach (Sombrero Rd, off MM 50 oceanside) is a peaceful haven with gentle, soothing surf and extra-clean facilities.

DIVING & KAYAKING

Good dive shops here include **Sombrero Reef Explorers** (☎ 305-743-0536; www.sombre roreef.com; 19 Sombrero Rd, off MM 50 oceanside) and **Aquatic Adventures Dive Center** (☎ 305-743-2421, 800-978-3483; Key Colony Beach, MM 54 oceanside), both offering snorkeling and diving expeditions through nearby sections of the coral reef.

Marathon Kayak (☎ 305-743-0561; 19 Sombrero Blvd, Marathon, MM 50 oceanside) provides three-hour guided mangrove ecotours (per person $40), full-day mangrove ecotours ($80) three-hour sunset tours ($40), instruction (included) and rentals (single/double half-day $30/40, full day $45/60).

Sleeping

Hawk's Cay Resort (☎ 305-743-9000, 800-432-2242; www.hawkscay.com; 61 Hawk's Cay Blvd, Duck Key, off MM 61 oceanside; r & ste low season $220-1100, high season $260-1100) This upscale Caribbean-style hotel has 400 rooms and is the most developed self-contained resort in the Keys. You'll find tightly packed townhouse villas, a sailing school, snorkeling, tennis, boat and kayak rentals, fishing programs, dolphin encounters and scuba-diving lessons.

Knights Key Campground (☎ 305-743-4343, 800-348-2267; MM 47 oceanside; tent sites without/with electricity $25/37, oceanfront/marina sites with electricity $30-50/47-72) On the northern end of the Seven Mile Bridge, this 200-site campground – overdeveloped and full of family campground bells and whistles – has many on-water sites and 17 sites specifically for tenters.

Seascape Ocean Resort (☎ 305-743-6455; 1075 75th St, off MM 50.5 oceanside; r $165-255) A photographer hailing from Boston has graced this little residential corner with a classy, understated-luxury B&B vibe. The nine rooms, several of which have a kitchen, all have a different feel, from old-fashioned cottage to sleek boutique. Seascape also has a lovely waterfront pool, kayaks for guests to use and a lovely lobby-lounge where you'll find breakfast and afternoon wine and snack (all included).

Siesta Motel (☎ 305-743-5671; www.siesta motel.net; MM 51 oceanside; r year-round average $70) Head here for one of the cheapest, cleanest flops in the Keys – and it's got great service, to boot.

Yellowtail Inn (☎ 305-743-8400; www.yellowtailinn.com; Grassy Key, MM 58.3 oceanside; efficiencies & cottages $109-329) This oceanfront Grassy Key complex, with a mix of quaint cottages and spare efficiencies,

has an old-school, wicker-furniture style and a homey feel. The best sleeps are in the oceanfront and oceanside cottages, which feel like private summer homes, and all the breezy units have use of barbecue grills, a private sandy beach and a pool.

Eating

7 Mile Grill (☎ 305-743-4481; MM 45 bayside; breakfast $3-9, dinner $8-11; ◷ 7am-9pm Fri-Tue) This popular short-order place has bar service and some covered tables overlooking the parking lot. Go for a hearty morning serving of two eggs and a Delmonico steak, or lunchtime grilled-fish sandwiches or dinnertime shrimp steamed in beer.

Barracuda Grill (☎ 305-743-3314; MM 49.5 bayside; mains $15-20; ◷ 5:55-10pm Mon-Sat) This stylishly casual New American grill makes waves with its creative dishes and friendly service.

Hideaway Café (☎ 305-289-1554; Rainbow Bend Resort, Grassy Key, MM 58; mains

Pigeon Key & Old Seven Mile Bridge

This 5-acre **island** (☎ 305-289-0025; MM 47; adult/child $8.50/5; ◷ tours 10am-3pm), about 2 miles west of Marathon and basically below the Old Seven Mile Bridge, is a National Historic District. As Henry Flagler's FEC Railway progressed southward, the construction of the Seven Mile Bridge between Marathon and Bahia Honda Key became an immense project. From 1908 to 1912, Pigeon Key housed about 400 workers. Later it housed the railroad maintenance workers. And after the hurricane that wiped out Flagler's railroad in 1935, the Key housed workers who converted the railroad to automobile bridges.

After a brief stint in the 1970s as a research facility leased by the University of Miami, the Pigeon Key Foundation preserved the island's buildings and began telling the story of the railroad and its workers. Today the Key is open for touring and you can visit the old town, including the 'honeymoon cottage,' assistant bridge tender and bridge tender's houses, the section gang's quarters and the 'negro quarters.'

You can park at the southwestern end of Marathon and take the hourly shuttle out to the island; it runs from 10am to 3pm, with the last shuttle returning at 4:45pm. You can also ride or walk across the bridge. The **Old Seven Mile Bridge** (admission free), meanwhile, serves as 'the World's Longest Fishing Bridge;' park at the northeastern foot of the bridge.

$18-30) Savor big-American fare with a slight French twist in this airy, oceanfront dining room, on the grounds of the upscale Rainbow Bend Resort.

Leigh Ann's Coffee House (☎ 305-743-2001; MM 50.5 oceanside; dishes $4-7; ☽ 7am-4pm) From breakfast frittatas to lunchtime bruschettas to smoothies and salads, the pleasant and friendly Leigh Ann's is a delightful oasis from the omnipresent Conch fritters and seafood platters.

Drinking & Entertainment

Brass Monkey Lounge (☎ 305-743-5737; Marathon, MM 52) It's got nightly live music, a daily happy hour and never a cover charge.

Gary's Pub & Billiards (☎ 305-743-0622; Marathon, MM 50) This macho sports bar has 22 beers on tap, eight pool tables and a big-screen TV.

Island Tiki Bar & Restaurant (☎ 305-743-4191; Marathon, MM 54 bayside) Slurp oysters and froofy cocktails on a patio overlooking the Gulf of Mexico.

Getting There & Around

You can fly into the **Marathon Airport** (☎ 305-743-2155, MM 50.5 bayside) or go Greyhound, which stops at the airport.

LOWER KEYS

The Lower Keys extend from Bahia Honda Key (MM 40) to Boca Chica Key (MM 7). As far as accommodation and dining choices in this stretch go, you might as well just keep driving to Key West. But if you're

in the area for beach and diving activities, there are plenty of decent lunch stops.

BIG PINE, BAHIA HONDA & LOOE KEY

Big Pine is home to endless stretches of quiet roads (once you leave the overdeveloped highway), Key West employees who found a way around astronomical real-estate prices, and packs of wandering key deer. Bahia Honda's got everyone's favorite sandy beach, while Looe is the place for amazing reef-diving opportunities.

Information

Big Pine Key public library (☎ 305-289-6303) In the Big Pine Shopping Center.

Lower Keys Chamber of Commerce (☎ 305-872-3580, 800-872-3722; www.lowerkeyschamber.com; MM 31 oceanside; ☽ 9am-5pm Mon-Fri, 9am-3pm Sat) Helpful office, on Big Pine Key.

Post office (MM 30 bayside) On Big Pine Key.

Sights & Activities
BAHIA HONDA STATE PARK

This is just a half-hour drive from Key West. Tourists and locals alike happily make the trip to this **park** (☎ 305-872-2353; www.bahiahondapark.com; MM 36.8 oceanside; per car $4, plus per person 50¢; ☽ 8am-sunset) to sample one of the Keys' best sparkling-white-sand beaches. It's got kayak, umbrella and snorkel-gear rentals; a small gift shop and concession area; and nature trails dedicated to butterflies and flora including sea

Sunset, Upper Keys (p165)

grapes, silver palms and yellow satinwood trees. All that said, be advised that this 524-acre park is a bit overrated: the 2½-mile strip of sand is annoyingly narrow and tangled with seaweed, and in the summer and fall it's infested with biting sandflies. Plus, no matter how far away from the crowds you hike for privacy, rangers can eject women who elect to sunbathe topless.

LOOE KEY NATIONAL MARINE SANCTUARY

Pronounced 'Loo,' this grove reef off Big Pine can only be visited through a specially arranged charter-boat trip (call ☎ 305-292-0311 for information). A National Marine Sanctuary, it was established in 1981 to protect sensitive areas within the Keys by providing a compromise between commerce and environmental protection (the sanctuary designation prohibits standing on, anchoring on or touching coral). Named for an English frigate that sank here in 1744, the Looe Key reef contains the 210ft *Adolphus Busch* – used in the 1957 film *Fire Down Below* – which was sunk in 110ft of water in 1998. Permissible activities include limited lobster-catching, crabbing, hook-and-line sport and commercial fishing.

NATIONAL KEY DEER REFUGE

Key deer, an endangered subspecies of white-tailed deer, live primarily on Big Pine and No Name Keys. The **National Key Deer Refuge Headquarters** (☎ 305-872-0774; http://nationalkeydeer.fws.gov; Big Pine Shopping Center, MM 30.5 bayside; ☻ 8am-5pm Mon-Fri) provides literature on the creatures and on the refuge, which actually sprawls over several Keys. But the sections that are open to the public – Blue Hole, Watson's Hammock and Watson's Nature Trail – are on Big Pine and No Name Keys.

Once mainland-dwellers, Key deer were stranded during the formation of the Keys, where they evolved a smaller stature. Since it's warmer here than on the mainland, the deer don't need as much body mass. And to compensate for reduced grazing lands and scarce freshwater, the deer now have single births rather than multiple litters. Though there are about 800 Key deer in this small area, don't expect to drive through any old time and find herds grazing along the highway. They prefer the shady, less populated areas away from the main drag, tend to vanish during the mid-

dle of the day and are best spotted in early morning and late afternoon.

To visit the various public areas of the refuge, take Key Deer Blvd north for 3½ miles from MM 30.5. You'll first come to **Blue Hole**, an old quarry that's now the largest freshwater body in the Keys. It's used as a small park, mainly by locals, and is home to lots of alligators, turtles, fish and wading birds (do not feed the wildlife!); don't expect to see much action at midday, though. Less than a mile long, **Watson's Nature Trail** and **Watson's Hammock** are a quarter mile further along the same road. **No Name Key** gets few visitors, but is also a good spot for deer spotting. Go on to Watson Blvd, turn right, then left onto Wilder Blvd. Cross Bogie Bridge and you'll be on No Name.

DIVING & SNORKELING

Looe Key Reef Resort & Dive Center (☎ 305-872-2215, 800-942-5397; MM 27.5 oceanside) and **Paradise Divers** (☎ 305-872-1114; MM 38.5 bayside) rent equipment and lead local reef dives. **Strike Zone Charters** (☎ 305-872-9863, 800-654-9560; MM 29.5 bayside) has four-hour snorkeling and diving trips aboard glass-bottom boats that explore the thousands of varieties of colorful tropical fish, coral and sea life in the Looe Key sanctuary. And the Bahia Honda **park concession** (☎ 305-872-3210) offers daily snorkeling trips at 9:30am and 1:30pm. Reservations are a good idea in high season.

Sleeping
BUDGET & MIDRANGE

Bahia Honda State Park Campground (☎ 305-872-2353, reservations 800-326-3521; www .reserveamerica.com; MM 37; sites without/with electricity $24/26, cabins mid-Sep–mid-Dec $97, other times $125) One of the Key's best camping places, this excellent park has six cabins, each sleeping six, and 200 almost bayside and oceanside sites. Reserve well in advance.

Big Pine Key Fishing Lodge (☎ 305-872-2351; MM 33 oceanside; sites without/with electricity $35/40, motel efficiencies $80-100) This tidy canalside place has 60 tent sites, 97 RV sites and 16 efficiencies. Even with an artificial beach, ocean swimming isn't great, but there is a pool. The lodge, geared to fishing and diving, also has boat rentals.

Casa Grande (☎ 305-872-2878; 1619 Long Beach Dr, Big Pine Key; r $90-140) A sophisticated B&B right on the ocean, the Casa will seduce you with its four-poster beds, private beach and hearty breakfasts. Guests also have use of snorkeling equipment, bicycles, windsurfers and kayaks.

Looe Key Reef Resort (☎ 305-872-2215, 800-942-5397; www.diveflakeys.com; MM 27.5 oceanside; r low season $75, high season $100) The focus of this Ramrod Key motel is diving, so, predictably, its 20 motel rooms are quite basic. The thatched-roof tiki bar is a happy-hour hit.

TOP END

Little Palm Island Resort & Spa (☎ 305-872-2524, 800-343-8567; www.littlepalmisland.com; ste $900-1200) Accessible only by plane or boat, this 30-bungalow luxe retreat on Little Torch Key rewards guests with pampering service, romantic surroundings, white-sand beaches, a lagoonlike pool, Zen-style gardens, plus a phenomenal spa and restaurant. Simply the best option (and it should be!).

Parmer's Place Guesthouse (☎ 305-872-2157; www.parmersresort.com; 565 Barry Ave, Big Pine Key, off MM 28.5 bayside; r, efficiencies & units $69-299) On 5 acres of Little Torch Key, this lush and tidy waterfront resort has motel rooms, efficiencies, one- and two-bedroom units and lots of aviaries with chattering birds. Its style is very highway-motel, though its setting is lovely and tropical. Rates include a Continental breakfast.

Eating

Coco's Kitchen (☎ 305-872-4495; Big Pine Key Shopping Center, MM 30.5 bayside; breakfast dishes $1-3, sandwiches & mains $2-5; ☻7am-7:30pm Tue-Sat) Enter through the oddly mirrored storefront into this tiny luncheonette, where local fishers join shoppers from the Winn Dixie next door for some of the best Cuban grub this side of Key West. The rice and beans, Cuban sandwiches and strong Cuban coffee are delicious.

Good Food Conspiracy (☎ 305-872-3945; MM 30 oceanside; ☻9:30am-7pm Mon-Sat, 9:30am-5pm Sun) This health-food place has a limited amount of prepared foods, a juice bar and smoothies, perfect for burger-free beach picnics.

No Name Pub (☎ 305-872-9115; N Watson Blvd, off MM 30.5 bayside; dishes $5-15; ☻11am-11pm) Perhaps the most colorful eatery in these parts, this smoky and hidden locals' roadhouse is wallpapered with dollar bills. The bar-cum-rustic restaurant serves great pizzas to families and drinkers.

Getting There & Around

Drive, go Greyhound or call the Keys Shuttle (p164).

SUGARLOAF & BOCA CHICA KEYS

This is the final stretch between the rest of the Keys and the holy grail of Key West. There's not much going on – just a few good eats and one thoroughly batty roadside attraction.

Orientation

This lowest section of the Lower Keys goes from about MM 20 to the start of Key West.

Sights
PERKY'S BAT TOWER

It resembles an Aztec-inspired fire lookout, but this wooden tower (Sugarloaf Key; MM17) is actually one real-estate developer's vision gone awry. His name was Richter C Perky, and in the 1920s he had the bright idea to transform this area into a vacation resort. There was just one problem: mosquitoes. His solution? Build a 35ft tower and move in a crowd of bats (he'd heard they eat mosquitoes). He imported the flying mammals, but they promptly took off and Perky never built anything else near here.

Sleeping

Sugarloaf Key Resort KOA (☎ 305-745-3549, 800-562-7731; 251 County Rd, off MM 20 oceanside; tent sites $42-70, RV sites $62-105) This highly developed KOA (Kampground of America) has about 200 tent sites and 200 RV sites, with amenities including beachfront volleyball, swimming pool, minigolf and new sunset cruises.

Sugarloaf Lodge (☎ 800-553-6097; Sugarloaf Key, MM 17; r $95-150) The 55 motel-like rooms are nothing special, though every single one has a killer bay view. There is also an on-site restaurant, a tiki bar, a marina and an airstrip, from which you can charter a seaplane tour or go skydiving.

Eating

Baby's Coffee (☎ 800-523-2326; MM 15 oceanside; ⏰ 7am-6pm Mon-Fri, 7am-5pm Sat & Sun) This very cool coffeehouse has an on-site bean-roasting plant and sells bags of the aromatic stuff along with excellent hot and cold java brews (as well as essentials from yummy baked goods to Dr Brommer's liquid soap). It's seriously popular – so much so that Baby's just opened a warehouse store in Miami.

Mangrove Mama's (☎ 305-745-3030; MM 20 oceanside; lunch $10-15, dinner mains $19-25; ⏰ 11:30am-3:30pm & 5:30-10pm) This groovy roadside eatery and rustic bar serves Caribbean-inspired seafood – coconut shrimp, spicy Conch stew, lobster – in a dining room and on a popular backyard patio, sometimes accompanied by live reggae. It's a great postbeach destination.

KEY WEST

Self-dubbed sophisticates like to think that Key West is over. Tell one of them that you're planning a visit to this hotspot and they'll likely warn you about how ticky-tacky touristy it's become. But pay them no mind.

While most of the main drag, Duval Street, has indeed become overridden with chain stores and shops hawking T-shirts that say 'I Love to Fart' (seriously), just leave that part to the cruise-ship tourists who dock here and you'll be OK. There is so much more to this town that it's practically impossible not to fall in love with everything from the tropical night breezes and Bahamian architecture to the warm people and precocious chickens that seem to have the run of the place. Just get off the beaten path and give yourself over to life in the Conch Republic.

ORIENTATION

The island of Key West is roughly oval-shaped, divided into Old Town and New Town. New Town is where the real working folks live – families with kids and hotel employees, who have been priced out of other neighborhoods. So Old Town, as you might have guessed, is where all the action is, from inns to eateries to museums. The main drags are Duval St and Truman Ave (US Hwy 1). Downtown streets are laid out in a grid, with street numbers (usually painted on lampposts) in a hundred-per-block format, counting upward from Front St (100)

Key West History

The area's first European settlers were the Spanish, who, upon finding Indian burial sites, named the place Cayo Hueso (pronounced kah-ya way-so, meaning Bone Island), a name that was later Anglicized into Key West. Purchased from a Spaniard by John Simonton in 1821, Key West was developed as a naval base in 1822, and for a long while, Key West's times of boom and bust were closely tied to a military presence.

The construction of forts at Key West and on the Dry Tortugas brought men and money. As well, the island's proximity to busy and treacherous shipping lanes (which attracted pirates) created a wrecking industry – salvaging goods from downed ships.

In the late 1800s, the area became the focus of mass immigration and political activity for Cubans, who were fleeing oppressive conditions under Spanish rule and trying to form a revolutionary army. Along with them came cigar manufacturers, who turned Key West into the USA's cigar manufacturing center. That would end when workers' demands convinced several large manufacturers, notably Vicente Martínez Ybor and Ignacio Haya, to relocate to Tampa in southwest Florida.

During the Spanish-American War, Key West was an important staging point for US troops, and the military buildup lasted through WWI. All of the Keys began to boom when Henry Flagler constructed his Overseas Hwy, running over a series of causeways from the mainland to Key West; he also constructed the Key West extension of his railroad in 1912.

In the late 1910s, with Prohibition on the horizon, Key West became a bootlegging center, as people stocked up on booze. To make matters worse, after the city went bankrupt during the Great Depression, a 1935 hurricane depleted what little enthusiasm remained. World War II, though, breathed new life into Key West when the naval base once again became an important staging area. And everyone in Washington was certainly happy about that presence when the Bay of Pigs crisis unfolded in 1961.

Key West has always been a place where people bucked trends. A large society of artists and craftspeople congregated here at the end of the Great Depression because of cheap real estate, and that community continues to grow (despite today's pricey real estate). While gay men have long been welcomed, the gay community really picked up in earnest in the 1970s. Today it's one of the most renowned and best organized in the country (p187).

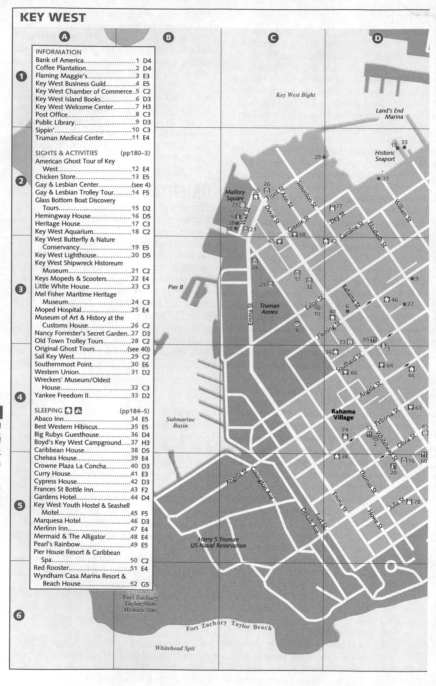

A

INFORMATION
Bank of America................................1 D4
Coffee Plantation..............................2 D4
Flaming Maggie's...............................3 E3
Key West Business Guild.................4 E5
Key West Chamber of Commerce..5 C2
Key West Island Books......................6 D3
Key West Welcome Center............7 H3
Post Office...8 C3
Public Library.....................................9 D3
Sippin'...10 C3
Truman Medical Center..................11 E4

SIGHTS & ACTIVITIES   (pp180–3)
American Ghost Tour of Key
   West..12 E4
Chicken Store..................................13 E5
Gay & Lesbian Center..................(see 4)
Gay & Lesbian Trolley Tour............14 F5
Glass Bottom Boat Discovery
   Tours..15 D2
Hemingway House...........................16 D5
Heritage House................................17 C3
Key West Aquarium.........................18 C2
Key West Butterfly & Nature
   Conservancy................................19 E5
Key West Lighthouse.......................20 D5
Key West Shipwreck Historeum
   Museum.......................................21 C2
Keys Mopeds & Scooters.................22 E4
Little White House...........................23 C3
Mel Fisher Maritime Heritage
   Museum.......................................24 C3
Moped Hospital...............................25 E4
Museum of Art & History at the
   Customs House.............................26 C2
Nancy Forrester's Secret Garden...27 D3
Old Town Trolley Tours...................28 C2
Original Ghost Tours....................(see 40)
Sail Key West..................................29 C2
Southernmost Point........................30 E6
Western Union.................................31 D2
Wreckers' Museum/Oldest
   House...32 C3
Yankee Freedom II..........................33 D2

SLEEPING   (pp184–5)
Abaco Inn..34 E5
Best Western Hibiscus.....................35 E5
Big Rubys Guesthouse.....................36 D4
Boyd's Key West Campground.........37 H3
Caribbean House..............................38 D5
Chelsea House.................................39 E4
Crowne Plaza La Concha.................40 D3
Curry House....................................41 E3
Cypress House.................................42 D3
Frances St Bottle Inn.......................43 F2
Gardens Hotel.................................44 D4
Key West Youth Hostel & Seashell
   Motel...45 F5
Marquesa Hotel...............................46 D3
Merlinn Inn.....................................47 E4
Mermaid & The Alligator................48 E4
Pearl's Rainbow..............................49 E5
Pier House Resort & Caribbean
   Spa..50 C2
Red Rooster....................................51 E4
Wyndham Casa Marina Resort &
   Beach House................................52 G5

B

C

Key West Bight

Pier B

*Submarine
Basin*

D

*Land's End
Marina*

*Historic
Seaport*

*Mallory
Square*

*Truman
Annex*

**Bahama
Village**

*Harry S Truman
US Naval Reservation*

Fort Zachary
Taylor State
Historic Site

Fort Zachary Taylor Beach

Whitehead Spit

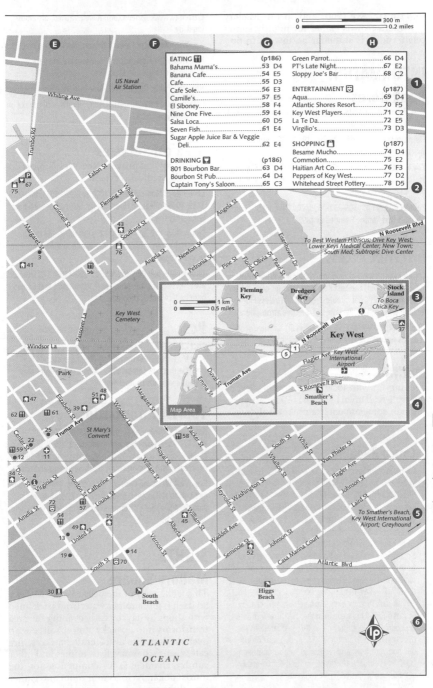

EATING 🍴 (p186)
Bahama Mama's...................53 D4
Banana Cafe.......................54 E5
Cafe..................................55 D3
Cafe Sole...........................56 E3
Camille's............................57 E5
El Siboney..........................58 F4
Nine One Five.....................59 E4
Salsa Loca..........................60 D5
Seven Fish..........................61 E4
Sugar Apple Juice Bar & Veggie
   Deli................................62 E4

DRINKING 🍷 (p186)
801 Bourbon Bar..................63 D4
Bourbon St Pub....................64 D4
Captain Tony's Saloon............65 C3

Green Parrot.......................66 D4
PT's Late Night....................67 E2
Sloppy Joe's Bar...................68 C2

ENTERTAINMENT 🎭 (p187)
Aqua.................................69 D4
Atlantic Shores Resort............70 F5
Key West Players...................71 C2
La Te Da.............................72 E5
Virgilio's............................73 D3

SHOPPING 🛍 (p187)
Besame Mucho......................74 D4
Commotion.........................75 E2
Haitian Art Co......................76 F3
Peppers of Key West...............77 D2
Whitehead Street Pottery.........78 D5

US Naval
Air Station

Whiting Ave

Eaton St

Grinnell St

Fleming St

White St

Angela St

Southard St

Angela St

Newton St

Petronia St

Pine St

Florida St

Olivia St

Pearl St

Eisenhower Dr

To Best Western Hibiscus; Dive Key West;
Lower Keys Medical Center; New Town;
South Med; Subtropic Dive Center

N Roosevelt Blvd

Fleming
Key

Dredgers
Key

Stock
Island
To Boca
Chica Key

Key West

N Roosevelt Blvd

Flagler Ave

Key West
International
Airport

S Roosevelt Blvd

Smather's
Beach

Map Area

Key West
Cemetery

Windsor La

Park

St Mary's
Convent

Truman Ave

Margaret St

Windsor La

Passover La

Elizabeth St

Center St

Duval St

Virginia St

Simonton St

Catherine St

Louisa St

United St

South St

Amelia St

Royal St

William St

Reynolds St

Whalton St

Washington St

Vernon St

Alberta St

Waddell Ave

Seminole St

William St

Packer St

South St

White St

Von Phister St

Flagler Ave

Johnson St

Laird St

Johnson St

Casa Marina Court

To Smather's Beach;
Key West International
Airport; Greyhound

Atlantic Blvd

South
Beach

Higgs
Beach

ATLANTIC
OCEAN

The Florida Keys – Key West

179

to Truman Ave (900) and so on. Mallory Sq, where crowds gather for nightly sunset celebrations, is at the far northwestern tip.

INFORMATION
Bookstores
For books in this very literary town, check out the following:

Flaming Maggie's (☎ 305-294-3931; 830 Fleming St) Specializes in gay books and periodicals.

Key West Island Books (☎ 305-294-2904; 513 Fleming St) Has an excellent selection of works by Key West writers both past and present.

Public Library (☎ 305-292-3535; 700 Fleming St) South Florida's first library. Founded in 1892.

Internet Access

Coffee Plantation (☎ 305-295-9808; 804 Whitehead St; ☼ 8am-6pm) The best Key West Internet café. It has computers for 20¢ per minute, free WiFi (Wireless Fidelity) for laptop users, kick-ass java and a festive atmosphere.

Sippin' (☎ 305-293-0555; 424 Eaton St) Another good spot. It's near the center of town. Costs 20¢ per minute.

Media
Keeping up with local goings-on is easy, as this well-read town has nearly 10 newspapers (though some are entertainment-only rags):

Conch Republic

Conchs (pronounced 'conk' as in 'bonk,' not 'contsh' as in 'bunch') are people who were born and raised in Key West. It's a rare title to achieve. Even after seven years of living here, residents only rise to the rank of 'Freshwater Conch.' You will hear reference to, and see the flag of, the Conch Republic, and therein lies an interesting tale.

In 1982 the US border patrol and US customs erected a roadblock at Key Largo to catch drug smugglers and illegal aliens. As traffic jams and anger mounted, many tourists disappeared. They decided they'd rather take the Shark Valley Tram in the Everglades, thank you very much. To voice their outrage, a bunch of fiery Conchs decided to secede from the USA. After forming the Conch Republic, they made three declarations (in this order): Secede from the USA; declare war on the USA and surrender; and request $1 million in foreign aid. Every February, Conchs celebrate the anniversary of those heady days with nonstop parties.

Citizen (www.keysnews.com) A well-written, oft-amusing daily.

Key West Keynoter (www.keynoter.com) A good weekly.

Key West: The Newspaper A semiweekly and very opinionated take on local politics.

National Public Radio (NPR) Tune into 91.3 FM.

Solares Hill (www.solareshill.com) Slightly activist take on community interests.

Medical Services
The following provide Key West's most accessible medical services:

Lower Keys Medical Center (☎ 305-294-5531, 800-233-3119; 5900 College Rd, Stock Island, MM 5) Has a 24-hour emergency room.

South Med (☎ 305-295-3838; 3138 Northside Dr) Dr Scott Hall caters especially to the gay community, but also serves visitors.

Truman Medical Center (☎ 305-296-4399; 540 Truman Ave; ☼ 9am-4:45pm Mon-Fri, 9:30am-noon Sat) Come here for less-critical problems.

Post

Post office (400 Whitehead St; ☼ main lobby 8:30am-9pm Mon-Fri, 9:30am-noon Sat) Mailing postcards is a cinch, with a new self-service machine (6am-9pm) that stamps and sends stuff for you.

Tourist Information

Key West Chamber of Commerce (☎ 305-294-2587, 800-527-8539; www.keywestchamber.org; 402 Wall St, Mallory Sq; ☼ 8:30am-6:30pm Mon-Sat, until 6pm Sun) An excellent source of information, brochures, maps and advice.

Key West Welcome Center (☎ 305-296-4444, 800-284-4482; 3840 N Roosevelt Blvd; ☼ 8am-7:30pm Mon-Sat, 9am-6pm Sun) Sells discounted attraction tickets and helps with accommodations.

SIGHTS
Mallory Square
This is the belly of the beast. While Mallory Sq itself is just another waterfront park lined with shops by day, by early evening the area transforms into a wacky sunset soiree – an over-the-top display of craft hawkers, fire eaters, singers, unicyclists, mimes and other sundry characters, all competing for the tourist dollar. As folks mill about and gather round the most outrageous performers, the

event quickly turns into a mob scene. But, love it or hate it, it's an integral part of Key West culture, so be sure to check it out at least once. You can always soothe yourself by actually watching the glorious sunset.

Hemingway House

Key West's biggest darling, Ernest Hemingway, lived in this gorgeous Spanish-colonial house (☎ 305-294-1575; www.hemingwayhome.com; 907 Whitehead St; adult/child 6-12 yrs $10/6; ⊙ 9am-5pm) from 1931 to 1940. It was here that he wrote books including *The Short Happy Life of Francis Macomber* and *To Have and Have Not*. But he didn't just write here; he procrastinated by installing Key West's first saltwater swimming pool in a kind of romantic garden. The construction project set him back so much that he pressed his 'last penny' into the cement on the pool's deck. It's still there today. Hemingway retained ownership of the house until his death in 1961; the furry descendants of his famous six-toed cat still rule the house and grounds, posing for photographs under the lush trees. Tours, departing every 15 minutes and lasting about 30 minutes, include fun stories about his wives, the chandeliers and the overgrown gardens.

Key West Butterfly & Nature Conservancy

The newest attraction in town is also one of the best – especially if you have children in tow. The vast domed conservatory (☎ 305-296-2988; www.keywestbutterfly.com; 1316 Duval St; adult/child $10/7.50; ⊙ 9am-5pm) lets you stroll through a magic garden of flowering plants, colorful birds and up to 1800 fluttering butterflies, all live imports from around the globe.

Nancy Forrester's Secret Garden

Choose this gem of a garden (☎ 305-294-0015; www.nfsgarden.com; One Free School Ln; admission $6; ⊙ 10am-5pm) over more touted gardens, as it truly feels secret and far-removed from the more raucous goings-on in town. Nancy, who lives on the property, invites you to bring lunch (but no cell phones!) into her oasis of lush palms, orchids and chatty caged parrots and macaws.

Museum of Art & History at the Customs House

This lovely museum (☎ 305-295-6616; www.kwahs.com; 281 Front St; adult/child $7/5; ⊙ 9am-5pm) deserves a look-see if only for its gorgeous home – the grand Customs House, long abandoned until its impressive renovation in the '90s. But the exhibits are great, too, and include temporary shows on Cuba or local artists as well as a permanent display of massive portraits, 'Who Is Key West?', by painter Paul Collins.

Key West Cemetery

This peaceful and fascinating cemetery (btwn Frances St & Windsor Ln at Olivia St), smack-dab in one of the most lovely residential areas of town, has above-ground tombs mixed with stout palm trees. Enjoy strolling in the quietude or searching for some of the more infamous headstone epitaphs, such as 'I told you I was sick' and 'At least I know where he is sleeping tonight.' Or get chaperoned by George Born, of the Historic Florida Keys Foundation (☎ 305-292-6718), who gives guided tours for $10 per person at 9:30am on Tuesday and Thursday from the main gate at Margaret and Angela Sts.

Wreckers' Museums

Three small museums are dedicated to the study of shipwrecks and their treasures. The home of Confederate blockade-runner Francis B Watlington, the Wreckers' Museum/Oldest House (☎ 305-294-9502; 322 Duval St; adult/child $5/1; ⊙ 10am-4pm), is filled with period antiques and has enjoyable, volunteer-led tours. The Key West Shipwreck Historeum Museum (☎ 305-292-8990; www.shipwreckhistoreum.com; 1 Whitehead St; adult/child 4-12 yrs $9/4.50; ⊙ 9:45am-4:45pm) is a bit more lively, with a cast of actors taking you back to 1856, when the *Issac Allerton* was destroyed by a hurricane in the Saddlebunch Keys. Finally, the worthy Mel Fisher Maritime Heritage Museum (☎ 305-294-2633; 200 Greene St; adult/child $10/6; ⊙ 9:30am-5:30pm) presents an impressive amount of artifacts salvaged by Fisher in 1985. Various jewels, tools, coins and navigational pieces are displayed on the ground floor, along with a world map showing shipping routes taken by the Spanish ships he discovered.

Off-beat Key West, Part One: the Gift of Fright

The mass influx of out-of-towners who have migrated to Key West over the years has made many of the longtime local proprietors a bit skittish, and you'll often notice stores and services touting themselves as 'locally owned and operated' or as a 'local family business' – code for 'we are not interlopers like the other guys!' And the very quirky and highly competitive Ghost Tours, offered by three companies, are no exception; each operator warns its potential customers to watch out for 'imitators.' All are comparable, though, lasting about an hour and a half, visiting local haunted sites and featuring guides in elaborate ghost costumes. The options are **American Ghost Tour of Key West** (☎ 305-942-6049; from cnr Duvall St & Truman Ave; adult/child $18/free; ☺ 7pm & 9pm), featuring accomplished actors posing as old-fashioned characters and story tellers who accompany you around town; **Original Ghost Tours** (☎ 305-294-9255; from Crowne Plaza La Concha Hotel; adult/child $18/10; ☺ 8pm & 9pm), operating since 1996 and featuring stories about the souls who inhabit 10 locations including the Hard Rock Café, of all places; and **Ghosts & Legends of Key West** (☎ 305-294-1713; adult/child $15/8; ☺ 7pm & 9pm), which promises to take you 'off the beaten track' to places 'only a Conch could show you,' including the old city morgue and a small cemetery. Reservations are recommended for each tour.

Southernmost Point

You'll find a steady stream of visitors pausing for photo ops at this official marker at the corner of South and Whitehead Sts, a simple red-and-black-striped buoy that's not much to look at – and not even the most southern point in the continental USA (there's land further south, within a naval base).

Key West Lighthouse

This functioning lighthouse (☎ 305-294-0012; www.kwahs.com; 938 Whitehead St; adult/student over 7 yrs/senior $8/4/6; ☺ 9:30am-4:30pm), built in 1846 after a hurricane destroyed the original tower on this coast, has 88 iron steps that you can climb for an OK Key West view, as well as a small museum of artifacts in the keeper's house. It's just as enjoyable to gaze up at the tower from the leafy street below.

Little White House

President Harry S Truman's former vacation house (☎ 305-294-9911; 111 Front St; adult/child 5-12 yrs $11/6; ☺ 9am-4:30pm), with restful, lush and lovely grounds, is open only for guided tours (though the two rooms of the Harry S Truman Annex, with displays on political and presidential trivia, are free). You'll see Truman's piano, lots of original furnishings and a 15-minute video about Truman's life. The knowledgeable guides rattle out trivia and fun facts for everyone from children to serious history buffs.

Heritage House

Of all the many historic Key West homes open to visitors, this Caribbean-Colonial house (☎ 305-296-3573; www.heritagehousemuseum.org; 410 Caroline St; admission $5; ☺ 10am-4pm Mon-Sat) is among the most wonderful to walk through. That's because it's rarely crowded, has lovely and passionate guides, and contains all original furnishings and antiques, from a piano from the court of Marie Antoinette to a set of dining chairs from the 1600s. All have been collected and preserved by seven generations of a local family. The Robert Frost Cottage, where the poet stayed for 16 winters, is out back, along with a wonderful garden.

Bahama Village

This Key West area, bordered by Whitehead St to the east and Petronia (its main drag) to the north, is the Afro-Caribbean center of Old Town. It once had more of a Bahamian feel, but second-homeowners and tourists have crept on in to begin the process of gentrification, though not completely – yet. Roam the side streets and you'll discover some wonderful eateries, boutiques and galleries.

ACTIVITIES
Beaches

Key West is *not* about beach-going. In fact, for true sun 'n' surf, locals escape to Bahia Honda (p174) whenever possible. Still, the three city beaches on the southern side of the island are lovely and narrow, with calm and clear water. **South Beach** is at the end of Simonton St. **Higgs Beach**, at the end of Reynolds St and Casa Marina Ct, has barbecue grills, picnic tables and a long wooden pier that draws gay sunbathers. **Smathers Beach**, further east off S Roosevelt Blvd, is more popular with jet skiers, parasailers, teens and college students. The best local beach, though, is **Fort Zachary Taylor** (☎ 305-292-6713; for 1 person in a car $2.50, for 2 $5, plus for each additional person in a car 50¢, per pedestrian $1.50; ☺ 8am-sunset), at the southwestern end of the island. The fort area operated from 1845 to 1866 and defended against blockade-running Union ships during the Civil War. The lovely park area has deep water, picnic tables, shady palms and a perfect sunset view.

Diving & Snorkeling

Because of pollution and activity, there's no snorkeling to speak of on Key West beaches, so most dive companies take you west, to sites including Cottrell, Barracuda, Boca Grande, Woman, Sand, Rock and Marquesas Keys. At some dive sites nondivers can go along and snorkel. Dive companies set up at kiosks around Mallory Sq and other places in town, notably the corner of Truman and Duval Sts. Check these well-established places: **Subtropic Dive Center** (☎ 305-296-9914, 800-853-3483; 1605 N Roosevelt Blvd) and **Dive Key West** (☎ 305-296-3823, 800-426-0707; 3128 N Roosevelt Blvd).

Boating

You'll also find plenty of folks hawking sails and other boat rides. The **Western Union** (☎ 305-292-1766; Schooner Wharf, William St; adult/child $25/59) offers sunset and stargazing sails aboard its 130ft historic schooner, while the family-owned **Sail Key West** (☎ 305-744-8335; 601 Front St; cruise $39) can take you out on its 60ft yacht, *Floridays,* for a champagne-fueled sunset cruise. The **Discovery** (right) does three glass-bottom boat trips daily.

TOURS

Old Town Trolley Tours (☎ 305-296-6688; adult/child $22/11) runs 90-minute narrated tram tours starting at Mallory Sq and making a large, lazy circle around the whole city, with nine stops along the way. You can get on and off, going in the same direction, as often as you want for one rotation. Trolleys depart every 15 to 30 minutes from 9am to 4:30pm daily. The narration is hokey and touristy, but you'll get a good overview of

Key West, its history and gossipy dirt about local issues and people in the news.

Conch Tour Train (☎ 305-294-5161; adult/child $22/11) is run by the same company as the trolley tours, though this one seats you in linked train cars that are more open, and therefore breezier. The 90-minute tour keeps moving, with no options to get on and off at various stops. From 9am to 4:30pm.

Glass Bottom Boat Discovery Tours (☎ 305-293-0099; foot of Margaret St, Historic Seaport; adult/child 5 yrs & under/child 8-11 yrs $30/free/16) depart daily in summer at 11:30am, 2:30pm and sunset, and in winter at 10:30am, 1:30pm and sunset. In Key West style, the sunset cruise includes a complimentary glass of bubbly.

Orchid Lady Orchid Tours (☎ 877-747-2718; Key West) is a thoroughly unique Key West experience, with guided walk-throughs of three lush, orchid-filled gardens with Orchid Lady Bobbi Mazer. Tours are 9:30am, 11am and in the afternoon by appointment (per person $25).

Also worth noting is **Sharon Wells' Walking & Biking Guide to Historic Key West** (www.seekeywest.com), a booklet of self-guided walks available for free at inns and businesses around town, written by a 30-year local.

FESTIVALS & EVENTS

Every day is a happening day in Key West, but for an all-out crazy celebration, don't

Off-beat Key West, Part Two: Where the Roosters are the Stars

Even in a town that's built on quirkiness, the **Chicken Store** (☎ 305-294-0070; www.thechickenstore.com; 1227-1229 Duval St; admission free; ☺ 10am-5pm) still stands out. This wayward-bird haven serves as a shelter and celebration of the local gypsy chickens, which roam through local streets, sidewalks and backyards. Originally brought by Key West settlers, the fowl friends have bred into a mass population – and some, seen as nuisances by wealthy newcomers, wind up poisoned or otherwise harassed by humans. The Chicken Store rescues these and other needy birds, nursing sick ones back to health and providing shelter – in the form of a furnished house with a TV! – for all feathered folk who need a home. You can also buy hip T-shirts ('Hot chicks of Key West'), magnets, postcards and other gift items here.

miss the annual **Fantasy Fest**, held throughout the week leading up to Halloween in late October. It's when all the inns get competitive about decorating their properties, and when everyone gets decked out in the most outrageous costumes they can cobble together. The **Goombay Festival**, held during the same out-of-control week, is a Bahamian celebration of food, crafts and culture. The **Annual Key West Literary Seminar**, now in its 23rd year, draws top writers from around the country each January, while the **Hemingway Days** festival, held in late July, brings parties, a 5km run and an Ernest look-alike contest. **WomenFest**, in early September, attracts thousands of lesbians who just want to party, while November's **Parrot Heads in Paradise Convention** is for, you guessed it, Jimmy Buffet fans (rabid ones only, natch).

SLEEPING

Key West is a sleeper's paradise! For an unforgettable, true Keys experience, choose from one of the endless B&Bs sporting ceiling fans, shady backyard gardens and Bahamian style (visit the Key West Innkeepers at www.keywestinns.com for a lineup of the best). But if all-amenity hotels are more your scene, you won't be disappointed – nor will budget travelers accustomed to tent poles rather than four-poster beds. Budget in Key West means $75 and under, while a midrange stay hovers at around $100 to $150; top-end options rise from there. High season generally refers to the time between mid-December and April.

Chain hotels include **Best Western Hibiscus** (☎ 305-294-3763; 1313 Simonton St); **Days Inn** ☎ 305-294-3742; 3852 N Roosevelt Blvd), one of the cheapest places in town, and **Crowne Plaza La Concha** (☎ 305-296-2991; 430 Duval St), which has a top-floor bar and observatory open to nonguests (though you'll mainly gaze at unexciting rooftops).

Though all people, gay and straight, will be welcome just about anywhere, there are some exclusively gay inns, noted below.

Budget & Midrange

Abaco Inn (☎ 305-296-2212; http://abaco-inn. com; 415 Julia St; r low season $69, high season $99-109) This intimate gem, tucked away on a quiet and diverse residential block, has three simple, airy and stylish rooms, all with wood floors and ceiling fans. There's

no breakfast, but there is a small, shaded garden and a couple of warm and knowledgeable hosts. An excellent find.

Boyd's Key West Campground (☎ 305-294-1465, 6401 Maloney Ave; sites low season non-waterfront/waterfront $35/41, mid-Nov–mid-Apr $41/48, water & electricity $10) Just outside town on Stock Island (turn south at MM 5), Boyd's has upwards of 300 sites. There's a bus stop for downtown practically at their front door.

Caribbean House (☎ 305-296-1600; www .caribbeanhousekeywest.com; 226 Petronia St; r low season $55, high season $75) Located in Bahama Village, this yellow house with pink trim has 10 brightly colored guest rooms. It's nothing fancy, but it's a happy, cozy bargain – with free breakfast, no less.

Chelsea House/Red Rooster (☎ 305-296-2211; www.chelseahousekw.com; 707 Truman Ave; r low season $79-130, high season $125-200) This pair of Victorian mansions is full of festive, happy people, and rooms have TV, air-conditioning, fridge and bath. There's a clothing-optional sundeck, paperback library, free parking and brick paths that lead to pools and tropical gardens.

Frances St Bottle Inn (☎ 305-294-8530, 800-294-8530; www.bottleinn.com; 535 Frances St; r low-season $80-149, high season $139-189) Gay-friendly and with a welcoming staff, this small inn at a quiet end of town has eight homey rooms, very tidy and clean bathrooms, a two-story veranda and a small patio with a hot tub. Rental bikes are available.

Key West Youth Hostel & Seashell Motel (☎ 305-296-5719; www.keywesthostel.com; 718 South St; dm members/nonmembers $25/28, motel r low season $75, high season $110-150) At the cheapest place in town, rates include sheets and use of the communal kitchen. The hostel also sells cheap breakfasts and dinners. Alcohol is prohibited. The grounds are social and comfortable, and rooms are basic, but neat and clean. Pass on the motel rooms, though, as there are plenty of classier – and cheaper – options.

Mermaid & the Alligator (☎ 305-294-1894, 800-773-1894; www.kwmermaid.com, 729 Truman Ave; r low season $88-168, high season $118-228) This 1904 Victorian mansion exudes equal parts classic and modern aesthetic, with nine individually decorated rooms, tons of character, a luxuriously comfortable common lounge and a small pool surrounded by tropical plantings and a charming brick patio.

Pearl's Rainbow (☎ 305-292-1450, 800-749-6696; www.pearlsrainbow.com; 525 United St; r & ste low season $99-199, high season $109-299) Key West's sole women-only place is a lesbian hotspot, 38 low-key rooms ranging from small 3rd-floor cubbies to deluxe poolside suites with balconies. An intimate backyard pool bar is the perfect spot for alfresco happy hour.

Top End

Big Rubys Guesthouse (☎ 305-296-2323, 800-477-7829; www.bigrubys.com; 409 Appelrouth Ln; r low season $85-187, mid-Dec–Mar $145-265) This sleek gay-only place is an impeccable 17-roomer. Highlights include a clothing-optional lagoon pool area with elegant decking and tropical palms, luxuriously full breakfasts, fine linens and lots of privacy. Low-key luxe sums it up.

Curry House (☎ 305-294-6777; www.curry housekeywest.com; 806 Fleming St; r low season $85-140, high season $140-190) This yellow, palm-shrouded century-old mansion is among Key West's quaintest properties. The oldest exclusively gay male guest house is housed in a 100-year-old, Victorian-style, three-story mansion, and the nine airy rooms have four-poster beds, verandas and pool or garden views. Rates include a full hot breakfast and daily happy hour.

Cypress House (☎ 800-525-2488; www.cyp resshousekw.com; 601 Caroline St; r low season $109-$278, high season $140-$320) This stately, plantationlike getaway has wraparound porches, leafy grounds, a secluded swimming pool and spacious bedrooms with four-poster beds. It's lazy, lovely luxury in the heart of Old Town.

Gardens Hotel (☎ 305-294-2661, 800-526-2664; www.gardenshotel.com; 526 Angela St; r & ste low season $155-425, high season $235-575) This walled, sprawling enclave has got it all. Recently renovated and under new management, the walled 17-room mansion is an ideal combination of new and old. It's nestled within an acre of tropical gardens and has a small pool and chichi bedrooms and suites sporting flat-screen TVs.

Marquesa Hotel (☎ 305-292-1919; www.mar quesa.com; 600 Fleming St; r low season $205-370, high season $285-430) Another high-end complex, the Marquesa blends classic Key West architecture with modern touches, and big-hotel amenities with a small-inn, intimate vibe. Rooms range from

---

Best Bets For Kids

Though your first images of Key West may include 7ft-tall drag queens or umbrella-topped cocktails, there are plenty of appropriate activities for your little ones as well. The best child attractions include the **Key West Aquarium** (☎ 305-296-2051; www .keywestaquarium.com; 1 Whitehead St at Mallory Sq; adult/child $9/4.50; ☼ 10am-6pm), which has touch-me tanks just for children, and the new **Key West Butterfly & Nature Conservancy** (p181). By day, grab a pail and shovel and head to one of the local beaches (p182) or take them for a festive ride on the **Conch Tour Train** (p183); by night, bring brave little ones on one of the highly theatrical ghost tours (p182). They'll also love the squawking chickens at the **Chicken Store** (p183) or the talking parrots at **Nancy Forrester's Secret Garden** (p181). When it's bedtime, skip the historic B&Bs and try one of the more family-friendly hotels, such as the **Wyndham Casa Marina Resort & Beach House** (below), which offers a full lineup of daily activities for kids.

---

cozy nests to massive suites, all with luxe linens and ceiling fans. A small, excellent restaurant is nestled on the property, too.

Merlinn Inn (☎ 305-296-3336, 800-642-4753; www.merlinnkeywest.com; 811 Simonton St; low season $89-225, high season $135-300) Set in a secluded garden with a pool and elevated wooden walkways, this 20-room B&B boasts airy, light and very tidy guest rooms. Everything is made from bamboo, rattan and wood; many rooms have high ceilings or exposed rafters.

Pier House Resort & Caribbean Spa (☎ 800-327-8340; www.pierhouse.com; 1 Duval St; r & ste low season $200-1400, high $290-1800) This all-inclusive waterfront resort was the first mammoth place in town. It still draws crowds of folks who enjoy getting everything they need in one complex, from private balconies and rooms with water views to a private beach and full-service spa.

Wyndham Casa Marina Resort & Beach House (☎ 305-296-3535, 800-949-3426; www.wynd ham.com; 1500 Reynolds St; r low season $169-359, late Dec-Mar $169-409, ste from $450) Next to Higgs Beach, this first-rate 311-room behemoth was built in the 1920s by railroad magnate Henry Flager. Look for three oceanside pools, every recreational pursuit imaginable, a kids' program, daily activities and plenty of dining and entertainment choices. Guest rooms and suites have private balconies or terraces.

The Florida Keys – Key West

EATING

The Key West dining scene has become more sophisticated in recent years, adding a delightful range of fusion and ethnic eateries to its already top-notch lineup of island seafood houses. The most ubiquitous local delicacies are Conch fritters – made from Conch obtained elsewhere these days, as the local batch has long been mined – and key lime pie (p171).

Bahama Mama's (☎ 305-294-3355; 324 Petronia St; mains $13-18; ☒ 10am-5pm) Chomp on the some of the lightest, tastiest Conch fritters around, along with melt-in-your-mouth curried Conch, coconut shrimp, jerk chicken and other Caribbean treats. Pair any and all with a chilled Red Stripe beer at the backyard bar or patio and you'll be perfectly satisfied.

Banana Café (☎ 305-294-7227; 1211 Duval St; mains $6-12; ☒ 8am-5pm Wed-Mon) A lovely, airy café at the quiet end of Duval, this is the perfect place for a fresh breakfast crepe and strong coffee served on a shady dining porch by friendly French servers.

Camille's (☎ 305-296-4811; 1202 Simonton St; breakfast $3-7, lunch $6-12, dinner $14-25; ☒ 8am-3pm, 4-10:30pm) An island fave since forever, Camille's is packed all day – especially at breakfast time – because of good, friendly service and creative dishes.

Café (☎ 305-296-5515; 509 Southard St; mains $7-13; ☒ 11am-10pm Mon-Sat) Vegetarians, rejoice! This new eatery is the only place in Key West that caters to herbivores. By day, it's a cute, sunny, earthy-crunchy luncheonette; by night, with flickering votive candles and a classy main dish (grilled, blackened tofu and polenta cakes), it's a sultry-but-healthy dining destination.

Café Sole (☎ 305-294-0230; 1029 Southard St; mains $16-29; ☒ 6-10pm) Eating at this eclectic house on a quiet residential corner is a special experience, from the funky, homey feel to the excellent French-flavored food, such as bouillabaisse and roasted duck. There's also a completely separate, and impressive, vegetarian menu.

El Siboney (☎ 305-296-4184; 900 Catherine St; dishes $5-13; ☒ 11am-9:30pm Mon-Sat) There are plenty of authentic Cuban eateries in Key West, but El Siboney is an institution. The ambience is lacking, but the service and the food are pure goodness.

Nine One Five (☎ 305-296-0669; 915 Duval St; tapas $6-12; ☒ 6pm-midnight) An excellent place right on Duval? Yes, it's true!

Settle into this upscale Victorian house for serious wines and perfect small plates, and watch the crazy crowds stagger by.

Salsa Loca (☎ 305-292-1865; 918 Duval St; mains $8-16; ☒ 11am-10pm Tue-Thu, 11am-11pm Fri-Sat, noon-10pm Sun). Locals and visitors are going *loco* for this new Mexican spot – which boasts frothy margaritas and delicious dishes from *chilaquiles* (tortilla chips in green sauce with scrambled eggs) to veggie *tortas* (Mexican-style sandwich in a roll).

Seven Fish (☎ 305-296-2777; 632 Olivia St; mains $14-21) This simple yet elegant tucked-away storefront is the perfect place for a romantic feast of homemade gnocchi or sublime banana chicken.

Sugar Apple Juice Bar & Veggie Deli (☎ 305-292-0043; 917 Simonton St; sandwiches $3-7; ☒ 11am-4pm Mon-Sat) The tiny juice and sandwich haven, attached to the town's only health-food store, is a great place to order a Thai tofu wrap, Tofurkey sub or fresh carrot-apple juice for a healthy beach picnic.

DRINKING

Drinking is a Key West institution with a long and illustrious history of lushes, from professional rumrunners to Hemingway. This tradition is immortalized in Jimmy Buffet's song 'Margaritaville.' Make your memories (or lack thereof) at one of the following. (For gay venues, see opposite.)

Captain Tony's Saloon (☎ 305-294-1838; 428 Greene St) This old-fashioned and very popular saloon features live music almost daily and nightly.

Green Parrot (☎ 305-294-6133; 601 Whitehead St) The perfect antidote to north-Duval tourist dives, this loud-music, strong-drink locals' bar has been pickling its patron's livers with booze since 1890. It's a fun place to while away an hour – or five.

PT's Late Night (☎ 305-296-4245; 920 Caroline St) Late-night means 3am at this sports bar, where the biggest draw is the fact that the kitchen serves until the end. The perfect spot to find nachos and burgers when you need help soaking up the sauce.

Sloppy Joe's Bar (☎ 305-294-5717; 201 Duval St) Hemingway, who used to tie one on here, would roll in his grave if he could see the dart-throwing, shot-slamming fratboy types who jam in here these days. But go see for yourself – you won't be able to resist – and then just walk on by.

Gay & Lesbian Key West

Though less true than in the past, visiting Key West is still a rite of passage for many LGBT (lesbian, gay, bisexual and transgender) Americans, as gays and lesbians have always had a major impact on the local culture. The best way to get a handle on the town's gay history is to hop aboard the **Gay & Lesbian Trolley Tour of Key West** (☎ 305-294-4603; $20), departing from the corner of South and Simonton Sts at 11am on Saturdays and providing commentary on local gay lore and businesses. It's organized by the **Key West Business Guild**, which represents many gay-owned businesses; the guild is housed at the **Gay & Lesbian Community Center** (☎ 305-292-3223; www.glcckeywest. org; 513 Truman Ave) in a lovely new location, where you can even access the Internet – for free! – on one of its few computers, plus pick up loads of information about local gay life. For details on gay parties and events, be sure to grab a copy of the free weekly *Celebrate* (www.celebratekeywest.com).

Gay nightlife, in many cases, blends into mainstream nightlife, with everybody kind of going everywhere these days. But the backbone of the gay bar scene can be found in a pair of cruisy-type watering holes that sit across the street from one another: **Bourbon St Pub** (724 Duval St) and **801 Bourbon Bar** (801 Duval St). For a peppier scene that includes dancing and occasional drag shows, men and women should head to **Aqua** (☎ 305-294-0555; 711 Duval St) or to **Atlantic Shores Resort** (☎ 305-296-2491; 510 South St) for two tea dances weekly, on Sunday and Wednesday. Women will enjoy the backyard pool bar at the women's inn **Pearl's Rainbow** (☎ 305-292-1450; 525 United St).

ENTERTAINMENT

Key West Players (☎ 305-294-5105; Waterfront Playhouse, Mallory Sq) Catch high-quality musicals and dramas from this 66-year-old theater troupe, which has a November through April season.

Key West Symphony Orchestra (☎ 305-292-1774; Tennessee Williams Theatre) Now in its eighth season, Key West's orchestra performs classics from Debussy, Beethoven and Mendelssohn from December through April. Sebrina Maria Alfonso conducts.

La Te Da (☎ 305-296-6706; 1125 Duval St) While the outside bar is where locals gather for mellow chats over beer, you can catch high-quality drag acts – big names come here from around the country – upstairs at the fabulous Crystal Room on weekends. More low-key cabaret acts grace the downstairs lounge.

Virgilio's (☎ 305-296-1075; 524 Duval St, entrance on Applerouth Ln) This is a hot spot for stylish locals and visitors alike. The dark and cozy lounge, in the back of the Italian La Trattoria restaurant, used to be a very cruisy men's bar; now it welcomes all with equal vigor, offering up a slew of specialty martinis accompanied by excellent live salsa or jazz bands nightly.

SHOPPING

Aside from the endless stream of tchotchke (knickknack) shops hawking crappy T-shirts, there are plenty of boutiques worth a spree.

Bésame Mucho (☎ 305-294-1928; 315 Petronia St) This place is stocked with high-end beauty products, eclectic jewelry, clothing and housewares.

Commotion (☎ 305-292-3364; 800 Caroline St) A great place for women's clothing of the linen-dress variety.

Peppers of Key West (☎ 305-295-9333; 602 Greene St) For a downright shopping party, bring your favorite six-pack with you right into this store and settle in at the tasting bar, where the entertaining owners use double entendres to hawk mouth-burning hot sauces like their own Right Wing Sauce (Use Liberally).

Whitehead Street Pottery (☎ 305-294-5067; 322 Julia St) and the **Haitian Art Co** (☎ 305-296-8932; 600 Frances St) are excellent art-gallery shops.

GETTING THERE & AROUND

Key West International Airport (EYW) is off S Roosevelt Blvd on the west side of the island. Expect to spend $150 to $180 for a round-trip flight between Miami and Key West. With a little luck and good timing, you can get a direct, round-trip flight between New York City and Key West for as low as $300. Flights from Los Angeles ($350 in summer, $575 in winter) and San Francisco ($400 year-round) usually have to stop in Tampa, Orlando or Miami first. **American Airlines** (☎ 800-433-7300) and **US Airways** (☎ 800-428-4322) all have several flights a day. **Cape Air** (☎ 305-352-0714, 800-352-0714; www.flycapeair.com) flies between Key West and Naples for round-trip fares ranging from $105 to $250. From the Key West airport, a quick and easy taxi ride into Old Town will cost about $10.

Detour: Dry Tortugas National Park

The Dry Tortugas (tor-too-guzz), a tiny archipelago of seven islands about 69 miles southwest of Key West, was first 'developed' 300 years after its discovery by Juan Ponce de León. He named Las Tortugas – 'The Turtles' – for the hawksbill, green, leatherback and loggerhead sea turtles that roam the islands. Sailors later changed it to Dry Tortugas since there was no freshwater here. Today it's a national park under the control of the **Everglades National Park office** (☎ 305-242-7700; www.nps.gov/drto). You can only reach it by boat or plane.

Since the island was surrounded by rocky shoals, the first item of business was to build a lighthouse at Garden Key. When the USA saw a need to protect and control the traffic flowing into the Gulf of Mexico, they began constructing Fort Jefferson in 1846. A federal garrison during the Civil War, Fort Jefferson was also a prison for Union deserters and for at least four people, among them Dr Samuel Mudd, arrested for complicity in the assassination of Abraham Lincoln. In 1867 a yellow fever outbreak killed 38 people, and after a hurricane in 1873, the fort was abandoned. It reopened in 1886 as a quarantine station for smallpox and cholera victims. It was declared a national monument in 1935 by President Franklin D Roosevelt, then, in 1992, President George Bush Sr upped its status to a national park.

The park is open for day trips and overnight camping, which provides a rare perspective: so close to the hubbub of Key West and yet so blissfully removed and peaceful. Garden Key has 13 campsites ($3 per person, per night) given out on a first-come, first-served basis. Reserve early by calling the Everglades National Park office. There are toilets, but no freshwater showers or drinking water; bring everything you'll need. The sparkling waters offer excellent snorkeling and diving opportunities. A visitor center is located within the fascinating Fort Jefferson.

As for food, most of the time you'll find Cuban-American fishing boats trolling the waters. They'll happily trade for lobster, crab and shrimp; you'll have the most leverage trading beverages. Just paddle up to them and start bargaining for your supper. In March and April, there is stupendous bird-watching, including aerial fighting. Star-gazing is mind-blowing any time of the year.

Getting There

If you have your own boat, the Dry Tortugas are covered under National Ocean Survey chart No 11438. Otherwise, the experienced and knowledgeable crew of the **Yankee Freedom II** (☎ 305-294-7009, 800-634-0939; www.yankeefleet.com; Key West Seaport) operates a fast ferry between Garden Key and the Key West Seaport (at the northern end of Margaret St). Round-trip fares cost adult/child $129/89. For an overnight drop-off (including gear), the cost is adult/child $159/119. Reservations are recommended. Continental breakfast, a picnic lunch, snorkeling gear and a 45-minute tour of the fort are all included.

Seaplanes of Key West (☎ 305-294-0709; www.seaplanesofkeywest.com) can take up to 10 passengers (flight time 40 minutes each way). A four-hour trip costs adult/child under 12 yrs $179/129, an eight-hour trip $305/225. They'll also fly you out to camp for $329/235 per person, including snorkeling equipment; reserve at least a week in advance.

For bus travel, **Greyhound** (☎ 305-296-9072; www.greyhound.com; 3535 S Roosevelt Blvd) has four buses daily between Key West and Downtown Miami. Buses leave Key West for the four-hour, 25-minute journey at 6am, 8:45am, 11:30am and 5:45pm ($35 one-way).

To drive the 160 miles (3½ hours) from Miami, simply follow US Hwy 1 to its end. Beware of serious traffic in high season.

Once you're in Key West, the best way to get around is by bicycle (rentals are about $10 a day), though other options include the **City Transit System** (☎ 305-292-8160; tickets 75¢), with color-coded buses running about every 15 minutes; the convenient **Bone Island Shuttle** (☎ 305-293-8710; 3-day pass $6, 5-day pass $10, kids free), which makes frequent loops around both New and Old Town; moped rentals (for about $20 a day); or the ridiculous electric tourist cars, or 'Conch cruisers,' which travel at 35mph and rent for about $30 an hour or $120 for an eight-hour day. As far as regular rental cars go, don't even bother in Key West.

The Everglades

The Everglades

South Florida is a truly weird and fascinating place – and there's nothing like a brush with the Everglades to remind you of that. Just south of Miami's glitz and glamour and north of the Keys' soft sand and clear seas is this incredibly unique ecosystem, filled with alligators, brackish swamps and strangely backwater towns.

The largest subtropical wilderness in the continental USA – containing the second-largest US national park (after Yellowstone) – the Everglades region is one of the most well-known and poorly understood areas of the USA. Visitors to South Florida hear about airboat tours, but many don't have time to find out more. Believe us when we say it's worth it to go further – whether you visit the **Ernest Coe Visitor Center** (p194) for an afternoon, take the **Shark Valley Tram Tour** (p194) or embrace canoeing and camping in the **10,000 Islands** (p200). Though the threat to the Everglades is very real (see History, below), it is a spectacular place to get into the real nature of South Florida. From the brackish waters of the mangrove and cypress swamps, hardwood hammocks, sawgrass flats, and Dade County pinelands and marshes, to creatures like crocodiles, alligators, bottle-nosed dolphins, manatees, snowy egrets, bald eagles and ospreys, there is simply no other place like the Everglades.

History

The Calusa Indians called the area Pa-hay-okee (grassy water). The late and much beloved conservationist Marjory Stoneman Douglas (1890–1998) called it the River of Grass. In her book *The Everglades: River of Grass,* she says surveyor Gerard de Brahm renamed the region the River Glades, which became Ever Glades on later English maps.

Top Five Experiences

Best swampy sunset
At the end of the Pa-hay-okee Overlook (p194), where you'll see vast grasslands aflame with pink and orange.

Most undisturbed trail
The Wilderness Waterway (p200), where you can kayak in utter peace through the 10,000 Islands.

Most romantic perspective
The Everglades photography of Clyde Butcher, on display at the sublime Big Cypress Gallery (p198).

Biggest relief from fried roadside grub
JT's Island Grill & Gallery (p201) on Chokoloskee, which serves up wholesome, yummy dishes in a funky, homey setting.

Most surprising night out
Homestead's Main St Café (p197), where locals gather for live folk music, beers and great food.

The Everglades are part of what's called a sheet-flow ecosystem, beginning at the Kissimmee River and emptying into Lake Okeechobee at the south center of the state. Before humankind's meddling, Okeechobee overflowed and sent sheets of water through the Everglades and finally into the Gulf of Mexico. The resulting ecosystem was home to thousands of species of flora and wildlife. Wading birds, amphibians, reptiles and mammals flourished.

Enter business, stage right. Sugar growers, attracted by mucky waters, swarmed in and pressured the government to make land available to them. In 1905, Florida governor Napoleon Bonaparte Broward personally dug the first shovelful of dirt for what was to become one of the largest and most destructive diversions of water in the world. The Caloosahatchee River was diverted and connected to Lake Okeechobee. Hundreds of canals were then dug, slicing through the Everglades to the coastline to 'reclaim' the land. The flow of lake water was then restricted by a series of dikes. Farmland began to sprout up in areas previously uninhabited by humans.

Unfortunately, farming diverted the freshwater desperately needed by nature in the Everglades, and it produced fertilizer-rich wastewater, which promotes foliage growth, which in turn clogs waterways and further complicates matters. Now, as chemicals spill into the Glades and local waters, the Florida Aquifer (the source of Florida's freshwater supply) is in great danger of being contaminated. It's also in danger of drying up, as evaporation and runoff (caused by the reflow of water) consume a large portion of the 40in to 56in of yearly rainfall. Autopsies of local animals, including Florida panthers, have shown that mercury levels are extremely high. Pollution from industry and farming is now killing foliage, and because of the freshwater diversion, saltwater from the Gulf of Mexico is flowing deeper into the park than ever before. The numbers of wading birds nesting in colonies in this region have declined 93% since the 1930s; the Florida Bay nurseries and shellfish industry have also been damaged. And currently, there are 15 endangered species (including the Florida panther and the green turtle) and eight threatened species (including the Southern bald eagle and American alligator) of animals within the park.

RESTORATION OF THE EVERGLADES

Efforts to save the Everglades began as early as the late 1920s, but they were sidelined by the Great Depression. In 1926 and 1928, two major hurricanes caused Lake Okeechobee to bust its banks; the resulting floods killed hundreds. So the Army Corps of Engineers came in and did a *really* good job of damming the lake. They constructed the Hoover Dike. Through the efforts of conservationists and prominent citizens like Douglas, the Everglades was declared a national park in 1947. But the threat is far from over.

Everglades restoration is one of the hottest potatoes in the US environmental community. In the mid-1990s, Congress voted to cut subsidies to Florida sugar growers by a penny a pound, and to use the savings to buy 126,000 acres of land to restore a natural flow of water through South Florida. The basic idea was to increase the quantity of freshwater within the Everglades, remove upstream phosphorus and maintain a diverse habitat to meet the needs of wildlife. An even bigger plan – one that'll cost $8.4 billion, to be exact – was approved by Congress in 2000. It calls for restoring the remaining Everglades lands to conditions prior to developmental impacts while maintaining flood protection, providing freshwater needs for the growing South Florida populace and protecting specifically earmarked regions against urban sprawl. It sounds great, but it's easier said than done. And so far, due to highly divisive politics,

the plan has basically been abused and ignored by those in power.

Thousands of scientists, environmentalists and business groups are still arguing about the best ways to meet the goals of restoration, and as of 2004, the yelling got much louder. The Everglades Coalition, with 35 subgroups including Florida Audubon and the Everglades Foundation, is the primary environmental group. But it lost a major member – the Sierra Club – in early 2004, when that organization claimed the federal government was turning the restoration effort into a huge water subsidy for farmers and developers. Other environmental groups disagreed at first, pointing to increased monetary support from Florida's Governor, Jeb Bush. But it became clear that Sierra was right when the federal government began efforts to bring the Scripps Biomedical Institute – a development that would span the area of 13 shopping malls – to land set aside for preservation. As a result, the Everglades Coalition and several other conservation groups including 1000 Friends of Florida and the Florida Wildlife Federation have filed suit against the state. Governor Bush has called the group 'legal terrorists'; the environmentalists say it was their last resort after many unsuccessful discussions. The outcome is anyone's guess but, until then, it'll be a long road of nail-biting litigation.

Orientation

The Everglades region refers to the 80 most southern miles of Florida; it's bound by the Atlantic Ocean to the east and the Gulf of Mexico to the west. The only road taking you south into the heart of the Everglades National Park (which comprises just the tip of the entire region) is Rte 9336. Traveling north to south along the park's eastern edge is Rte 997; the Tamiami Trail (US Hwy 41) goes east–west, parallel to the more northern (and less interesting) Alligator Alley (I-75).

Information

Everglades Area Chamber of Commerce (☎ 941-695-3941; cnr US Hwy 41 & Hwy 29, Everglades City; ☺ 9am-5pm) Provides general information about businesses and attractions in the region.

Everglades National Park (☎ 305-242-7700; www .nps.gov/ever; 40,001 State Rd 9336, Homestead) Provides details about park trails, entrances and conditions.

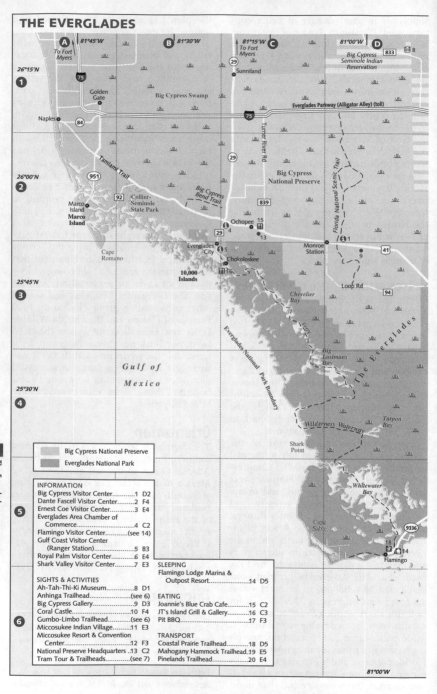

THE EVERGLADES

INFORMATION
Big Cypress Visitor Center............1 D2
Dante Fascell Visitor Center........2 F4
Ernest Coe Visitor Center...........3 E4
Everglades Area Chamber of
   Commerce................................4 C2
Flamingo Visitor Center............(see 14)
Gulf Coast Visitor Center
   (Ranger Station).....................5 B3
Royal Palm Visitor Center...........6 E4
Shark Valley Visitor Center.........7 E3

SIGHTS & ACTIVITIES
Ah-Tah-Thi-Ki Museum..............8 D1
Anhinga Trailhead....................(see 6)
Big Cypress Gallery....................9 D3
Coral Castle............................10 F4
Gumbo-Limbo Trailhead..........(see 6)
Miccosukee Indian Village.........11 E3
Miccosukee Resort & Convention
   Center..................................12 F3
National Preserve Headquarters ..13 C2
Tram Tour & Trailheads.........(see 7)

SLEEPING
Flamingo Lodge Marina &
   Outpost Resort.....................14 D5

EATING
Joannie's Blue Crab Cafe...........15 C2
JT's Island Grill & Gallery..........16 C3
Pit BBQ..................................17 F3

TRANSPORT
Coastal Prairie Trailhead...........18 D5
Mahogany Hammock Trailhead.19 E5
Pinelands Trailhead...................20 E4

The Everglades

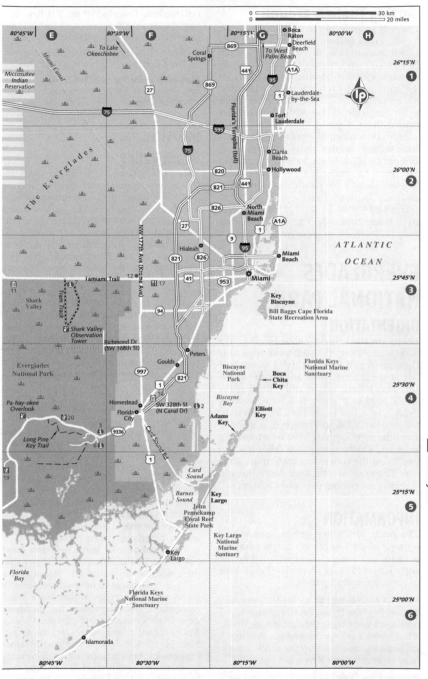

Getting There & Around

The only sensible way to explore the area is by car. From Miami, take Florida's Turnpike Extension (toll) or US Hwy 1 to reach Florida City and Homestead; it's about 45 minutes with light traffic. From there to the entrance of Everglades National Park, it's another 15 minutes. And from there to Flamingo along Hwy 9336, add another hour without stopping.

From Downtown Miami (assuming moderate traffic), it takes about 45 minutes to an hour to reach Shark Valley, or just over two hours to reach the Gulf Coast Visitor Center. There's no public transportation along the Tamiami Trail.

Greyhound (☎ 800-231-2222) bus services go to Homestead only. There are five buses daily ($11 each way) there from Miami.

EVERGLADES NATIONAL PARK

ORIENTATION

There are three main entrances into the park – one along the southeast edge near Homestead and Florida City (Ernest Coe), one at the central-north side on the Tamiami Trail (Shark Valley) and a third at the lovely northwest shore (Gulf Coast), past Everglades City. From the Coe entrance, follow Hwy 9336 to Flamingo, a visitors' area offering everything from boat tours to a lodge and a restaurant. Shark Valley is where you'll find the convenient tram tour, while Gulf Coast region is the least developed and is geared toward campers and kayakers.

INFORMATION

The main park entry points have visitor centers, where you can get maps, camping permits and ranger information. Pay the entrance fee ($10 for seven days) only once to gain access at all points.

Ernest Coe Visitor Center (☎ 305-242-7700; www.nps .gov/ever; Hwy 9336; ⊙ 8am-5pm) The principal visitor center is packed with excellent information in the form of both pamphlets and museumlike exhibits. There are also rangers who can answer any of your questions, plus a bookstore. The gate is open 24 hours daily.

Flamingo Visitor Center (☎ 941-695-3094; ⊙ 7:30am-5pm) On the park's southern coast.

Gulf Coast Visitor Center (☎ 941-695-3311; Hwy 29, Everglades City; ⊙ 8:30am-5pm) This northwesternmost ranger station provides access to the 10,000 Islands area.

Royal Palm Visitor Center (☎ 305-242-7700; Hwy 9336; ⊙ 8am-4:15pm) Adjacent to Ernest Coe Visitor Centre.

Shark Valley Visitor Center (☎ 305-221-8776; Tamiami Trail; ⊙ 9am-5pm) Sells tickets for the tram tour and has a good little bookstore.

SIGHTS
Shark Valley

This park entrance (⊙ 8:30am-5pm) offers a very popular and painless way to immerse yourself in the Everglades prairie. You can bike (per hour $5), walk or take a two-hour tram tour (☎ 305-221-8455; adult/child under 12 yrs/senior $13.25/8/12.25) along the 15-mile asphalt trail. If you only have time for one Everglades activity, this should be it, as the guides are informative and witty (especially ranger John McKinney, who likes to use an alligator hand puppet to liven the crowd), and the area is teeming with flora and fauna – including gators who sun themselves on the road. Halfway along the trail you'll come to the 50ft-high Shark Valley Observation Tower, an ugly concrete structure that happens to offer a dramatically beautiful view of the park.

Flamingo

Flamingo is the low-key resort complex (and small residential community of park employees) that lies 38 miles past the Ernest Coe Visitor Center (left). Along the road that leads here, Rte 9336, you'll find plenty of trails for hiking and canoeing, as well as a couple of lovely (and easy) boardwalk trails: Pa-hay-okee Overlook, a quarter-mile walk that ends with a startling view of the sunset, and Mahogany Hammock, a half-mile walk leading into lush and overgrown vegetation.

The Flamingo Lodge Marina & Outpost Resort (☎ 941-695-3101, 800-600-3813; www.fla mingolodge.com) supplies all the activities and gear you might desire in these parts. A rental and tour center (which has a small souvenir shop selling those vital mosquito nets) rents kayaks for $11 per hour plus a $100 deposit, as well as bicycles for $3 per hour plus a $50 deposit. It has naturalist-lead boat tours through the back country for two hours (adult/child $18/10) and sailboat cruises ($18/9; December to May only) on a 50ft schooner.

Gulf Coast

The northwest park entrance, near Everglades City, has a small waterfront complex offering a picnic area with gorgeous vistas, plus daily boat tours ($20), which take you into the mangrove estuary of the Gulf of Mexico, motoring around the 10,000 Islands, where you'll see dolphins, roseate spoonbills, alligators, eagles and the occasional manatee. The main activity out of the Gulf Coast center, though, is kayaking (p200).

ACTIVITIES
Hiking

The **Royal Palm Visitor Center** (opposite) is the starting point for two good trails: the three-quarter-mile **Gumbo-Limbo Trail**, with gumbo-limbo and royal palm trees, orchids and lush vegetation; and the **Anhinga Trail**, named for the odd anhinga birds (also called the snake bird, for the way it swims with its long neck and head above water). You'll probably run into alligators, turtles, waterfowl, lizards and snakes on this half-mile hike. Other good options include the **Pinelands**, a half-mile trail through Dade County pine forest that features exposed limestone bedrock, and the 7.5-mile (one-way) **Coastal Prairie Trail**, which follows an old road once used by cotton pickers; it's only partially shaded by buttonwood trees, so bring plenty of sunscreen. Finally, **Long Pine Key** is the starting point of a 15-mile series of walking trails, where you may see many species indigenous to the Everglades, including, if you're very quiet and patient, Florida panthers. In Shark Valley, the easy **Otter Cave** walk, which enters a tropical hardwood hammock, is a one-mile round-trip walk from the visitor center.

Canoeing & Kayaking

From Flamingo, hit the visitor center for a map of local canoe trails, such as the **Nine Mile Pond Trail**, a 5.5-mile loop that leads you into Florida Bay. You can rent canoes and kayaks (per hour $12, per day $50) at the Flamingo Marina, and be transported to various trailheads for an additional fee (☎ 305-695-3101 ext 322 for reservations). For extensive kayak trips and kayak camping, make a beeline to the **Gulf Coast Visitor Center** (opposite), which also rents canoes for

Panthers, Gators & Crocs, Oh My!

Panthers, gators and crocs lurk in the Everglades, but the biggest threats are actually insects and strong sun.

Gators

While alligators are common in the park, they are not very common in the 10,000 Islands area, as they tend to avoid saltwater. If you do see an alligator, it probably won't bother you, unless you do something overtly threatening or angle your boat between it and its young. If you hear an alligator making a loud hissing sound, you should get the hell out of Dodge. That hissing sound is a call to other alligators when a young gator is in danger. Finally, never, ever, ever feed an alligator – it's stupid and illegal.

Crocs

Crocodiles are less common in the park, as they prefer coastal and saltwater habitats. They are more aggressive than alligators, however, so the same rules apply. With perhaps only a few hundred remaining in the USA, they are also an endangered species.

Weather

Thunderstorms and lightning are more common in summer than winter. But in summer the insects are so bad you won't want to be outside anyway. In emergency weather, rangers will search for registered campers, but under ordinary conditions, they won't unless they receive information that someone's missing. If camping, have a friend or family member ready to contact rangers if you do not report back by a certain day.

Insects

You can't overestimate the problem of mosquito and no-see-ums (tiny biting flies) in the Everglades. While in most national parks around the country there are warning signs showing how high the forest-fire risk is, here there are charts showing the mosquito level (☎ 305-242-7700 for a report). In summer and fall, the sign almost always says 'extremely high.' You'll be set upon the second you open your car door. The only protections are 100% DEET or, even better, a pricey net suit. Trust us: go in winter.

Snakes

There are four types of poisonous snake in the Everglades: diamondback rattlesnake (*Crotalus adamanteus*); pigmy rattlesnake (*Sistrurus miliarius*); cottonmouth or water moccasin (*Agkistrodon piscivorus conanti*), which swim along the surface of water; and the coral snake (*Micrurus fulvius*). Wear long, thick socks and lace-up boots – and keep the hell away from them.

three-, five- or eight-hour daytrips around the 10,000 Islands (for more on kayaking in this region, see boxed text, p200).

SLEEPING & EATING

Flamingo Lodge Marina & Outpost Resort (☎ 941-695-3101, 800-600-3813; www.flamingo lodge.com; Hwy 9336; r off-season/mid-Dec–Mar $65/98, ste & cottages $89-140) All 102 perfunctory units have two double beds, TV and air con. It's better than camping in a rainstorm or with the mosquitoes, but don't expect much more than that. Suite and cottage rates are for four people (so they're a bargain, really) and cottages have full kitchens.

National Park Service (NPS; ☎ 800-365-2267; www.nps.gov/ever/visit/backcoun.htm; sites off-season free, Nov-Apr $14) The campgrounds here are run by the NPS. None of these primitive, barely shaded sites have hookups. Depending on the time of year, cold-water showers are either bracing or a welcome relief (though Flamingo sites offer hot showers for $3 extra).

Long Pine Key (☎ 800-365-2267; free off-season, Nov-Apr $14) In addition to camping in Flamingo and Big Cypress (p198), car campers shouldn't overlook this place, just west of the Royal Palm Visitor Center.

Flamingo Restaurant (☎ 239-695-3101 ext 275; ☽ 7-10:30am, 11:30am-2:30pm, 5:30-9pm Oct-May) This offers everything from eggs and bacon for breakfast to burgers or shrimp for dinner. And if you've caught your own supper, the eatery offers 'fish service,' and will cook up your already cleaned and filleted catch. For after-dinner drinks, hit the Anglers Bar at the front of the restaurant.

FLORIDA CITY & HOMESTEAD

Hurricane Andrew ripped through Homestead in 1992 at speeds of 200mph (320km/h), leveling everything in its path. Even though it's been rebuilt, Homestead's economy has never completely recovered, as evidenced by the feeling of working-class heartache and after-dark edginess that grips the place. Stretches of the areas between Florida City and Homestead host highway prostitutes after nightfall, especially around the roadside go-go bars; don't be surprised

if you witness a disturbing scene that resembles the TV show *Cops*. If you stick to Krome Ave, though – the main strip favored by locals – you'll find a surprisingly good selection of Mexican restaurants, local pubs and welcoming motels. The surrounding countryside, serving as the 'gateway to the Everglades,' supports lots of excellent farms, nurseries and produce stands.

ORIENTATION

Krome Ave (Hwy 997) and Rte 1 cut through both towns; Krome Ave has the best, most indie offerings, while chain hotels and fast-food spots (and those strip joints) line Rte 1.

INFORMATION

Chamber of Commerce (☎ 305-247-2332; 43 N Krome Ave; ☽ 9am-noon & 1-5pm Mon-Fri) Be sure to stop here for information on all surrounding Everglades areas.

SIGHTS
Coral Castle

South Florida has its fair share of strange attractions, half-truths, embellishments and wacky stories, and **Coral Castle** (☎ 305-248-6345; www.coralcastle.com; 28,655 S Dixie Hwy; adult/youth 7-18 yrs/senior & student $9.75/5/6.50; ☽ 7am-8pm), on the National Register of Historic Places, is one if not all of the above. Here's the rumor and legend: after a Latvian was snubbed at the altar by a younger woman, he was so distraught he fled the country and immigrated to the States. He then spent the next 28 years (from 1923 to 1951), using only handmade tools, to single-handedly carve these coral rocks into a monument to unrequited love. The largest stone weighs 29 tons and the swinging gate weighs in at 9 tons. Strangely, no one ever saw him actually building the prehistoric-looking structures. But scholars have come here hoping to unlock the mysteries of how the pyramids were built. (It's actually a mistake to refer to it as a castle, since there are no turrets, ramparts or other architectural elements typical of castles.)

SLEEPING

Best Western Florida City/Homestead Gateway to the Keys (☎ 305-246-5100, 800-937-8376; www

.bestwestern.com; 411 S Krome Ave, Florida City; r off-season $74-89, Dec-May $94-109) This two-story motel has a pool and 114 standard-issue rooms with either two queen-sized or one king-sized bed. Some rooms have a microwave and refrigerator.

Hampton Inn (☎ 305-247-8833; www.hamptoninnfloridacity.com; 124 E Palm Dr, Florida City; r $120-165) The absolute best place in town is this new chain, which gets booked up quickly.

Everglades International Hostel (☎ 305-248-1122, 800-372-3874; www.evergladeshostel.com; 20 SW 2nd Ave, Florida City; dm $13-16, d $33-35) This friendly hostel, in a 1930s boarding house, has six-bed dorm rooms and private doubles with shared bath. You'll find lots of information about Glades canoeing, kayaking and bicycling, and can rent canoes and kayaks ($20 to $60 daily) and sign up for various types of tours ($12.50 to $45). The hostel has a full kitchen, garden, Internet connections and laundry facilities.

Greenstone Motel (☎ 305-247-8334; http://greenstone.gzinc.com; 304 N Krome Ave, Homestead; r $65-100). Though it looks just like any other roadside motor lodge from the outside, the inside of several 'signature rooms' have been decorated in funky (not fancy) style by local artists who live and work at the Art South art colony, located in an adjacent building.

Redland Hotel (☎ 305-246-1904; 5 S Flagler Ave, Homestead; r $75-150) This historic inn, right in the center of town, has clean and cozy rooms. The building has served as the town's first hotel, mercantile store, post office, library and boarding house (for real!) and is now favored by regional businessmen and folks who want more of a personal touch than you can get from the chains.

EATING

Casita Tejas (☎ 305-248-8224; 27 N Krome Ave, Homestead; dishes $6.50-11) This popular storefront eatery on the main drag has affordable, delicious, authentic Mexican lunches and dinners.

El Toro Taco (☎ 305-245-8182; 1 S Krome Ave, Homestead; dishes $2-9; ☑ 11am-9pm Tue-Thu & Sun, 11am-10pm Fri & Sat) The fajitas, burritos, other Mexican specialties and fresh salsa – as well as the hearty Mexican breakfasts of *huevos* (eggs) and warm tortillas – are exceptional at this family-run restaurant. Bring your own beer (at night only, *por favor*).

Air Boats & Swamp Buggies

Air boats are flat-bottomed skiffs that use powerful fans to propel themselves through the water. While capable of traveling in shallow water, they are very loud, and their environmental impact has not been determined. One thing is clear: air boats can't be doing much good.

Swamp buggies are enormous balloon-tired vehicles that can go through swamps, creating ruts and damaging wildlife.

Air boat and swamp buggy rides are offered all along US Hwy 41 (Tamiami Trail). Please think twice before getting on a 'nature' tour. You may be helping to disturb the Everglades' delicate balance

Farmer's Market Restaurant (☎ 305-242-0008; 300 N Krome Ave, Florida City; lunch dishes $8-10, dinner dishes $12-14; ☑ 5:30am-9pm) This simple restaurant prepares homemade everything, from hot cakes and hearty breakfasts to fried-fish baskets at lunch, to seafood combos and snapper at dinner.

Main St Café (☎ 305-245-7575; www.mainstreetcafe.net; 128 N Krome Ave, Homestead; mains $6-12) This bright spot on Krome is a warm and lively locals' hotspot, serving everything from tofu sandwiches and fresh salad to charbroiled burgers and homemade Caribbean stews. Thursday is open-mike night and weekends have live folk and blues shows, and there's a small Internet café near the bar up front.

Robert Is Here (☎ 305-246-1592; 19,200 SW 344th St, Homestead; ☑ 8am-7pm Nov-Aug) For a slice of Old Florida, not to mention some exotic fruits and slices of heady mango (in summer), stop at Robert's, one of the best-known farmers' markets in the country. The mango shakes are sweet and refreshing, but if you're here in the winter, try a Key lime milkshake.

ALONG THE TAMIAMI TRAIL

Although the main attraction on the Tamiami Trail (US Hwy 41) – which blazes between Miami and Tampa – is Shark Valley (p194), a few other stops are worthy of your time, namely the Big Cypress National Preserve. For the most part, the Tamiami Trail runs straight as an arrow through

Kayaking (p200), Everglades

eerily beautiful swampland until you reach Everglades City and the western edge of the park.

SIGHTS & ACTIVITIES
Miccosukee Resort & Convention Center

About 15 minutes west of the Miami airport, this imposing, high-rise Miccosukee Resort (☎ 305-925-2555, 877-242-6464; www .miccosukee.com; 500 SW 177th Ave) has 302 contemporary guest rooms and suites ($99 November to April, inquire about off-season packages); wall-to-wall gaming tables that are open around the clock; second-tier nationally known entertainers; and five restaurants, including a deli and an all-you-can-eat buffet. If it's actually an introduction to Native American traditions you're looking for, skip this (and the nearby inauthentic Miccosukee Indian Village) and make a beeline for the Ah-Tah-Thi-Ki Museum (opposite).

Big Cypress Gallery

Clyde Butcher's photography gallery (☎ 941-695-2428; www.clydebutcher.com; Tamiami Trail; ☯ 10am-5pm Wed-Mon) is a highlight of any trip to the Everglades, so by all means stop here. In the great tradition of Ansel Adams, Clyde's large-format black and white images elevate the swamps to a higher level, and locals, appreciative of his appreciation, are often major fans (look for his images on the walls of hotels and restaurants throughout the region). Butcher has found a quiet spirituality in the brackish waters and you just might, too, with the help of his eyes.

Big Cypress National Preserve

This 1139-sq-mile, federally protected preserve is the result of a compromise between environmentalists, cattle ranchers and oil-and-gas explorers. While allowing preexisting development to proceed to a certain extent, the preserve generally protects the land. The area is integral to the Everglades' ecosystem: rains that flood the prairies and wetlands here slowly filter down through the Glades. Recently, the park entered into an interesting 'Sister Park Understanding' with a similar park in Guatemala, Laguna del Tigre National Park. The two parks share closely related habitats and management issues, and will now be able to share technical assistance and resource expertise.

About 45% of the cypress swamp (which is not a swamp at all but a group of mangrove islands, hardwood hammocks, islands of slash pine, prairie and marshes) is protected preserve. Great bald cypress trees are nearly gone from the area, as lumbering and other industry took its toll before the preserve was established. These days, dwarf pond cypress trees fill the area.

Why is it called Big Cypress, then? Because of the size of the preserve, not the cypress trees within it. Resident fauna include alligators, snakes, wading birds (white ibis, wood storks, tri-color herons and egrets), Florida panthers (rarely seen), wild turkeys and red cockaded woodpeckers. Find more information at the **Big Cypress Visitor Center** (☎ 941-695-4111; ✹ 8:30am-4:30pm), about 20 miles west of Shark Valley, or at the **National Preserve Headquarters** (☎ 941-695-2000; ✹ 8am-4:30pm Mon-Fri), just east of Ochopee.

You'll find 31 miles of the **Florida National Scenic Trail** (FNST), maintained by the Florida Trail Association, within Big Cypress National Preserve. From the southern terminus, which can be accessed by car via Loop Rd, the trail runs 8.3 miles north to the Tamiami Trail, passing the Big Cypress Visitor Center. There are two primitive campsites with water wells along the trail. Off-road vehicles are permitted to cross, but not operate on, the FNST. For the less adventurous, there's the short **Tree Snail Hammock Nature Trail**, off Loop Rd.

On-road vehicles can drive on Loop Rd, a potholed dirt road, and Turner River Rd, which shoots straight as an arrow north off the Tamiami Trail. There are excellent wildlife-viewing opportunities along the entire stretch of Turner River Rd, especially in the Turner River Canal, which runs along the east side of it. The road leads to the northern area of the preserve where off-road vehicles are permitted.

In addition to the two sites on the FNST, there are six primitive campgrounds on the preserve. You can pick up a map at the visitor center. Be sure to bring your own water and food. Most campsites – Bear Island, Midway, Loop Rd, Mitchell Landing and Pinecrest – are free, and you needn't register. Mitchell Landing, Loop Rd and Pinecrest do not accommodate recreational vehicles (RVs). **Monument Lake** (off-season free, Nov-Apr $14) has water and toilets.

Ochopee

Drive to the tiny hamlet of Ochopee (population about four)…no…wait…turn around, you missed it! Then pull over and

Ah-Tah-Thi-Ki Museum

The best Everglades tourism news in years is the advent of this **Seminole museum** (☎ 863-902-1113; www.seminoletribe.com/museum; Big Cypress Seminole Indian Reservation, Clewiston; adult/senior & child $6/4; ✹ 9am-5pm Tue-Sun), 17 miles north of I-75. With educational exhibits on Seminole life, history and the tribe today, the museum was founded with Seminole gaming proceeds. Gambling receipts, an economic powerhouse, provide most of the Seminole tribe's multimillion-dollar operating budget.

Never before have the Seminoles opened so much up to the public. Sure, it's good for business, but they really are dedicated to giving visitors a closer understanding of the Seminole and Miccosukee people, and to enabling them to experience Seminole life. It's not the wild Glades, and there are aspects of this 60-acre cypress forest – such as alligator wrestling – that leave something to be desired, but it's a breakthrough for the tribe. Until recently, they had kept to themselves where tourism was concerned. Its **Seminole Safari excursions** (☎ 941-949-6101, 800-617-7516; www.seminoletours.com) offer day ($46) and overnight ($112) very touristy packages. Overnights include sleeping in a screened-in chickee hut, listening to campfire storytelling, taking an airboat or swamp buggy ride and having Indian meals (catfish, fry bread, gator nuggets).

break out the cameras: Ochopee's claim to fame is the country's smallest official post office. Housed in a former toolshed and set against big park skies, a friendly postal worker patiently poses for snapshots.

EATING

Joannie's Blue Crab Café (☎ 941-695-2682; Tamiami Trail, east of Ochopee; dishes $10-13; ✹ 9am-5pm) This quintessential shack, with open rafters, shellacked picnic tables, wooden floors and alligator kitsch serves OK food on paper plates. While stone crabs are a decided specialty, you can also get swamp dinners (with gator nuggets, gator fritters, frogs' legs and Indian fry bread) and peel-and-eat shrimp.

Pit BBQ (☎ 305-226-2272; 16,400 SW 8th St, btwn Miami & Shark Valley; dishes $4-9; ✹ 11am-11:30pm) It doesn't get more real than this: authentic barbecue served on picnic tables in a dumpy joint with

Canoe Camping on 10,000 Islands

The finest way to experience the serenity and beauty of the Everglades – which is somehow desolate yet lush, tropical yet foreboding – is by canoeing or kayaking through the excellent network of waterways that skirt the northwest portion of the park. The **10,000 Islands** consist of many (but not really 10,000) tiny islands and a mangrove swamp that hugs the southwesternmost border of Florida. The **Wilderness Waterway**, a 99-mile path between Everglades City and Flamingo, is the longest canoe trail in the area, but there are shorter trails near Flamingo.

Most islands are fringed by narrow beaches with sugar-white sand, but note that the water is brackish, not clear, and very shallow most of the time. It's not Tahiti, but it's fascinating. The best part is that you can camp on your own island for up to a week.

Getting around the 10,000 Islands is pretty straightforward if you religiously adhere to National Oceanic & Atmospheric Administration (NOAA) tide and nautical charts. Going against the tides is the fastest way to make it a miserable trip. The Gulf Coast Visitor Center sells nautical charts and gives out free tidal charts. You can also purchase charts prior to your visit – call ☎ 305-247-1216 and ask for chart Nos 11430, 11432 and 11433.

Canoe & Kayak Itineraries

Near Everglades City, you can take a downstream trip on the Turner River alone or with a group. Take a drift-with-the-current trip to Chokoloskee Island, or add a bit of a challenge at the end and paddle upstream in the boating canal to the Gulf Coast Visitor Center. For an easy day of paddling, just cross the bay from the Gulf Coast Visitor Center and paddle out and around the mangroves to Sandfly Island or on the Chokoloskee Bay Loop. For an easy one- or two-night trip, head to islands closest to the ranger station: Tiger, Picnic, Rabbit, New Turkey, Turkey and Hog Keys, all with beach campsites. There are hundreds of other combinations; check with a ranger at the Gulf Coast Visitor Center for more recommendations.

If you're going to make the eight- to 10-day Wilderness Waterway trek between Everglades City and Flamingo, you'll probably need help portaging (shuttling your car from one point to the other). Contact the very nice folks at the **Everglades International Hostel** (☎ 305-248-1122, 800-372-3874; www.evergladeshostel.com; 20 SW 2nd Ave, Florida City). They're the only ones in the area who provide this service ($200 if you rent with them, $300 if you don't.) However you cut it, count on sacrificing one day for logistics: one person ferries the car around while another pulls permits for the backcountry trip.

Wilderness Camping

Three types of backcountry campsites are available from the Flamingo and Gulf Coast Visitor Centers: beach sites, on coastal shell beaches and in the 10,000 Islands; ground sites, which are basically mounds of dirt built up above the mangroves along the interior bays and rivers; and 'chickees,' wooden platforms built above the water line on which you can pitch a free-standing (no spikes) tent. Chickees, which have toilets, are the most civilized; they're certainly unique. There's a serenity in sleeping on what feels like a raft levitating above the water in the middle of nature. Beach sites are the most comfortable, though biting insects are rife, even in winter. Ground sites tend to be the most bug-infested.

Warning: if you're just paddling around and you see an island that looks perfectly pleasant for camping but it's not a designated campsite, beware – you may end up submerged when the tides change.

From November to April, camping permits cost $10; in the off-season sites are free, but you must still self-register at the Flamingo and Gulf Coast Visitor Centers.

country-and-western music on the jukebox. You gotta love it (otherwise, don't stop).

EVERGLADES CITY

Everglades City survives rather than thrives from the trade of fisherfolk, who pull into the marina and live in RVs, and tourists passing through to visit the Everglades. It's perfectly pleasant, in a fisherfolk's paradise kind of way – and it's a sensible place to spend the night to get an early start on canoe trips in the 10,000 Islands.

ORIENTATION

Highway 29 runs south through town, soon leading you onto the peaceful, residential island of Chokoloskee.

INFORMATION

Everglades Area Chamber of Commerce (☎ 941-695-3941; cnr US Hwy 41 & Hwy 29; ☼ 9am-5pm) Dispenses basic information, with much about this corner of the region.

Gulf Coast Visitor Center (☎ 941-695-3311; Hwy 29; ☼ 8:30am-5pm) At the southern end of town; has loads of information on the 10,000 Islands and the Everglades.

SIGHTS & ACTIVITIES

North American Canoe Tours (NACT; ☎ 941-695-3299/4666; www.evergladesadventures.com; Ivey House Bed & Breakfast, 107 Camellia St; ☑ Nov–mid-Apr), is the best outfit for equipment and guided tours. It rents camping equipment and first-rate canoes for full or half days ($25 to $45) and touring kayaks ($25 to $65), which have rudders and upgraded paddles that make going against the current a whole lot easier. You get 20% off most of these services and rentals if you're staying at the **Ivey House Bed & Breakfast** (below), which NACT owns. Bike rentals are available for $5 per hour or $20 per day (free to Ivey House guests). Tours are varied; get shuttled to places including Chokoloskee Island, Collier Seminole State Park, Rabbit Key or Tiger Key for afternoon or overnight excursions ($16 to $250).

For those making the eight- to 10-day trip between the Gulf Coast and Flamingo Visitor Centers with an NACT rental boat, you'll pick up boats in Flamingo for $100, but you'll still have to get yourself back to Everglades City. Call the **Everglades International Hostel** (☎ 305-248-1122, 800-372-3874) to make arrangements for that.

SLEEPING

Note that all rates in town go up for the annual Everglades Seafood Festival, held the first weekend in February.

Captain's Table (☎ 941-695-4211, 800-741-6430; Hwy 29; r off-season $50-115, late Dec-Apr $70-130) At the jig in Hwy 29 east of the downtown traffic circle, Captain's Table has a nice staff and 48 old but tidy rooms and suites (with kitchen facilities).

Glades Haven Cozy Cabins (☎ 941-695-2746; www.gladeshaven.com; Hwy 29; cabins $60-100) This complex of 23 log cabins, many with stoves and refrigerators, is an easy way to feel at one with nature. It's sandwiched between the road and a lovely marina, and the quarters are spic-and-span.

Ivey House Bed & Breakfast (☎ 941-695-3299; www.iveyhouse.com; 107 Camellia St; inn $75-175, lodge $60-100) This interesting inn consists of two halves: the lodge, an extremely bare-bones row of motel rooms in a 1928 boarding house (the former flop for workers who constructed the Tamiami Trail), and the newly constructed inn (2001), which offers bigger, more comfort-able rooms set around a lovely pool area. This family-run place also serves good breakfasts in its small Ghost Orchid Grill, and it operates some of the best nature trips around (left).

Rod & Gun Club Lodge (☎ 941-695-2101; 200 Riverside Dr; r off-season $75, mid-Oct–Jun $105) Built in the 1920s as a hunting lodge by Barron Collier (who needed a place to chill after watching workers dig his Tamiami Trail), this masculine lodge, fronted by a lovely porch, harkens back to Olde Florida.

EATING

JT's Island Grill & Gallery (☎ 239-695-3633; 238 Mamie St, Chokoloskee; ☑ lunch only, 11am-3pm, late Oct-May) It's slim pickings in Everglade City, so hooray for JT's! Just a mile or so past the edge of town, this awesome café sits in a restored 1890 general store that sits in the midst of a residential neighborhood. It's outfitted with bright, retro furniture and piles of kitschy books, pottery, clothing and maps that are for sale. But the best part is the food – fresh crab cakes, salads, fish platters and veggie wraps, made with locally grown organic vegetables. JT's is also home to the new Gumbo Limbo Natural Foods, which has the best selection of produce and health-food groceries for miles around.

Susie's Station (Hwy 29; dishes $6-9) The atmosphere at Susie's is pleasant enough, but she only serves fried stuff: chicken strips, fried shrimp, french fries and the like. It's on the west side of the traffic circle.

BISCAYNE NATIONAL PARK

ORIENTATION

Located just to the east of the Everglades National Park, this park offers a stark contrast: clear waters, sandy beaches and not a gator in sight. Biscayne contains a portion of the world's third-largest reef (after Australia's Great Barrier Reef and offshore Belize). Fortunately, this unique 300-sq-mile park, 95% of which is under water, is very easy to explore independently with a canoe or via a glass-bottom-boat tour. Its offshore keys, accessible only by boat, also offer pristine opportunities for camping. Generally, summer and fall are the best times to visit the park; you'll want to snorkel when the water is calm.

INFORMATION

Dante Fascell Visitor Center (☎ 305-230-7275; www.nps.gov/bisc; 9700 SW 328th St; ⊙ 8:30am-5pm) shows a great introductory film for a good overview of the park and has maps and information.

SIGHTS & ACTIVITIES

Biscayne National Underwater Park (☎ 305-230-1100) offers glass-bottom-boat viewing of the exceptional reefs, canoe rentals, transportation to the keys, and snorkeling and scuba-diving trips. All tours require a minimum of six people, so call to make reservations. Three-hour glass-bottom-boat trips depart at 10am daily (adult/child under 12 $25/17). Canoe rentals cost $10 per hour and kayaks $17; they're rented from 9am to 3pm. Transportation to Elliott Key for hiking or camping costs $25 per person round-trip (make reservations at least a day in advance). A three-hour snorkeling trip (per person $35) departs at 1:15pm daily; you'll have about 1½ hours in the water. Scuba trips depart at 8:30am Friday to Sunday ($45).

Long **Elliott Key** has picnicking, camping and hiking among mangrove forests; tiny **Adams Key** has only picnicking; and equally tiny **Boca Chita Key** has an ornamental lighthouse, picnicking and camping. No-see-ums (tiny biting flies) are invasive, and their bites are devastating. Make sure your tent is devoid of miniscule entry points. Primitive camping costs $10 per night; you pay on a trust system (there is no cashier) with exact change on the harbor (rangers cruise the Keys to check your receipt). Bring in all supplies, including water, and carry everything out. There is no water on Boca Chita (only saltwater toilets), and since it has a deeper port, it tends to attract bigger (and louder) boaters. There are cold-water showers and potable water on Elliott, but it's always good to bring your own since the generator might go out.

Fort Lauderdale

Fort Lauderdale

Once upon a time, Fort Lauderdale was known as a main destination for beer swilling college students on raucous Spring Break vacations. And up until the mid-'80s, it was this accurate set of images – of drunk 19-year-old girls in wet-T-shirt contests, bands of boys drinking beer in the streets and round-the-clock parties at unfortunate beachside hotels – that dominated most people's knowledge of the place. But my, what a difference a couple of decades make! Today, after a concerted effort to clean itself up by outlawing activities that lead to such alcohol-fueled bacchanalia, Fort Lauderdale has been successful in attracting a more mature and sophisticated sort of visitor with its myriad offerings (though there's still plenty of carrying on within the confines of many a bar and nightclub). The city's Port Everglades is even the winter home to the new swanky *Queen Mary II* cruise ship, for heaven's sake. Though much of the inland portion of the city consists of endless, unattractive strip malls, seek out the good stuff and you'll find yourself rewarded with beautiful beaches, a system of Venice-like waterways, an international yachting scene, spiffy new hotels, top-notch restaurants, and gay hotspots – all just 40 minutes up the coast from Miami.

ORIENTATION

Fort Lauderdale, about 40 miles north of Miami, is laid out in a grid wherever physically possible (it's difficult with all the water breaking things up). It's also divided into three distinct sections: the beach, east of the Intracoastal Waterway; downtown, on the mainland; and Port Everglades, the cruise port south of the city. US Hwy 1 (also called Federal Highway) cuts through downtown, while Hwy A1A runs along the ocean and is also called Atlantic Blvd and Ocean Blvd, depending if you're north or south of Sunrise Blvd. The main arteries between downtown and the beach are Sunrise Blvd to the north, Las Olas Blvd in the center and 17th St to the south.

INFORMATION

Broward General Medical Center (☎ 954-355-4400; 1600 S Andrews Ave, Port Everglades) This is the largest public hospital in the area.

Clark's Out of Town News (☎ 954-467-1543; 303 S Andrews Ave) Gather both local and foreign newspapers at Clark's. You can also pick up a copy of the alternative weekly *New Times* (it's a Fort Lauderdale version of the main Miami paper) to find out the latest on eating, arts and nightlife.

Greater Fort Lauderdale Convention & Visitors Bureau (☎ 954-765-4466; www.sunny.org; 1850 Eller Dr, Port Everglades; ☺ 8:30am-5pm Mon-Fri) Come here for an excellent array of visitor information. It offers informa-

Top Five Experiences

Best unofficial tour
On one of the water taxis (p214) that wind through Fort Lauderdale's gleaming waterways.

Most gorgeous facelift
The Fort Lauderdale Beach Promenade (p208), which looks fabulous after a $26-million renovation.

Best reason to leave Miami on a Saturday night
The Coliseum (p213), a gay nightclub that gets rocked by the country's hottest DJs, attracting boatloads of boys from South Beach.

Coolest vegetarian surprise
The restaurant Sublime (p212), home of exquisite vegan cuisine, a café and a boutique of cruelty-free products.

Best reason to bust out the credit card
The beautiful Las Olas Riverfront (opposite), home to lovely shops and eateries.

tion on hotels and attractions in the entire greater Fort Lauderdale region.

Lauderdale-by-the-Sea Chamber of Commerce (☎ 954-776-1000; 4201 Ocean Dr) Offers information on businesses throughout Fort Lauderdale.

Main post office (☎ 800-275-8777; 1900 W Oakland Park Blvd) Send your snail mail here, west of I-95.

New Millennium Internet Café (☎ 954-566-2111; 3337 NE 33rd St) Check your email here.

SIGHTS & ACTIVITIES

Museum of Art

This **museum** (☎ 954-525-5500; www.moafl
.org; 1 E Las Olas Blvd; adult/student & child
over 12 yrs/senior $6/3/5; ☯ 11am-5pm
Fri-Wed, 11am-9pm Thu) is simply one of
Florida's best. The impressive permanent
collection includes works by Pablo Picasso,
Henri Matisse, Henry Moore, Salvador Dalí
and Andy Warhol, plus growing and impressive collections of Cuban, ethnographic,
African and South American collections. A
recent quirky and popular show included
'Diana, A Celebration,' about the beloved
princess. Also, check out the great new
Stork's Café and Bakery, and the brand-new
Saturday jazz series, held in the museum's
auditorium.

Museum of Discovery & Science

Fronted by the 52ft Great Gravity Clock,
Florida's largest kinetic energy sculpture, this
environmentally oriented **museum** (☎ 954-
467-6637; www.mods.org; 401 SW 2nd St;
adult/child/senior & student $14/12/13;
☯ 10am-5pm Mon-Sat, noon-6pm Sun) is
a treat for kids of all ages, with exhibits on
topics including rocket ships, electricity and
the Everglades restoration. The admission
also includes one **IMAX 3D show** in the impressive five-story theater. Before leaving, check
out the **parabolic display** across the street: two
dishes face each other about 60ft apart. Turn
toward one dish and have a friend turn toward the other. Whisper into the dish and
you'll hear each other perfectly.

Fort Lauderdale Historical Society

This **organization** (☎ 954-463-4431; www.old
fortlauderdale.org; 231 SW 2nd Ave; admission $5; ☯ 11am-5pm Tue-Sun) maintains
the brand new **Hoch Heritage Center**, a historic
research facility; the century-old **New River
Inn**, **Philemon Bryan House** and **King-Cromartie
House**, open for tours; and the 1899 **Replica
Schoolhouse**. The museum mounts exhibits on
Fort Lauderdale and Broward County history and Seminole folk art and also offers
guided walking tours of historic downtown.
Call for details and reservations.

Fort Lauderdale For Kids

Museum of Discovery & Science (left) You'll find
several exhibits geared especially to little ones.

Fort Lauderdale Beach (p208) Pail, shovel, done.

Water Bus taxi ride (p214) What kid doesn't love a
boat adventure?

Lago Mar Resort (p210) This top-notch hotel features a complete children's activity program during
the winter holiday season.

Mai Kai (p213) It's wacky and wild, plus it's got a
children's menu.

Wannado City (☎ 954-838-7100; www.wannado
city.com; Purple Parrot Way, Sawgrass Mills Mall;
over/under 14 yrs $27.95/15.95) It's worth a short
day trip to the nearby City of Sunrise for this new
kids' theme park, which asks children, 'Whatchya
wanna do?' and then lets them do it. Kids can try
all sorts of real-life jobs and tasks through little vil-
lages, costumes and games that let them star in an
action movie, act as circus ringmaster, use an ATM,
perform surgery, investigate a crime scene and, of
course, have mom and dad buy plenty of souvenirs
to always remember the day. Daily hours vary by
season; call for more info.

Riverwalk/Las Olas Riverfront

This meandering **pathway** (☎ 954-468-1541;
www.goriverwalk.com), along New River,
runs from Stranahan House to Broward
Center for the Performing Arts. It's pleasant and lovely, and connects a number of
city sights, restaurants and shops. **Las Olas
Riverfront** (☎ 954-522-6556, SW 1st Ave at
Las Olas Blvd) is a giant shopping mall with
stores, restaurants, a movie theater and live
entertainment nightly; it's also the place to
catch many river cruises (p209).

Stranahan House

One of Florida's oldest residences, the land-
marked **Stranahan House** (☎ 954-524-4736;
www.stranahanhouse.com; 335 SE 6th St; admission $6; ☯ 10am-3pm Wed-Sat, 1-3pm
Sun) is a fine example of Florida frontier desi
gn. Constructed from Dade County pine,
the house has wide porches, tall windows,
a Victorian parlor, original furnishings and
fine tropical gardens. It was built as the home
and store for Ohio transplant Frank Stranahan, who built a small empire trading with
the Seminole but killed himself by jumping

FORT LAUDERDALE

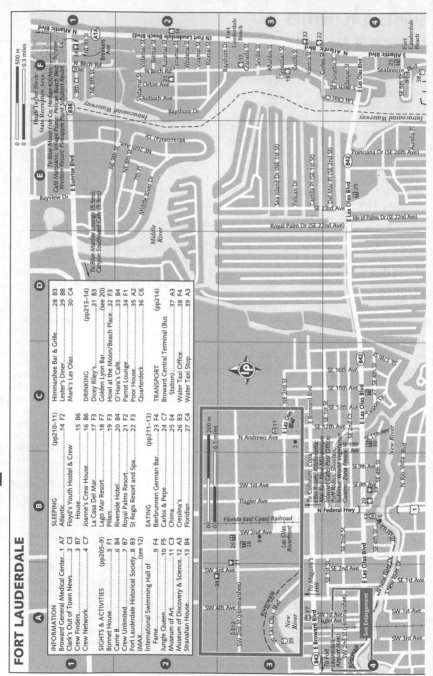

INFORMATION (pp210–11)
Broward General Medical Center....1 A7
Clark's Out of Town News...............2 C3
Crew Finders....................................3 B7
Crew Network...................................4 C7

SIGHTS & ACTIVITIES (pp205–9)
Bonnet B...5 F1
Carrie B..6 B4
Crew Unlimited.................................7 B7
Fort Lauderdale Historical Society...8 B3
IMAX...(see 12)
International Swimming Hall of
  Fame...9 F4
Jungle Queen..................................10 F5
Museum of Art................................11 C3
Museum of Discovery & Science...12 A3
Stranahan House.............................13 B4

SLEEPING (pp210–11)
Atlantic..14 F2
Floyd's Youth Hostel & Crew
  House..15 B6
Joanne's Crew House.......................16 B6
La Casa Del Mar.............................17 F3
Lago Mar Resort.............................18 F7
Pillars...19 F3
Riverside Hotel...............................20 B4
Royal Palms Resort.........................21 F2
St Regis Resort and Spa..................22 F3

Himmarshee Bar & Grille...............28 B3
Lester's Diner..................................29 B8
Mark's Las Olas..............................30 C4

DRINKING (pp213–14)
Dicey Riley's...................................31 B3
Golden Lyon Bar........................(see 20)
Howl at the Moon/Beach Place.....32 F3
O'Hara's Café.................................33 B4
Parrot Lounge.................................34 F1
Poor House.....................................35 A2
Quarterdeck....................................36 C6

TRANSPORT (pp214)
Broward Central Terminal (Bus
  Station)..37 A3
Water Taxi Office............................38 F4
Water Taxi Stop...............................39 A3

EATING (pp211–13)
Bierbrunnen German Bar................23 F4
Carlos & Pepe.................................24 C7
Chima...25 E4
Creolina's.......................................26 B3
Floridian...27 C4

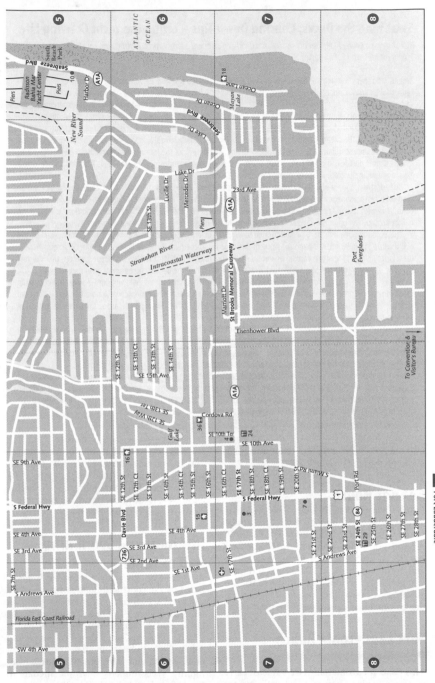

Swabbing the Decks, Chasing Down Tips – Living the Yacht Crewing Life

Rick Starey is a Lonely Planet author as well as a deckhand on board a luxury yacht. Here he gives Lonely Planet readers an insight into the world of megayachts.

Among its other nicknames – Venice of America (for its waterways) and Liquordale (for obvious reasons) – Fort Lauderdale is known among the nautical set as the yachting capital of the world. It's home to thousands of luxury motoryachts and sailboats, and somebody's gotta make them run. Enter a water-loving workforce with varying experience, many of whom divide their time between Fort Lauderdale (winter) and places up north such as New England (summer).

For those who join this workforce, it means great coin, idyllic destinations, divine cuisine, incredible cultures and the mystic beauty of the ocean. Combine that with scrubbing decks, polishing stainless steel, detailing acute and minute features and then scrubbing a few more decks. Reveling in a portion of the former and getting down and dirty in a lot of the latter is the life of a deckhand aboard a luxury yacht. Here is an industry where money is flaunted for fun, excess is paramount and bottom lines are ignored at all costs.

Boat destinations are mouth-watering. Megayachts roam the world's hot spots of culture, style and ecology. In the space of a few seasons you could soak up Rio de Janeiro's sexy samba, experience the European cultural hub of Monte Carlo, chill with the polar bears of Alaska, be dazzled by Miami's nightlife, revel in Spain's rich traditions, carve up the Italian pizzazz, sun up in the Caribbean and explore the ecological fantasy that is the Galapagos Islands.

These floating beauties have been designed to overwhelm, entertain and exude a lifestyle that's far beyond 99.9% of the world's population. Although the value of these megayachts equals the Gross Domestic Product of a small nation, these pricey pieces of fiberglass are, in essence, just very big toys for rather loaded boys. So loaded, in fact, that the vast majority of megayachts run at a monumental loss, to the delight of the owners' accountants, year in, year out.

Life on board requires a certain type of individual, as close quarters, communal living and a stacked dictatorship come together to provide a unique atmosphere. Always present is a heavily regimented pecking order that is essential in any offshore activity. Another aspect is that you can't leave the office, meaning you are at the ship's beck and call 24/7. Even when you're nursing a nasty hangover.

The job of a 'decky' could best be described as a jack-of-all-trades gig. You become a world-class cleaner, meaning you're chamois is not only your best mate but also your greatest tool. You'll learn a bit about engines, fiddle with radars, paint anchors, throw heaving lines, study weather patterns and may even learn to read a chart or two. But, above all, the quality of a deckhand is best judged in two simple departments, work ethic and an eye for detail.

Fort Lauderdale is the place to be for aspiring crewmen as it's justifiably regarded as the luxury yachting capital of the world with thousands of captains looking for their next crew. The megayacht industry can be a postcard lifestyle: sailing off into another perfect sunset with tax-free cash, lifelong friends and crystal-clear memories. The yachting game at its best is almost unbeatable; at its worst, well, did I mention the decks?

---

into the New River after real estate and stock market losses in the late 1920s.

Bonnet House

Lovely **Bonnet House** (☎ 954-563-5393; www .bonnethouse.org; 900 N Birch Rd; adult/ senior/student & child 6-18 yrs $10/8/9, grounds only $6; ☒ 10am-4pm Tue-Sat) has 35 subtropical acres filled with native and imported tropical plants, including a vast orchid collection. Tours of the house are guided (1¼ hours), but you are free to walk the grounds and nature trails on your own.

Fort Lauderdale Beach Promenade

This peaceful promenade (well at least early in the morning, before the traffic starts)

recently received a $26-million renovation, and it's quite evident. The wide pathway, which runs along the beach, with A1A running parallel and palm trees swaying alongside, is an understandable magnet for runners, walkers and cyclists.

International Swimming Hall of Fame

Anyone who loves swimming or is fascinated by the sport and its greatest achievers will get a splash out of this **museum** (☎ 954-462-6536; www.ishof.org; 1 Hall of Fame Dr/SE 5th St; adult/senior & student/family $3/1/5; ☒ 9am-7pm Mon-Fri, 9am-5pm Sat & Sun). Exhibits include thousands of photographs and Olympic mementos, from Johnny Weissmuller's Olympic medals to Mark Spitz's starting block. You can also

Joining a Crew

Some crew jobs, such as captain and engineer, require particular skills and experience. These jobs can pay up to $2500 a week on board, while other jobs, such as deckhands and cooks, are open to hard workers with a sense of adventure, with salaries of about $400 to $800 a week. As the industry is developing, it is becoming basically essential to obtain the STCW95 certificate. Although it costs $895, it displays an investment of sorts from the applicant and makes finding a job a whole lot easier.

Agencies

Placing agencies include **Crew Finders** (☎ 954-522-2739; www.crewfinders.com; 408 SE 17th St), **Crew4Crew** (www.crew4crew.net), and the **Crew Network** (☎ 954-467-9777; 1053 SE 17th St). Though Smallwood's **Yachtware** (☎ 954-523-2282; 1001 SE 17th St), with its famed three-ring binder, is a good starting point, in my time I have not met anybody that gained employment through it. A much more successful plan of attack is 'dock walking' with a bunch of resumes under one arm and your confidence in the other.

When to Go

A great time to make your presence felt is the month or so leading up to any boat show (October to November), as there is plenty of work in preparing the boats, and if you make the right impressions, there is a solid chance you may be taken on. If not, you will build up your contacts list so you, as a product, will get more airtime.

What to Bring

For international arrivals, along with the STCW95, getting hold of a B1B2 visa sets you on sail for the job of your choice. Pack half as many clothes as you'd planned, and twice as much money.

Women Crew Members

The role of women with the industry is developing. However, women seeking crew work should only get on a boat that they're happy with.

Networking

Two great places to network are **Waxy O'Connor's Irish Pub** (☎ 954-525-WAXY; 1095 17th St Causeway) and **Quarterdeck** (☎ 954-423-4197; 1541 Cordova Rd).

view, upon request, some fun films featuring famous water rats such as Tarzan and Esther Williams.

Hugh Taylor Birch State Recreation Area

This **state park** (☎ 954-564-4521; 3109 E Sunrise Blvd; per vehicle of 2-8 people $4, per pedestrian or bicyclist $1; ☀ 8am-sunset), which has recently undergone a major renovation of trails and landscaping, contains one of the last significant maritime hammocks left in Broward County, as well as mangroves, a freshwater lagoon system and several endangered plant and animal species (including the gopher tortoise and golden leather fern). You can fish, picnic, hike, canoe or bike. Canoe rentals, to be used on the half-mile trail, cost about $6 per hour.

TOURS

Carrie B (☎ 954-768-9920; from Las Olas at SE 5th Ave; tour $13) is a kitschy waterfront tour on a 19th-century riverboat replica. It lasts an hour and a half.

On the first Saturday of the month the Fort Lauderdale Historical Society runs the **Historic Walking Tour** (☎ 954-463-4431; from New River Inn lobby; $5), a one-hour stroll focusing on the area's rich historic district; there's also a full-moon evening tour monthly. Reservations are required.

Jungle Queen Riverboat (☎ 954-462-5596; www.junglequeen.com; from Bahia Mar Yacht Center; tour/tour with dinner $13.50/30) runs three-hour tours of the waterfront, Millionaires' Row and part of the Everglades on a paddlewheeler; four-hour evening excursions include all-you-can-eat shrimp or barbecue dinners.

SLEEPING

The splashiest hotel experiences – offering spa services, a restaurant, a pool area and other amenities – can be found on the beach (they're also usually the priciest). Meander inland, and you'll discover some wonderful inns with old-Florida charm, many of which exclusively cater to gay guests (these are listed below and noted). Expect to pay an average of $200 a night for top-end hotels and less for budget and midrange stays. And stay tuned, style seekers: a W Fort Lauderdale hotel is scheduled to open in a 27-floor oceanfront tower in early 2006, and is sure to instantly up the hip factor in these parts.

Budget & Midrange

Beach Hostel (☎ 954-567-7275; www.fortlauderdalehostel.com; 2115 N Ocean Blvd; dm $18) Just a few years old and so not yet infused with that musty scent that's typical of creakier youth hostels, this hot-pink, 61-bed backpacker home is just one block from the beach and about a mile north of the main beach area. Help yourself to breakfast foods (scramble the eggs yourself), log onto the Internet and borrow snorkeling gear. Just know that you'll need a passport to bunk here.

Courtyard Villa (☎ 954-776-1164, 800-291-3560; www.courtyardvilla.com; 4312 El Mar Dr; efficiencies & ste $115-275) This Mediterranean-style quartet of courtyard suites and efficiencies are infused with a breezy style with its ceiling fans, parquet floors and four-poster beds. You also get free use of the bikes, barbecue grills, tennis courts and there's a rooftop patio. It's no wonder the rooms here go fast.

Floyd's Youth Hostel & Crew House (☎ 954-462-0631; www.floydshostel.com; 445 SE 16th St; dm $18) This is close to most crew-placement agencies and a short bus ride from the beach. Before you can stay you'll be vetted on the telephone.

Joanne's Crew House (☎ 954-527-1636; 916 SE 12th St; per week $135) Fort Lauderdale's most established crew house, Joanne's is set in a residential area in a sprawling, ranch-style house. Fifteen people can await employment in five bedrooms (four bathrooms) in style. There's a big screened-in backyard, a pool and a barbecue area on the 1-acre property. Joanne calls boat owners to tell them who's staying at the house.

La Casa Del Mar (☎ 954-467-2037; www.lacasadelmar.com; 3003 Granada St; r $80-119, kitchenette $89-149, large units $179-240) This family-owned, homey B&B has very basic rooms, studios and one-bedroom units. They're not stylish, but they're comfortable, and are nestled in a tropical garden. A full breakfast is included.

Riverside Hotel (☎ 954-467-0671, 800-325-3280; www.riversidehotel.com; 620 E Las Olas Blvd; r $99-200) This 1936 historic hotel, sitting right in the center of downtown and fronted by stately columns, has an old-fashioned Main Street feel to it. It's never been one of the most stylish sleeps in Fort Lauderdale, but a recent renovation has helped by adding glass-enclosed showers and some new carpeting (though the bedspreads and curtains are a bit old-school). Its Las Olas location is a big plus.

Schubert Resort (☎ 866-763-7435, 954-763-7434; www.schubertresort.com; 855 NE 20th Ave; r $99-199) Why should Miami be the only place with deco style? The Schubert, one of the newest gay inns, is a retro inn with newly renovated rooms housed in the shell of a 1953 motel. Behind the neon sign out front you'll find sleek rooms with marble baths and boldly striped bedspreads; many of them surround a lovely pool area. Note the inn's frisky, clothing-optional policy.

Folks seeking work aboard Fort Lauderdale's luxury yachts (see p209) have tried and true options for bunking while they're finding a sweet gig.

Top End

Atlantic (☎ 954-567-8020; www.theatlantichotelfortlauderdale.com; 601 N Fort Lauderdale Beach Blvd; r $269-859) One of the newest games in town, opened in 2004, the Atlantic has raised the bar for Fort Lauderdale luxury. Part of the Starwood's resort group, the design is bathed in rich hues of orange and brown, while spacious rooms are lighter in tone. Each have balconies with sliding glass doors and gorgeous sea views, and the grounds have a lovely pool and deck, private beach, spa and top-end restaurant, Trina, from New York City's Don Pintabona (of Tribeca Grill).

Lago Mar Resort (☎ 954-523-6511, 800-524-6627; www.lagomar.com; 1700 S Ocean Ln; r $150-560) A wonderfully noncorporate traditional resort, the Lago Mar has it all:

a private beach, over-the-top grand lobby, massive island-style rooms, a full-service spa, on-site eateries and the personal touch of family ownership.

Pelican Beach Resort Best Western (☎ 954-568-9431; www.pelicanbeach.com; 2000 N Atlantic Blvd; r & ste $120-230) It may be part of the world's largest hotel chain, but it's one of the newest gigs in town, opened in 2004. Expect rooms that are slightly sterile – but extremely new and clean – in a high-rise that fronts a lovely private beachfront.

Pillars (☎ 954-467-9639, 800-800-7666; www.pillarshotel.com; 111 N Birch Rd; r $150-550) A lovely Key West–style lodge, this luxe retreat features plantation-style rooms surrounding a courtyard pool, a private waterway dock with outdoor dining tables, a beautiful lobby with hardwood floors and lushly landscaped grounds.

Pineapple Point (☎ 888-844-7295; www.pine applepoint.com; 315 NE 16th Tce; r $159-195, ste $235-449) A supremely stylish gay guest house set in intimate, verdant surroundings, the Point boasts tasteful rooms with four-poster beds, sumptuous duvets, hardwood floors and sun porches. There's a clothing-optional pool, but of course.

Royal Palms Resort (☎ 954-564-6444, 800-237-7256; www.royalpalms.com; 2901 Terramar St; r $169-319). This serene, isolated gay guest house is a clothing-optional place that features 12 large rooms (complete with CD/TV/VCR and library), a tropical garden, a pool with a waterfall and lots of perks, such as free parking and breakfast.

St Regis Resort & Spa (☎ 954-465-2300; 1 N Fort Lauderdale Beach Blvd; r from $250) This is the newest and most exclusive Fort Lauderdale hotel. Starwood opened the St Regis in spring 2005, and plans to drop the second part of its double whammy in early 2006, with the nearby W Fort Lauderdale. The St Regis has five stars, 24 stories and endless amenities, including a prime beachfront location, an upscale restaurant, a huge full-service spa and large rooms blessed with ocean and intracoastal views.

EATING

No longer cowering in the shadow of Miami's foodie scene, Fort Lauderdale has finally come into its own when it comes to gourmet dining options. You'll find everything from good, cheap Mexican to top-end Italian. Bon appetite!

Budget & Midrange

Bierbrunnen German Bar (☎ 954-462-1008; 425 Fort Lauderdale Beach Rd; dishes $7-15; ⊗ 11am-2am Sun-Fri, 11am-3am Sat) Down a little alley, this super-casual bar-cum-restaurant serves authentic schnitzel (pork loin breaded and pan-fried), sauerbraten (sour roast beef with mashed potatoes and red cabbage), fresh bratwurst and, of course, excellent draft beer. You can always get something light such as a mahimahi sandwich. It's a fun, beachside, partially alfresco sort of place.

Blue Moon Fish Co (☎ 954-267-9888; 4405 Tradewinds Ave W; lunch mains $10-15, dinner mains $26-38; ⊗ 11:30am-3pm daily, 6-10pm Sun-Thu, 6-11pm Fri & Sat) Seafood lovers flock to Blue Moon for its excellent and eclectic menu, solid service and spectacular waterside setting. The Sunday brunch ($25 per person), with frequent live jazz, provides a particularly bountiful meal of all-you-can-peel-and-eat shrimp, Louisiana crawfish, shucked oysters, a seafood buffet, mains such as seafood gumbo or salmon strudel, dessert and either a Bloody Mary, mimosa or champagne.

Carlos & Pepe (☎ 954-467-7192; 1302 SE 17th St; dishes $7-15; ⊗ 11:30am-11pm Mon-Thu, 11:30am-11pm Fri & Sat, noon-10:30pm Sun) Ignore the strip-mall location and the casual interior, because this

Lifeguard's lookout hut

authentic Mexican place has excellent salsa, fajitas and burritos, plus potent margaritas, all at affordable prices.

Creolina's (☎ 954-524-2003, 209 SW 2nd St; lunch mains $7-10, dinner mains $10-18; ☽ 11:30am-2:30pm Mon-Fri, 5-9pm Sun & Mon, 5-10pm Tue-Thu, 5-11pm Fri & Sat) Get transported to the backwaters of Louisiana for some serious Cajun and Creole dishes such as jambalaya at this Riverwalk hotspot. The Sunday New Orleans brunch is a wonderful choice.

Floridian (☎ 954-463-4041; 1410 E Las Olas Blvd; dishes $5-15; ☽ 24hr) This breakfast institution (also serving good round-the-clock diner food) has drawn fans since the late 1930s. It's particularly crowded on weekend mornings, with diners clamoring for huge omelettes and scrambled-egg concoctions.

Herban Kitchen (☎ 954-566-1110; 2823 E Oakland Park Blvd; mains $12-16; ☽ 4-10pm Tue-Sat) Especially popular with gay locals, this small, recently renovated storefront packs 'em in for a huge and diverse menu of Italian and Mediterranean basics, including grilled pork medallions, crab cakes, veal Milanese and eggplant parm, which are a great bargain, too, with soup, salad and dessert thrown in for free.

Lester's Diner (☎ 954-525-5641; 250 Hwy 84; dishes $6-8; ☽ 24hr) Universally hailed, endearingly, as a greasy spoon, campy Lester's has been keeping folks happy since the late 1960s. Everyone makes their way here at some point, from business types on cell phones and late-night clubbers to blue-haired ladies with third husbands.

Sublime: World Vegetarian Cuisine (☎ 954-615-1431; 1431 N Federal Hwy; mains $10-17; ☽ 5:30-9pm Sun-Thu, 5:30-10pm Fri-Sat) Vegans frustrated by Miami's lack of dining options will rejoice over this find – a vegan palace boasting a massive menu, a take-out café and a shopping boutique offering cruelty-free products from chips to soaps. The menu changes daily, but always reflects various world cuisines, with options such as ancho-orange glazed soy steak, pueblo corn enchiladas, red lentil-quinoa loaf and mushroom burgers, plus a slew of veggie sushi rolls and salads.

Zona Fresca (☎ 954-566-1777; 1635 N Federal Hwy; mains $3-7) The food may come quickly at this jumpin' highway stop, but Zona is no fast-food joint. Follow the local hipsters inside for cheap, fresh and delicious

Mexican eats, such as grilled-veggie or shrimp burritos, taco combo plates and tostada salads, washed down with some Mexican beer.

Top End

Café Martorano (☎ 954-561-2554; 3343 E Oakland Park Blvd; mains $15-30; ☽ 5-11pm) Pop into this newish spot for upscale, delicious Italian dinners featuring everything from fresh pastas to fish. Don't expect an intimate, romantic scene: it's loud, bustling and popular enough for people to wait an hour or two for a table, due to its no-reservations policy.

Canyon Southwest Café (☎ 954-765-1950; 1818 E Sunrise Blvd; mains $18-30) This popular eatery is Santa Fe–chic, specializing in tasty Southwestern fusion grub such as smoked-salmon tostadas and filet mignon with a rich poblano-pepper goat cheese. Don't miss the fine tequilas or the sweet prickly-pear margarita, which fuel the raucous din from late-night diners.

Chima (☎ 954-712-0580; 2400 E Las Olas Blvd; all-you-can-eat $35) Currently the trendiest eatery on the Las Olas strip, this new Brazilian steakhouse is drawing the hordes with its big-food concept, yummy offerings, sleek interior and romantic torch-lit courtyard. Start with the appetizer buffet, which could fill you up with its carpaccio, salads and blue-cheese mousse, but save room for the main draw: meat, and lots of it. There is meat, chicken and fish, cooked *churrascaria* style (over open-flame pits) and served, in abundance, by cowboys who slide them off skewers and onto your plate.

Himmarshee Bar & Grille (☎ 954-524-1818; 210 SW 2nd St; mains $16-25; ☽ 11am-2:30pm Mon-Fri, 6-10:30pm) This upscale yuppie place has creative burgers and imaginative American dishes. Outdoor tables are coveted, though the indoor mezzanine provides a perfect perch to people-watch at the bar, where there's always a hip scene unfolding.

Kitchenetta (☎ 954-567-3333; 2850 N Federal Hwy; mains $16-28) The interior is sleek-industrial – stainless-steel tables, high ceilings and cement floors – but the food at this new Italian delight is warm-delicious, with portions offered in either single or family servings. Start with made-to-order flatbread and a choice from the extensive wine list, then move on to linger over options such as tomato salad, risotto balls or macaroni with peas and prosciutto.

Mai Kai (☎ 954-563-3272; 3599 N Federal Hwy; mains $15-30; ⏰ 5-10:30pm Mon-Thu, 5-11:30pm Fri-Sat) This old-school Polynesian joint is pure kitsch – with some good food and amusing entertainment thrown in for good measure. Las Vegas–style shows ($9.95 additional) can accompany your weekend-evening meals, which range from Hawaiian chicken and seafood with noodles to the massive oak-roasted filet mignon Madagascar for two ($60). And don't forget the froofy cocktails, including run punch, pina passion and the potent 'mystery drink.'

Mark's Las Olas (☎ 954-463-1000; 1032 E Las Olas Blvd; mains $30-40; ⏰ 11:30am-2:30pm Mon-Fri, 6-10pm Sun-Thu, 6-11pm Fri & Sat) Mark's, an upscale dining room with excellent service, has been one of the most exceptional South Florida restaurants since it opened in 1994. From your cozy booth and mahogany table, you can gaze into the open kitchen, which lovingly churns out signature treats including cracked conch with black-bean mango salsa and vanilla rum butter sauce; crispy-skin yellowtail snapper with clams, mussels, chorizo and fennel; and pancetta-wrapped rabbit loin with soft polenta.

DRINKING

Fort Lauderdale bars can stay open until 4am on weekends and 2am during the week. For gay and lesbian venues, see the boxed text, below.

Blue Martini Lounge (☎ 954-653-2583; 2432 E Sunrise Blvd) A yuppified sip spot in the Galleria Mall, this sleek lounge strives for sophistication with low lighting and dozens of specialty martinis, from Almond Joy to Green Demon.

Dicey Riley's (☎ 954-522-2202; 217 SW 2nd St) At this standard Irish pub expect traditional cuisine and draft Guinness, Bass and others. Dicey's is particularly packed on weekends, but traditional and contemporary live Irish tunes headline Tuesday to Saturday.

Elbo Room (☎ 954-563-7889; 3339 N Federal Hwy) This dive bar achieved immortality thanks to the 1960s classic *Where the Boys Are*. It hit its stride during the Spring Break years, but keeps itself going with plenty of drink specials that attract the young elbow-bending set.

Golden Lyon Bar (☎ 954-467-0671; Riverside Hotel, 620 E Las Olas Blvd) This mellow alternative features a cabaret-like piano bar scene and swank cocktails.

Howl at the Moon (☎ 954-522-7553; 17 N Fort Lauderdale Beach Blvd) Part of the popular Beach Place complex, this fun spot has folks playing piano and inebriated revelers singing along.

Maguire's Hill (☎ 954-764-4453; 535 N Andrews Ave) Another classic Irish pub, this one has Irish bands Thursday to Sunday.

O'Hara's Jazz Café (☎ 954-524-1764; 722 E Las Olas Blvd) For nightly jazz – and occasional rhythm-and-blues or pop performances – paired with cool cocktails and a

---

Gay & Lesbian Fort Lauderdale

What Cherry Grove is to its neighbor, the Fire Island Pines, Fort Lauderdale is to South Beach – a little more rainbow-flag-oriented and a little less exclusive. And for the hordes of gay boys who flock here, either to party or to settle down, therein lies the charm. You don't need to be A-list to feel at home at any of the many gay bars, clubs or restaurants here, and you won't have any trouble finding 'the scene.' Fort Lauderdale is home to more than 25 gay bars and clubs; about a dozen gay guest houses; and a couple of way-gay residential hubs, including Victoria Park, which is the more established gay ghetto, and Wilton Manors, more recently gay-gentrified and boasting endless nightlife options, including the very popular **Hamburger Mary's** (☎ 954-567-1320; 2449 Wilton Dr) and **Georgie's Alibi** (☎ 954-565-2626; 2266 Wilton Dr). Even the Miami boys make the trip here for the dance parties held at **Coliseum** (☎ 954-832-0100; 2520 S Federal Hwy), especially on Saturdays, when circuit DJs such as Monty Q and Brett Henrichsen blow in for gigs. The neighboring **Copa** (2800 S Federal Hwy) is also a big hit. For information on everything queer here, stop by the helpful **Gay & Lesbian Community Center** (☎ 954-463-9005; www.glccftl.org; 1717 N Andrews Ave), which provides information, meeting space and events such as bingo parties. To shop for hot duds (from hot dudes), try the exclusive T-shirts, jeans, belts and accessories at the **Ruff Riders** (☎ 954-828-1401; 918 N Federal Hwy) boutique, which has a cultish following at its Provincetown location up north. Gay guest houses are plentiful; see Sleeping (p210) for some suggestions, or visit www.gayftlauderdale.com. And consult the glossy, weekly listings rag *Hot Spots* to keep updated on the best of gay nightlife; it's available at local gay bars, inns and eateries

small bar menu, head to this warm, comfortable place after 9pm.

Parrot Lounge (☎ 954-563-1493; 911 Sunrise Ln) A mainstay since the 1970s, this popular dive bar draws a beer-and-peanuts kind of crowd.

Poor House (☎ 954-522-5145; 110 SW 3rd Ave) Enjoy great microbrews, diverse live music and a multigenerational crowd.

Shooters (☎ 954-566-2855; 3033 NE 32nd Ave) It's old-school Fort Lauderdale raucousness in here, with lots of great live music, waterfront views and strong drinks.

Village Pump (☎ 954-776-5840; 4404 El Mar Dr) This is a fun local dive bar, serving full meals throughout the day.

GETTING THERE & AROUND

The **Fort Lauderdale–Hollywood International Airport** (FLL; ☎ 954-359-1200; www.fll.net) is served by more than 35 airlines, including some with nonstop flights from Europe. It's so hassle-free and accessible that many Miami-bound visitors choose to fly in and out of here instead. **Jet Blue** (www.jetblue.com) has great fares from New York's Kennedy and LaGuardia airports. From the airport, it's a 20-minute drive to downtown, or a $16 cab ride. By boat, the **Port Everglades Authority** (☎ 954-523-3404) runs the enormous Port Everglades cruise port (the second busiest in the world after Miami). From the port, walk to SE 17th St and take bus No 40 to the beach or to Broward Central Terminal. If you're coming here in your own boat (not unlikely here), head for the **Radisson Bahia Mar Yacht Center** (☎ 954-764-2233). By bus, the **Greyhound station** (☎ 954-764-6551; www.greyhound.com; 515 NE 3rd St at Federal Hwy) is about four blocks from Broward Central Terminal, the central transfer point for buses in the Fort Lauderdale area. Buses to Miami leave throughout the day ($5 one-way, 30 to 60 minutes) but, depending on when you arrive, you might have to wait as long as 2½ hours for the next one. By train, **Tri-Rail** (☎ 800-874-7245; www.tri-rail.com) runs between Miami and Fort Lauderdale ($6.75 round-trip, 45 minutes). A feeder system of buses has connections for no extra charge. Free parking is provided at most stations. The **Amtrak** (☎ 800-872-7245; www.amtrak.com) passenger trains also run on Tri-Rail tracks. The **Fort Lauderdale station** (200 SW 21st Tce) is just south of Broward Blvd and just west of I-95. If you're driv-

Palm Beach & West Palm Beach

Looking for something a little glitzier than the spoils of Lauderdale? Then by all means, hop into your rental car and head due north for about 45 minutes and you'll encounter the Beverly Hills of the east: Palm Beach, a haven for the very wealthy. There's not much to do here but gawk – at the sprawling oceanfront mansions (including Trump's Mar-a-Lago, on Southern Blvd at S Ocean Blvd), gorgeous salty seascapes and fancy shop windows lining the aptly named **Worth Avenue**, the local Rodeo Drive. The historical **Henry Morrison Flagler Museum** (1 Whitehall Way) is also worth a look, as is the classic **Breakers** (1 South County Rd) – Flagler's opulent oceanfront hotel where you could opt for a room ($260 and way up) and stay the night.

Just across the waterway, back on the mainland, is the much more accessible West Palm Beach, fast becoming a hip and happening place to shop, dine and hobnob with martinis. **CityPlace** (700 Rosemary Ave), similar to Coconut Grove's CocoWalk, is an alfresco mall and dining complex that has unfortunately become the center of West Palm's universe. Still, it has a breezy, friendly vibe and isn't far from the well-regarded **Norton Museum of Art** (1451 S Olive Ave). To make it a night, check in to West Palm's coolest inn: **Hotel Biba** (320 Belvedere Rd; r $120-180), a sleek boutique hotel sporting a chic and popular wine bar, to boot.

ing here, I-95 and Florida's Turnpike run north–south. The major east–west artery, I-595, intersects I-95, Florida's Turnpike and the Sawgrass Expressway. It also feeds into I-75, which runs to Florida's west coast.

Once you're in town, driving provides the best way to access every part of spread-out Fort Lauderdale. But the flatness here makes it easy to get around by bike. Check with your hotel – many have bikes to loan or rent. **TMAX** (☎ 954-761-3543), a free shuttle with service every 15 minutes or so, runs between downtown sights, between the beach and E Las Olas Blvd and the Riverfront, and between Tri-Rail and E Las Olas Blvd and the beaches. Finally, the fun **Water Taxi** (☎ 954-467-6677; www.watertaxi.com; 651 Seabreeze Blvd) plies the canals and waterways between 17th St to the south, Atlantic Blvd/Pompano Beach to the north, the New River to the west and the Atlantic Ocean to the east. A $5 daily pass entitles you to unlimited rides.

Directory

Directory

TRANSPORTATION

AIR

Miami is served by nearly 100 airlines via two main airports: **Miami International Airport** (MIA) and the **Fort Lauderdale-Hollywood International Airport** (FLL), half an hour north. **MIA** (☎ 305-876-7000; www.miami-mia.com) is the third busiest airport (after JFK and LaGuardia in New York City) in the country. Just 6 miles west of Downtown, the airport is open 24 hours and is laid out in a horseshoe design; it's a quick cinch to get there from just about anyplace in Miami, especially from Mid-Beach. If you're driving, just follow the Julia Tuttle Causeway, or I-195, west until you hit Rte 112, which goes directly into the airport. Other options include the free shuttles offered by most hotels, a taxi ($27 flat rate to South Beach; metered, from South Beach, is only about $10), the Airport Owl night-only public bus, or the **SuperShuttle** (☎ 800-874-8885; www.supershuttle.com) shared-van service, which will cost about $14 to South Beach. Be sure to reserve a seat the day before. There are left-luggage facilities on two concourses at MIA, between B and C and on G; prices vary according to bag size.

The **Fort Lauderdale-Hollywood International Airport** (☎ 954-359-1200; www.broward.org/airport; 320 Terminal Dr), about 30 miles north of Miami just off I-95, often serves as a lower-cost alternative to MIA, especially because it's serviced by popular, cut-rate flyers including Southwest Airlines and JetBlue. Put the money you save toward getting to Miami once you land; either rent a car at one of the many Fort Lauderdale agencies (opposite), or take the free shuttle from terminals one and three to the airport's **Tri-Rail** (☎ 800-874-7245; www.tri-rail.com) station; you can ride this commuter train into Miami. The schedule is infrequent, though, so you may want to opt for the **Bahama Link** (☎ 800-854-2182; 1-2 people $45-60) shared-van service or the cheaper **SuperShuttle** (☎ 800-874-8885; www.supershuttle.com), which will cost about $25 to South Beach.

BICYCLE

Miami may be flat as a pancake, but it's also plagued by traffic backups and speedy thoroughfares, so judge the bikeability of your desired route carefully. It's a perfectly sensible option in South Beach, though, as well as through most Miami Beach 'hoods and, of course, on Key Biscayne. Use a sturdy U-type bike lock, as mere chains and padlocks do not deter people in these parts.

Bicycles are allowed only on specific Metrorail or Tri-Rail bus routes; you can also bike across the causeways. There are several places in South Beach and on Key Biscayne to rent bicycles for a fee of about $20 a day; see p129.

BOAT

Though it's doubtful you'll be catching a steamer to make a trans-Atlantic journey, it is quite possible that you'll arrive in Miami via a cruise ship, as the **Port of Miami** (Map pp252–3; ☎ 305-371-7678; www.miamidade.gov/portofmiami), which received nearly four million passengers in 2003, is known as the 'cruise capital of the world.' Arriving in the port will put you on the edge of Downtown Miami; taxis and public buses to other local points are available from nearby Biscayne Blvd.

BUS

Greyhound (☎ 800-231-2222; www.greyhound.com) is the major carrier in and out of town. There are four major terminals: **Airport terminal** (☎ 305-871-1810; 4111 NW 27th St); **Main Downtown terminal** (Map pp252–3; ☎ 305-374-6160; 100 NW 6th St); **North Miami terminal** (Map pp244–5; ☎ 305-945-0801; 16560 NE 6th Ave);

and the **Southern Miami terminal** (Map pp244–5; ☎ 305-296-9072; Cutler Ridge Mall, 20,505 S Dixie Hwy). There are several buses daily each to New York City ($115 one-way, 27 to 30 hours) and Washington, DC ($109, 23 to 25 hours); five to New Orleans ($95, 20 to 22 hours); and 10 daily to Atlanta ($95, 16 to 18 hours).

The local bus system is called **Metrobus** (☎ 305-770-3131; www.miamidade.gov/transit) and, though it has an extensive route system, know that you may very well spend more time waiting for a bus than you will riding on one. Each bus route has a different schedule and routes generally run from about 5:30am to about 11pm, though some are 24 hours. Rides cost $1.25 and must be paid in exact change with a token, coins or a combination of a dollar bill and coins (most locals use the monthly Metropass). An easy-to-read route map is available online.

In South Beach, an excellent option is the **Electrowave** (☎ 305-535-9160), an electric, nonpolluting shuttle bus with disabled-rider access that operates along Washington Ave (as well as sections of 5th St, West Ave and 17th St) between South Pointe Dr and 17th St. Rides cost only 25¢ and come along every few minutes between 8am-1am Mon-Sat and 10am-1am Sun and holidays. Look for official bus stops, every couple of blocks, marked by posts with colorful Electrowave signs.

Coral Gables has its own new shuttle in the form of a hybrid-electric bus disguised as a Trolley. It's free, but good for getting around Gables only. Its north–south route runs along Ponce de León Blvd from the Douglas Metrorail Station to SW 8th St (between 6:30am and 8pm Monday to Thursday, 6:30am to 11pm Friday), while the east–west twilight route runs along Miracle Mile from Anderson Rd to Douglas Rd (between 3pm and 7pm Monday to Thursday, 3pm until 10pm Friday). Trolleys run about every 10 to 15 minutes.

CAR & MOTORCYCLE

Finding your way here from other points in the USA is not hard; follow any other major Interstate to I-95 south, which will eventually take you directly into Downtown Miami. Be aware that gasoline prices are not so cheap these days: in early 2005 they averaged $2 a gallon (a bit less than 4L) in Miami. From New York, expect a 19-hour trip without stops. And remember that speed limits change from state to state.

The urban sprawl of metro Miami means that most visitors, unless staying in one neighborhood, will end up driving. Though getting around is quite easy to figure out, do expect serious rush hour traffic from 7am to 9am and 4pm to 6pm weekdays, as well as constant snarls along Collins Ave and Ocean Dr during high season, especially on weekends.

Vehicle Rentals

All the big operators, and a host of smaller or local ones, have bases in the Miami/Fort Lauderdale area, and advance reservations are advisable, especially in high season. For motorcycles, try **Harley Davidson Rentals** (Map pp246–7; ☎ 305-673-8113; 1770 Bay Rd, South Beach). Car rental companies in the area include the following:

Alamo (☎ 800-327-9633; www.alamo.com)

Avis (☎ 800-831-2847; www.avis.com)

Budget (☎ 800-527-0700; www.budget.com)

Continental (☎ 305-871-4663; www.continentalcar.com)

Thrifty (☎ 800-367-2277; www.thrifty.com)

Rental rates in Florida tend to be lower than in other big American cities, though they do fluctuate, depending on the company, day of the week and the season. Expect to pay about $200 a week for a typical economy car at most times; around the Christmas-holiday time, however, you could pay upwards of $900 a week for the same vehicle. Phone around to compare prices, and know that booking ahead usually ensures the best rates. Most companies include unlimited mileage at no extra cost, but taxes and a host of surcharges increase the final bill, as could insurance. While many credit cards cover a loss/damage waiver, or LDW, (sometimes called a collision/damage waiver, or CDW), meaning that you don't pay if you damage the car, as well as liability insurance, you should make *absolutely* certain before driving in the litigious USA.

Bring your driver's license if you intend to rent a car; visitors from some countries may find it wise to back up their national license with an International Driving Permit, available from many local auto clubs (including the Automobile Association of America, www.aaa.com). Most operators require that you be at least 25 years of age and have a major credit card in your own name.

Navigating

Miami Beach is linked to the mainland by four causeways built over Biscayne Bay. They are, from south to north: the MacArthur (also the extension of US Hwy 41 and Hwy A1A), Venetian (50¢ toll), Julia Tuttle and John F Kennedy. The most important north–south highway is I-95, which ends at US Hwy 1 south of Downtown. US Hwy 1, which runs from Key West all the way north to Maine, hugs the coastline. It's called Dixie Hwy south of Downtown and Biscayne Blvd north of Downtown. The Palmetto Expressway (Hwy 826) makes a rough loop around the city and spurs off below SW 40th St to the Don Shula Expressway (Hwy 874, a toll road). Florida's Turnpike Extension makes the most western outer loop around the city. Hwy A1A becomes Collins Ave in Miami Beach.

Besides the causeways to Miami Beach, the major east–west roads are SW 8th St (also called Calle Ocho in Little Havana and the Tamiami Trail west of the city); Hwy 112 (also called Airport Expressway); and Hwy 836 (also called Dolphin Expressway), which slices through Downtown and connects with I-395 and the MacArthur Causeway, and which runs west to the Palmetto Expressway and Florida's Turnpike Extension.

Parking

Though it can get annoying (especially when you have to feed quarters into meters), parking around town is pretty straightforward. Regulations are well-signed and meters are plentiful (except perhaps on holiday-weekend evenings in South Beach). The situation Downtown, near the Bayside Marketplace, is cheap but a bit confusing: you must find a place in the head-on parking lots, buy a ticket from a central machine, and display it in your windshield.

On Miami Beach there's metered street parking along Washington & Collins Aves and Ocean Dr – and on most other streets (except Lincoln Rd and residential areas). Meters are enforced from 9am to midnight. Most allow you to pay for up to three hours. If you use a meter, be sure you're armed with quarters – or use the much more civilized Meter Card options, available from the **Miami Beach City Hall** (Map pp246–7; 1st fl, 1700 Convention Center Dr); the **Chamber of Commerce** (Map pp246–7; 1920 Meridian Ave); any municipal parking lot or any Publix grocery store. Denominations come in $10, $20 and $25 (and meters cost $1 per hour).

There are many municipal parking garages, which are usually the easiest and cheapest option; look for giant blue 'P' signs. Find them at Collins Ave at 7th St, Collins Ave at 14th St, Washington Ave at 12th St, Washington Ave at 16th St, and 17th St across from the Jackie Gleason Theater of the Performing Arts (perfect if you're headed to Lincoln Rd). If you park illegally or if the meter runs out, parking fines are about $20, but a tow could cost $75.

TAXI

Outside of MIA and the Port of Miami where taxis buzz around like bees at a hive, you will use a phone to hail a cab. A consortium of drivers has banded together and formed a **Dispatch Service** (☎ 305-888-4444) for a ride. If the dispatch service is busy, try **Metro** (☎ 305-888-8888), **Sunshine** (☎ 305-445-3333) or **Yellow** (☎ 305-444-4444).

Taxis in Miami have flat and metered rates. The metered fare is $3.90 for the first mile, and $2.20 each additional mile. You will not have to pay extra for luggage or extra people in the cab, though you are expected to tip an additional 10% to 15%.

If you have a bad experience, get the driver's chauffeur license number, name and license plate number and contact the **Taxi Complaints Line** (☎ 305-375-2460).

TRAIN

The main Miami terminal of **Amtrak** (☎ 305-835-1222, 800-872-7245; www.amtrak.com; 8303 NW 37th Ave) connects the city with the rest of continental USA and Canada. Travel time between New York and Miami is a severe 27 to 30 hours and costs $99 to $246 one-way. The Miami Amtrak station has a left luggage station, which costs $2 per bag.

Around Miami the **Metromover** (www.miami dade.gov/transit), equal parts bus, monorail and train, is helpful for getting around the Downtown area. It offers visitors a great perspective on the city and a cheap – it's free! – orientation tour of the area (see p81). The one- and two-car, rubber-wheeled, computer-controlled (and therefore driverless) vehicles operate on three lines on two elevated-track 'loops,' covering Downtown as far south as the Financial District Station of Brickell Ave and as far north as the School Board Station up on NW 15th St and NE 1st Ave. You can transfer to the Metrorail at Government Center.

Metrorail (www.miamidade.gov/transit), meanwhile, is a 21-mile-long heavy rail system that has one elevated line running from Hialeah through Downtown Miami and south to Kendall/Dadeland. Trains run every five to 15 minutes from 6am to midnight. The fare is

$1.25, or $1 with a Metromover transfer. The regional **Tri-Rail** (☎ 800-874-7245; www.tri-rail .com) double-decker commuter trains run the 71 miles between Dade, Broward and Palm Beach counties. For longer trips, to Palm Beach, for instance, Tri-Rail is very inefficient. Fares are calculated on a zone basis, and the route spans six zones. The shortest distance traveled costs $3.50 round-trip. The most you'll ever pay is for the ride between MIA and West Palm Beach ($9.25 round-trip). No tickets are sold on the train, so allow time to make your purchase before boarding. All trains and stations are accessible to riders with disabilities. For a list of stations, go to the Tri-Rail website.

PRACTICALITIES

ACCOMMODATIONS

The Sleeping chapter of this book (p150) lists mid- to high-range accommodations in alphabetical order by neighborhood, with each list followed by some Cheap Sleeps options, meaning places that charge under $150 per night. (When we refer to efficiencies, we mean very small, one-room apartments with kitchenettes.) You'll pay about $200 for a midrange place and $300 and up for high-range. Prices vary depending on the time of year, with high season (defined in the Miami hotel business as the time between December and April) being the costliest time of the year. A typical check-in time is 2pm or 3pm, with check-out time at either 11am or noon. For a guide to websites and booking services that offer discounts off hotels' rack rates – the official, published rates – see boxed text, p150.

You could also consider an apartment rental for longer stays, thriftiness and use of a kitchen. **Interhome** (☎ 305-940-2299; www .interhome.com), **Vacation Home Rentals Worldwide** (☎ 800-633-3284) or **Craig's List** (http://miami .craigslist.org) are a few places to start.

BUSINESS HOURS

Office hours in Miami operate on the usual 9am to 5pm Monday to Friday schedule, with some larger branches having Saturday morning hours. Shops usually stay open later, depending on the neighborhood, with 9pm being the typical closing time in malls or other shopping districts. Some restaurants close on Mondays, while many nightclubs only operate from Wednesday or Thursday through the weekend.

CHILDREN

Miami is very kid-friendly. All the public parks and recreation areas help, too, along with the attractions that star animals, from **Seaquarium** (p68) to **Parrot Jungle** (p78). Rainy-day activities abound, and include the new **Miami Children's Museum** (p76). See the boxed text on p77 for detailed advice. And just be sure to check with your hotel – especially if it's in South Beach – to make sure it's kid-friendly and not too full of loud partiers.

For more information, advice and anecdotes, read *South Florida Parenting Magazine*, available at major booksellers, and Lonely Planet's *Travel with Children* by Cathy Lanigan.

Baby-sitting

When it's time to head out for some adult time, check with your hotel, as many offer child-care services – especially the big resorts, including the Four Seasons, Loews, the Conrad and the Fontainebleau Hilton. The local **Nanny Poppinz** (☎ 305-607-1170; www.nannypoppinz.com) will do the job for $10 per hour.

CLIMATE

Ideal conditions exist between December and May, when temperatures average between 60°F and 85°F (16°C and 30°C), and average rainfall is a scant 2.14in per month. Summer is very hot and humid, with thunderstorms rolling in at 3pm or 4pm – not to mention the

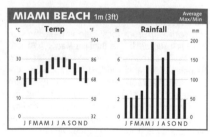

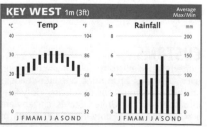

constant threat of hurricanes. June is the raini-est month, while August is the hottest (in an oppressive sort of way). You can call ☎ 305-229-4522 for a weather report. See the climate chart (p219), as well as the Environment section (p25), for more information.

COURSES

It never hurts to learn a thing or two while you're on vacation – especially if it's a skill that could come in particularly handy while you're here. For up-to-date listings of general classes, seminars and lectures on a variety of topics, visit www.miamiintelligence.com.

Salsa Dancing

Going out to a Latin club and being a wall-flower feels awful. Drop into a class or two at **Latin Rhythm Studios** (☎ 305-552-9110; 9704 Coral Way; per class $6) or **Latin Heat Salsa Studio** (☎ 305-868-9418; www.latin-heat.com; Miami Beach locations vary; per class $10).

Spanish

Take a crash course in the language at **Miami English Center** (Map pp248–9; ☎ 305-815-4271; www.miamispanishclasses.com; 1210 Washington Ave; monthly classes) or the **University of Miami** (Map pp256–7; ☎ 305-284-4727; 7-day intensives). Or head to Miami for total immersion classes in Little Havana at **Amerispan** (☎ 800-879-6640).

Cooking

You can learn from local celeb chefs through various programs: the **Burdines-Macy's** (☎ 305-662-3550; admission free; ⊙ 1pm) in both **Aventura** (p142) and **Dadeland** (p147) malls offer Saturday afternoon classes for the public, with a different local chef each week (a recent lec-turer was chef Tom Parlo of Azul); also, the Ritz-Carlton South Beach offers weekly Saturday classes, kitchen tours and lunch with executive chef Thomas Connell (Map pp246–7; ☎ 786-276-4033; 1 Lincoln Rd at Collins Ave; admission $95; ⊙ 11am-2pm).

CUSTOMS

United States customs allows each person over the age of 21 to bring one liter of liquor and 200 cigarettes or 50 cigars, duty-free, into the country. United States citizens are allowed to import, duty-free, $400 worth of gifts from abroad, while non-US citizens are allowed to bring in $100 worth. United States law permits you to bring in, or take out, as much as US$10,000 in American or foreign currency, traveler's checks or letters of credit without formality. Larger amounts of any or all of the above – there are no limits – must be declared to customs. It's forbidden to bring in to the USA chocolate liqueurs, porn-ography, lottery tickets and items with fake brand names, among other sundry items. For a complete and ever-changing list, visit www .customs.ustreas.gov.

Due to Miami's infamous popularity as a drug-smuggling gateway, customs officers in Miami are known to be quite thorough in their examination of backpackers and other travel-ers who may fit a particular profile. They may not be very polite – but you should be, and you should dress neatly and carry lots of trav-eler's checks and credit cards, or show other signs of prosperity lest they think you're here to work illegally.

DISABLED TRAVELERS

Miami is mainly wheelchair friendly, although many Deco District doorways may be too tight. Many buses, all Tri-Rail trains and stations, and Metromovers are wheelchair accessible. Special-needs travelers can contact the Metro-Dade Transit Agency **Special Transportation Service** (STS; ☎ 305-263-5406), which provides door-to-door transportation for disabled people; contact them a few weeks before your visit since the application process takes a bit of time.

The **Deaf Services Bureau** (☎ 305-668-4407, 800-955-8770; Suite 760, 1320 S Dixie Hwy) has inter-preters and an information and referral service. The **Florida Relay Service** (☎ 305-579-8644, TDD 800-955-8771, voice 800-955-8770, customer service 800-955-8013) connects TDD (Telecom-munication Device for the Deaf) users to people without TDDs, 24 hours a day. For information for the blind, contact the **Lighthouse for the Blind** (☎ 305-856-2288; 601 SW 8th Ave).

A number of organizations and tour op-erators specialize in serving disabled travelers. Among them are the **Access-Able Travel Source** (☎ 303-232-2979; www.access-able.com), an excellent website with many links; **Society for Accessible Travel & Hospitality** (SATH; ☎ 212-447-7284; www.sath.org), which lobbies for better facilities and publishes *Open World* magazine; and **Travelin' Talk Network** (☎ 615-552-6670; www .travelintalk.net), which offers a global network of people providing services to the disabled.

DISCOUNT CARDS

If you qualify, you can sometimes use an International Student Identity Card (ISIC) for discounts to museums, tourist attractions and on some airfares. And parents, take note: the new South Florida Parenting Kids Fun Pass, a promotional tool of *South Florida Parenting* magazine, is now available at all Publix supermarkets and the information booths at the Dadeland Mall. Each pass is $11.95 and grants free entry for kids 12 and under (when accompanied by a full-paying adult) to a slew of family attractions including **Miami Metrozoo** (p77), the **Gold Coast Railroad Museum** (p76), **Miami Children's Museum** (p76), **Miami Seaquarium** (p68) and many more.

ELECTRICITY

Electric current in the USA is 110V to 115V, 60Hz. Outlets may be suited for flat two- or three-prong plugs. If your appliance is made for another electrical system, you will need a transformer or adapter; if you didn't bring one along, check any major drugstore, hardware or electronics store.

EMBASSIES
US Embassies & Consulates Abroad

In addition to those listed here, US embassies and consulates overseas can be found at http://usembassy.state.gov.

Australia (☎ 2-6214-5600, 21 Moonah Place, Yarralumla, ACT 2600; ☎ 2-9373-9200, Level 59 MLC Center, 19-29 Martin Place, Sydney, NSW 2000; ☎ 3-9526-5900, 553 St Kilda Rd, Melbourne, Victoria 3004)

Canada (☎ 613-238-5335, 490 Sussex Dr, Ottawa, Ontario, K1N 1G8; ☎ 604-685-4311, 1095 W Pender St, Vancouver, BC, V6E 2M6; ☎ 514-398-9695, 1155 Rue St-Alexandre, Montréal, Québec, H2Z 1Z2)

France (☎ 1-4312-2222, 2 Av Gabriel, 75382 Paris)

Germany (☎ 30-238-5174, Neustaedtische Kirchstrasse 4-5, 10017 Berlin)

Japan (☎ 3-224-5000, 1-10-5 Akasaka, Minato-ku, Tokyo)

Mexico (☎ 5-209-9100, Paseo de la Reforma 305, Cuauhtémoc, 06500 Mexico City)

Spain (☎ 1-91587-2200, Calle Serrano 75, 28006 Madrid)

UK (☎ 020-7499-9000, 24/31 Grosvenor Sq, London W1A 1AE; ☎ 131-556-8315, 3 Regent Tce, Edinburgh EH7 5BW; ☎ 2890-328-239, Queens House, 14 Queens St, Belfast BT1 6EQ)

Embassies & Consulates in Miami

Check under consulates in the telephone book for diplomatic representation here. Most consulates are in Miami, but a few are in Coral Gables. Citizens of Australia and New Zealand may contact the **British consulate** (Map pp252–3) or the **Canadian consulate** (Map pp252–3) for emergency assistance, as neither country maintains consular offices in Miami.

EMERGENCY

Dial ☎ 911 for police, fire and medical emergencies, which is a free call from any phone. The inside front cover of the Miami *White Pages* lists a slew of emergency numbers. Some useful ones include the following:

Beach Patrol (☎ 305-673-7711)

Coast Guard Search (☎ 305-535-4314)

Hurricane Hotline (☎ 305-229-4483)

Poison Information Center (☎ 800-282-3171)

Rape Hotline (☎ 305-585-7273)

Suicide Intervention (☎ 305-358-4357)

GAY & LESBIAN TRAVELERS

LGBT visitors account for nearly $100 million in annual revenues to the Miami area. Expect to feel comfortable being open with your same-sex partner – holding hands, canoodling and other usual displays of affection won't raise an eyebrow in most places or with most hotel check-in clerks, especially in South Beach. For information on gay businesses, get the *Miami Gay & Lesbian Yellow Pages,* widely available at South Beach shops, or visit their website at www.glyp.com and click on 'Miami.' Or give a call to the **South Beach Business Guild** (☎ 305-534-3336), a sort of LGBT chamber of commerce. Local gay publications include *The Weekly News, Express Gay News, Hot Spots, Scoop* and *Wire.* Find them all, and much more, at the gay bookstore **Lambda Passage** (Map p251; ☎ 305-754-6900; 7545 Biscayne Blvd, North Miami).

HOLIDAYS

Below are national or public holidays – days on which you can expect government offices (and some restaurants and shops) to be closed.

New Year's Day January 1

Martin Luther King Jr Day Third Monday in January

Presidents Day Third Monday in February

Easter A Sunday in March or April

Memorial Day Last Monday in May

Independence Day July 4

Labor Day First Monday in September

Columbus Day Second Monday in October

Veterans Day November 11

Thanksgiving Fourth Thursday in November

Christmas December 25

INTERNET ACCESS

Finding access to your email is a cinch in this technologically savvy city. The majority of hotels and hostels these days have either computers for you to log onto or wireless service that's free or cheap to its laptop-toting guests. You can also find plenty of strong connections at places including **public libraries** (☎ 305-535-4219; www.mdpls.org) and Internet cafés. Wireless Fidelity (WiFi) hotspots are also becoming quite commonplace; for a list of hotspots visit www.wi-fihotspotlist.com and click on Miami.

Though you won't have any trouble finding an Internet café in your travels, here are two suggestions: **Kafka's Inc** (☎ 305-673-9669; 1464 Washington Ave; per hr $6), **D'Vine Cyber Lounge** (Map pp248–9; ☎ 305-534-1414; 910 Collins Ave; per hr $5, WiFi per hr $3).

LEGAL MATTERS

Florida law tends to be tougher than most states north when it comes to drug possession, with dozens of people arrested on minor drug charges each week. If you are approached by a police officer, just use common sense: be polite and do what they ask – up to a point; you are to be presumed innocent until proven guilty in a court of law, and you cannot be searched without good reason. If you are arrested, you must be read your rights under the Miranda Law. Whatever you do, don't try to bribe the officer – that's a crime.

To purchase alcohol or cigarettes you must be at least 21; to drive or give sexual consent you must be 17. Know that it's illegal to walk around on the street with an open alcoholic drink – beer, liquor, frozen cocktail, whatever – even though you'll see tipsy tourists doing it. If you're driving, all liquor has to be unopened (not just sealed, but new and untouched) and stored in the trunk. Florida's drunk-driving laws are among the toughest in the country. Driving under the influence of alcohol (technically a

0.08 blood-alcohol content) or drugs in Florida carries a $5000 fine in addition to suspension of your license and possibly imprisonment.

MAPS

All rental car companies are required by law to hand out decent city and area maps when they rent a car. But you can purchase ones that are even better: Rand McNally, AAA and Dolph Map Company all make maps of the Miami area, and Lonely Planet produces a laminated foldout map of the Miami area that includes Key West and Fort Lauderdale. The best free map is from the **Greater Miami & the Beaches Convention & Visitors Bureau** (p226).

MEDIA

News junkies in Miami have plenty to keep them satiated – a top-rated daily newspaper, public radio and alternative newsweeklies. Expect a vaguely left-leaning editorial bias, like in most big cities, but a more conservative (as in anti-Castro) one in some Spanish-language papers.

Newspapers & Magazines

The best is the much-lauded *Miami Herald*, which covers local, national and international news and began achieving fame back in the late '80s and early '90s when the murder rate was at its peak. Writers from the *Herald* – Edna Buchanan, Carl Hiassen and the just-retired columnist Dave Barry – have achieved national fame, and coverage is go-getter. It doesn't have much competition, though, with other daily newspapers including the *Sun-Sentinel*, covering South Florida, plus the Spanish-language dailies *El Nuevo Herald* and *Diario Las Americas*. The hip, alternative take on goings-on include the weeklies the *Street* and the *Miami New Times*, both free, politically progressive and heavy on arts and entertainment coverage. The *Biscayne Boulevard Times*, a free weekly, is a great source of local news on the mainland, as is *Miami Today News*, a community-news daily.

There are several good local magazines: the excellent *ML: Miami Living Magazine*, a glossy filled with quirky features and food and nightlife listings; *Home Miami*, about real estate and home design; and *Loft*, about the visual arts and design scene.

Television & Radio

Local TV news is about as cheesy as in any other American municipality, but there is a local cable channel that's oddly mesmerizing – the Beach Channel (www.thebeachchannel .tv), on channel 19, which is a 24-hour broadcast, like a constant infomercial, of quirky programs about what's going on in Miami Beach, from dining to real estate. Also, the local Public Broadcasting Station, WLRN, is on cable 17 and satellite 20. You'll find quality documentaries, series and local programs, including *Art Street,* about the South Florida arts scene.

Radio options are quite good: 91.3-FM WLRN is the public NPR affiliate, with intelligent discussion shows, both national and local, as well as jazz music; 90.5-FM WVUM is the University of Miami's alternative-rock station; and 88.9-FM WDNA is the community public radio station. Also tune into 1320-AM WLQY for French and Creole news and 96-FM for hip-hop.

MEDICAL SERVICES
Clinics

For physician referrals 24 hours daily, contact the **Visitor's Medical Line** (☎ 305-674-2222) of the Mount Sinai Medical Center. The **Miami Beach Community Health Center** (Map pp248–9; ☎ 305-538-8835; 710 Alton Rd; ☺ 7am-3:30pm Mon-Fri) charges fees based on your income. Arrive early since walk-in clinic lines are usually very long. Bring ID. If you're foreign born, bring your passport and I-94 card, the arrival/departure document for nonimmigrant visitors that's issued by the Immigration & Naturalization Service (INS). United States citizens should bring proof of residence and income. For more information, contact the INS (☎ 305-536-574; 7880 Biscayne Blvd). If you need dental attention, try ☎ 800-DENTIST (☎ 800-336-8478), a free referral service.

Emergency Rooms

In a serious emergency, call ☎ 911 for an ambulance to take you to the nearest hospital's emergency room (ER). **Mount Sinai Medical Center** (Map p251; ☎ 305-674-2121; 4300 Alton Rd) is the area's best. Whatever your deal is – visitor, no insurance, etc – the hospital must treat you. But, in return, you must eventually pay. And the ER fees are stellar: Mount Sinai charges a *minimum* ER fee of $300. Then there are additional charges for X rays, casting, medicines, analysis…*everything,* so the cost of a visit can easily top $1000.

MONEY

Formerly one of the strongest currencies in the world, the US dollar (US$ or just $) has recently been worth about half of its former equal, the Euro (take note, Europeans); it's still worth more than most South American, South Asian or Canadian currencies, though. The dollar is divided into 100 cents (100¢) with coins of one cent (penny), five cents (nickel), 10 cents (dime), 25 cents (quarter) and relatively rare 50 cents (half dollar). There are even a few gold-colored $1 coins in circulation.

Bank notes are called bills. Be sure to check the corners for amounts, as they're all the same size and color. Circulated bills come in denominations of $1, $5, $10, $20, $50 and $100. The US has two designs of bills in circulation, but you'd have to study them closely to notice. On the newer bills the portrait is bigger and off-center.

There are three straightforward ways to handle payments: cash, US-dollar traveler's checks (just as good as cash, but replaceable if lost or stolen) and credit/debit cards. The ubiquitous ATMs facilitate the process of acquiring cash; find them on just about any corner – in banks, delis, supermarkets, even some restaurants and nightclubs. Most accept bank cards from the Plus and Cirrus systems, and also charge you a slight fee (from $1 to $2.50) if you're not at your own bank. Credit/debit cards are the simplest option; easy to carry and accepted just about everywhere.

If you prefer cash, try to change a good chunk in your own country, before you arrive in Miami, as exchange rates here are notoriously skimpy. If you must change money here, do it at banks. Try **Bank of America** (☎ 305-350-6350), which offers foreign-exchange services in its branches – or money-changing operations such as **Thomas Cook** (☎ 305-285-2348,

800-287-7362). Exchange rates change constantly, but to get an idea, see the exchange-rate chart inside this book's front cover.

PHARMACIES

The most ubiquitous drugstores are the following chains: the blue-signed **Eckerd** (☎ 305-538-1571) and the red-signed **Walgreens** (☎ 305-261-2213), both of which have some 24-hour branches. Call for the nearest location.

PHOTOGRAPHY

Though a majority of travelers use digital cameras these days – and can easily download their photos at an Internet café to be sent to friends back home – folks sticking to old-school film won't have trouble finding gear. Color print film, widely available at supermarkets and drugstores, has greater latitude than color slide film. This means that print film can handle a wider range of light and shadow than slide film, and that the printer can fix your mistakes. However, slide film, particularly the slower speeds (under 100 ASA), has better resolution than print film. Black-and-white film is most likely found at camera shops. With the abundance of reflective surfaces in Miami, consider using a polarizing filter.

Drugstores process film cheaply. If you drop it off by noon, you can usually pick it up the next day. Processing a roll of 100 ASA 35mm color film with 24 exposures costs about $8 to $10. One-hour processing services are listed in the *Yellow Pages* under 'Photo Processing.' Expect to pay double the drugstore price.

Film can be damaged by excessive heat, so don't leave your camera and film in the sun on hot days (most of the year). For equipment, try **Tropicolor Photo** (Map pp248–9; ☎ 305-672-3720; 1442 Alton Rd, South Beach), or **LIB Color Labs** (Map pp248–9; ☎ 305-538-5600; 851 Washington Ave, South Beach) for film and processing. Pros go to **Aperture Pro Supply** (Map pp246–7; ☎ 305-673-4327; 1330 18th St, South Beach).

POST

Currently, rates for 1st-class mail within the USA are 37¢ for letters up to 1 ounce (28g) and 23¢ for postcards. International airmail rates differ from country to country, but in general run about 85¢ for a half-ounce letter (65¢ to Mexico and Canada). International postcard rates are 75¢ (55¢ to Mexico and Canada). Aerogrammes are 70¢. You can check for updates and other

details at www.usps.gov. Convenient post offices include the main branch in **South Beach** (Map pp248–9; 1300 Washington Ave; ☺ 8am-5pm Mon-Fri, 8:30am-2pm Sat) and the branch in **Ocean View** (Map p251; 445 W 40th St; ☺ 8am-5pm Mon-Fri, 8:30am-2pm Sat), both of which have extended hours due to excellent self-serve machines in the lobbies.

SAFETY

There are a few areas considered by locals to be dangerous: Liberty City, in northwest Miami, Little Haiti and stretches of the Miami riverfront, and newly gentrified Biscayne Blvd (after dark). Obviously, in these and other reputedly 'bad' areas, you should avoid walking around alone late at night, use common sense and travel in groups.

Deserted areas below 5th St in South Beach are more dangerous at night. In Downtown Miami, use particular caution near the Greyhound station and around causeways, bridges and overpasses where homeless people and some refugees have set up shantytowns.

Natural dangers include the strong sun (use a high SPF sunscreen!), mosquitoes (use a spray-on repellent) and hurricanes (between June and November). There's a **hurricane hot line** (☎ 305-229-4483), which will give you information about approaching storms, storm tracks, warnings, estimated time till touchdown…all the things you need to make a decision about if and when to leave.

TAXES

You must add tax to rates listed in this book. In Miami the tax on goods and services is 6.5% (6% state and 0.5% local). The tax on hotel accommodations varies with each community, but ranges from 9.5% to 12.5%. In Miami Beach it is 11.5%. If you eat and drink in a hotel the tax is also 11.5%. Rental cars are subjected to the 6.5% sales tax and a myriad of other surcharges.

TELEPHONE

All phone numbers within the USA consist of a three-digit area code followed by a seven-digit local number. If you are calling locally in Miami, you must dial the area code plus the seven-digit number. (Leave off the preceding 1 before local calls – just start with ☎ 305 or ☎ 786.) If you are calling locally in the Keys or Key West, you only have to dial the seven-digit number. If you are calling long distance, dial 1 plus the three-digit area code and then the seven-digit number. If you're calling from abroad, the international country code for the USA is '1.'

The ☎ 800, ☎ 888, ☎ 877 and ☎ 866 area codes are toll-free numbers within the USA and sometimes from Canada as well.

Directory assistance is reached locally by dialing ☎ 411. This is free from most pay phones, but costs as much as $1.25 from a private phone. For directory assistance outside your area code, dial ☎ 1 plus the three-digit area code followed by 555-1212.

To place an international call direct, dial ☎ 011 plus the country code and area code (dropping the leading 0) and then the number. From a pay phone, dial all those numbers before inserting coins; a voice will come on telling you how much to put in the phone after you dial the number. For international operator assistance and rates dial ☎ 00. Canada is treated like a domestic call. In general, it's cheaper to make international calls at night.

Cell Phones

Anyone who's anyone in Miami has a cell phone, and you can rent one almost as easily as you can buy soda from a machine. You can bring your own, but since the USA doesn't have a standardized system, call and check with your service provider to see if your phone will work in Miami. (Most of the world works on the GSM network at 900 or 1800 MHz, though Miami offers GSM access at 1900 MHz; Europeans should be okay with a tri-band phone.)

You can often rent cell phones in larger hotels and at rental-car agencies, as well as at a slew of shops (check the local phone book). One well-situated option is **Unicomm** (Map p250; ☎ 305-538-9494; 742 Alton Rd) in South Beach. You can make local calls with a national card, but not national calls with a local card.

Phonecards

Phone debit cards in denominations of $5, $10, $20 and $50 allow purchasers to pay in advance, with access through a toll-free number. Look for these ubiquitous cards in small convenience stores and large drugstores. You shouldn't have to pay more than 25¢ per minute on domestic long-distance calls, but some are as high as 45¢ per minute. Wal-Mart and other discount retailers sell them for as little as 6¢ a minute. When using phone debit or calling cards, you will have

to punch in an access code rather than be able to stick the card into the phone like you can in places outside of the US; be cautious of people watching you dial in the numbers – thieves will memorize numbers and use your card to make calls to all corners of the earth.

Public Phones

Local calls cost 35¢, and they don't give change. They're cheaper than using the phone in your hotel room, as almost all hotels add a service charge of 50¢ to $1 for each local – and sometimes even toll-free – call made from a room phone. They also add hefty surcharges for long-distance calls, 50% or even 100% on top of their carrier's rates.

To use a public phone, pick up the receiver, listen for a dial tone, put in your change (nickels, dimes and quarters only) and dial. Many area pay phones accept incoming calls; the number will be posted on the phone.

TIME

Miami is in the US Eastern standard time zone, three hours ahead of San Francisco and Los Angeles, and five hours behind GMT/UTC (so when it's noon in Miami, it's 5pm in London, for example). Daylight saving time takes place from the first Sunday in April through the last Sunday in October. The clocks 'spring forward' one hour in April and 'fall back' one hour in October, both at 1am.

TIPPING

Waitstaff at restaurants, bartenders, taxi drivers, bellhops, hotel cleaning staff and others are paid a mere stipend, and tips are counted as part of their salary. In a bar or restaurant a tip is customarily 15% to 20% (for a standard tip, double the tax and add a smidge) of the bill. Hotel cleaning staff should be tipped about $2 a day; tip daily, as they rotate shifts. Add about 10% to taxi fares. Hotel porters who carry bags a long way expect $3 to $5, or add it up at $1 per bag. Valet parking is worth about $2, to be given when your car is returned to you.

TOILETS

There are public toilets at several spots on South Beach (such as South Pointe Park and the Art Deco Welcome Center), but generally speaking, the area doesn't offer much in the way of public facilities. Usually restaurants will allow you to use their toilets if you're reasonably presentable and ask politely. Bars and Starbucks are also a good bet; just walk to the back and to the right or left, as if you're a customer.

TOURIST INFORMATION

There are several tourist offices in the Greater Miami area, all of which give advice of varying usefulness and hand out visitors' guides, pamphlets and flyers and discount tickets to many area attractions.

In South Beach, there's the **Art Deco Welcome Center** (Map pp248–9; ☎ 305-672-2014, www .mdpl.org; 1001 Ocean Dr; ❧ 10am-10pm), with tons of Deco District information, and the **Miami Beach Chamber of Commerce** (Map pp246–7; ☎ 305-672-1270, www.miamibeachchamber .com; 1920 Meridian Ave; ❧ 9am-5pm Mon-Fri). On the mainland, the **Greater Miami & the Beaches Convention & Visitors Bureau** (Map pp252–3; ☎ 305-539-3000; www.gmcvb.com; 27th fl, 701 Brickell Ave; ❧ 8:30am-5pm Mon-Fri) is helpful, but housed in a confusing high-rise with an attached mazelike parking-garage. You can also visit the **Downtown Miami Partnership** (Map pp252–3; ☎ 305-379-7070; www .downtownmiami.net; Downtown Miami Welcome Center, Olympia Theater, 174 E Flagler St; ❧ 9am-5pm).

VISAS

A reciprocal visa-waiver program applies to citizens of certain countries – UK, Japan, Australia, New Zealand and all West European countries (except for Portugal and Greece). Citizens of these countries may enter the USA for stays of 90 days or less without having to obtain a visa.

Other travelers (except Canadians) will need to obtain a visa from a US consulate or embassy. In most countries you can do this by mail; for others, you'll need show up at the nearest US consulate or embassy.

WOMEN TRAVELERS

Women travelers, especially solo travelers, should develop the habit of traveling with a little extra awareness of their surroundings. Men may interpret a woman drinking alone in a bar as a bid for male company, whether it's intended that way or not. If you don't want company, most men will respect a firm but polite 'no thank you.' Use common sense, and you'll be fine in most Miami nabes.

WORK

Foreigners cannot work legally in the USA without the appropriate work visa, and recent legislative changes specifically target illegal immigrants, which is what you will be if you try to work while on a tourist visa.

Miami has been ground zero for large numbers of refugees from the Caribbean area, notably Haiti and Cuba, so INS checks are frequent. Local businesses are probably more concerned here than anywhere outside Southern California and Texas when it comes to verifying your legal status.

One viable option is to find work on the cruise liners or yachts in the region, which can employ anyone since they operate in international waters. For more information on crew work, see the boxed text, p209.

Language

Language

Although visitors to Miami can get away with using only English, to do so is essentially to write off experiencing a huge chunk of the city's culture and life. Spanish may be more widely spoken in the metropolitan area than English, and you will certainly run into people who do not speak any English at all.

If you plan to spend a lot of time in Spanish-speaking neighborhoods, take along Lonely Planet's comprehensive and compact *Latin American Spanish Phrasebook*. If you're planning on romancing some Latin types, the finest resources are *Hot Spanish for Guys and Girls* and *Hot Spanish for Guys and Guys*, both of which contain an amazing number of useful phrases.

A Social Life

Hi!	¡Hola!
Good morning/ day.	Buenos días.
Good evening/ night.	Buenas noches.
Pleased to meet you.	Mucho gusto.
Goodbye!	¡Adiós!
See you later.	Hasta luego.
Please.	Por favor.
Thank you (very much).	(Muchas) Gracias.
You're welcome/ Don't mention it.	De nada.
Yes/No.	Sí/No.
Excuse me. (to get past)	Permiso.
Excuse me. (eg before asking directions)	Perdóneme.
Sorry!	¡Perdón!
Pardon? (as in 'what did you say?')	¿Cómo?
I understand.	Entiendo.
I don't understand.	No entiendo.
Please speak slowly.	Por favor hable despacio.

What's on ...?	
¿Qué pasa ...?	
around here	para acá
this weekend	este fin de semana
today	hoy
tonight	esta noche

Where are the ...?	
¿Dónde hay ...?	
places to eat	lugares para comer
clubs/pubs	boliches/pubs
gay venues	lugares para gays

Is there a local entertainment guide?
¿Hay una guía de entretenimiento de la zona?

A Practical Life

to the left	a la izquierda
to the right	a la derecha
straight ahead	adelante
bus	gua gua or autobús
taxi	taxi
toilet	sanitario
train	tren

Where is ... ?	Donde está ... ?
the bus station	el terminal de gua gua/autobús
the train station	la estación del tren

How much is it?	¿Cuanto cuesta?
Can I look at it?	¿Puedo mirarlo?
I want ...	Quiero ...
good/OK	bueno/a (m/f)
bad	malo/a (m/f)
best	mejor
more	más
less	menos

0	cero	14	catorce
1	uno	15	quince
2	dos	16	dieciséis
3	tres	17	diecisiete
4	cuatro	18	dieciocho
5	cinco	19	diecinueve
6	seis	20	veinte
7	siete	21	veintiuno
8	ocho	30	treinta
9	nueve	40	cuarenta
10	diez	50	cincuenta
11	once	100	cien
12	doce	500	quinientos
13	trece	1000	mil

Behind the Scenes

THE LONELY PLANET STORY

The story begins with a classic travel adventure: Tony and Maureen Wheeler's 1972 journey across Europe and Asia to Australia. There was no useful information about the overland trail then, so Tony and Maureen published the first Lonely Planet guidebook to meet a growing need.

From a kitchen table, Lonely Planet has grown to become the largest independent travel publisher in the world, with offices in Melbourne (Australia), Oakland (USA) and London (UK). Today Lonely Planet guidebooks cover the globe. There is an ever-growing list of books and information in a variety of media. Some things haven't changed. The main aim is still to make it possible for adventurous travelers to get out there – to explore and better understand the world.

At Lonely Planet we believe travelers can make a positive contribution to the countries they visit – if they respect their host communities and spend their money wisely. Every year 5% of company profit is donated to charities around the world.

THIS BOOK

This 4th edition of *Miami & the Keys* was written by Beth Greenfield. Rick Starey wrote the 'Swabbing the Decks, Chasing Down Tips' boxed text. The 3rd edition was written by Kim Grant. Earlier editions of *Miami & the Keys* were written by Nick and Corinna Selby. This guidebook was commissioned in Lonely Planet's Oakland office, and produced by the following:

Commissioning Editor Jay Cooke
Coordinating Editor Simon Williamson
Coordinating Cartographers Laurie Mikkelsen & Herman So
Coordinating Layout Designers Michael Ruff & Laura Jane
Managing Cartographer Alison Lyall
Proofreader Kate Evans
Assisting Editor Suzannah Shwer
Assisting Cartographers Owen Eszeki & Helen Rowley
Cover Designer Marika Kozak
Project Manager Rachel Imeson
Language Content Coordinator Quentin Frayne

Cover photographs: Miami Beach, Florida, Panoramic Images/Getty Images (top); Ocean Drive Miami, Florida, Peter Griffith/Masterfile (bottom); Roller blader on Ocean Drive, Art Deco District, Miami Beach, Witold Skrypczak/Lonely Planet Images (back).

Internal photographs by Lonely Planet Images as following: p28, p35, p108, p115, p198 Lee Foster; p46 Kim Grant; p54 John Neubauer; p72 Jon Davison; p85 Witold Skrypczak; p125, p140, p211 Richard Cummins; p174 William Harrigan. All images are the copyright of the photographers unless otherwise indicated. Many of the images in this guide are available for licensing from Lonely Planet Images: www.lonelyplanetimages.com.

THANKS
BETH GREENFIELD

To Tony and Etta Rodriguez, George Fontana and Debbie Stephens, David Lafond, Bruce at Miss Yip, Ted Norton, Erin McHugh, Jaye Harkowe and Glorya, Pauline Fischer, Meredith Bollong, Andrew Berman, Dayna Blossom, Bea Blanco, Aunt Helen and Uncle Jack, Jacky Cummings, Mom and Dad. Big thanks to Kim Grant for great copy, Jay Cooke (phew!) for being an awesome editor, Rod Schimko and Meade Dickerson for lending your home and for indispensable advice, Kiki Herold for being the best partner in the world, and Grandma Lil and Grandpa Norman for starting this whole Miami thing.

OUR READERS

Many thanks to the travelers who used the last edition and wrote to us with helpful hints, useful advice and interesting anecdotes. Your names follow:

Lui Brandt, Carl Danzig, Denise Davies, Raphael Elimelech, Katherine Fernandez, Douglas Frazer, Alexander Frix, Melissa Geerlings, Lars Gentzen, Grainne Hogan, Henrick Hollesen, Helena Jones, Marjorie and Michael Kinch, Sophie Lefebvre-Blachet, Gillian MacKenzie, Benjamin Poor, Liz Raleigh, Jeff Rothman, Virginia and Gilbert Roy, Tina Ruchti, Chris Simmons, Dagmar Spichale, Sheri Thrasher, Cian Traynor, Anita Verma, Marcella Vinciguerra, Clive Williams, Andrew Wilson, Andrew Young

SEND US YOUR FEEDBACK

We love to hear from travelers – your comments keep us on our toes and help make our books better. Our well-traveled team reads every word on what you loved or loathed about this book. Although we cannot reply individually to postal submissions, we always guarantee that your feedback goes straight to the appropriate authors, in time for the next edition. Each person who sends us information is thanked in the next edition – and the most useful submissions are rewarded with a free book.

To send us your updates – and find out about Lonely Planet events, newsletters and travel news – visit our award-winning website: www.lonelyplanet.com/feedback

Note: We may edit, reproduce and incorporate your comments in Lonely Planet products such as guidebooks, websites and digital products, so let us know if you don't want your comments reproduced or your name acknowledged. For a copy of our privacy policy visit www.lonelyplanet.com/privacy.

Notes

Notes

Notes

Notes

Index

Index

000 map pages
000 photographs

Index

000 map pages
000 photographs

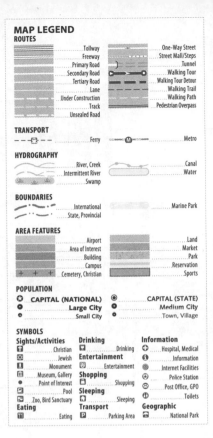

MAP LEGEND

ROUTES

Tollway
Freeway
Primary Road
Secondary Road
Tertiary Road
Lane
Under Construction
Track
Unsealed Road

One-Way Street
Street Mall/Steps
Tunnel
Walking Tour
Walking Tour Detour
Walking Trail
Walking Path
Pedestrian Overpass

TRANSPORT

Ferry
Metro

HYDROGRAPHY

River, Creek
Intermittent River
Swamp

Canal
Water

BOUNDARIES

International
State, Provincial

Marine Park

AREA FEATURES

Airport
Area of Interest
Building
Campus
Cemetery, Christian

Land
Market
Park
Reservation
Sports

POPULATION

CAPITAL (NATIONAL)
Large City
Small City

CAPITAL (STATE)
Medium City
Town, Village

SYMBOLS

Sights/Activities
Christian
Jewish
Monument
Museum, Gallery
Point of Interest
Pool
Zoo, Bird Sanctuary

Eating
Eating

Drinking
Drinking

Entertainment
Entertainment

Shopping
Shopping

Sleeping
Sleeping

Transport
Parking Area

Information
Hospital, Medical
Information
Internet Facilities
Police Station
Post Office, GPO
Toilets

Geographic
National Park

Map Section

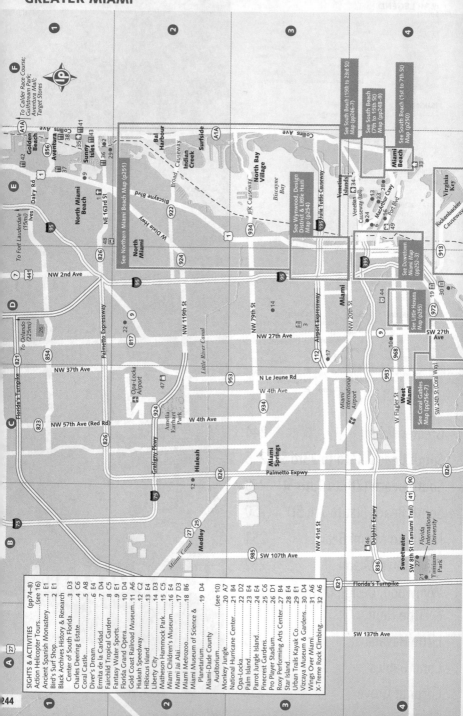

GREATER MIAMI

To Calder Race Course;
Cultural Park;
Aventura Mall;
Target Stores

To Fort Lauderdale
(15mi)

To Orlando
(225mi)

Florida's Turnpike

NW 2nd Ave

NW 37th Ave

NW 57th Ave (Red Rd)

Palmetto Expy

SW 107th Ave

SW 137th Ave

Florida's Turnpike

Golden
Beach

Aventura

Sunny
Isles

Bal
Harbour

Surfside

Indian
Creek

North Bay
Village

Biscayne
Bay

Venetian
Islands

Miami
Beach

Virginia
Key

Rickenbacker
Causeway

Collins Ave

JFK Causeway

Broad Causeway

Julia Tuttle Causeway

Venetian
Causeway (toll)

MacArthur Cwy

Port Blvd

North Miami
Beach

North
Miami

Miami

West
Miami

Miami
Springs

Hialeah

Opa-Locka
Airport

Amelia
Earhart
Park

Miami
International
Airport

Sweetwater

Medley

Florida
International
University

Tamiami
Park

See Northern Miami Beach Map (p251)

See Wynwood, Design
District & Little Haiti
Map (p254)

See Downtown
Miami Map
(pp252-3)

See Little Havana
Map (p255)

See Coral Gables
Map (p256-7)

Dairy Rd

Ives Dairy Rd

NE 163rd St

W Dixie Hwy

Biscayne Blvd

Collins Ave

Little River Canal

NW 119th St

NW 79th St

NW 27th Ave

NW 20th St

N Le Jeune Rd

W 4th Ave

W 4th Ave

Gratigny Pkwy

Miami Canal

Miami Canal

NW 41st St

Palmetto Expwy

W Flagler St

SW 24th St (Coral Way)

SW 27th
Ave

SW 8th St (Tamiami Trail)

Dolphin Expwy

Airport Expressway

SW 107th Ave

SIGHTS & ACTIVITIES (pp74-8)

Action Helicopter Tours.....................(see 16)	
Ancient Spanish Monastery.................1	E1
Bird's Surf Shop...............................2	E1
Black Archives History & Research	
Center of South Florida................3	D3
Charles Deering Estate......................4	C6
Coral Castle..................................5	A8
Diver's Dream................................6	F4
Ermita de la Caridad.......................7	D4
Fairchild Tropical Garden...................8	C5
Fantasy Water Sports........................9	E1
Florida Grand Opera........................10	D4
Gold Coast Railroad Museum............11	A6
Hialeah Speedway..........................12	C2
Hibiscus Island..............................13	E4
Liberty City..................................14	D3
Matheson Hammock Park..................15	C5
Miami Children's Museum.................16	E4
Miami Jai Alai...............................17	D3
Miami Metrozoo............................18	B6
Miami Museum of Science &	
Planetarium...............................19	D4
Miami-Dade County	
Auditorium.........................(see 10)	
Monkey Jungle...............................20	A7
National Hurricane Center.................21	B4
Opa-Locka....................................22	D2
Palm Island..................................23	E4
Parrot Jungle Island.........................24	E4
Pinecrest Gardens...........................25	C6
Pro Player Stadium..........................26	D1
Roxy Performing Arts Center..............27	B4
Star Island...................................28	E4
Urban Trails Kayak Co......................29	E1
Vizcaya Museum & Gardens..............30	D4
Wings Over Miami..........................31	A6
X-Treme Rock Climbing....................32	A6

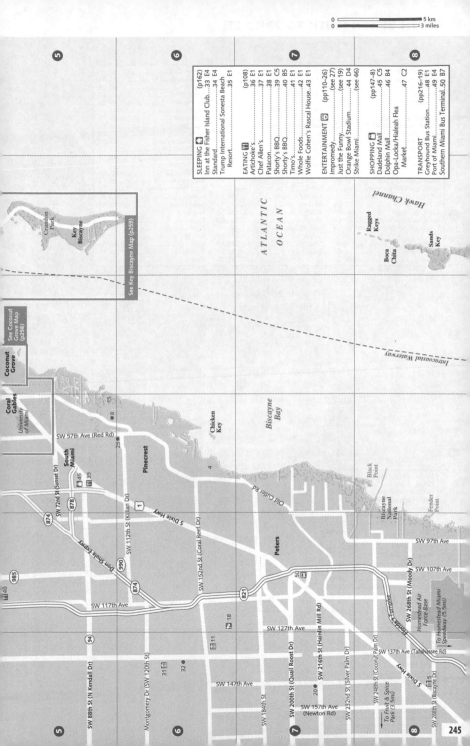

ATLANTIC
OCEAN

Hawk Channel

Ragged
Keys

Boca
Chita

Sands
Key

Intracoastal Waterway

See Key Biscayne Map (p259)

Crandon Park

Key
Biscayne

See Coconut
Grove Map
(p258)

Coconut
Grove

Coral
Gables

University
of Miami

SW 57th Ave (Red Rd)

South
Miami

Pinecrest

Chicken
Key

Biscayne Bay

Black
Point

Biscayne
National
Park

Fender
Point

SW 72nd St (Sunset Dr)

SW 88th St (N Kendall Dr)

Montgomery Dr (SW 120th St)

SW 112th St (Killian Dr)

Old Cutler Rd

Don Shula Expwy

SW 117th Ave

SW 147th Ave

SW 184th St

SW 200th St (Quail Roost Dr)

SW 157th Ave
(Newton Rd)

SW 232nd St (Silver Palm Dr)

SW 216th St (Hainlin Mill Rd)

SW 248th St (Coconut Palm Dr)

SW 127th Ave

SW 137th Ave (Tallahassee Rd)

SW 152nd St (Coral Reef Dr)

Peters

SW 97th Ave

SW 107th Ave

SW 268th St (Moody Dr)

Homestead Air
Force Base

To Homestead Miami
Speedway (5.5mi)

To Fruit & Spice
Park (3.5mi)

SW 288th St (Biscayne Dr)

245

SOUTH BEACH (15TH TO 23RD ST)

W 24th St

Ⓐ Ⓑ Ⓒ Ⓓ

INFORMATION	
Aperture Pro Supply	1 B3
Harley Davidson Rentals	2 B4
Miami Beach Chamber of Commerce	3 E3

SIGHTS & ACTIVITIES	(pp50–5)
ArtCenter/South Florida	4 E5
Bass Museum of Art	5 G1
David Barton Gym	(see 20)
Fritz's Skate Shop	6 E5
Holocaust Memorial	7 E2
Idol's Gym	8 E4
Miami Beach Botanical Garden	9 E2
Miami Beach City Hall	10 E4
Miami Beach Convention Center	11 F3
Miami Duck Tours	12 G4
Miami Yogashala	(see 46)
South Beach Ironworks	13 C4
Temple Emanu El Synagogue	14 G4

SLEEPING	(pp151–9)
Abbey Hotel	15 G2
Albion	16 G4

EATING	(pp89–96)
190 at the Albion	(see 16)
Altamar	31 C5
Balans	32 D5
Blue Door	(see 20)
Café Papillon	33 F5
Cafeteria	34 F5
Casa Tua	35 G4
David's Cafe II	36 E4
Epicure Market	37 C5

Aqua Hotel	17 G6
Creek Hotel	18 H1
Crest Hotel Suites	19 G4
Delano Hotel	20 G4
Greenview	21 G4
Loews Miami Beach	22 G5
National Hotel	23 G4
Raleigh Hotel	24 H3
Ritz-Carlton South Beach	25 G4
Sagamore	26 G4
Setai	27 H2
Shore Club	28 H3
Townhouse Hotel	29 H2
Tropics Hotel & Hostel	30 G6

Ice Box Café	38 D5
Joe Allen Miami Beach	39 B3
Miss Yip	40 E4
Pacific Time	41 D5
Panizza Bistro	42 C5
Pasha's	43 D5
Pizza Rustica	44 E5
Sushi Samba	45 F5
Talula	46 H1
Tiger Oak Room	(see 24)
Van Dyke Café	47 D5
Yuca	48 F5

DRINKING	(pp110–13)
Abbey Brewery	49 C5
Bond Street Lounge	(see 29)
Buck 15	(see 40)
Jade Lounge	50 B4
Laundry Bar	51 E4
Mynt	52 H2
Purdy Lounge	53 B3
Rose Bar	(see 20)
Rumi	54 G5
Six2Six	55 E5
SkyBar	(see 28)

Bayshore
Municipal
Golf Course

19th St

Collins Canal

Jefferson Ave

🍴39 18th St 1 West Ave Dade Blvd 18th St

Purdy Ave
Bay Rd

Island View Park

2 ●
50 🍴

17th St

P P

ENTERTAINMENT	(pp113–26)
Colony Theatre	56 C5
Concert Association of Florida	57 F4
Jackie Gleason Theater	58 F4
Lincoln Theatre	59 F5
New World Symphony	(see 59)
Regal South Beach Cinema	60 E5
Score	61 E5

Courtyard

13 ●

Sun Trust Bank

64 65 77 41 73 66 79

Lincoln Rd Mall

🍴56 🍴32 🍴38

42 37 🍴
🍴🍴31

68 43 47 72

Lincoln Rd Alton Rd Lenox Ave Michigan Ave Jefferson Ave

West Ave
Alton Ct

Belle
Isle

Bay Rd

Lincoln La S

60

SHOPPING	(pp137–42)
Absolutely Suitable	62 G5
Alexa & Jack	63 E5
Base	64 D5
Books & Books	65 D5
Brownes & Co Apothecary	66 D5
Burdines-Macy's	67 E4
Chroma	68 D5
Daszign New York	69 G4
En Avance	70 E5
Ete	(see 33)
Intermix	71 G5
Joyella	(see 66)
Kiehl's	72 D5
Me & Ro	(see 28)
Miss Sixty	73 D5
Neo Accessario	74 E5
Neo Scarpa	75 E5
Recycled Blues	76 G6
Scoop	(see 28)
See	77 D5
Senzatempo	78 E4
Sobe Shoe Company	79 D5

49

16th St

15th Tce

P

15th St

LP

Index

Index

241

Index

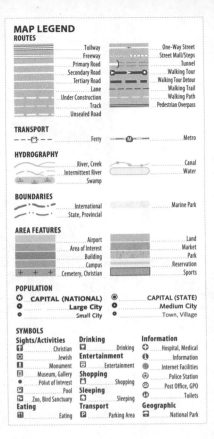

MAP LEGEND

ROUTES

Tollway	One-Way Street
Freeway	Street Mall/Steps
Primary Road	Tunnel
Secondary Road	Walking Tour
Tertiary Road	Walking Tour Detour
Lane	Walking Trail
Under Construction	Walking Path
Track	Pedestrian Overpass
Unsealed Road	

TRANSPORT

Ferry	Metro

HYDROGRAPHY

River, Creek	Canal
Intermittent River	Water
Swamp	

BOUNDARIES

International	Marine Park
State, Provincial	

AREA FEATURES

Airport	Land
Area of Interest	Market
Building	Park
Campus	Reservation
Cemetery, Christian	Sports

POPULATION

CAPITAL (NATIONAL)	CAPITAL (STATE)
Large City	Medium City
Small City	Town, Village

SYMBOLS

Sights/Activities	Drinking	Information
Christian	Drinking	Hospital, Medical
Jewish	**Entertainment**	Information
Monument	Entertainment	Internet Facilities
Museum, Gallery	**Shopping**	Police Station
Point of Interest	Shopping	Post Office, GPO
Pool	**Sleeping**	Toilets
Zoo, Bird Sanctuary	Sleeping	**Geographic**
Eating	**Transport**	National Park
Eating	Parking Area	

Map Section

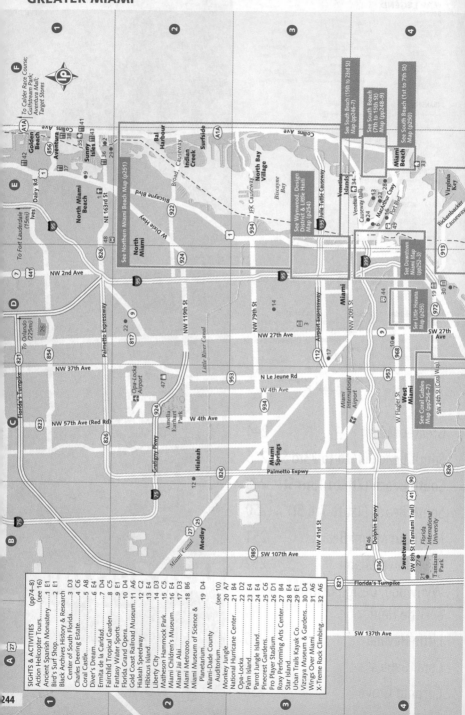

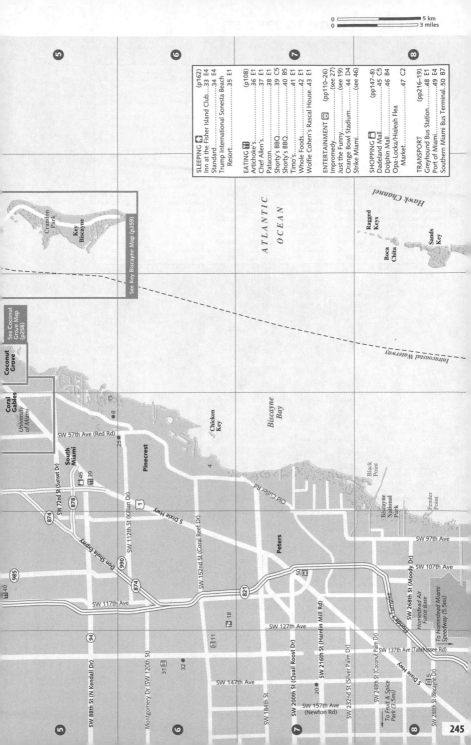

0   5 km
0   3 miles

SLEEPING 🛏 (p162)
Inn at the Fisher Island Club....33 E4
Standard...............................34 E4
Trump International Sonesta Beach
Resort...................................35 E1

EATING 🍴 (p108)
Artichoke's...........................36 E1
Chef Allen's..........................37 E1
Patacon................................38 E1
Shorty's BBQ.........................39 C5
Shorty's BBQ.........................40 B5
Timo's..................................41 E1
Whole Foods..........................42 E1
Wolfie Cohen's Rascal House....43 E1

ENTERTAINMENT 🎭 (pp110–26)
Impromedy...........................(see 27)
Just the Funny........................(see 19)
Orange Bowl Stadium...............44 D4
Strike Miami...........................(see 46)

SHOPPING 🛍 (pp147–8)
Dadeland Mall........................45 C5
Dolphin Mall...........................46 B4
Opa-Locka/Hialeah Flea
Market.................................47 C2

TRANSPORT 🚍 (pp216–19)
Greyhound Bus Station............48 E1
Port of Miami.........................49 E4
Southern Miami Bus Terminal...50 B7

ATLANTIC
OCEAN

Hawk Channel

Ragged Keys

Boca Chita

Sands Key

Intracoastal Waterway

See Key Biscayne Map (p259)

Crandon Park
Key Biscayne

See Coconut Grove Map (p258)

Coconut Grove

Coral Gables
University of Miami

Biscayne Bay

Chicken Key

Black Point

Fender Point

Biscayne National Park

South Miami

Pinecrest

Peters

SW 57th Ave (Red Rd)
SW 72nd St (Sunset Dr)
SW 88th St (N Kendall Dr)
Montgomery Dr (SW 120th St)
SW 112th St (Killian Dr)
S Dixie Hwy
Old Cutler Rd
SW 152nd St (Coral Reef Dr)
SW 117th Ave
SW 127th Ave
SW 97th Ave
SW 107th Ave
SW 147th Ave
SW 184th St
SW 200th St (Quail Roost Dr)
SW 216th St (Hainlin Mill Rd)
SW 232nd St (Silver Palm Dr)
SW 248th St (Coconut Palm Dr)
SW 137th Ave (Tallahassee Rd)
SW 157th Ave (Newton Rd)
SW 268th St (Moody Dr)
SW 288th St (Biscayne Dr)

Homestead Air Force Base

To Homestead Miami Speedway (5.5mi)

To Fruit & Spice Park (3.5mi)

Don Shula Expwy

S Dixie Hwy

SOUTH BEACH (15TH TO 23RD ST)

W 24th St

Ⓐ　　　　Ⓑ　　　　Ⓒ　　　　Ⓓ

INFORMATION
Aperture Pro Supply.....................1 B3
Harley Davidson Rentals..............2 B4
Miami Beach Chamber of
　Commerce...............................3 E3

SIGHTS & ACTIVITIES (pp50–5)
ArtCenter/South Florida...............4 E5
Bass Museum of Art.....................5 G1
David Barton Gym...............(see 20)
Fritz's Skate Shop........................6 E5
Holocaust Memorial.....................7 E2
Idol's Gym...................................8 E4
Miami Beach Botanical Garden..9 E2
Miami Beach City Hall.................10 E4
Miami Beach Convention
　Center......................................11 F3
Miami Duck Tours......................12 G4
Miami Yogashala.................(see 46)
South Beach Ironworks...............13 C4
Temple Emanu El Synagogue....14 G4

SLEEPING (pp151–9)
Abbey Hotel..............................15 G2
Albion.......................................16 G4

Aqua Hotel................................17 G6
Creek Hotel...............................18 H1
Crest Hotel Suites......................19 G4
Delano Hotel.............................20 G4
Greenview.................................21 G4
Loews Miami Beach...................22 G5
National Hotel...........................23 G4
Raleigh Hotel............................24 H3
Ritz-Carlton South Beach...........25 G4
Sagamore..................................26 G4
Setai...27 H2
Shore Club................................28 H3
Townhouse Hotel.......................29 H2
Tropics Hotel & Hostel...............30 G6

EATING (pp89–96)
190 at the Albion................(see 16)
Altamar....................................31 C5
Balans......................................32 D5
Blue Door...........................(see 20)
Café Papillon............................33 F5
Cafeteria..................................34 F5
Casa Tua...................................35 G4
David's Cafe II..........................36 E4
Epicure Market..........................37 C5

Ice Box Café.............................38 D5
Joe Allen Miami Beach..............39 B3
Miss Yip...................................40 E4
Pacific Time..............................41 D5
Panizza Bistro...........................42 C5
Pasha's.....................................43 D5
Pizza Rustica............................44 E5
Sushi Samba.............................45 F5
Talula.......................................46 H1
Tiger Oak Room...................(see 24)
Van Dyke Café..........................47 D5
Yuca...48 F5

DRINKING (pp110–13)
Abbey Brewery..........................49 C5
Bond Street Lounge..............(see 29)
Buck 15..............................(see 40)
Jade Lounge..............................50 B4
Laundry Bar..............................51 E4
Mynt..52 H2
Purdy Lounge............................53 B3
Rose Bar.............................(see 20)
Rumi..54 G5
Six2Six.....................................55 E5
SkyBar.................................(see 28)

ENTERTAINMENT (pp113–26)
Colony Theatre..........................56 C5
Concert Association of Florida.57 F4
Jackie Gleason Theater..............58 F4
Lincoln Theatre.........................59 F5
New World Symphony...........(see 59)
Regal South Beach Cinema........60 C5
Score..61 E5

SHOPPING (pp137–42)
Absolutely Suitable....................62 G5
Alexa & Jack.............................63 E5
Base...64 D5
Books & Books..........................65 D5
Brownes & Co Apothecary........66 D5
Burdines-Macy's........................67 E4
Chroma....................................68 D5
Daszign New York.....................69 G4
En Avance.................................70 E5
Ete.....................................(see 33)
Intermix....................................71 G5
Joyella.................................(see 66)
Kiehl's......................................72 D5
Me & Ro..............................(see 28)
Miss Sixty.................................73 D5
Neo Accessario.........................74 E5
Neo Scarpa...............................75 E5
Recycled Blues..........................76 G6
Scoop..................................(see 28)
See...77 D5
Senzatempo..............................78 E4
Sobe Shoe Company..................79 D5

Bayshore
Municipal
Golf Course

19th St

Collins Canal

Jefferson Ave

Dade Blvd

18th St

🚌39

Purdy Ave

Bay Rd

18th St
1

West Ave

Island
View
Park

2
50🚌

17th St

🅿

🅿

Belle
Isle

13

Courtyard

Sun Trust
Bank

42　37🍴
🍴🍴31

64 65 77 41　73 66 79

Lincoln Rd

Lincoln Rd Mall

🎬56

🍴32

38

68　43　47　72

Alton Rd

Lincoln La S

Alton Ct

Lenox Ave

Michigan Ave

Jefferson Ave

🎬60

16th St

🍺49

15th Tce

🅿

15th St

15th St

246

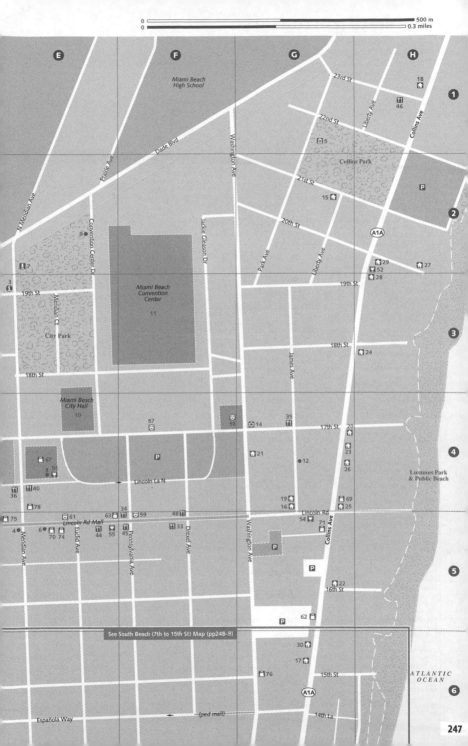

0 —————————— 500 m
0 —————————— 0.3 miles

Miami Beach
High School

23rd St

18

46

22nd St

5

Collins Park

21st St

Liberty Ave

Collins Ave

Dade Blvd

Prairie Ave

N Meridian Ave

Convention Center Dr

Washington Ave

Jackie Gleason Dr

9

15

20th St

Park Ave

Liberty Ave

A1A

7

3

19th St

Meridian Ct

Miami Beach
Convention
Center

11

29
52
28

27

19th St

18th St

24

James Ave

City Park

18th St

Miami Beach
City Hall

10

57

58

14

35

17th St

20

23

26

Lummus Park
& Public Beach

67

8 51

36   40

78

21

12

Lincoln La N

19
16

69
25

75

61

Lincoln Rd Mall

34
63   59

48

54

71

Lincoln Rd

Collins Ave

4

6
70 74

Meridian Ave

Euclid Ave

44   55

45

Pennsylvania Ave

33

Drexel Ave

Washington Ave

22
16th St

62

See South Beach (7th to 15th St) Map (pp248–9)

30

17

76

15th St

A1A

ATLANTIC
OCEAN

Española Way

(ped mall)

14th La

SOUTH BEACH (7TH TO 15TH ST)

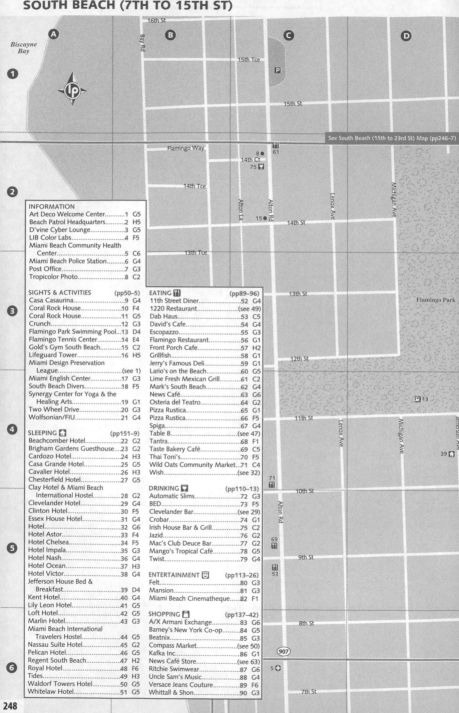

Biscayne Bay

See South Beach (15th to 23rd St) Map (pp246–7)

INFORMATION
Art Deco Welcome Center	1 G5
Beach Patrol Headquarters	2 H5
D'vine Cyber Lounge	3 G5
LIB Color Labs	4 F5
Miami Beach Community Health Center	5 C6
Miami Beach Police Station	6 G4
Post Office	7 G3
Tropicolor Photo	8 C2

SIGHTS & ACTIVITIES (pp50–9)
Casa Casaurina	9 G4
Coral Rock House	10 F4
Coral Rock House	11 G5
Crunch	12 G3
Flamingo Park Swimming Pool	13 D4
Flamingo Tennis Center	14 E4
Gold's Gym South Beach	15 C2
Lifeguard Tower	16 H5
Miami Design Preservation League	(see 1)
Miami English Center	17 G3
South Beach Divers	18 F5
Synergy Center for Yoga & the Healing Arts	19 G1
Two Wheel Drive	20 G3
Wolfsonian/FIU	21 G4

SLEEPING (pp151–9)
Beachcomber Hotel	22 G2
Brigham Gardens Guesthouse	23 G2
Cardozo Hotel	24 H3
Casa Grande Hotel	25 G5
Cavalier Hotel	26 H3
Chesterfield Hotel	27 G5
Clay Hotel & Miami Beach International Hostel	28 G2
Clevelander Hotel	29 G4
Clinton Hotel	30 F5
Essex House Hotel	31 G4
Hotel	32 G6
Hotel Astor	33 F4
Hotel Chelsea	34 F5
Hotel Impala	35 G3
Hotel Nash	36 G4
Hotel Ocean	37 H3
Hotel Victor	38 G4
Jefferson House Bed & Breakfast	39 D4
Kent Hotel	40 G4
Lily Leon Hotel	41 G5
Loft Hotel	42 G5
Marlin Hotel	43 G3
Miami Beach International Travelers Hostel	44 G5
Nassau Suite Hotel	45 G2
Pelican Hotel	46 G5
Regent South Beach	47 H2
Royal Hotel	48 F6
Tides	49 H3
Waldorf Towers Hotel	50 G5
Whitelaw Hotel	51 G5

EATING (pp89–96)
11th Street Diner	52 G4
1220 Restaurant	(see 49)
Dab Haus	53 C5
David's Cafe	54 G4
Escopazzo	55 G3
Flamingo Restaurant	56 G1
Front Porch Cafe	57 H2
Grillfish	58 G1
Jerry's Famous Deli	59 G1
Lario's on the Beach	60 G5
Lime Fresh Mexican Grill	61 C2
Mark's South Beach	62 G4
News Café	63 G6
Osteria del Teatro	64 G2
Pizza Rustica	65 G1
Pizza Rustica	66 F5
Spiga	67 G4
Table 8	(see 47)
Tantra	68 F1
Taste Bakery Café	69 C5
Thai Toni's	70 F5
Wild Oats Community Market	71 C4
Wish	(see 32)

DRINKING (pp110–13)
Automatic Slims	72 G3
BED	73 F5
Clevelander Bar	(see 29)
Crobar	74 G1
Irish House Bar & Grill	75 C2
Jazid	76 G2
Mac's Club Deuce Bar	77 G2
Mango's Tropical Café	78 G5
Twist	79 G4

ENTERTAINMENT (pp113–26)
Felt	80 G3
Mansion	81 G3
Miami Beach Cinematheque	82 F1

SHOPPING (pp137–42)
A/X Armani Exchange	83 G6
Barney's New York Co-op	84 G5
Beatnix	85 G3
Compass Market	(see 50)
Kafka Inc	86 G1
News Café Store	(see 63)
Ritchie Swimwear	87 G5
Uncle Sam's Music	88 G4
Versace Jeans Couture	89 F6
Whittall & Shon	90 G3

0   300 m
0   0.2 miles

E   F   G   P   H

1

15th St   15th St
86
19 56 65   59
68   58
Española Way   82   74   14th La
64
28

2
14th Pl
14th St   Pennsylvania Ave   47   Lummus
45   57   Park &
23   Public Beach
14th St
77
14th St

76   Collins Ave
22   26
Washington Ave   90
7   55
3
13th St   20   13th St   24
80   12   Ocean Ct   37   Ocean Dr
72   81   35   49
17
43
12th St   12th St   12th St
85

Old City   38   The Promenade
Hall
67   40
6   88   62
14   11th St   36   11th St   South
52   9   Beach
79   54

10   ATLANTIC
21
OCEAN
33   31
10th St   10th St
29   2
34   42   16
73   3   1
ATLANTIC
70   11   OCEAN
66   44   9th St
9th St   78
4   50   Lummus
18   30   84 27   25   Park &
51   41   46   Public Beach
60

8th St   89   32
83   8th St   63
48   87
A1A

See South Beach (1st to 7th St) Map (p250)

6
7th St
7th St

Playground

249

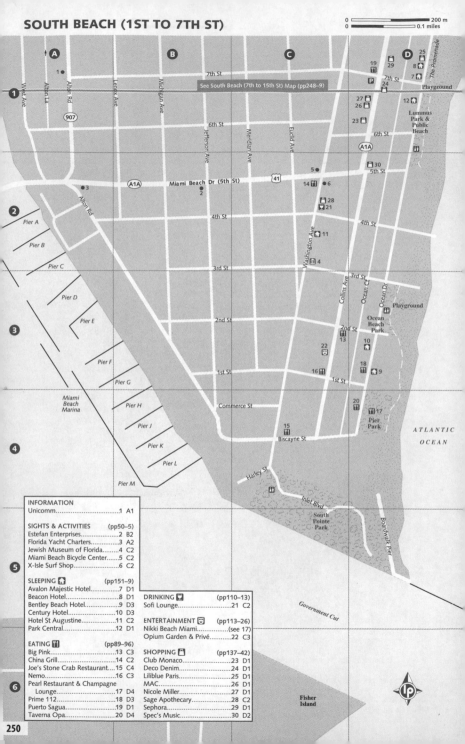

SOUTH BEACH (1ST TO 7TH ST)

See South Beach (7th to 15th St) Map (pp248–9)

INFORMATION
Unicomm..................................1 A1

SIGHTS & ACTIVITIES (pp50–5)
Estefan Enterprises......................2 B2
Florida Yacht Charters..................3 A2
Jewish Museum of Florida..........4 C2
Miami Beach Bicycle Center........5 C2
X-Isle Surf Shop..........................6 C2

SLEEPING (pp151–9)
Avalon Majestic Hotel.................7 D1
Beacon Hotel..............................8 D1
Bentley Beach Hotel....................9 D3
Century Hotel............................10 D3
Hotel St Augustine....................11 C2
Park Central.............................12 D1

EATING (pp89–96)
Big Pink....................................13 C3
China Grill................................14 C2
Joe's Stone Crab Restaurant....15 C4
Nemo.......................................16 C3
Pearl Restaurant & Champagne
Lounge.................................17 D4
Prime 112.................................18 D3
Puerto Sagua...........................19 D1
Taverna Opa.............................20 D4

DRINKING (pp110–13)
Sofi Lounge.............................21 C2

ENTERTAINMENT (pp113–26)
Nikki Beach Miami..............(see 17)
Opium Garden & Privé..........22 C3

SHOPPING (pp137–42)
Club Monaco...........................23 D1
Deco Denim............................24 D1
Liliblue Paris...........................25 D1
MAC..26 D1
Nicole Miller...........................27 D1
Sage Apothecary.....................28 C2
Sephora..................................29 D1
Spec's Music...........................30 D2

250

NORTHERN MIAMI BEACH

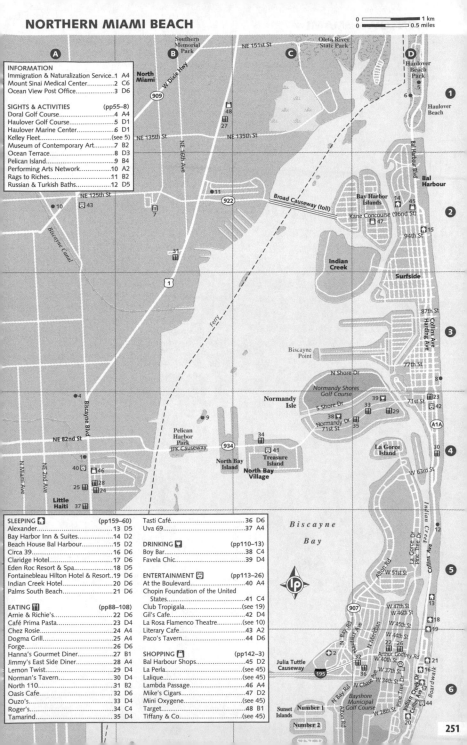

0 —————— 1 km
0 —————— 0.5 miles

INFORMATION
Immigration & Naturalization Service..1 A4
Mount Sinai Medical Center................2 C6
Ocean View Post Office......................3 D6

SIGHTS & ACTIVITIES (pp55–8)
Doral Golf Course..............................4 A4
Haulover Golf Course.........................5 D1
Haulover Marine Center......................6 D1
Kelley Fleet.................................(see 5)
Museum of Contemporary Art.........7 B2
Ocean Terrace..................................8 D3
Pelican Island..................................9 B4
Performing Arts Network.................10 A2
Rags to Riches...............................11 B2
Russian & Turkish Baths.................12 D5

SLEEPING (pp159–60)
Alexander......................................13 D5
Bay Harbor Inn & Suites................14 D2
Beach House Bal Harbour..............15 D2
Circa 39...16 D6
Claridge Hotel...............................17 D6
Eden Roc Resort & Spa..................18 D5
Fontainebleau Hilton Hotel & Resort.19 D6
Indian Creek Hotel........................20 D6
Palms South Beach.........................21 D6

EATING (pp88–108)
Arnie & Richie's.............................22 D6
Café Prima Pasta...........................23 D4
Chez Rosie.....................................24 A4
Dogma Grill...................................25 D6
Forge...26 D6
Hanna's Gourmet Diner.................27 B1
Jimmy's East Side Diner.................28 A4
Lemon Twist...................................29 D4
Norman's Tavern............................30 D6
North 110......................................31 B2
Oasis Cafe......................................32 D6
Ouzo's..33 D4
Roger's...34 C4
Tamarind.......................................35 D4
Tasti Café.......................................36 D6
Uva 69...37 A4

DRINKING (pp110–13)
Boy Bar..38 C4
Favela Chic.....................................39 D4

ENTERTAINMENT (pp113–26)
At the Boulevard............................40 A4
Chopin Foundation of the United
States..41 C4
Club Tropigala............................(see 19)
Gil's Cafe.......................................42 D4
La Rosa Flamenco Theatre..........(see 10)
Literary Cafe..................................43 A2
Paco's Tavern.................................44 D6

SHOPPING (pp142–3)
Bal Harbour Shops.........................45 D2
La Perla......................................(see 45)
Lalique..(see 45)
Lambda Passage............................46 A4
Mike's Cigars................................47 D2
Mini Oxygene.............................(see 45)
Target...48 B1
Tiffany & Co...............................(see 45)

251

To Alton Rd (0.3mi)

To Watson Island

Intracoastal Waterway

Biscayne Bay

Venetian Causeway (toll)

41 A1A MacArthur Causeway

To Port of Miami (0.1mi)

Piers

Bicentennial Park

Bicentennial Park

Herald Plaza

N Bayshore Dr

Omni

M Omni

Marina

AT&T Amphitheater

Bayfront Park

Pepper Fountain

Bayside Marketplace

16

33

Biscayne Blvd

Biscayne Blvd

Biscayne Blvd

35

40

Port Blvd

12

31

32

10

College/Bayside

NE 1st St

Biscayne Blvd

NE 2nd Ave

NE 2nd Ave

NE 1st Ave

39

School Board

38

Park West

Freedom Tower

Freedom Tower

College North

13

4

1st St

968

25

NE 16th St

NE 15th St

NE 14th St

NE 13th St

NE 12th St

NE 11th St

NE 10th St

NE 9th St

NE 8th St

NE 7th St

NE 6th St

NE 5th St

NE 4th St

NE 3rd St

NE 2nd St

9

14

41

43

26

34

8

N Miami Ave

N Miami Ave

42

E Flagler St

24

W Flagler St

37

Arena/State Plaza

Metromover

Government Center

Government Center

11

Miami-Dade Cultural Center

44

Overtown

NW 1st Ave

NW 1st Ct

36

NW 2nd Ave

NW 1st Pl

NW 2nd Ave

NW 3rd St

NW 2nd St

Government Center

95

NW 3rd Ave

NW 3rd Ct

Gibson Park

North-South Expwy

North-South Expwy

NW 4th Ave

NW 5th Ave

NW 4th St

Lummus Park

SW N River Dr

968

Reeves Park

NW 9th St

NW 6th Ave

NW N River Dr

23

Miami River

SW S River Dr

Metrorail

NW 12th St

NW 10th St

NW 8th St

NW 7th St

NW 6th St

NW 5th St

NW 4th St

NW 3rd St

NW 2nd St

NW 1st St

NW 7th Ave

To Miami International Airport (5mi)

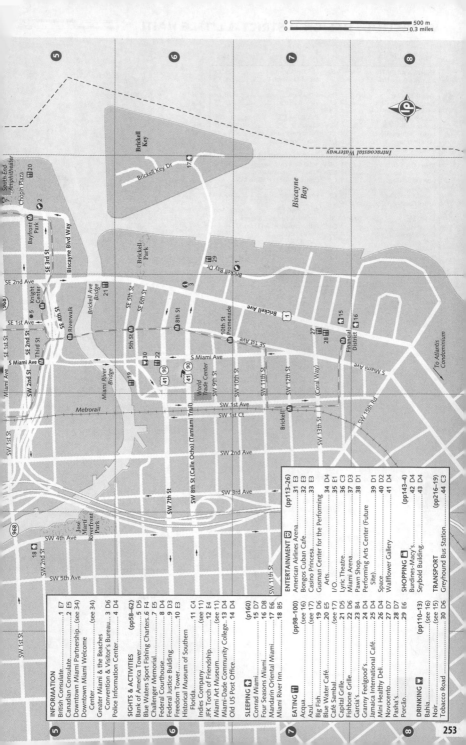

0 ━━━━━ 500
0 ━━━━━ 0.3 m

A

SIGHTS & ACTIVITIES	(pp62–5)
American Police Hall of Fame & Museum	1 D3
Bacardi Building	2 D6
Barbara Gillman Gallery	3 C1
Bernice Steinbaum Gallery	4 C4
Buick Building	5 C3
Dorsch Gallery	6 B5
Haitian Refugee Center	7 C1
Libreri Mapou	8 C1
Living Room	9 C3
Melin Building	10 C3
Miami City Cemetery	11 C6
Moore Space	12 C3
Newton Building	13 C3
Pilates Miami	14 C3
Placemaker Gallery	15 C3
Rubell Family Art Collection	16 B5

EATING 🍴	(pp100–3)
Andiamo!	17 D1
Cane á Sucre	18 C4
District	19 C3
Enriqueta's	20 C5
Grass Restaurant & Lounge	21 C3
Honeytree	22 D2
OLA	23 D2
Pasha's	24 C3

B

S&S Restaurant	25 C6
Secret Sandwich Co	26 C3
Soyka	27 D1
Sushi Siam	28 D1
Tree of Zion	29 C5

DRINKING 🍷	(pp110–13)
Coma's	(see 10)
Polish American Club	30 A6
Soho Lounge	31 B4

ENTERTAINMENT 🎭	(pp113–26)
4400 Club Live Comedy	32 A3
Churchill's Hideaway	33 C1
Light Box Theatre/Miami Light Project	34 C4
Power Studios	35 C4

SHOPPING 🛍	(pp144–5)
Annabella Bucheli Collection	36 C3
Artisan Antiques Art Deco	37 C3
Holly Hunt	38 C3
Kartell	39 C3
Kuma Central	40 C3
Luxe	41 C3
M-80	42 C4
Soye	43 D1
World Resources	44 C3

See Northern Miami Beach Map (p251)

LITTLE HAVANA

0 ――――― 500 m
0 ――――― 0.3 miles

SIGHTS & ACTIVITIES (pp65–6)
Bay of Pigs Museum & Library...1 C4
Casa Elián...............................2 A1
Cuba Brass Relief.....................3 F4
Eternal Torch in Honor of the
2506th Brigade.....................4 F4
José Martí Memorial.................5 F4
La Plaza De la Cubanidad (Alpha
66).....................................6 D1
Latin Quarter Cultural Center of
Miami.................................7 E4
Los Pinareños.........................8 F4
Madonna Statue......................9 F4
Máximo Gómez Park (Domino
Park)...................................10 E4
Maxoly Art Cuba Gallery..........11 D4
Nestor Izquierdo Statue...........12 F4

EATING (pp103–4)
Casa Juancho.........................13 A4
Chimichurri.............................14 E3
El Cristo.................................15 E4

Exquisito Restaurant................16 E4
Guayacan...............................17 C4
I Love Calle Ocho....................18 D4

DRINKING (pp110–13)
Casa Panza............................19 D4
Hoy Como Ayer.......................20 B4

ENTERTAINMENT (p125)
Tower Theater.........................21 E4

SHOPPING (pp145–6)
Botánica Mystica.....................22 C4
Cervantes Book Store..............23 C4
Do Re Mi Music Center............24 C4
El Crédito Cigars......................25 F4
Havana-to-go..........................26 E4
La Tradición Cubana................27 C4
La Tradición Cubana...........(see 23)
Moore & Bode Cigars..............28 D4
Old Cuba: The Collection.........29 D4
Power Records........................30 E3

To Taquerias
el Mexicano (0.3mi)

SW 11th Ave
SW 12th Ave
SW 12th Ct
SW 13th Ave   Cuban Memorial Blvd
SW 13th Ct
SW 14th Ave
SW 14th Ave
SW 15th Ave
SW 16th Ave
SW 17th Ave
SW 17th Ct
SW 18th Ave
SW 18th Ct
SW 19th Ave
SW 20th Ave
SW 21st Ave   Calle Ocho (SW 8th St) (Tamiami Trail)
SW 22nd Ave
SW 23rd Ave

SW 3rd St
SW 4th St
SW 5th St
SW 6th St

NW 17th Ave

To Miami
Hispanic
Ballet

W Flagler St
SW 1st St
SW 2nd St
SW 3rd St
SW 4th St
SW 5th St
SW 6th St
SW 7th St

NW 2nd St
NW 1st Ter
NW 1st St
NW Flagler Ter
NW 22nd Ave

To Islas
Canarias
(4mi)
2 NW 2nd St

To Miami-Dade
Auditorium
(3.5mi)

To Versailles; La Carreta;
Hy Vong Vietnamese
Restaurant; Botánica Las
Mercedes; Versailles Bakery;
La Casa de las Guayaberas

22nd (Beacon Rd) Ave Rd

SW 9th St
SW 10th St

255

CORAL GABLES

1

2

3

4

To Latin
American (1mi)

SW 22nd
Tce
SW 23rd St
SW 23rd
Tce
SW 24th St

SW 37th Ave (Douglas Rd)

See Coconut Grove Map (p258)

F

Bird Ave

Douglas
Road

1

SW 37th Ct
SW 38th Ave
SW 38th Ct
SW 39th Ave
Ponce de León Blv

Alhambra
Entrance
Monuments

21

Alhambra Plaza

Merrick Way

Galiano St

Monegro St

Alhambra Cir

Antiquera Ct

To Biltmore
(0.3mi)

Ponce de León Blvd

16

20

1

San Sebastián Ave

Santo Ave

Camilo Ave

Aledo Ave

Cadima Ave

Alesio Ave

Viscaya Ave

Fluvia Ave

Candia Ave

Velarde Ave

SW 40th St (Bird Rd)

Altara Ave

Le Lorenzo Ave

33

24

29

26

23

18

22

32

30

19

31

953

Laguna St

E

Navarre Ave

Minorca Ave

Alcazar Ave

Giralda Ave

Aragon Ave

SW 22nd St (Miracle Mile)

Andalusia Ave

Salzedo St

Palermo Ave

Malaga Ave

Romano Ave

Ponce
Circle
Park

12

976

SW 42nd Ave (Le Jeune Rd)

5

Hernando St

972

Biltmore Way

Valencia Ave

Almeria Ave

Sevilla Ave

Palermo Ave

Catalonia Ave

Santander Ave

Malaga Ave

Anastasia Ave

San Antonio Ave

Altara Ave

Segovia St

D

Cardena St

Segovia Cir

Greenway Dr

Anderson Rd

Riviera Dr

University Dr

Monserrate St

Toledo St

Granada
Entrance
Monuments

Toledo St

11

SW 24th St (Coral Way)

PMB 50th Dr

14

7

C

Granada Blvd

Cordova St

Andalusia Ave

Palermo Ave

Catalonia Ave

Malaga Ave

Anastasia Ave

13

Salvadore
Park

6

15

27

Mariola Ct

Algardi Ave

Columbus Blvd

Indian Mound Trail

Coral Gables Canal

Biltmore
Golf Course

3

San Amaro Dr

Alhambra Cir

N Greenway Dr

Granada Golf
Course

S Greenway Dr

Astulia Ave

Castile Ave

Madrid St

San Domingo St

N Greenway Dr

SW 40th St (Bird Rd)

Algardi Ave

B

Greenway
Ct

Ferdinand St

Alhambra Cir

Coral Way
Entrance
Monuments

17

Country Club Prado

SW 57th Ave (Red Rd)

To Latin Rhythm
Studios (3mi)

Valencia Ave

Sevilla Ave

To Miami Twice (1mi;
Tropical Park Tennis
Center (2.5mi)

A

1

2

3

4

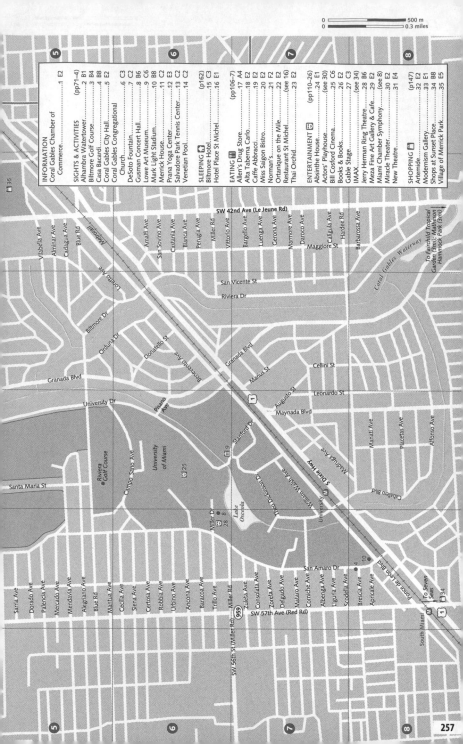

0 ——— 500 m
0 ——— 0.3 miles

INFORMATION	
Coral Gables Chamber of Commerce...............................1	E2

SIGHTS & ACTIVITIES	(pp71–4)
Alhambra Watertower..................2	B1
Biltmore Golf Course....................3	B4
Casa Bacardi.................................4	B8
Coral Gables City Hall...................5	E2
Coral Gables Congregational Church...................................6	C3
DeSoto Fountain...........................7	C2
Gusman Concert Hall....................8	B6
Lowe Art Museum.........................9	C6
Mark Light Stadium.....................10	B8
Merrick House.............................11	C2
Prana Yoga Center.......................12	E3
Salvadore Park Tennis Center.....13	C2
Venetian Pool.............................14	C2

SLEEPING	(p162)
Biltmore Hotel............................15	C3
Hotel Place St Michel..................16	E1

EATING	(pp106–7)
Allen's Drug Store.......................17	A4
Alta Taberna Carlo......................18	E2
Caffe Abbracci............................19	E2
Miss Saigon Bistro.......................20	E2
Norman's....................................21	F2
Ortanique on the Mile.................22	F2
Restaurant St Michel...............(see 16)
Thai Orchid................................23	E2

ENTERTAINMENT	(pp110–26)
Absinthe House............................24	E1
Actors' Playhouse....................(see 30)
Bill Cosford Cinema.....................25	C6
Books & Books.............................26	E2
Gable Stage.................................27	C3
IMAX.......................................(see 34)
Jerry Herman Ring Theatre..........28	B6
Meza Fine Art Gallery & Cafe......29	E2
Miami Chamber Symphony......(see 8)
Miracle Theater...........................30	E2
New Theatre................................31	E4

SHOPPING	(p147)
Artemide.....................................32	E1
Modernism Gallery.......................33	E1
Shops at Sunset Place..................34	B8
Village of Merrick Park................35	E5

257

COCONUT GROVE

INFORMATION	
Coconut Grove Chamber of Commerce...............................1	C5

SIGHTS & ACTIVITIES	(pp68–71)
Barnacle State Historic Site..........2	C5
Bubbles Dive Center.....................3	C2
Coconut Grove Exhibition Center..4	D4
Dinner Key Marina........................5	D5
Miami City Hall.............................6	D4
Miami Improv................................7	C4
Monty's Marina.............................8	D4
Plymouth Congregational Church.9	B5
Yoga Grove.................................10	B3

SLEEPING	(p161)
Mayfair House.............................11	C4
Ritz-Carlton Coconut Grove........12	C4
Sonesta Hotel & Suites Coconut Grove.......................................13	C5
The Mutiny Hotel.........................14	C5

EATING	(pp105–6)
Anokha.......................................15	B5
Berries Restaurant......................16	C3
Daily Bread Marketplace............17	C2
Green Street Cafe.......................18	B5
Latin American...........................19	C2
Le Bouchon du Grove.................20	C5
Mr Moe's....................................21	B5
Paulo Luigi's..............................22	C4
Somoto......................................23	B5

ENTERTAINMENT	(pp110–26)
Book Addiction...........................24	A5
Coconut Grove Playhouse..........25	B5
DQ Bookstore.............................26	B5
Oxygen Lounge....................(see 29)

SHOPPING	(p146)
Architectural Antiques...............27	D2
CocoWalk...................................28	C4
Streets of Mayfair......................29	C4

To Kampong (2mi); Florida Grand Opera

KEY BISCAYNE

0 — 1 km
0 — 0.5 miles

A Rickenbacker Park
Hobie Island
Rickenbacker Causeway (toll)

8

11 B 18

C Virginia Key

D 15

Duck Lake

4

Rickenbacker Causeway

Virginia Key Beach

1

Bear Cut

Northwest Point

Crandon Blvd

3

2

Biscayne Bay

Crandon Park

6

West Point

Crandon Park Beach

Key Biscayne

10

19

17 16

Ocean Lane Dr

21

5

East Dr

Harbor Dr

Fernwood Rd

Crandon Blvd

13 Ocean Dr

ATLANTIC OCEAN

W Heather Dr

E Heather Dr

20

14

Galen Dr

Harbor Point

Ocean Dr

Hurricane Harbor

W Wood Dr

E Wood Dr

Southwest Point

S Mashta Dr

W Mashta Dr

Crandon Blvd

12

Bill Baggs Cape Florida State Recreation Area

Cape Florida Channel

Crandon Dr

1

Cape Florida

9

259

SIGHTS & ACTIVITIES (pp67–8)
Cape Florida Lighthouse............1 C6
Crandon Golf Course................2 C2
Crandon Park Marina................3 C2
Divers' Paradise......................(see 3)
Fishing Charters.....................(see 3)
Hobie Beach..........................4 B1
Mangrove Cycles......................5 C4
Marjory Stoneman Douglas
  Biscayne Nature Center............6 C3
Miami Seaquarium.....................7 C1
Sailboards Miami.....................8 A1
Sailboats of Key Biscayne...........(see 3)
Stiltsville...........................9 C6
Tennis Center at Crandon Park......10 C4
Tony's Ultralight Adventures.......11 B1

SLEEPING (p161)
Ritz-Carlton Key Biscayne..........12 C5
Silver Sands Beach Resort..........13 C4
Sonesta Beach Resort Key
  Biscayne...........................14 C4

EATING (p105)
Aria.................................(see 12)
Jimbo's.............................15 D1
Le Croisic..........................16 C4
Oasis...............................17 C4
Rusty Pelican.......................18 B1
Stefano's...........................19 C4

SHOPPING (p146)
Palm Produce Resortwear.............20 C4
Toy Town............................21 C4

MIAMI METRO MAP

NW 16 St.

NW 15 St.

I-395

NW 14 St.

SCHOOL BOARD STATION

BISCAYNE BLVD.

NE 2 AVE

OMNI STATION

NE 14 St.

VENETIAN CAUSEWAY

NE 13 St.   **OMNI**

HERALD PLAZA

MacARTHUR CAUSEWAY

NW 12 St.

NE 12 St.

NW 2 AVE

NW 1 AVE

N. MIAMI AVE

NE 1 AVE

BICENTENNIAL PARK STATION (closed)

NW 11 St.   NE 11 St.

ELEVENTH STREET STATION

NW 10 St.   NE 10 St.

NW 9 St.   NE 9 St.

NW 8 St.   NE 8 St.

PARK WEST STATION

NE 7 St.

FREEDOM TOWER STATION

PORT BOULEVARD

METRORAIL

ARENA/ STATE PLAZA STATION

COLLEGE NORTH STATION

NW 6 St.

NW 5 St.

NW 4 St.

NW 3 St.

LOOP   LOOP   LOOP

N. MIAMI AVE

NE 1 AVE

NE 2 St.

COLLEGE/BAYSIDE STATION

FIRST STREET STATION

N

GOVERNMENT CENTER STATION

NW 1 St.

BISCAYNE BLVD.

W. Flagler St.

BRICKELL   OMNI   DOWNTOWN

MIAMI AVENUE STATION

SW 1 St.

DOWNTOWN

SW 2 St.

THIRD STREET STATION

KNIGHT CENTER STATION

SW 3 St.

BAYFRONT PARK STATION

RIVERWALK STATION

MIAMI RIVER

SE 5 St.

SE 2 AVE

FIFTH STREET STATION

SOUTH MIAMI AVE

SE 6 St.

SW 7 St.

SW 1 AVE

SE 8 St

EIGHTH STREET STATION

SW 8 St

SW 9 St.

METRORAIL

SW 10 St.

BRICKELL AVENUE

BAYSHORE DR.

SW 11 St.

SW 12 St.

TENTH STREET/ PROMENADE STATION

BRICKELL STATION

BRICKELL

SW 13 St.

SW 14 St.

FINANCIAL DISTRICT STATION

260